THE FRESHWATER FISHES OF ALASKA

THE FRESHWATER FISHES

OF ALASKA

JAMES E. MORROW

ILLUSTRATIONS BY
MARION J. DALEN

ALASKA
NORTHWEST
PUBLISHING
COMPANY
Anchorage, Alaska

Library of Congress cataloging in publication data:
Morrow, James Edwin, 1918-
The freshwater fishes of Alaska.
Bibliography: p.
Includes index.
1. Fishes, Fresh-water—Alaska. 2. Fishes—Alaska. I. Title.
QL628.A4M66 597.092'9798 80-11160
ISBN 0-88240-134-3

COVER ILLUSTRATIONS:
Details from carbon dust illustrations, page 129-141.
TITLE PAGE ILLUSTRATION:
Inconnu (or sheefish), *Stenodus leucichthys*

Design by Val Paul Taylor
Photographs by the author, except as noted
Maps by the author

Alaska Northwest Publishing Company
Box 4-EEE, Anchorage, Alaska 99509
Printed in U.S.A.

CONTENTS

LIST OF PHOTOGRAPHS

The Illustrator and Illustration Techniques

In any work involving identification, accurate illustrations are important. The paintings and carbon dust illustrations of Marion J. Dalen are the most accurate we have ever seen. We had originally hoped to include a Dalen illustration of each species in this book, but the carbon dust technique is so time-consuming that this was not possible; so we have included an illustration of at least one representative of each family and paintings of all the more spectacularly colored forms. A surprisingly large percentage of the fishes included here have never been illustrated before, at least not in any North American work known to us, and certainly not with the high degree of scientific accuracy and artistic ability which Mrs. Dalen's work exhibits.

Born in Red Wing, Minnesota, Marion Johnson Dalen grew up on the banks of the Mississippi River. As a child she often accompanied her brother and father when they pulled in setlines, and from those trips acquired a lifelong fascination with fish.

Dalen began her education in art in Minneapolis, ventured west, and continued her studies in Seattle. She became a fashion illustrator, married, moved to a ranch in Oregon, and raised six children. When the last of her children went to college Dalen returned to her early interests in fish and art, studying at Humboldt State University in California and setting as her goal a job at the Smithsonian Institution. Determination and talent paid off, and she became a science illustrator for the Smithsonian's Division of Fishes, her work—especially drawings of deep-sea fishes—appearing in numerous museum publications.

A charter member of the Guild of Natural Science Illustrators, Dalen now lives in Port Orford, Oregon, occasionally taking on assignments as an illustrator and exhibiting her paintings and drawings of natural history.

Techniques used for the watercolor and carbon dust illustrations in this book

Marion Dalen's color paintings for *The Freshwater Fishes of Alaska* were done in watercolor or in a transparent acrylic technique that is similar to watercolor. The black and white illustrations were done in a more unusual method: carbon dust. When Marion Dalen makes a carbon dust illustration, the first step is a base, or preliminary, drawing done in great detail from a zoological specimen. This is checked, in this case by an ichthyologist, and she is ready to begin the illustration itself.

The artist works on coated paper with hard carbon drawing pencils and, for fine detail, a silverpoint pencil— silver jeweler's wire in a mechanical pencil.

To shade an area, the artist uses flat sable brushes dipped in carbon dust, making some areas darker than others by painting layer over layer. To anchor the dust, dark areas are rubbed into the paper with a wine bottle cork carved to a fine point. In Marion Dalen's work all but the lightest areas must be rubbed in. Then areas to be highlighted are erased and fine details such as scales are drawn in with the hard carbon pencil or with the silverpoint.

While using this technique the artist must keep a piece of paper under her hand to protect the drawing; Dalen points out that fingerprints or a sneeze could be disastrous to a carbon dust illustration. Fixative is sprayed on the drawing as soon as it is finished and, until the illustration is framed, it must always be covered with a protective plastic sheet.

LIST OF PLATES

FOREWORD

For good reason ''Alaska'' and ''fish'' have a synonymy to thousands who know our largest state, or to those who would visit this great land. Uncounted lakes and ponds and thousands of miles of rivers and creeks in Alaska are home to northern fish—from scattered numbers to concentrations that are truly incredible.

Alaska's early inhabitants depended heavily upon fish as food, for fish is among the most easily caught in wild foods; this has scarcely changed, and fish is still a major item in the diets of many Alaskans.

The waters of Alaska are home to that family of fishes that thrive where it is cool—the salmon. Alaska's five species of salmon and their relatives the trout, charr, grayling, whitefish and sheefish, dominate the fresh waters of the state. These are among the finest food fishes, and among their numbers are those species most prized by sportsmen.

In the past century hundreds of books have been published on Alaska's natural resources. Many of these have detailed Alaska's abundance and variety of fish. In recent years scientific fishery studies have proliferated in Alaska. Hundreds of millions of dollars have been earned from the sale and processing of Alaska's fish and fishery products, largely salmon.

Yet until this book, no author has listed all the known freshwater fishes of Alaska, with details of their life histories, and their importance to man. This is partly because of the uncertainty of which species lived in Alaskan waters, as well as lack of documentation of the ranges of those species known to exist in the vastness that is Alaska.

''The initial stimulus (for this book) came from my students who, over the years, asked many questions that I couldn't answer,'' says author Jim Morrow, about this much needed, carefully researched book. Morrow has been Professor of Fisheries and of Zoology at the University of Alaska since 1960. In 1977 he was named professor emeritus at that university.

Because it is both the *first* book to concentrate exclusively on Alaska's variety of freshwater fishes and because it represents the summa of a distinguished career of ''answering questions'' about the fishes of a vast area for which there was little documentation prior to that provided by Morrow, his colleagues and students, *The Freshwater Fishes of Alaska* is a major scientific contribution: it establishes the foundation for all future study of Alaska's freshwater fishes.

Jim Rearden
OUTDOORS EDITOR
ALASKA® magazine

Preface

Comments on the Past and Future of Freshwater Fishes and Studies of Fishes in Alaska

When I came to the University of Alaska in 1960 to teach ichthyology and fisheries biology, little was known about Alaskan fishes save for those salmonids that were important to sport, commercial and subsistence fisheries. The need for a book on the state's freshwater fishes was apparent, but the information on which to base it did not exist. In many instances the basic information still does not exist, but progress has been made.

The scarcity of information regarding the freshwater fishes of Alaska had been due in part to the vastness of the state and the great range of its climate. Alaska has an area equal to about one-fifth of all the rest of the United States and climates varying from warm, rainy southeastern Alaska to the cold, dry interior, where winter temperatures of -45 °C are common. In the interior, snow lies on the ground from October to May, resulting in short summer field seasons.

Transportation in this land has been a major problem for students of fishes. Small aircraft, snow machines, river boats, all-terrain vehicles, dog teams and, often, long hikes on foot have been the means of reaching remote areas.

Further, much of Alaska is covered by water, with thousands of lakes and ponds, and rivers great and small, creating something of a problem in sampling. Although important food fishes are usually well known locally, other species have often been of scant interest except to students of fishes.

In the early 1960s considerable controversy arose over the proposed construction of the Rampart Dam, and this led to studies of the Yukon River fishes. Later, pressure to construct the trans-Alaska pipeline resulted in investigations of Alaskan freshwater fishes—more investigations than had ever been made previously. The pressures of development resulted in better transportation that finally made it practical to acquire fish specimens from remote places.

The future of Alaska's freshwater fishes now depends on how well the state can balance the needs of the fish populations against the needs and desires of the human population. Fishes can't give way much—they aren't that adaptable—but if Alaskans will learn from the mistakes of the past and will make small sacrifices to keep water fit for fishes (which will make it better for people, too), then there is probably little to worry about. On the other hand, if irresponsibility and greed are allowed to prevail, then the fishes must inevitably disappear.

Another aspect of increased population and tourism is an increase in the number of fish caught, probably leading to reduced fish populations in accessible areas, especially along the roads and around the larger cities. Reduced populations can already be observed in certain streams near Anchorage and Fairbanks. Further, some fishes, such as lake trout, arctic charr and Dolly Varden, which reproduce annually in more temperate climates, breed only every second or third year in the arctic. These populations will have to be managed most carefully, for, with their reduced reproductive capacity, they could easily come close to extinction by overexploitation. Fortunately, the Alaska Department of Fish & Game keeps a close watch on all sport fishes in the state and has established regulations and bag limits that will help to ensure recreation for years to come. A few "fishing for fun" areas, where all fish caught must be returned to the water unharmed, have already been established.

In its Department of Fish & Game and in its state university, Alaska has ongoing research programs regarding fishes. Fish & Game has of necessity concentrated on management aspects of important sport and commercial species, while the university has often reflected the personal interests of individual investigators. It has been encouraging to see in recent years increased cooperation between the two groups and to note an increased tendency toward environmental, rather than single-species, investigations—a recognition of the fact that no species, not even man, lives in isolation. What is still needed is increased education of the public concerning the value of research, its needs, objectives and results.

Surprisingly, considering the size and contrasts of Alaska, there are relatively few varieties of freshwater fishes in the state. Including the anadromous salmonids and smelts and the several marine forms that occasionally enter rivers, only 56 different species—one of which was introduced—are known from Alaska's lakes and streams.

I had some difficulty in deciding which fishes to include in this book. If I confined myself to strictly freshwater forms, then the salmons and other anadromous fishes would have to be left out, but these are very important fishes in their freshwater stages and surely deserve a place in the book. Still, if anadromous fishes were included, why leave out those marine forms that more or less frequently enter rivers? Finally I decided to include all the fishes that have been recorded from fresh water, including more or less brackish estuaries, in Alaska. For this reason, several normally marine herrings, cods, surfperches, sculpins and flounders have found their way into these pages.

The names of the fishes and the arrangement of families here follow, with a few exceptions, the recommendations of the American Fisheries Society Committee on Names of Fishes. Within each family, species descriptions are arranged in the order in which the species key out. The keys for identification are based on my *Illustrated Keys to the Fresh-water Fishes of Alaska* (Morrow, 1974). These keys were tested by my ichthyology students for a number of years before publication and have been further improved since then by suggestions from biologists and fishermen.

We still do not know nearly as much as we should about the freshwater fishes of Alaska. In order to provide as well-rounded a picture of their biology and behavior as possible, I have therefore drawn extensively on studies made elsewhere, on the assumption, perhaps not wholly warranted, that the situation in Alaska will not be very different from that in other places. Extrapolations from other areas must be treated with some caution, however, for fishes, like other animals, are capable of adapting to local conditions. Therefore, this book should not be considered the final word but rather a summary of what is known, a source of background information and, I hope, a stimulus for further research.

Acknowledgments

A great many people have helped in the preparation of this book. The initial stimulus came from my students, both graduate and undergraduate, who, over the years, asked many questions that I couldn't answer. As the book took shape, a number of biologists in the Alaska Department of Fish & Game and the Auke Bay Fisheries Laboratory of the National Marine Fisheries Service (NMFS) helped by providing specimens and information that I could not have obtained otherwise. The staff of the Elmer E. Rasmuson Library at the University of Alaska was most helpful in obtaining obscure books and journals. Grants and research contracts from the National Science Foundation, the Sport Fishing Institute and the Alaska Department of Fish & Game provided financial support for field work and the graduate students and technicians without whom there would have been serious gaps in this project. The writing of the book was supported in part by a grant from the Environmental Protection Agency. Kenneth Coyle, Marine Sorting Center, University of Alaska, translated some of the Russian literature.

Very few comprehensive books on fishes have provided color photographs of every species covered, so I am grateful to all those people who went out of their way to help in the search for slides and prints of rarely photographed fishes. Special thanks are due to the personnel of the Northwest and Alaska Fisheries Center, NMFS, Seattle, and to the Fisheries Research Institute (FRI), University of Washington, Robert L. Burgner, Director. Staff members of the FRI who contributed slides were Quentin Stober, Richard Whitney (Washington Cooperative Fishery Unit) and Charles Simenstad. In particular, Simenstad's personal contacts and detective work were especially productive. Loaned photographs are credited in the color insert. Abbreviations appearing in credits are for the College of Fisheries and the Fisheries Research Institute, University of Washington (CF, UW and FRI, UW); University of Alaska (UA); Oregon State University (OSU); University of Oregon (UO); University of Manitoba (UM); Massachusetts Division of Fish & Game (MDFG); Washington State Department of Fisheries (WSDF); Alaska Department of Fish & Game (ADFG); National Museum of Natural Science, Ottawa (NMNS); and United States Fish & Wildlife Service (USFWS).

Photographs of the breeding behavior of the arctic charr, northern pike and fourhorn sculpin are printed through the courtesy of the Institute for Freshwater Research, Drottningham, Sweden, and photographers Fabricius, Gustafson and Westin.

Dianne Hofbeck, Val Paul Taylor and editors at Alaska Northwest Publishing Company have done a tremendous job of editing and composing.

My wife, Kay, has been a constant source of encouragement and inspiration and has patiently endured all the trials and tribulations incidental to involvement in this work.

—James E. Morrow

INTRODUCTION

Classification and Nomenclature of Fishes

Everything in the living world is divided into several categories and subcategories; starting from the largest and going down, these are phylum, class, order, family, genus, species, and subspecies. In this book we are concerned mostly with the last four.

The scientific name of a species consists of two words. The first word, which is always written with a capital letter, is the generic name: the name of the genus to which the species belongs. The second word, never capitalized, is the specific name, and the two words together are the species name. In some cases there is a third word, also not capitalized. This is the name of the subspecies, indicating that the species is represented by two or more slightly different forms that do not live in the same area (for example, the Pacific herring is *Clupea harengus pallasi,* while the closely related Atlantic herring is *Clupea harengus harengus*). In general, I have not employed subspecific names in this book because subspecies of most of our Alaskan fishes are unknown. (A subspecies cannot be assumed to exist only on the basis of single specimens. As a rule very large samples, 50 to 100 or more specimens, are required.)

The system of naming is not unlike that used for people; Smith, for example, indicates a group of related people—the Smith family—and John tells us which one of the Smiths. In scientific names, the genus name indicates the group of related species and the specific name indicates a particular species within the genus.

It is customary, and I have followed the custom, to add to the scientific name the name of the author who first described the species. If this scientist used the name exactly in the modern sense (for example, referring to the green sturgeon as *Acipenser medirostris* Ayres), then the author's name stands without parentheses. However, if the author originally assigned the species to a genus other than that now used, the author's name is placed in parentheses. Thus, the name of the sheefish is written *Stenodus leucichthys* (Güldenstadt) because Güldenstadt originally placed the sheefish with the salmons and trouts in the genus *Salmo.* Later studies showed that this species did not belong with *Salmo* and a new genus, *Stenodus,* was created for it.

Measurement of Fishes

The length of a fish may be expressed as total length, fork length or standard length. The first is the longest, from the tip of the snout (or lower jaw, if it projects beyond the snout) to the tip of the tail. This is not a very accurate measurement because it depends partly on how much the two lobes of the tail are squeezed together. If the lobes are spread as wide apart as possible, the measurement will be shorter, sometimes significantly so, than if the lobes are pushed together. Fork length, used especially by fishery biologists, is the distance from the tip of the snout or lower jaw (whichever projects farther) to the tip of the middle rays of the tail fin. Standard length, used almost exclusively by taxonomic ichthyologists, is the distance from the tip of the snout to the end of the backbone. Because it is impossible to derive precise relationships among these three measurements, and because different authors use different lengths, all three are mentioned from time to time in this book. Where there is no indication to indicate if a measurement is of total, fork or standard length, that is because the source did not supply that information.

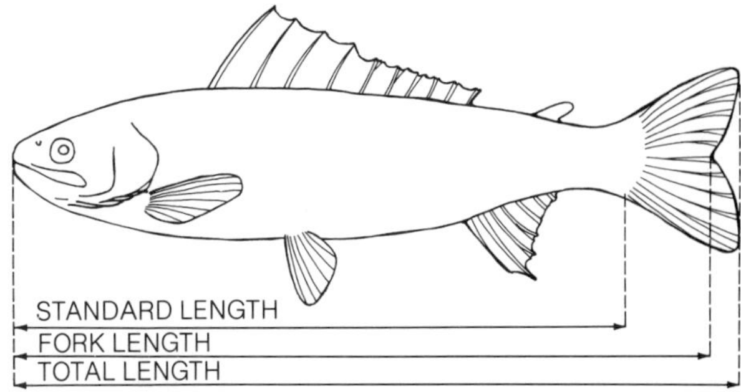

FIGURE 1. Various measurements of fish length.

System of Indicating Ages of Fishes

The age of a fish is usually determined by an annulus, or age mark, formed on the scale although age can also be determined from various bones such as gill covers, vertebrae or otoliths (ear stones). Age marks form in the late winter or spring, and in most cases provide as accurate a measurement of age as do the rings of a tree.

In this book the age of fish has generally been indicated with an arabic figure and a plus sign—3+, for example—meaning that the fish is more than 3 years old and less than 4. In a few cases, however, roman numerals have been used to indicate that the age was measured at a specific time: when the annulus was formed.

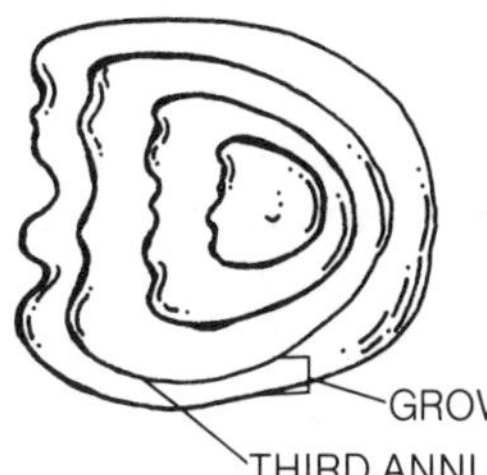

FIGURE 2. The arctic grayling, found in clear water streams of interior Alaska, is one of many fish having age rings (annuli) on its scales. By counting these rings, you can find the grayling's age. This one is 4 years old.

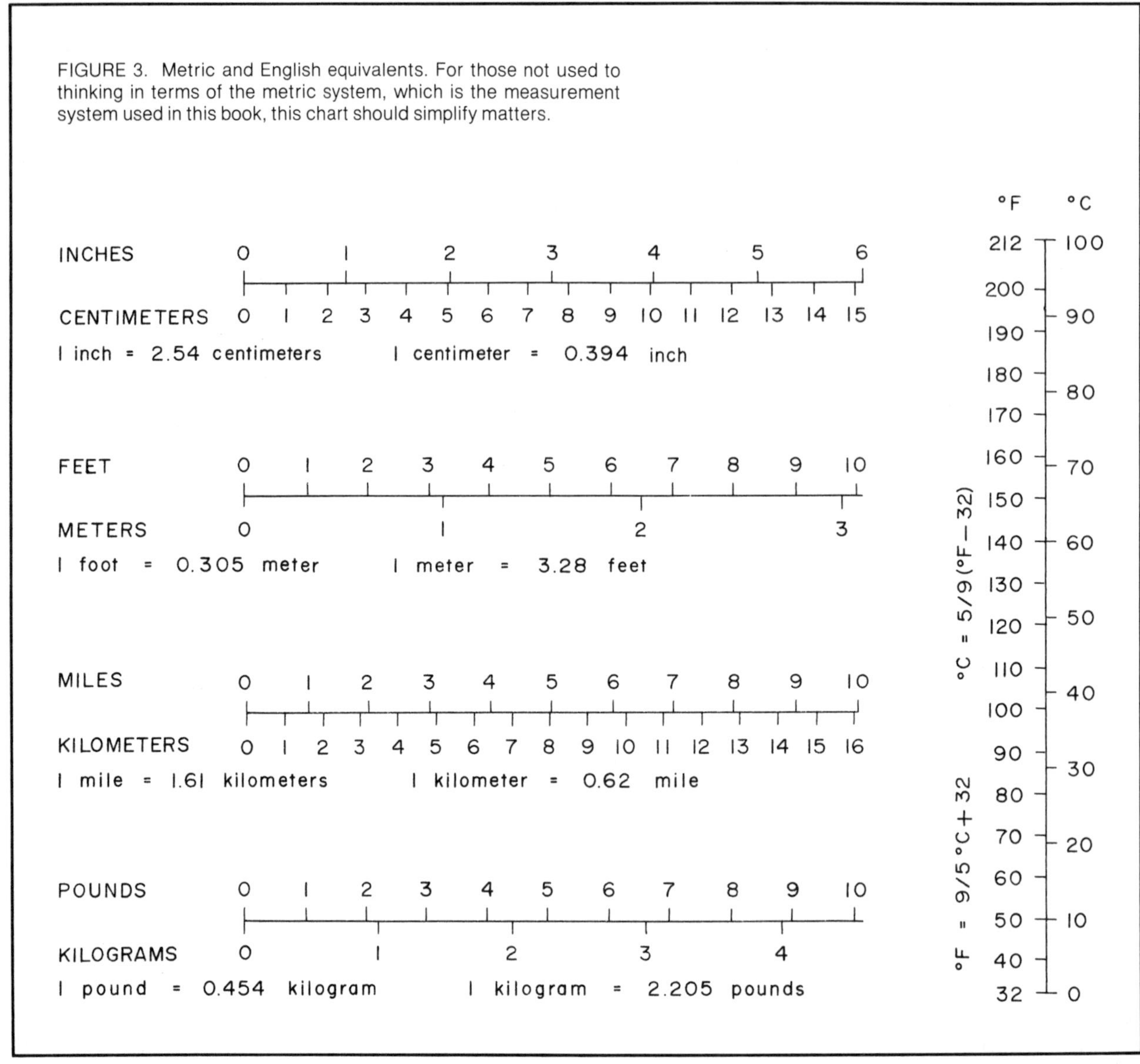

FIGURE 3. Metric and English equivalents. For those not used to thinking in terms of the metric system, which is the measurement system used in this book, this chart should simplify matters.

Keys

A key is simply a list of characteristics arranged to aid in identification. In one form or another, keys are used in all branches of science where identification is required, for example in analytical chemistry, mineralogy and, perhaps especially, in taxonomic zoology and botany. Keys of one sort or another are just about as old as modern biological classification. In their most primitive form, keys date from the 18th century. An early key consisted of a statement describing a general character followed by brief descriptions of all the animals (or plants) to which this character applied. Then came another character and more descriptions. This key was better than nothing, but it meant that the user had to wade through pages of descriptions while hoping to find something that matched the specimen in hand.

Some improvements, notably in the use of secondary characters to make groupings smaller, appeared in the 19th century, but the general format remained the same. It was not until near the end of the 19th century that the modern form of dichotomous key, with its either-or choices, appeared.

The physical format of modern keys varies with the custom and needs of the particular scientific field and the preferences of the author. However, in all dichotomous (two-choice) keys, each statement or description of a characteristic is matched by a contrasting description; for example, *Mouth without jaws* is followed by *Mouth with jaws.* After each statement is either the name of the group or species to which the statement applies, or a reference leading the searcher to another set of paired statements of additional characters.

How to Use the Keys

Begin with the Key to the Families, where you will find pairs of numbered statements. If your fish agrees with the description in 1a, the fish is a lamprey and you go to the key to lampreys on the page indicated. If 1a does not describe your fish, go to 1b. If the fish agrees with the description in 1b, go to the key section indicated at the end of the statement, in this case 2. In like manner, follow pair by pair until you reach a statement that leads to a name and page number. To identify a herring, for example, you would go to 1a (which disagrees, so go to 1b); 1b (agrees, go to 2); 2a (agrees, go to 3); 3a (disagrees, go to 3b); 3b (agrees, go to 4); 4a (agrees, go to the key to herrings and shads in Chapter 3 and repeat the process).

Having identified your specimen from the key, it's a good idea to check the specimen against the illustration and the detailed description. Even the most experienced of us can make mistakes in keying out.

FIGURE 4.
A. Sketch of a generalized fish showing various structures referred to in the keys.
B. Roof of mouth of a fish showing bones and teeth.
C. Gill arch with gill filaments and gill rakers.

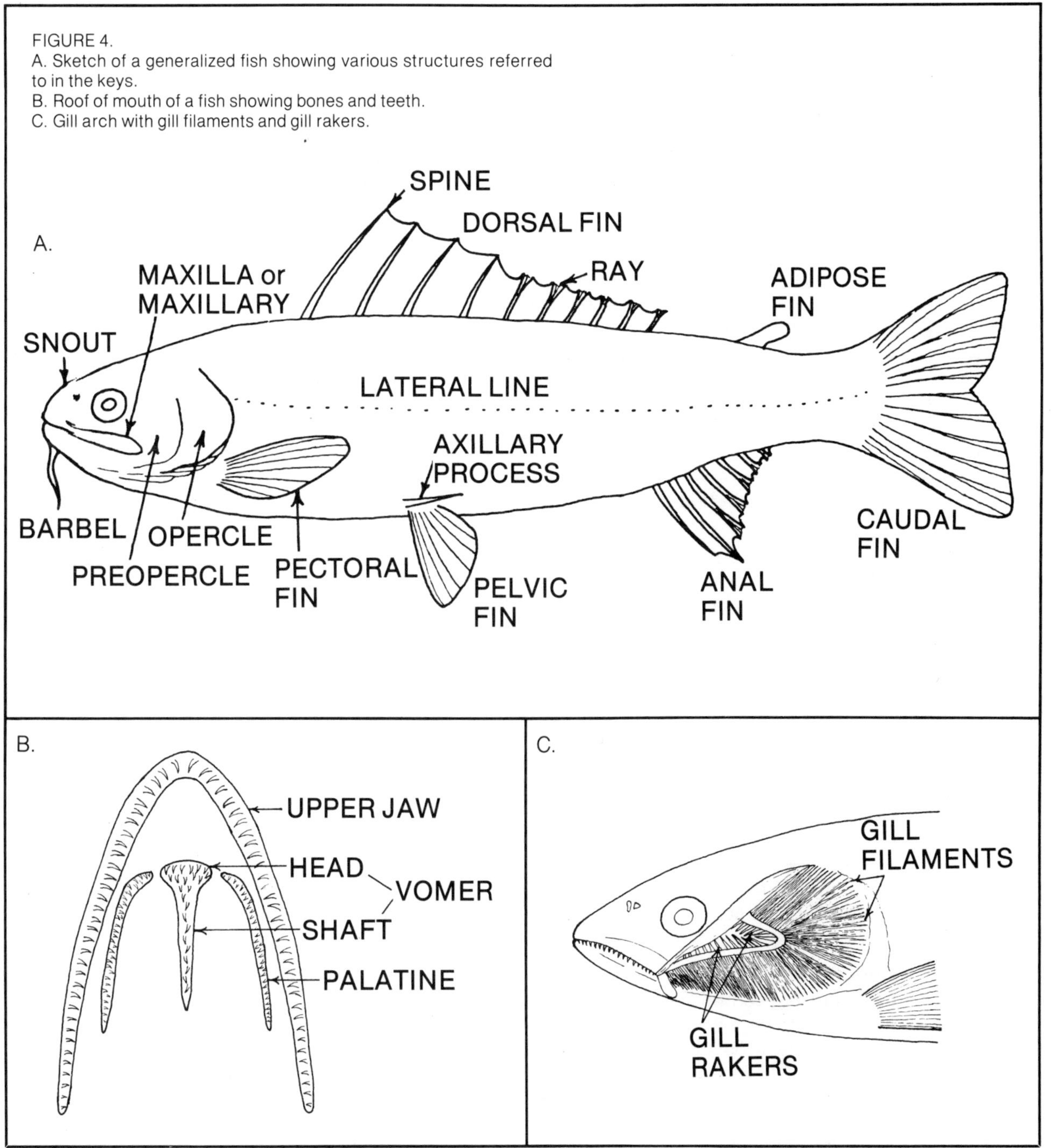

KEY TO THE FAMILIES

SECTION	DESCRIPTION	TURN TO	PROCEED IN THIS KEY TO SECTION
1 a.	No jaws, mouth a round sucking disc. A single dorsal median nostril present.	Lampreys, Family Petromyzontidae, page 7.	
b.	Mouth with jaws. Nostrils paired, not median.		**2**
2 a.	Pelvic fins far back, abdominal in position.		**3**
b.	Pelvic fins forward, just behind head or under head, thoracic or jugular in position.		**13**
3 a.	Five rows of keeled bony shields present along body; 4 well-developed barbels present under snout in front of mouth.	Sturgeons, Family Acipenseridae, page 13.	
b.	No keeled bony shields on body, although flat shields present in one family; no barbels under snout, but a single barbel present on tip of lower jaw in some groups.		**4**
4 a.	No lateral line (Figure 4A, page 3).	Herrings and Shads, Family Clupeidae, page 17.	
b.	Lateral line present.		**5**
5 a.	Adipose fin present (Figure 4A, page 3).		**6**
b.	No adipose fin.		**10**
6 a.	Adipose fin well behind base of anal fin. Pectoral fin reaches past base of pelvic fins. Dorsal fin has 2 spines, anal fin has a single spine anteriorly.	Trout-perch, Family Percopsidae, page 177.	
b.	Adipose fin about over base of anal fin. Pectoral fin does not reach base of pelvic fins. No spines in dorsal or anal fins.		**7**
7 a.	Pelvic axillary process present (Figure 4A, page 3).		**8**
b.	No pelvic axillary process.	Smelts, Family Osmeridae, page 149.	
8 a.	Dorsal fin, which has 18 or more soft rays, is long, its anterior end ahead of posterior tip of pectoral fin.	Grayling, Subfamily Thymallinae of the Family Salmonidae, page 145.	
b.	Dorsal fin has 15 or fewer rays; anterior end behind tip of pectoral fin.		**9**
9 a.	Teeth in jaws are small and weak or absent. Scales large, in 4 to 11 rows above lateral line.	Whitefishes, Subfamily Coregoninae of the Family Salmonidae, page 23.	

9 b.	Teeth in jaws are well developed. Scales small, difficult to count, in 20 to 27 rows above lateral line.	Salmons and Trouts, Subfamily Salmoninae of the Family Salmonidae, page 43.	
10 a.	Teeth present in mouth. Front of dorsal fin nearer to base of tail than to tip of snout.		**11**
b.	No teeth in jaws. Front of dorsal fin closer to tip of snout than to base of tail.		**12**
11 a.	Caudal fin forked. Snout long, nearly half of head length, and flattened like a duck's bill. Pelvic fin has 10 or 11 rays.	Pikes, Family Esocidae, page 165.	
b.	Caudal fin rounded. Snout not long, about a third of head length, not duck-billed. Pelvic fin has 0 to 3 rays.	Alaska blackfish, Family Umbridae, page 161.	
12 a.	Mouth on ventral side, lips are thick and covered with papillae. Distance from snout tip to anus more than 2.5 times distance from anus to base of tail.	Suckers, Family Catostomidae, page 173.	
b.	Mouth normal, lips not covered with papillae. Distance from snout to anus about 1.5 times distance from anus to base of tail.	Minnows, Family Cyprinidae, page 171.	
13 a.	Both eyes on same side of head.	Flounders, Family Pleuronectidae, page 211.	
b.	Eyes in normal position, one eye on each side of head.		**14**
14 a.	Several free spines in front of dorsal fin, the spines not connected to each other by membranes. Pelvic fin formed of a single spine.	Sticklebacks, Family Gasterosteidae, page 189.	
b.	No free spines in front of dorsal fin. Pelvic fin not reduced to a single spine.		**15**
15 a.	First dorsal fin made up of spines connected by a membrane. No barbel under chin.		**16**
b.	No spines in any fins (only soft rays). A barbel, which may be very small, present under chin.	Codfishes, Family Gadidae, page 181.	
16 a.	Body covered with distinct scales. Anal fin has 3 spines.	Surfperches, Family Embiotocidae, page 195.	
b.	Body naked or partly covered with bony tubercles or prickles. No spines in anal fin.	Sculpins, Family Cottidae, page 199.	

Chapter One

LAMPREYS

Family Petromyzontidae

KEY TO THE ALASKAN SPECIES

SECTION	DESCRIPTION	THE LAMPREY IS	PROCEED IN THIS KEY TO SECTION
1 a.	Supraoral bar has 3 (in rare cases 2) sharp teeth; infraoral bar has about 5 teeth. Four pairs of lateral tooth plates, the two central pairs each having 3 points (Figure 5A, page 7).	Pacific lamprey, *Entosphenus tridentatus* (Gairdner), page 8.	
b.	Supraoral bar has 2 teeth (and in rare cases a small central third tooth); infraoral bar has 5 to 10 (usually 7 or 8) teeth. Three pairs of lateral tooth plates (Figures 5B-5D, page 7).		**2**
2 a.	Semicircular row of posterial teeth present below infraoral bar (teeth may be hidden in mucus) (Figure 5B, page 7); lateral tooth plates all have 2 points.	Arctic lamprey, *Lampetra japonica* (Martens), page 9.	
b.	No posterial teeth. Central pair of lateral tooth plates with 2 or 3 points (Figures 5C and 5D, page 7).		**3**
3 a.	Teeth sharp and strong. Tongue has large middle tooth. Three (in rare cases 2) points on central lateral tooth plates (Figure 5C, page 7).	River lamprey, *Lampetra ayresi* (Günther), page 10.	
b.	Teeth blunt. No median tooth on tongue. Two (in rare cases 3) blunt points on central lateral tooth plates (Figure 5D, page 7).	Western brook lamprey, *Lampetra richardsoni* Vladykov and Follett, page 11.	

The lampreys are a primitive group of fish-like creatures. Characteristically they have no jaws, the mouth being a round sucking opening on the ventral side of the head. There is only a single nostril, located on the dorsal side of the head just in front of the eyes. The gill openings are a row of seven round holes on each side of the head behind the eyes. The body is long and eellike, with no paired fins. The dorsal fin is in two parts, the anal fin in one, and both fins merge more or less into the caudal fin. The dorsal fin is larger and better developed in males than in females, while the anal fin is well developed in females but is almost nonexistent in males. The skeleton is entirely of cartilage and contains no bone.

Some species of lampreys are parasitic on fishes. They attach themselves to the host with the oral sucker, rasp away the skin and scales with their horny teeth, and suck the body juices. Parasitism appears to be found chiefly in anadromous species and is confined almost entirely to the marine phase of the life history. Nonparasitic species are much smaller than the parasitic and generally have blunt rather than sharp teeth.

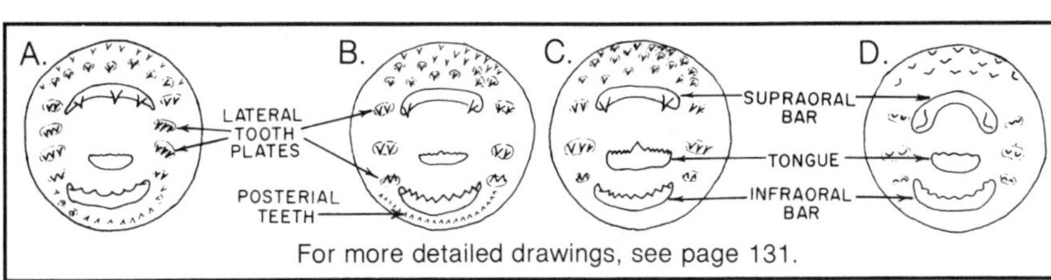

FIGURE 5. Tooth patterns of Alaska lampreys.
A. Pacific lamprey, *Entosphenus tridentatus.*
B. Arctic lamprey, *Lampetra japonica.*
C. River lamprey, *Lampetra ayresi.*
D. Western brook lamprey, *Lampetra richardsoni.*

PACIFIC LAMPREY

Entosphenus tridentatus (Gairdner)

DISTINCTIVE CHARACTERS

The Pacific lamprey is characterized by the presence of three (or, in rare cases, two) large sharp teeth on the supraoral bar and three sharp points on each of the central lateral tooth plates. (Plate 20A, page 131).

DESCRIPTION

Body elongate, eellike, more or less cylindrical toward the head, compressed toward the tail. Body depth about 7% of total length. Head moderate, its length about 15% of total length. Snout rounded, its length about 66% of head length. Eye round, small, its diameter about 19% of head length and about equal to postorbital distance. A single nostril is on median dorsal line just in front of the eyes, in a short tube. Oral sucker round to oval. Seven gill openings on each side of head, the vertical height of each opening about 60% of eye diameter; spaces between openings 43% to 53% of the eye diameter. There are 58 to 74 myotomes between last gill opening and anus. Anus at anterior end of anal fin. A slender, fairly prominent genital papilla present in males.

TEETH. Supraoral bar has 3 large, sharp points (in rare cases 2, the center point being reduced or absent). Lateral tooth plates have 3 sharp points on each of the central plates. A row of posterial teeth is present. Tongue has 15 to 25 small, fine teeth, all about the same size. Infraoral bar has 5 to 8 points (Figure 5A, page 7; Plate 20A, page 131).

FINS. Two dorsal fins arise far back on the body, the anterior fin lower and shorter than the posterior, the 2 fins separated by a notch. Dorsal fins higher in males than in females. Caudal fin more or less pointed, lower lobe larger than upper, the lobes joined to dorsal and anal fins. Anal fin rudimentary, virtually absent in males. No paired fins.

COLOR. Adults fresh from the sea are usually blue-black to greenish above, silvery to white below. Spawning adults become reddish brown.

SIZE. The Pacific lamprey reaches a length of 76 cm and a weight of about .5 kg.

RANGE AND ABUNDANCE

The Pacific lamprey has been recorded from the waters of Hokkaido Island, Japan, and one was taken from the stomach of a whale captured off Bering Island, near the Kamchatka Peninsula. In Alaskan waters, the Pacific lamprey has been recorded from Nome (UAFC #1119), Saint Matthew Island, Wood River, Unalaska Island and southward. The range in North America extends from the northern Bering Sea south to southern California. This lamprey is fairly abundant throughout its range.

HABITS

Adults return from the sea and run upstream in fresh water in the spring and summer, showing considerable ability to overcome obstacles such as dams and waterfalls. To accomplish this, a lamprey holds on with its oral sucker to the smooth face of an obstruction, then lets go and swims vigorously upward and catches onto a new hold. This procedure is repeated until the obstacle has been passed. At the time of upstream migration, lampreys are not yet sexually mature. They spend the following fall and winter in the streams, often burrowing into stream bottoms. Spawning takes place in the spring following the migration into fresh water. Spawning areas are usually in the upper reaches of the streams, most often in fine gravel at the upper ends of riffles. The nest is a shallow pit, about 55 cm in diameter, and is dug by both the male and female. To do the digging, each lamprey affixes itself to a stone by means of its oral sucker; then both members of the pair thrash about with their bodies, disturbing the fine sand and debris, which are carried downstream by the current. They may also pick up small stones with their suckers and carry them out of the nest.

In the spawning act, the female attaches herself to a stone and the male fastens his sucker on the head of the female. The two arch and twist their bodies toward each other, the male more or less wrapping his body around the female. This brings the male's genital papilla in close proximity to the genital pore of the female. The two then vibrate and eggs and sperm are released. A large female can produce up to about 100,000 eggs. The adults die soon after spawning.

The small, whitish eggs fall to the bottom of the nest, where the parents leave them. Hatching occurs a week or two after spawning, the time depending largely on temperature. The newly hatched larvae (ammocoetes) are blind and have no sucking disc. They remain for several years more or less buried in the fine sand and mud of the stream bottom, feeding by filtering plankton and tiny particles of algae and debris from the water. Finally, they metamorphose into the adult form and go to sea. A number of landlocked populations are known; in these the adults remain in fresh water throughout their entire lives (Pletcher, 1963).The adults of the nonlandlocked populations do not feed in fresh water.

During the marine life of the Pacific lamprey, the adults are parasitic, attaching themselves by means of the oral sucker to the bodies of larger fishes. With their sharp, horny teeth, they rasp through the scales and skin of the host and feed on the blood and body fluids. They will probably attack any fish of suitable size, but are known to parasitize especially the various species of salmons and trouts. The lampreys in turn are fed upon by many predacious fishes such as pike, trout and salmon.

IMPORTANCE TO MAN

The Pacific lamprey is of greatest importance as a parasite of more desirable fishes. It is not known whether this lamprey actually kills a significant number of fishes, but certainly a fair percentage of fishes are found bearing scars that may be attributable to *E. tridentatus.* The Pacific lamprey is not marketed as food, but there is no reason to think that it is any less edible than the European lampreys, which have long been considered a delicacy.

ARCTIC LAMPREY

Lampetra japonica (Martens)

DISTINCTIVE CHARACTERS

The arctic lamprey is distinguished by two large teeth on the supraoral bar, the presence of only two points on the central pair of lateral tooth plates, and the presence of a row of posterial teeth (Figure 6, below; Plate 20B, page 131).

DESCRIPTION

Body elongate and eellike; depth about equal to width near the head, becoming compressed toward the tail, equal to 5.8% to 9.1% of total length. Head short, 11.7% to 13.3% of total length. Snout rounded, its length 55% to 68% of head. Eye round, its diameter 15% to 28% of head and 114% to 152% of postorbital distance. In specimens less than 15 cm in total length, the eye is relatively large, more than 20% of the head length, while in individuals more than 20 cm long the eye is only 15% to 17% of head length. The relationship between the eye and the postorbital distance appears to remain constant. A single nostril is present on median dorsal line, just in front of eyes, in a short, fairly prominent tube. Oral sucker more or less round. Seven gill openings, approximately round, on each side of head, the diameter of each being 22% to 62% of size of eye. Spaces between gill openings average a little more than half the eye diameter. There are 65 to 80 myotomes between last gill opening and anus. Anus located at anterior end of anal fin. A slender, fairly prominent genital papilla present in males, barely developed in females (Figures 6A and 6B).

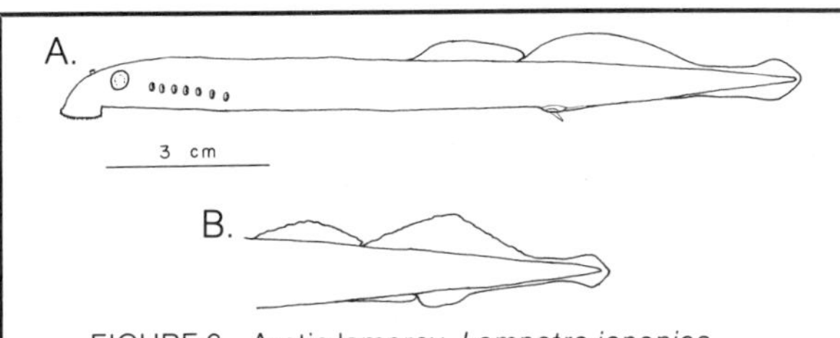

FIGURE 6. Arctic lamprey, *Lampetra japonica.*
A. Male.
B. Posterior end of female. Note presence of anal fin and lack of urogenital papilla in the female.
All four Alaskan lampreys are much alike in general appearance, so only the one species is illustrated.

Sensory pores on head region, each in a small tubercle, as follows: on each side a row of about 6 pores extending backward from tip of snout; a row of about 9 running upward and forward from ventral margin of the eye; a row of about 7 extending backward from upper part of posterior margin of eye. On dorsal side, a transverse row, often broken, of 4 to 6 pores across top of head at level of posterior margin of eye; 2 rows of widely spaced pores extending backward from just in front of first gill opening, the more dorsal row reaching somewhat behind the last opening and the more lateral row reaching the last opening. On ventral side, a fairly prominent row of sensory pores more or less encircling posterior part of oral sucker; 2 rows from behind oral sucker to a point about even with the fourth gill opening.

TEETH. Supraoral bar normally has 2 large points (rarely, a small third central point); lateral tooth plates with 2 points on central pair; a row of posterial teeth present. Tongue has a large median tooth point and 6 or 7 small points on each side. Infraoral bar has 5 to 10 points, usually blunt (Figure 5B, page 7; Plate 20B, page 131).

FINS. Two dorsal fins, the anterior lower than the posterior, arise far back on body, the fins separated from each other by at least a definite notch, fins higher in males than in females. On caudal fin, lower lobe is somewhat larger than upper, the fin joined to both dorsal and anal fins. Anal fin small, in males represented only by a low ridge.

COLOR. Variable, from brown to olive or grayish above, paler beneath (photograph, page 81; Plate 19, page 130).

SIZE. Known to reach a length of over 60 cm, but generally smaller. The strictly freshwater, nonanadromous form rarely exceeds 18 cm.

RANGE AND ABUNDANCE

In Alaska, the arctic lamprey ranges from the Kenai Peninsula north to the arctic coast and east as far as the Anderson River in Canada. It has also been found on Saint Lawrence Island. Inland, it ranges up the Yukon River into the Yukon Territory and is also present in the Kuskokwim and Tanana river drainages. Worldwide, this species is almost completely circumpolar, ranging from Lapland south to the Caspian Sea, eastward to Kamchatka, south to Korea, and eastward across North America to the Northwest Territories of Canada.

Abundance varies locally and seasonally. Large numbers are known to ascend the lower Yukon River, and the population in the Naknek River also seems to be relatively large. A small population is known to spawn in the Chatanika River a few kilometers below the Elliott Highway Bridge.

HABITS

Relatively little is known of the life history of this species. In the Naknek River of Alaska, and doubtless in other areas as well, the populations are composed of both anadromous and completely freshwater forms. The lampreys of the Chatanika River are strictly freshwater. This dwarf freshwater form has recently been described as a new species, *Lethenteron alaskense,* by Vladykov and Kott (1978). Lampreys of the lower Yukon are mostly anadromous. Both the anadromous and freshwater forms have been reported to be parasitic, but the blunt teeth of the freshwater form suggest that it is nonparasitic.

Spawning takes place in the spring. Both the male and female engage in nest-building, removing pebbles and small rocks from the stream bottom either by picking the rocks up with their suckers and depositing them downstream from the nest or by attaching themselves to large rocks and thrashing violently, thus raising small stones and silt which are then carried downstream by the current. Nests are located out of the main current in water from a few centimeters to nearly a meter deep, flowing at .16 to .3m per second. In the breeding act, the male attaches himself by means of his sucker to the head of the female. The two arch their bodies and the male wraps himself around the female so that his genital papilla is close to her genital pore. Both of the lampreys vibrate rapidly and eggs and sperm are extruded into the nest. Occasionally two males may mate simultaneously with a single female. A female will mate several times before her egg supply is exhausted, usually with several males. A large female may produce more than 100,000 eggs.

Time for development of the eggs is probably a few weeks. The larvae (ammocoetes) apparently spend at least one and possibly two years in this stage, for in the Naknek River two distinct size groups have been observed. Upon metamorphosis, the young adults descend the stream either to the sea or to lakes or larger rivers. The adult is parasitic on many species of fishes, attaching itself to the host by means of the oral sucker, rasping through the skin and scales and sucking the host's blood and body fluids. Host species that have been recorded include sockeye salmon *(Oncorhynchus nerka),* pink salmon *(O. gorbuscha),* chum salmon *(O. keta),* chinook salmon *(O. tshawytscha),* starry flounder *(Platichthys stellatus),* pygmy whitefish *(Prosopium coulteri)* and three-spine stickleback *(Gasterosteus aculeatus)* (Berg, 1948; Birman, 1950; Heard, 1966; McPhail and Lindsey, 1970). It is probable that this lamprey will parasitize any species of fish, providing only that the host be of suitable size.

Length of life is unknown, but must be at least 3 years, probably more.

IMPORTANCE TO MAN

The arctic lamprey is probably of no direct importance to man. It is possible that lamprey parasitism may have a bad effect on the health of the host, but, at least in the Naknek River, there is no evidence that the arctic lamprey has had an adverse effect on the fisheries (Heard, 1966). In the Yukon River, lampreys were once taken in large numbers with dip nets and used for food (Evermann and Goldsborough, 1907). However, at the present time this species is little used for any purpose, although a market for smoked lampreys might well be developed.

RIVER LAMPREY

Lampetra ayresi (Günther)

DISTINCTIVE CHARACTERS

The river lamprey is distinguished by two large teeth on the supraoral bar, a large middle tooth on the tongue, three points (in rare cases, two) on each central lateral tooth plate, and the absence of posterial teeth (Plate 20C, page 131).

DESCRIPTION

Body elongate, eellike, nearly cylindrical as far back as the dorsal and anal fins, where it becomes compressed. Depth about 8% to 11% of total length. Head moderate, 11% to 14% of total length. Snout rounded, its length about 60% of head. Eye large, round, its diameter 100% to 200% of postorbital length. A single nostril on median dorsal line, barely in front of eyes, in a short tube. Seven gill openings on each side of head, vertical height of each about 24% of eye diameter, spaces between openings equal to about 50% of eye. Usually 65 to 71 trunk myotomes, in rare cases as few as 60, between last gill opening and anus. Anus at anterior end of anal fin. A slender anal papilla present in males.

TEETH. Supraoral bar has 2 sharp points. Three lateral tooth plates present on each side of mouth, the central ones with 3 points, the others with 2. Tongue has a large triangular central tooth and about 7 small teeth on each side. Infraoral bar with 7 to 10 (usually 9) teeth. No posterial teeth (Figure 5C, page 7; Plate 20C, page 131).

FINS. Two dorsal fins, the anterior fin being the lower, the fins separate in nonbreeding individuals but coming in contact at spawning. Caudal fin pointed, lobes about equal, lower lobe joined to anal fin. Anal fin virtually absent in males.

COLOR. Dark brown or brownish gray on sides and back; belly whitish, silvery around head, gill openings and lower sides. Caudal fin has a band of dark pigment inside its margin, symmetrical on each lobe.

SIZE. Maximum length about 31.1 cm. Average length of adults seems to be about 17 cm (Vladykov and Follett, 1958).

RANGE AND ABUNDANCE

The river lamprey is confined to the west coast of North America and is found from as far south as San Francisco Bay (Vladykov and Follett, 1958) to as far north as Tee Harbor, 24 km northwest of Juneau (Scott and Crossman, 1973). It does not appear to be particularly abundant anywhere within its range.

HABITS

Like most parasitic lampreys, *L. ayresi* is anadromous. Spawning occurs in the spring (in late April through May in California). No written description of spawning behavior exists, nor is the length of larval or adult life known. Egg numbers per female have been estimated at 37,288 for a specimen 17.5 cm long, and 11,398 for one of 23 cm. The river lamprey is known to parasitize small coho and kokanee salmon, and is in turn eaten by other fishes such as ling cod (Vladykov and Follett, 1958).

IMPORTANCE TO MAN

As with other lampreys, the importance of this species is indirect in that it parasitizes more desirable fishes. However, its limited abundance makes it of little concern.

WESTERN BROOK LAMPREY

Lampetra richardsoni Vladykov and Follett

DISTINCTIVE CHARACTERS

The very blunt teeth, the lack of a distinct median tooth on the tongue and the lack of posterial teeth distinguish this species of lamprey from others found in Alaska (Plate 20D, page 131).

DESCRIPTION

Body elongate and eellike, more or less cylindrical near the head but becoming compressed toward the tail. Depth of body about 7% of total length. Head short, about 12.5% of total length. Snout rounded, its length about 60% of head. Eye small, round; diameter about 2.3% of total length, about equal to postorbital distance. A single nostril on median dorsal line of head, a short distance in front of eyes, in a short, fairly prominent tube. Oral sucker round, its diameter about 59% to 60% of snout length. Seven gill openings on each side. From 60 to 67 myotomes between last gill opening and anus. Anus just before anal fin. A small but obvious genital papilla in males. The number and arrangement of

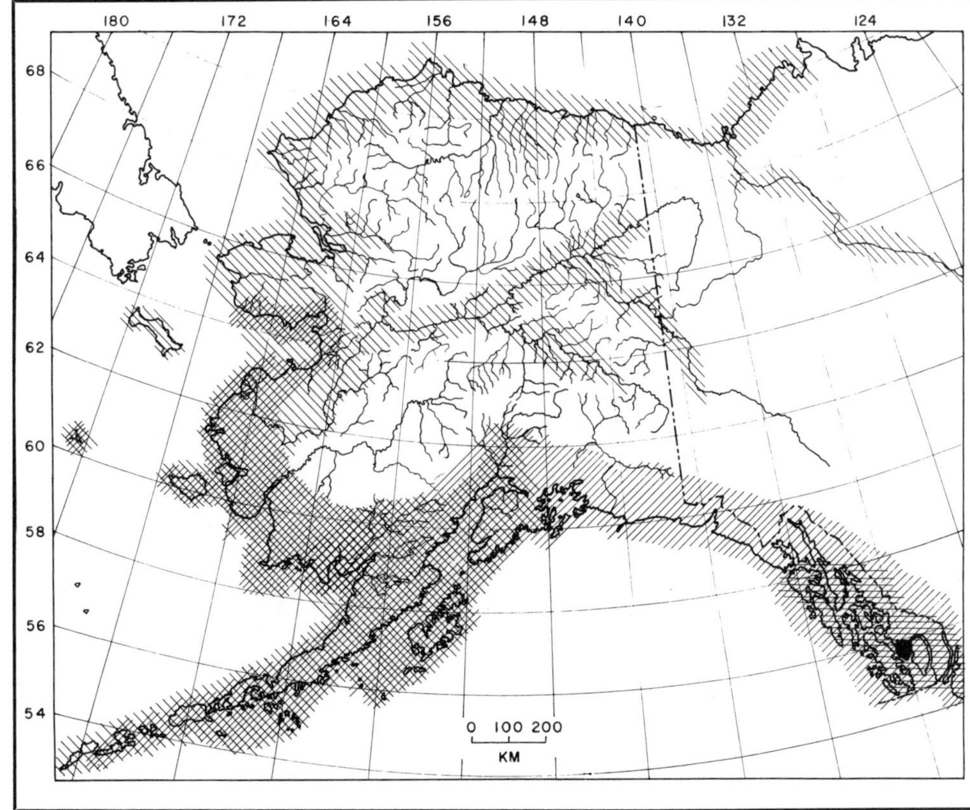

Range in Alaska and northwestern Canada of the Pacific lamprey ▨, arctic lamprey ▧, river lamprey ▤ and western brook lamprey ●

the sensory pores on the head seems to be as in *L. japonica.*

TEETH. Two broad, blunt teeth present on supraoral bar. Two blunt teeth on each lateral tooth plate. About 5 blunt teeth on tongue. Infraoral bar with about 7 blunt teeth. No posterial teeth (Figure 5D, page 7; Plate 20D, page 131).

FINS. Two dorsal fins, the anterior lower than the posterior, arising well back on body. Fins are separate from each other in the young, but come together and at least touch (and may fuse) with onset of sexual maturity. Caudal fin joined to both dorsal and anal fins. Anal fin small, represented in males only by a low ridge.

COLOR. Sides and back dark gray to brown, ventral side of body whitish. Caudal fin and posterior tip of body conspicuously dark.

SIZE. This is quite a small species, the largest specimen recorded being only 15.4 cm long. Ammocoetes range up to 17.5 cm (Vladykov and Follett, 1965).

RANGE AND ABUNDANCE

In Alaska the western brook lamprey has been recorded only from McDonald Lake, on the Cleveland Peninsula in southeastern Alaska, just north of Yes Bay. However, it ranges southward in coastal streams in British Columbia, Washington and Oregon as far south as the Umpqua River near Reedsport, Oregon. It is not particularly abundant anywhere as far as is known.

HABITS

Nothing is known of the biology of this species. Presumably its life history is like that of other nonparasitic lampreys; the larvae burrow into the bottoms of brooks or hide under stones, hence are not easily discovered. The adults do not feed and probably do not live more than a few months. They die after spawning.

IMPORTANCE TO MAN

Except for its scientific and esthetic interest, this species is of no importance to man. It probably serves as a minor portion of the food of predacious insects and fishes wherever it is found.

Chapter Two

STURGEONS

Family Acipenseridae

KEY TO THE ALASKAN SPECIES

SECTION	DESCRIPTION	THE STURGEON IS	
a.	Bony plates between pelvic fins and anal fin in a single row of 1 to 4 plates (Figure 7A, below). About 33 dorsal fin rays.	Green sturgeon, *Acipenser medirostris* Ayres, below.	
b.	Bony plates between pelvic fins and anal fin in two rows of 4 to 8 plates each (Figure 8A, page 14). About 45 dorsal fin rays.	White sturgeon, *Acipenser transmontanus* Richardson, page 14.	

This group includes some of the largest fishes in the world, some of them exceeding 1,000 kg in weight and 6 m in length. The sturgeon is a heavy fish with a more or less cylindrical body; a flat, extended snout and a toothless, protrusible mouth with four barbels in front of it on the underside of the snout. The tail is upturned, like that of a shark, with the upper lobe notably longer than the lower. The body has five rows of large bony plates: a row along the back, a row on each side, and two ventrolateral rows. The plates are sharp-pointed in the young but blunt in adults. The skin between the plates appears naked but actually bears patches of fine denticles. The head is covered by bony plates. The first ray of the pectoral fin is heavy and ossified. The two species of sturgeon found in Alaska are anadromous, spending most of their lives in the sea but breeding in fresh water.

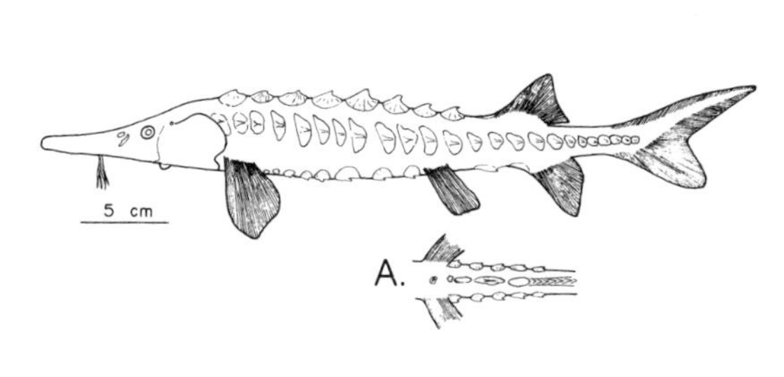

FIGURE 7. Green sturgeon, *Acipenser medirostris*.
A. The single row of bony plates in front of the anal fin.

GREEN STURGEON

Acipenser medirostris Ayres

DISTINCTIVE CHARACTERS

A single row of one to four bony plates along the midventral line between the anus and the anal fin, and about 33 to 35 rays in the dorsal fin characterize the green sturgeon (Figure 7).

DESCRIPTION

Body rather robust, more or less 5-sided in cross-section, depth about 10% of total length. Head flattened, its length about 25% of total length. Snout elongate, flattened, somewhat concave in profile. Mouth toothless, small, transverse, protrusible and located on ventral side. Four sensory barbels in front of mouth, their bases nearer to mouth than to tip of snout. Eyes small, round. Gill rakers: 18 to 20. Body has 5 longitudinal rows of bony, keeled plates, the keels sharp-pointed in the young but becoming more blunt and rounded in older individuals. Plates are in one dorsal row of 8 to 11 plates; in 2 lateral rows of 23 to 30 plates each, and in 2 ventrolateral rows of 7 to 10 plates each. Skin between plates has numerous small rough plates or denticles. A single row of 1 to 4 small bony plates is present on ventral midline between anus and origin of anal fin.

FINS. Dorsal arises at posterior third of total length; usually has 33 to 35 rays. Anal originates under posterior part of dorsal; 22 to 28 rays. Pectorals orginate low on body just behind gill openings, and are large and rounded. Pelvics arise near anus. Caudal is heterocercal, lower lobe about three-quarters as long as upper.

COLOR. Generally olive to dark green, lower parts more or less whitish green. A longitudinal olive-green stripe is on side between lateral and ventrolateral plates, another on midventral surface. Fins grayish to pale green (photograph, page 81; Plate 1, page 112).

SIZE. Reaches a length of over 2 m and a weight of about 160 kg (Dees, 1961).

RANGE AND ABUNDANCE

In Alaska, the green sturgeon has been found as far north as the northwest side of Unalaska Island in the Aleutians, but it is rather uncommon in the state (Wilimovsky, 1964). The range extends southward along the Pacific coast of North America to southern California, with two specimens recorded from just south of Los Angeles (Roedel, 1941; Norris, 1957). It has also been reported from Ensenada, Baja California (Miller and Lea, 1972). On the western side of the Pacific, this species ranges from the Amur River of eastern Siberia, south to the Japanese island of Hokkaido (Ueno and Abe, 1966); and from Peter the Great Bay in the U.S.S.R. south to Kunsan, Korea. The area of greatest abundance seems to be from the Columbia River in Washington and Oregon to the Fraser River in British Columbia.

HABITS

Very little is known of the biology of the green sturgeon. Available information suggests that the life history is like that of other anadromous sturgeons. However, the green sturgeon is not known to ascend streams to any great distance. It is most commonly found in estuaries, in the lower reaches of large rivers and in salt or brackish water off river mouths.

The green sturgeon probably spawns in fresh water. It is captured in nets and by anglers in the lower Columbia and Fraser rivers from late summer to winter. Presumably these fish move into the fresh water in the late summer and fall to spawn the following spring.

Green sturgeon may cover considerable distances in the ocean. Three fish tagged in 1954 in San Pablo Bay, California, near the mouth of the Sacramento River, were recovered one to four years later in Oregon. One was recaptured in Winchester Bay, the other two in the lower Columbia River (Chadwick, 1959).

Nothing is known of growth rates or age.

Food of the green sturgeon probably consists largely of bottom-dwelling invertebrates and small fishes. There is one report of a green sturgeon having fed on sand lance (Anonymous, 1954). The young eat mostly amphipods and mysids (Radtke, 1966).

IMPORTANCE TO MAN

The green sturgeon is virtually unused in North America, although it is taken commercially in the Bering Sea by Russian fishermen (Magnin, 1959). As a food fish, the green sturgeon is considered inferior. The flesh, which was once thought to be poisonous, is said to be dark, with a strong disagreeable taste and an unpleasant odor. We know that in the past the roe was not used (Jordan and Evermann, 1908). The green sturgeon does not seem to be particularly common, although occasional concentrations (possibly feeding aggregations) may be encountered. One such was reported off Kyuquot Sound on the northwest coast of Vancouver Island, where 75 fish were taken in a single day (Anonymous, 1954).

WHITE STURGEON

Acipenser transmontanus Richardson

DISTINCTIVE CHARACTERS

Two rows of four to eight bony plates on a midventral line between the anus and anal fin, and about 45 rays in the dorsal fin distinguish the white sturgeon (Figure 8).

DESCRIPTION

Body elongate, subcylindrical, depth about 10% of total length. Head more or less conical, somewhat flattened above, its length 19% to 23% of total length. Snout moderately produced, blunt, relatively shorter in adults than in young. Eyes small. Nostrils prominent. Mouth wide, transverse, protrusible and toothless; located on ventral side of head below eyes. Four tactile barbels on ventral side of snout in front of mouth, a little closer to tip of snout than to mouth. Gill rakers: 34 to 36. Five longitudinal rows of keeled, bony plates on body: dorsal row contains 11 to 14 plates; lateral rows, 38 to 48 each; ventrolateral rows, 9 to 12 each. In rare cases there may be

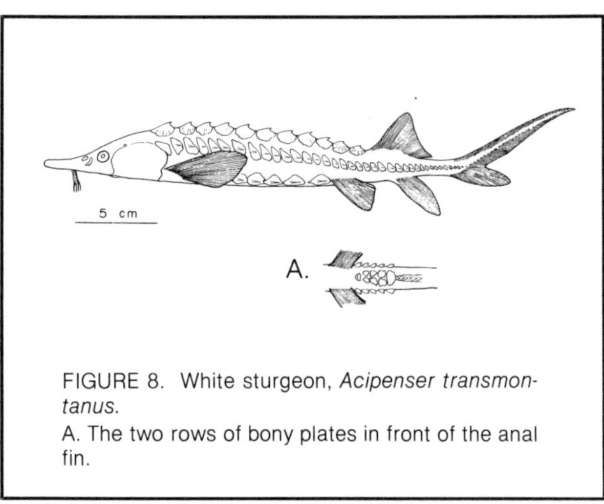

FIGURE 8. White sturgeon, *Acipenser transmontanus*.
A. The two rows of bony plates in front of the anal fin.

a secondary row on each side between the dorsal and lateral rows (Bajkov, 1955). Skin between plates has numerous, rather inconspicuous, stellate tubercles. Two rows of 4 to 8 plates each on ventral side between anus and anal fin.

FINS. Dorsal originates near posterior third of total length and has 44 to 48 rays. Anal originates under posterior part of dorsal; 28 to 31 rays. Pectorals arise low on body just behind gill openings; upper rays longer than lower, first ray notably enlarged and bony. Pelvics originate slightly before anus. Caudal is heterocercal, upper lobe about twice as long as lower.

COLOR. Generally gray or brownish above, paler below. Fins gray (photograph, page 82).

SIZE. The largest freshwater fish in North America, the white sturgeon is reputed to attain a length of 6 m and a weight of over 860 kg. However, the heaviest specimen actually documented weighed 630 kg (Hart, 1973).

RANGE AND ABUNDANCE

The white sturgeon inhabits the Pacific coast of North America from Ensenada, Baja California, in the south (Miller and Lea, 1972) to the Gulf of Alaska in the north. Found in rivers and estuaries and in the sea as deep as 122 m, the white sturgeon is most abundant in and around the mouth of the Columbia River. It has been suggested that the "sea monster" of Lake Iliamna may be a large white sturgeon. This species is not common in Alaska.

HABITS

The white sturgeon is anadromous, but some individuals apparently spend much of their lives in fresh water. Mature fish enter the estuaries and lower reaches of large rivers any time from fall to early spring, although the majority seem to leave the sea in the spring. Upstream migration begins in April or May, with spawning taking place in May and June in most areas (Bajkov, 1951). Some fish may move great distances, for example going up the Columbia River as far as Flathead Lake, Montana (Brunson and Block, 1957). Such fish may well start their upstream migration earlier (perhaps even in the previous year) and spawn later than fish moving shorter distances.

Spawning areas are said to be in swift water over rocky bottoms. Water temperature during the spawning period has been reported as 8.9° to 16.7°C (Scott and Crossman, 1973).

For fish of southern stock, first spawning occurs at about 10 years of age for males, 11 to 12 years for females (Pycha, 1956; Carlander, 1969). In the Fraser River, males mature at 11 to 22 years, females at 26 to 34 (Semakula and Larkin, 1968). Adults return to the sea after spawning and do not breed annually. Intervals of 2 to 9 years may occur between breeding periods in the Fraser River stock (Semakula and Larkin, 1968).

Fecundity varies with the size of the individual, from a few hundred thousand eggs in small females to about 2 million or more in the largest. Ovary weights may reach more than 110 kg.

The eggs, which are brown in color, are sticky and adhere to the stream bottom. Time required for hatching is unknown. Growth of the young is quite rapid for the first few years. One-year-old fish from San Pablo Bay, California, averaged about 26 cm total length; five-year-olds, about 80 cm. After the eighth year, the fish grew at a fairly constant rate of 5 to 6 cm per year. Similar growth rates were found in white sturgeon of the Fraser River (Pycha, 1956; Semakula and Larkin, 1968).

Adult white sturgeon may reach great size, but exceptionally large fish are rare nowadays. The average weight of net-caught fish seems to be on the order of 16 to 25 kg. Around the turn of the century, however, unusually large fish appear to have been more common. One of 862 kg was claimed to have been taken at Astoria, Oregon. Another (possibly the same fish) of about 908 kg is supposed to have been exhibited at the Chicago World's Fair in 1893, but neither the specimens nor records of them now exist (Jordan et al., 1930; Gudger, 1942). Other large white sturgeon include one of 817 kg from the Fraser River at Mission, British Columbia, sometime before 1897; one of 630 kg from the Fraser at New Westminster in 1897; and one of 583 kg and 3.81 m long from the Columbia River at Vancouver, Washington, in 1912 (Gudger, 1942; Clemens and Wilby, 1946, 1961).

The maximum age recorded for the white sturgeon is 82 years (Carlander, 1969). Extrapolation of growth-rate date given by Pycha (1956) suggests that the several unusually large fish mentioned above must have been on the order of 100 years old, possibly older.

The white sturgeon spends much of its life in the sea, where it is thought to remain fairly close to shore. It is known from depths of 30 m or less and has been taken in salt, brackish and fresh waters that had temperatures between 0° and 23.3°C. Migrations and movements in the sea are not well known, but they certainly exist, for a specimen tagged in San Pablo Bay, California, was recaptured about 10 months later at the mouth of the Columbia River, a minimum distance of 1,056 km (Chadwick, 1959).

The white sturgeon is primarily an omnivorous scavenger, but seems also to be actively piscivorous—much more so than other sturgeons. Eulachon and lampreys appear to be favored foods; other foods the white sturgeon commonly eats are sculpins, sticklebacks, salmonids, crayfish, frogs, mollusks, insect larvae and various other organisms (Gudger, 1942; Merrell, 1961; Carlander, 1969; Scott and Crossman, 1973). The young feed primarily on plankton, amphipods, shrimp and tendepedid larvae. Other food organisms include mysids, *Daphnia, Chaoborus* larvae, copepods and various immature insects (Schreiber, 1961; Radtke, 1966; Carlander, 1969; Scott and Crossman, 1973).

IMPORTANCE TO MAN

Before about 1880, white sturgeon were used almost solely in subsistence fisheries. As the Pacific salmon fisheries developed, the sturgeon came to be considered a nuisance. However, in 1886 or 1887, a commercial firm began to ship frozen sturgeon to eastern markets. The enterprise was successful, and by 1892 the Oregon landings from the Columbia River were about 1.5 million kg. The greater part of the flesh was smoked after arrival in the east, the eggs made into caviar and the air bladder into isinglass. (Isinglass was a translucent or transparent gelatin used, among other things, as transparent plastic is used today: for example, as roll-down curtains to keep out rain.) Indeed, every part of the fish was used, even the backbone (McGuire, 1896). But this state of affairs did not last long. By 1897 the total catch for Washington and Oregon had dropped to just under 629,142 kg and by 1900 had declined to a mere 55,152 kg. The fishery continued at a low ebb until the mid-1940s, when catches began to rise. Landings in 1970 were on the order of 227,000 kg. The catch from the Fraser River has averaged about 13,600 kg annually since 1941 (Hart, 1973).

Flesh of the white sturgeon is highly esteemed, either fresh or smoked, and the eggs make excellent caviar. However, there is no demand for isinglass nowadays.

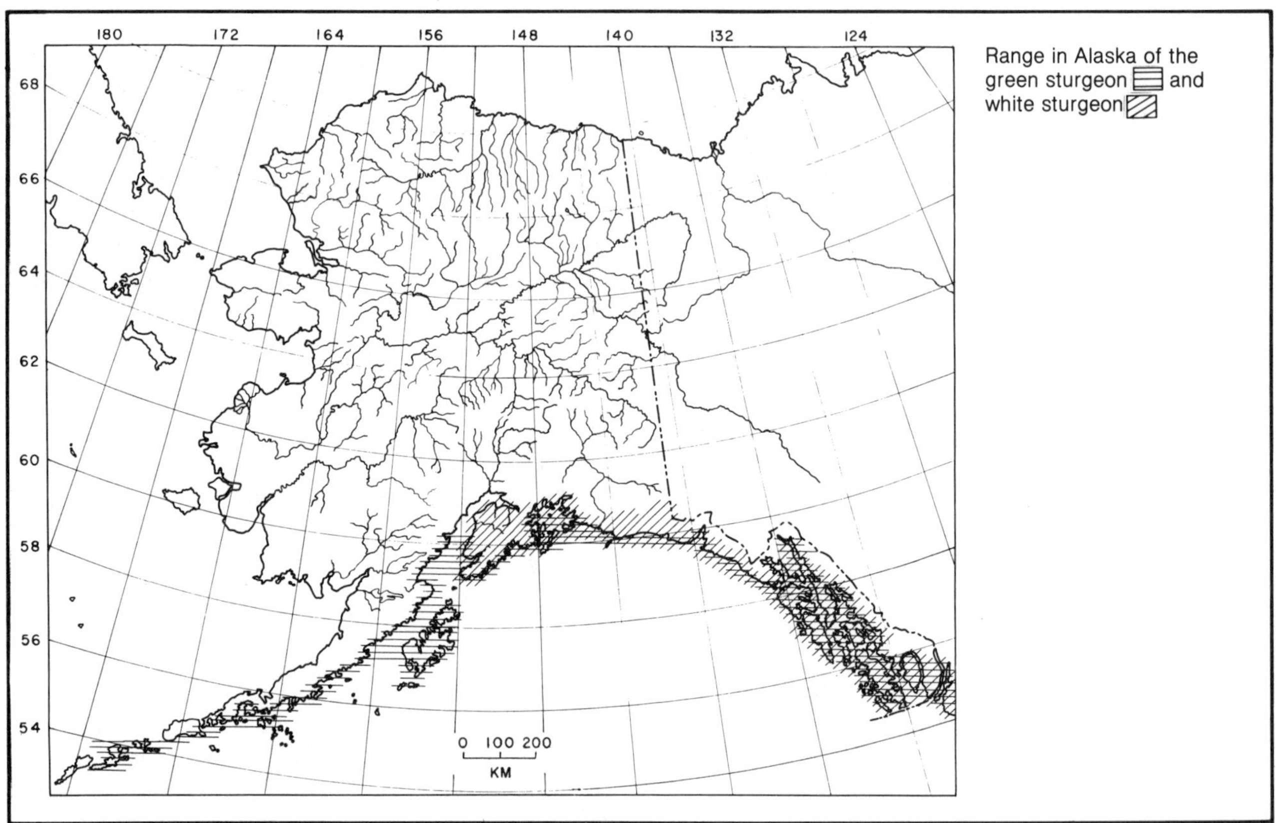

Range in Alaska of the green sturgeon and white sturgeon

Chapter Three

HERRING AND SHAD

Family Clupeidae

KEY TO THE ALASKAN SPECIES

SECTION	DESCRIPTION	THE FISH IS	
a.	Distance from front of dorsal fin to tip of snout about equal to distance from front of dorsal fin to base of tail. Teeth present on vomer.	Pacific herring, *Clupea harengus pallasi* Valenciennes, below.	
b.	Distance from front of dorsal fin to tip of snout much less than distance from front of dorsal fin to base of tail. No teeth on vomer.	American shad, *Alosa sapidissima* Wilson, page 20.	

The family Clupeidae is a large one, containing about 70 genera and more than 150 species, but only two members—the Pacific herring, *Clupea harengus pallasi,* and the American shad, *Alosa sapidissima*—are found in Alaska.

Characteristically, the members of this group have slender, compressed bodies, although some species are short and deep and a few are subcylindrical. The scales are cycloid and in most cases are extremely deciduous. The ventral side of the body is compressed to a sharp edge, usually serrate. There is no lateral line. The mouth is large, and teeth are small or absent in almost all members of this family. The dorsal fin is located about at the center of the body length and there is no adipose fin. The caudal fin is forked.

From the economic standpoint, this is one of the most important of the families of fishes. Vast numbers are taken for food to be eaten fresh, canned, smoked or pickled. Other species are used for fish meal and oil. The smaller species and the young of the larger ones serve as food for a tremendous variety of large fishes, aquatic mammals, birds and turtles.

PACIFIC HERRING

Clupea harengus pallasi Valenciennes

DISTINCTIVE CHARACTERS

The Pacific herring can be distinguished from its relative, the American shad, by the place of origin of the dorsal fin, which is about midway between the tip of the snout and the base of the tail (the fin originates farther forward in the shad); the body depth, which is 25% or less of the length (more in the shad); and the presence of teeth on the vomer which are absent in the shad (Figure 9).

DESCRIPTION

Body elongate, compressed, its depth less than 25% of total length. Head compressed, its length about equal to body depth. Snout of moderate length, about equal to eye diameter. Eyes round, adipose lids present. Mouth fairly large; no teeth on jaws, but a patch of fine teeth on vomer in roof of mouth. Gill rakers fine and long; those at angle of gill arch about as long as eye diameter; the number—63 to 73—apparently increases with size of fish. Lateral line absent. Number of vertebrae—51 to 57—increases with latitude.

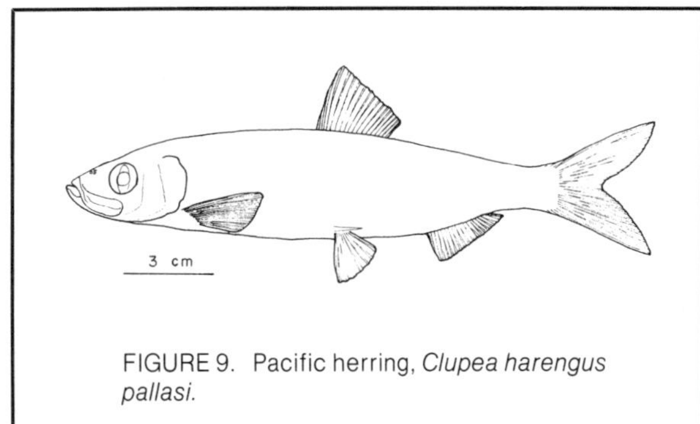

FIGURE 9. Pacific herring, *Clupea harengus pallasi.*

FINS. Dorsal, originates about midway between tip of snout and base of tail; 15 to 21 rays. Anal, 14 to 20 rays; pectorals, 17 to 19. Pelvics, which are abdominal in position, have 8 to 9 rays and a fleshy axillary process above the origin of the fin. Caudal forked.

SCALES. Large, cycloid, deciduous, in 38 to 54 rows along side of body. On midventral line scales are modified; moderate keels are present on scales in front of pelvic fins, strong keels on scales between pelvics and anal.

COLOR. Dark blue to olivaceous above shading to silver below (photograph, page 82).

SIZE. Said to reach 38 cm in Alaskan waters, but the average adult is probably around 25 cm.

RANGE AND ABUNDANCE

On the North American coast, the Pacific herring is found from northern Baja California (Miller and Lea, 1972) to Bathurst Inlet in the eastern Beaufort Sea (Richardson, 1836). Commercial fisheries exist as far south as San Francisco, but the region of greatest abundance is along the coasts of British Columbia and Southeastern and Central Alaska. Large Pacific herring populations probably exist in the Bering Sea (Warner, 1977). It is uncertain whether the herring of the Chukchi and Beaufort seas are self-sustaining populations or represent migrants from farther south.

On the western side of the Pacific, this herring ranges from the Japanese islands and Korea north and west to the Laptev Sea on the arctic coast of Siberia. Very closely related forms are found still farther west in the Kara Sea, Barents Sea and White Sea (Andriyashev, 1954; Nikolskii, 1961).

Although generally considered a marine species, the Pacific herring occasionally enters estuaries. Freshwater, landlocked races have been reported from Japan (Fujita and Kokubo, 1927).

The Pacific herring is, by and large, one of the more abundant fishes along the coast of Alaska, although this abundance tends to be seasonal and varies tremendously from year to year. Occasionally, enormous schools may congregate in very limited areas. One of these aggregations occurred on January 1, 1912, when millions of herring followed the incoming tide into Klawock harbor on the west coast of Prince of Wales Island. The fish arrived in such numbers that they filled the bay ". . . solid with herring from top to bottom. . . . Big halibut . . . skittered along the surface, unable to bore down into the jam of dead and dying herring" (Gould, 1938). In the middle harbor alone, a conservative estimate reported 40 million cubic feet of solidly packed dead herring, and a year later the propellers of ships docking at Klawock stirred up still-undecomposed herring from the harbor bottom (Gould, 1938).

Even aside from such enormous and abnormal examples as this, herring schools can be of great size. On April 12, 1974, 28 purse-seiners and 12 gill-netters at Sitka took about 1.4 million kg of herring in 2.5 hours (Rearden, 1975b).

HABITS

The Pacific herring spawns from December to July. Winter spawning occurs at the southern end of its range, around San Diego, California, and occurs progressively later in the year in more northern populations (Schaefer, 1937; Scattergood et al., 1959; Barraclough, 1967). In Alaska most spawning activity goes on between mid-March and mid-April in southeastern; from April to May in Prince William Sound; and from May to June around Kodiak Island (Scattergood et al., 1959). Spawning has been recorded in the Bering Sea near Saint Michael in June (Nelson, 1887). Spawning activity is roughly related to temperature and occurs at water temperatures between 3° and 12.3°C.

The eggs are .12 cm to .17 cm in diameter after being spawned. Fecundity is related to size and age, with northern fish apparently producing more eggs than do southern ones of the same size (Nagasaki, 1958), although there is considerable variation among populations (Katz, 1948). Average egg numbers along the coast of North America range from a little over 8,000 in two-year-old fish from southern British Columbia to more than 59,000 in seven-year-olds (Nagasaki, 1958). A fish from Peter the Great Bay, near Vladivostok, was reported to contain more than 134,000 eggs (Katz, 1948, citing Russian data).

Spawning of the Pacific herring appears to be a mass proposition, with no definite pairing of males and females, although Rounsefell (1930) described the male following "a few inches behind the female covering the attached eggs with a stream of milt."

Spawning takes place in shallow water, from the very edge of the high-tide line to a depth of about 7 m, most commonly over vegetation such as eelgrass or seaweed, or on brush, pilings or rocks, and begins in Alaskan waters when the temperature rises to about 4° C.

In the spawning act the female turns on her side, fins extended and body nearly rigid. Vibrating her tail, she moves slowly forward, brushing the eel grass or other substrate with her vent and depositing her eggs as she goes. The posterior edge of the vent is equipped with a fleshy lobe which blocks extrusion of the eggs. Brushing the vent against the substrate pulls this lobe out of the way, allowing the eggs to escape. The female remains on her side for 2 to 5 seconds, then resumes an upright posture. This procedure is repeated again and again until all the eggs have been laid, which may take several days (Schaefer, 1937).

While the females are depositing their eggs, the males in the area are releasing milt. The milt mixes and spreads in the water, fertilizing the eggs, and the whitish, milt-filled water may extend for several kilometers along the shore (photograph, page 83).

The eggs are sticky and adhere to whatever they touch. If temperatures are normal, the eggs hatch in about 10 days, yielding yolk-sac larvae approximately .75 cm long. Feeding begins two weeks or less after hatching, as soon as the yolk has been absorbed. The first foods are mainly copepods, invertebrate eggs and diatoms. The young fish are in turn eaten by various filter feeders such as pilchards and by entanglers such as jellyfishes as well as by amphipods and young salmons (von Westernhagen and Rosenthal, 1976).

During the early growth period the young herring may be dispersed by waves and currents. Those that are carried out to sea apparently perish, and this offshore transport seems to be the major cause of mortality at this time (Stevenson, 1962). Those not carried out to sea subsequently congregate in suitable shallow bays, inlets and channels (Hourston, 1958; 1959). By the end of the summer, the young may be as long as 10 cm. They move into deeper water in the fall and virtually disappear from the fishing grounds for the next couple of years.

After the first year or two, northern herring grow faster than those from California, and they also live longer and grow bigger. The oldest known California herring was a 9+, but a 19+ has been recorded from Alaska. Most herring in the Alaskan catch are between 4+ and 9+ (Rounsefell, 1930; Miller and Schmidtke, 1956).

As the fish grow, larger food items become more important in the diet. Copepods remain important to the young, but the diet also includes euphausiids, amphipods, cladocerans and decapod and mollusk larvae. Adults have a similar diet but also eat larger crustaceans and a wide variety of small fishes. In turn, adult herring are preyed upon by virtually every animal large enough to eat them: dogfish and other sharks, salmon, cods, mackerel, squid, seals, sea lions and man.

Pacific herring usually move offshore in the winter and back onshore for spawning, but apparently do not undertake extensive coastal migrations. Mixing of local populations is relatively rare, so particular groups can be recognized by distinctive physical characteristics all the way from Alaska to southern California.

IMPORTANCE TO MAN

The Pacific herring has never rivaled its Atlantic relative in terms of tonnage landed, but it is nevertheless a significant part of the fisheries of the North Pacific. Along the Siberian coast, "the annual catch exceeds 6,000,000 centners"—300 million kg (Andriyashev, 1954). Tonnage figures for the North American coast are generally slightly lower. Almost all the North American Pacific herring catch comes from Alaska and British Columbia.

The Alaskan herring fishery began in the late 19th century. Statistics for 1882 show landings of 1.36 million kg. Over the next 34 years the catch fluctuated between 2.5 and 14.6 million kg, averaging about 6.6 million. The majority of the catch went into salted herring in various forms. World War I increased the demand for salted herring from Alaska and catches increased accordingly. By the mid-1920s, however, the Alaskan salteries could no longer compete, either in price or in quality of product, with the resurgent European industry. Nevertheless, a great expansion of the reduction industry led to further increased landings. From 1924 to 1941, Alaskan landings were more than 45.5 million kg per year, peaking at more than 118.6 million kg in 1937. For the next 10 years or so, catches varied widely; then, beginning in the early 1950s, they dropped rapidly. This has been attributed to a sudden drop in the number of fish, increased competition from foreign sources, and other factors such as greater profit in competing fisheries, which attracted workers away from herring. Probably all three causes were important. In recent years, the Alaskan herring fishery has produced between 4.5 and 9.1 million kg annually, most of it being used for bait (Anderson and Power, 1946, 1957; Anderson and Peterson, 1953; Power, 1962; Lyles, 1969; Anonymous, 1971, 1972, 1973; Browning, 1974).

Dwellers along the Pacific coast have long made use of herring eggs spawned on kelp or on brush placed at appropriate places to collect the spawn. In the early 1960s, the Japanese began buying herring eggs on kelp. This product, called *kazunoka kombu,* is a great delicacy in Japan and commands a high price. In Alaska, this commercial fishery started in the southeastern area and soon spread northward to Prince William Sound, Cook Inlet and Bristol Bay. However, in 1974 the Alaska Department of Fish & Game, in response to concern about the apparent scarcity of herring in southeastern, closed the eggs-on-kelp fishery there. The product is now taken only in Prince William Sound and Bristol Bay.

Another use of herring eggs is as sac roe, the skein of unspawned eggs. This also is considered a delicacy in Japan and brings a high price. In the early days of this fishery, processors allowed the fish to spoil for a day or two, as the softened flesh made it easier for workers to remove the roe quickly. The carcasses of the de-egged females and of all males taken were then dumped, with unfortunate effects on the local atmosphere. Nowadays, the unused fish must be ground to a slurry and dumped in water not less than 13 m deep. Several processors have recently turned to fileting herring. This produces roe from the females for the Japanese trade; milt from the males for a European market; two fine filets per fish, most of which are frozen and shipped to Germany; and gurry, which is processed into fish meal. Thus, every bit of the fish is used. The vast majority of herring taken for these fisheries is caught by purse seine (Rearden, 1975a, b).

The uses of herring vary with the time of year and the condition of the fish. Herring are fattest in the fall, when the filets are about 20% oil and are best for pickling and general home use. In the spring, when the oil content of the flesh is only about 8%, the fish are best for making smoked herring. Small herring are generally lean all year round.

AMERICAN SHAD

Alosa sapidissima Wilson

DISTINCTIVE CHARACTERS

The American shad is easily distinguished from apparently similar Alaskan fishes by its rather pointed lower jaw, which fits into a deep notch in the upper jaw; the coarse, curved, radiating striae on its gill cover; and the row (or sometimes two or even three rows) of dark spots on the upper sides behind the head (Figure 10).

DESCRIPTION

Body compressed, fairly deep; depth 30% to 37% of standard length. Head moderate, compressed; length 23% to 28% of standard length. Snout moderate, 27% to 32% of head length. Eye about equal to snout; adipose lids well developed. Mouth terminal, lower jaw fitting into a notch in upper jaw in adults, but this notch lacking in young less than about 15 cm long. Upper jaw reaches middle of eye in the young and to below posterior margin of the eye in adults. Teeth absent, or at most are few and small in adults, present but minute on jaws and midline of tongue in the young. Gill rakers long and slender; those at angle of gill arch are shorter than snout in young but longer than snout in adults; number increases with age and size; 26 to 43 on lower limb in young, 59 to 73 in adults. Lateral line absent. Vertebrae: 53 to 59.

FINS. Dorsal elevated anteriorly, its margin slightly concave; origin of fin slightly forward of pelvic bases; 15 to 19 rays, usually 17 or 18. Anal long and low; 20 to 23 rays. Pectorals small, low on sides; 14 to 18 rays; pelvics, 9 rays. Pelvic axillary process present. Caudal deeply forked, upper and lower lobes about equal.

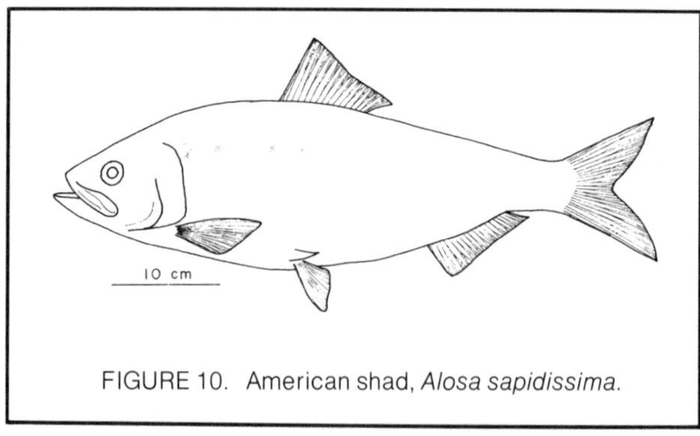

FIGURE 10. American shad, *Alosa sapidissima*.

SCALES. Moderately adherent, cycloid, with crenulate borders, in 52 to 62 rows along middle of side, in 15 to 16 rows between pelvic base and dorsal origin. Ventral scutes well developed; 20 to 22 scutes in front of pelvics, 14 to 17 behind.

COLOR. Metallic greenish or bluish above shading to silvery on sides and belly. A row of dark spots present on upper part of sides behind head and sometimes a second row (and in rare cases a third) present below the first. Fins colorless to greenish; dorsal and caudal fins dusky in large specimens; tips of caudal sometimes dark (photograph, page 83).

SIZE. The largest North American member of its family, the shad reaches a length of 76 cm and a weight of 6.4 kg. However, the average weight of an adult shad is probably around 2 to 2.5 kg. Females are usually larger and heavier than males.

RANGE AND ABUNDANCE

The normal range of the shad on the east coast is from the Saint Lawrence River and Nova Scotia south to the Indian River, Florida. The shad has been reported from as far north as Bull's Bay, Newfoundland. In the Pacific Ocean the shad ranges from Todos Santos Bay, Baja California, to southeastern Alaska, with strays north and west to Cook Inlet, Kodiak Island and Kamchatka.

In the major portions of its range the shad is abundant, but it is quite scarce in Alaska. Fishermen in southeastern pick up a few in salmon nets every year but, as far as is known, there are no breeding populations of shad in the state.

HABITS

The shad is anadromous, spending most of its life in the sea but returning to freshwater streams to breed. Some shad spawn almost immediately on entering fresh water while others may undertake fairly long journeys, as much as 630 km upstream, to their favored spawning grounds (Hildebrand, 1963). Timing of the run is governed by water temperature. Shad enter a river when the temperature is between 10° and 13°C. Thus, in the southern part of the range spawning may occur as early as March but will not take place until late June at the northernmost end.

Spawning usually occurs in the evening, between dusk and 10 p.m., on sandy or pebbly shallows. No nest or redd is made. The fish pair and swim close together, side by side, releasing eggs and milt. A single female may require several evenings to complete spawning, as not all eggs, apparently, are shed at once. The eggs, which are slightly denser than water and are nonadhesive, drop loosely and singly to the bottom, where they lodge in crevices between pebbles. Estimates of fecundity range from 116,000 to 616,000 eggs per female, with egg number directly related to the size and age of the individual fish. Early estimates of average egg counts ranging from 30,000 to 156,000 apparently referred to egg-takes in hatcheries in the late 19th century. On the Atlantic coast, fish in the southern part of the range produce more eggs than fish in the northern part, but it is not known if this also holds true along the Pacific coast (Lehman, 1953; Davis, 1957).

The spent fish return to the sea immediately after spawning. They begin to feed while still in fresh water and may recover a good deal of fat before reaching the sea. Adult shad return to fresh water year after year to spawn in their natal streams (Hollis, 1948; Talbot and Sykes, 1958; Cheek, 1968).

The fertile eggs, about .35 cm in diameter and pale pink to amber in color, hatch in 12 to 15 days at 12°C; in 11 days at 13.3°C; in 6 to 8 days at 14° to 17°C; and in only 3 days at 23.3°C (Rice, 1884; Ryder, 1884b; Leim, 1924). The young are about .9 cm to 1 cm long at hatching. The yolk sac is absorbed in 4 to 5 days and the young begin to feed 10 to 12 days after hatching. The first food consists primarily of copepods and chironomid larvae (Ryder, 1884a; Leim, 1924), but as the young fish grow they take larger and larger particles of food. They have doubled their length, reaching about 2 cm, in three to four weeks, by which time the fins are fully developed and metamorphosis is virtually complete.

A young shad about 5 cm long closely resembles the adult except that the body is more slender, the shoulder spots are not developed and the ventral scutes are more prominent. Adult fish feed on copepods, mysids, shrimps, barnacle larvae, ostracods, amphipods, insects and, in rare cases, small fishes (Bigelow and Schroeder, 1953; Hildebrand, 1963).

Growth proceeds rapidly in fresh water during the summer. By the time the young fish move downstream in the fall, they are between 3.7 and 11.2 cm long. The growth rate of the young in salt water is unknown. However, on the basis of back calculations made in scale studies, the lengths at various ages are approximately as follows: 1+, 12.7 to 19.3 cm; 2+, 22.9 to 29.5 cm; 3+, 25.4 to 37.6 cm; 4+, 37.6 to 42.9 cm; 5+, 40.4 to 48.3 cm; 6+, 51.3 cm (LaPointe, 1958; Cheek, 1968). Growth rates vary from one population to another. Shad live to be at least 11 years old, but it is difficult to determine the age of old fish because of the extensive regression of the edges of the scales at spawning (Cating, 1953).

After leaving the natal streams, the young shad spend 3 or 4 years in the sea. Sexual maturity usually occurs in the fourth year for males, in the fifth for females, and spawning occurs annually thereafter. An exception seems to be the fish of the southern Atlantic states, from North Carolina south, which spawn but once and then die (Cheek, 1968).

Aside from facts concerning spawning migrations, little is known of the movements of the shad. Atlantic fish, from Chesapeake Bay north, congregate in the Gulf of Maine after spawning and they presumably winter in deep water off the mid-Atlantic coast (Talbot and Sykes, 1958). What happens with Pacific populations is not known but, at least in the early years following the first transplants, the shad in the Pacific must have wandered considerably.

The American shad was first introduced into Pacific waters in 1871, when about 10,000 eggs were placed in the Sacramento River at Tehama, California, on June 26. Another 35,000 eggs were planted on July 2, 1873, and between 1876 and 1880 almost 600,000 more were added to the Sacramento. Plants of 910,000 were made in the Columbia River Basin in 1885 and 1886. Additional plants totaling more than 9.6 million eggs were made in the Colorado River and in Utah and Idaho between 1873 and 1891, but these seem to have been unsuccessful (Smith, 1896). Shad appeared at Vancouver Island, British Columbia, in 1876 (McDonald, 1891; Clemens and Wilby, 1946); in the Stikine River near Wrangell, Alaska, in 1891 (Smith, 1896); and by 1904 had reached Cook Inlet (Evermann and Goldsborough, 1907). In 1926 and again in 1937, single individuals were taken at Kodiak Island (Welander, 1940). Expansion southward also took place, with shad found near San Diego in 1916 (Starks, 1918) and in Todos Santos Bay, Baja California, in 1958 (Claussen, 1959). Occasional specimens are taken in Kamchatkan waters (Nikolskii, 1961). Thus, although the shad normally returns to the natal stream, it has been something of a wanderer in the new environment of the Pacific.

Despite the rapid expansion of range, however, shad have never been more than strays in Alaska. The statement by Evermann and Goldsborough (1907) that "the cannery at Fairhaven took one about

July 1, 1903, and the fishermen at Birch Point got about 3,000 in one day'' has at times been taken to indicate that shad were once abundant in Alaska. However, there is no Birch Point in the state, and Fairhaven, near Juneau, was not officially named until 1962 (Orth, 1967). The Fairhaven and Birch Point referred to by Evermann and Goldsborough are undoubtedly at Bellingham, Washington.

IMPORTANCE TO MAN

The shad is an important sport and commercial fish on the east coast, with total commercial landings in excess of 4.5 million kg in most years. Pacific coast landings as a rule are about a third of this figure. As a sport fish, the shad is highly regarded in the east, for it readily takes a fly or small spinner and is a game fighter. Because of its tender mouth, light tackle is imperative. Oddly enough, there is relatively little sport fishing for shad on the west coast. Because of its scarcity in the state, the shad is of no importance in the Alaskan fisheries, either for sport or for commercial purposes.

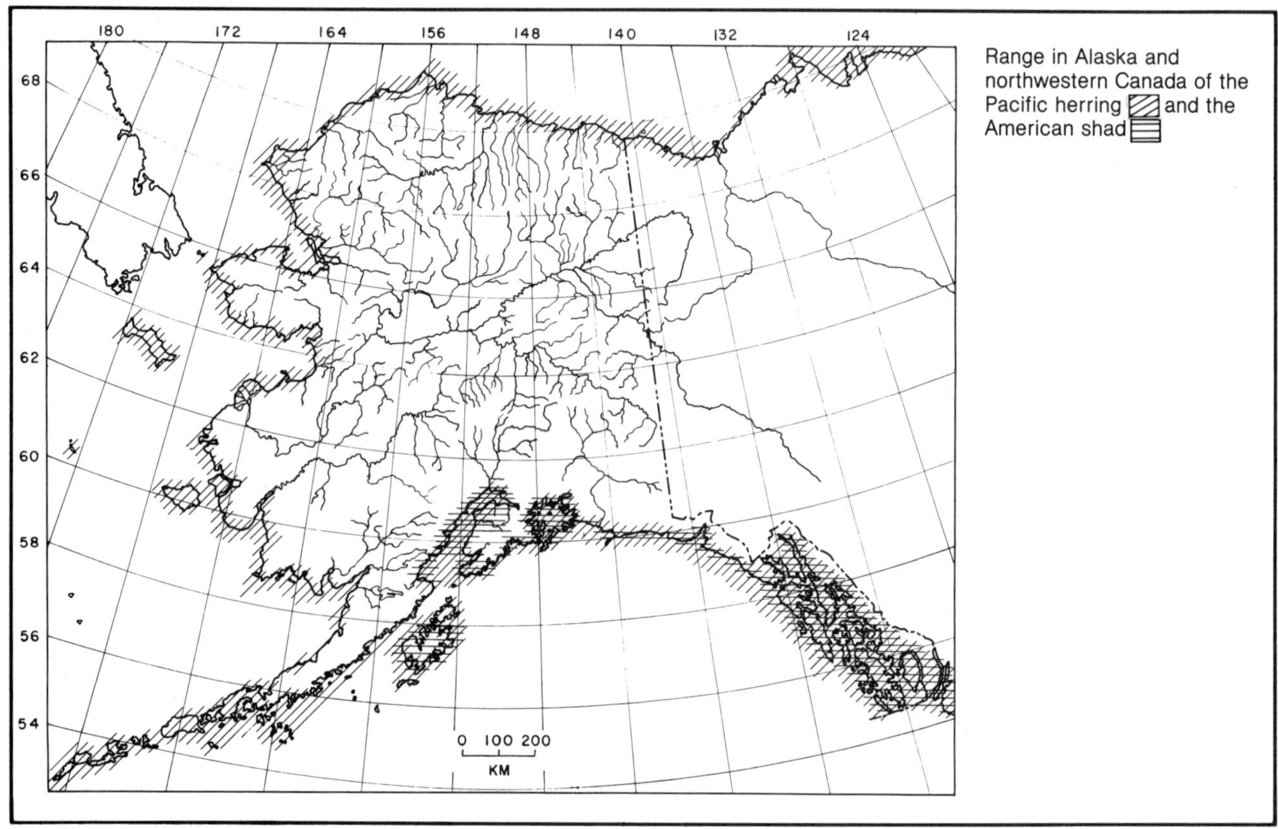

Range in Alaska and northwestern Canada of the Pacific herring and the American shad

Chapter Four

WHITEFISHES

Subfamily Coregoninae of the Family Salmonidae

FAMILY SALMONIDAE

The salmonoids are freshwater or anadromous fishes, generally medium-size or large in comparison to most other freshwater fishes. The body of the salmonoid is somewhat round or moderately compressed; the fins are all soft-rayed and an adipose fin is present. Scales are cycloid and a distinct, elongate, axillary process is present at the base of each pelvic fin. The mouth may range from large and well toothed to small and toothless. The swim bladder is connected to the esophagus. Pyloric caeca are numerous. Sexual dimorphism is often apparent at spawning time.

The group is conveniently divided into three subfamilies; Coregoninae, the whitefishes and ciscoes; Salmoninae, the salmons, trouts and charrs; and Thymallinae, the graylings. (See Chapters 5 and 6.)

The Salmonidae is the dominant family of fishes in the northern parts of Europe, Asia and North America, with a number of species reaching the high arctic. Various members of the group, especially the Pacific salmons, genus *Oncorhynchus,* are of great commercial importance, while others such as the trouts *(Salmo),* charrs *(Salvelinus)* and grayling *(Thymallus)* are noted chiefly as sport fishes.

KEY TO THE ALASKAN SPECIES

SECTION	DESCRIPTION	THE FISH IS	PROCEED IN THIS KEY TO SECTION
1 a.	Lower jaw equal to or longer than upper jaw. Profile of upper lip not overhanging lower jaw (Figures 11A and 11B, page 25).		**2**
b.	Lower jaw distinctly shorter than upper jaw. Profile of upper lip vertical or overhanging (Figure 11C, page 25).		**5**
2 a.	Mouth large, with posterior end of maxilla reaching to below posterior edge of pupil of eye. Gill rakers: 13 to 17 on lower limb of first arch.	Inconnu or sheefish, *Stenodus leucichthys* (Güldenstadt), page 25.	
b.	Mouth moderate, upper jaw not reaching posterior edge of pupil. Gill rakers: at least 20 on lower limb of first arch.		**3**
3 a.	Mouth superior, with tip of lower jaw generally projecting slightly beyond upper jaw (Figure 11B, page 25). Pelvic fins dusky or black in adults.	Least cisco, *Coregonus sardinella* Valenciennes, page 27.	
b.	Mouth terminal, the tip of lower jaw not projecting beyond tip of upper jaw (Figure 11A, page 25). Pelvic fins always pale.		**4**

KEY TO THE ALASKAN SPECIES (CONT.)

SECTION	DESCRIPTION	THE FISH IS	PROCEED IN THIS KEY TO SECTION
4 a.	Gill rakers: 21 to 25 on lower limb of first arch.	Bering cisco, *Coregonus laurettae* Bean, page 29.	
b.	Gill rakers: 26 to 31 on lower limb of first arch.	Arctic cisco, *Coregonus autumnalis* Pallas, page 30.	
5 a.	Membrane around eye has a distinct notch below posterior edge of pupil (Figure 11C, page 25). A single flap present between nostrils on each side (Figure 11D, page 25).		**6**
b.	Membrane around eye has no notch. A double flap between nostrils on each side (Figure 11E, page 25).		**7**
6 a.	Snout blunt when seen from above. Lateral line has less than 70 pored scales. Pyloric caeca: 14 to 33.	Pygmy whitefish, *Prosopium coulteri* (Eigenmann and Eigenmann), page 31.	
b.	Snout rather pointed when seen from above. Lateral line has more than 70 pored scales. Pyloric caeca: 50 or more.	Round whitefish, *Prosopium cylindraceum* (Pallas), page 32.	
7 a.	Gill rakers short, the longest less than a fifth of the interorbital width. Profile of head smoothly convex or only barely concave. Hump behind head absent, or not at all prominent.	Broad whitefish, *Coregonus nasus* (Pallas), page 34.	
b.	Profile of head distinctly concave between snout and nape. A pronounced hump behind head in adults. Longest gill raker longer than a fifth of interorbital width.		**8**
8 a.	Total gill rakers: 19 to 24, average counts about 21 or 22.	Humpback whitefish, *Coregonus pidschian* (Gmelin), page 37.	
b.	Total gill rakers: 23 to 31.		**9**
9 a.	Total gill rakers: 23 to 27, average counts about 24 or 25.	Alaska whitefish, *Coregonus nelsoni* Bean, page 35.	
b.	Total gill rakers: 24 to 31, average counts about 26 or more.	Lake whitefish, *Coregonus clupeaformis* (Mitchill), page 38.	

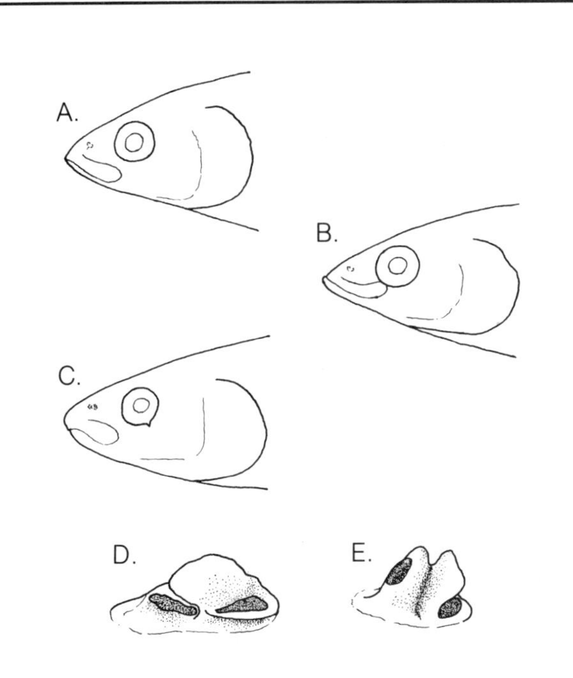

FIGURE 11.
A. Head of Bering cisco, both jaws equal.
B. Head of least cisco, tip of lower jaw projecting slightly.
C. Head of round whitefish, lower jaw shorter than upper, profile of upper lip overhanging; notch in lower margin of eye membrane.
D. Nostrils of round whitefish with a single flap between openings.
E. Nostrils of Alaska whitefish with double flap between openings.
(One needs a strong magnifying glass to see these flaps clearly.)

SUBFAMILY COREGONINAE OF THE FAMILY SALMONIDAE

Distinguishing characteristics of the subfamily Coregoninae are the relatively large scales, of which there are never more than 100 along the lateral line; teeth that are small and weak or absent; and the absence of parr marks except in the genus *Prosopium*.

INCONNU OR SHEEFISH

Stenodus leucichthys (Güldenstadt)

DISTINCTIVE CHARACTERS

The inconnu is easily distinguished from other coregonines by its large mouth, the protruding lower jaw, and the presence of only 13 to 17 gill rakers on the lower limb of the first gill arch (Figure 12).

DESCRIPTION

Body elongate, little compressed; depth 20% to 23% of total length, deepest just behind pectoral fins. Head long, 24% to 28% of total length; depth of head about half its length. Snout prominent, approximately 23% of head length. Eye round, its diameter averaging 15% of head length. Two nostrils on each side of head, with a double flap between the openings. Mouth large, lower jaw protruding, maxilla reaching at least to below the middle of the eye. Teeth very small, in velvetlike bands on anterior portion of both jaws and on tongue, vomer and palatines. Gill rakers: 17 to 24. Branchiostegals: 9 to 12. Lateral line scales: 90 to 115. Pyloric caeca: 144 to 211. Vertebrae: 63 to 69.

FINS. Dorsal, which is high and pointed, has 11 to 19 rays. Adipose fin present. Anal, 14 to 19; pectorals, 14 to 17; pelvics, 11 to 12. Axillary process well developed. Caudal forked.

SCALES. Large, cycloid.

COLOR. Generally silvery, with the back usually rather green, blue or pale brown. Silvery white below. Dorsal and caudal fins have dusky margins; other fins pale (photograph, page 84; Plate 18, page 129).

SIZE. Up to 27 kg in the Kobuk River, Alaska (Alt, 1969), to 28.6 kg in the Mackenzie River (Dymond, 1943) and to 40 kg in Siberia (Wynne-Edwards, 1952).

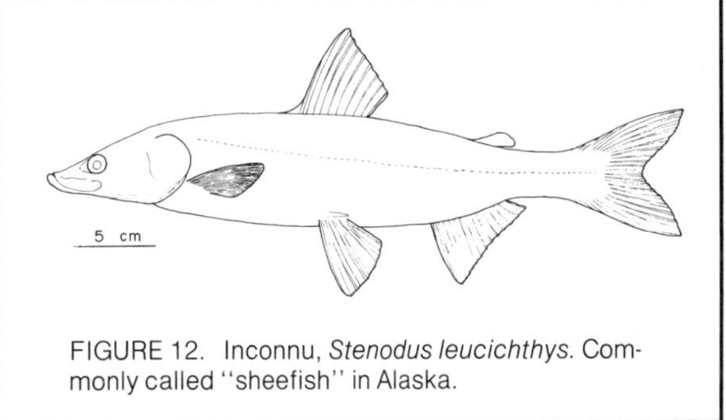

FIGURE 12. Inconnu, *Stenodus leucichthys*. Commonly called "sheefish" in Alaska.

RANGE AND ABUNDANCE

In Alaska the inconnu is known from the Kuskokwim, Yukon, Selawik and Kobuk river drainages. It is found in the Yukon River and in Yukon tributaries all the way from the mouth to Teslin Lake, Yukon Territory, but apparently does not ascend the Tanana much beyond Fairbanks. It migrates up the Koyukuk River at least as far as Alatna. Except for a few fish reported from the Meade River, the inconnu is not found north or east of the Kobuk River. In Canada the inconnu is present in most of the Mackenzie drainage and east to the Anderson River.

The inconnu ranges westward across Siberia to the White Sea and south to Kamchatka. Another subspecies is present in Caspian Sea drainages.

Because of its migratory habits, the abundance of the inconnu varies according to place and season. However, aside from that limitation, it is abundant in most areas where it is found.

HABITS

Inconnu in Alaska spawn in late September and early October, in water temperatures of 1.4° to 4.6°C. The spawning grounds are located in clear, fairly swift streams, over bottoms composed of different-size gravel and sand under 1 to 3 m of water. Spawning takes place in the evening, usually beginning about dusk and continuing well into the night. In the spawning act a female accompanied by a male (in rare cases by two or more males) rises to the surface near the upstream end of the spawning grounds. She moves rapidly across the current, usually in an upright position but sometimes almost completely on her side, with the abdomen upstream, extruding eggs as she goes. This activity lasts for 1 to 3 seconds. The male, meanwhile, stays below the female. The eggs, averaging about .25 cm in diameter, sink to the bottom through the cloud of sperm released by the male and are fertilized as they sink. Apparently, it is important that gravel be of different sizes on the stream bottom to insure that the eggs lodge in the bottom and are not carried away by the current.

After completing a spawning pass the female drifts downstream. She may repeat the spawning act over the downstream portion of the spawning area or may move upstream to the head of the grounds before releasing more eggs. It is not known how many spawning passes are required to extrude all the eggs, but Alt (1969) noted one female that released eggs six times in a single pass. Since large females may contain as many as 400,000 eggs, several passes are undoubtedly needed to complete a spawning.

Development of the eggs is slow. The young hatch sometime from late February to April and are about .7 cm long. The yolk sac is absorbed in a week to 10 days and the young inconnu then feed actively on plankton. Growth rates of the early young are unknown. In hatcheries, although eggs can be easily cared for, mortality of the young after absorption of the yolk sac has so far been virtually 100% (La Perriere, 1973).* However, Russian workers apparently have had good success with hatchery rearing of inconnu (Karzinkin, 1951; Nikolskii, 1961).

The distribution of young fish appears to differ from one drainage to another. In the Kobuk and Selawik rivers, and indeed in most areas, the young inconnu are probably swept downstream by spring floods. Alt (1969) found no fish younger than 4+ in the Kobuk and Selawik rivers. On the other hand, he found young-of-the-year as well as 1-year-old and 2-year-old fish in the upper Yukon, and Fuller (1955) believed the young remained for two years in rivers emptying into Great Slave Lake.

Growth of the young is quite rapid for the first two years of life. One-year-olds in Alaska are 11 to 15 cm long, with 2-year-olds averaging about 20 cm. After that, growth slows down. At 5 years, Alaskan inconnu average about 43 cm in total length; at 10 years, about 70 cm; and at 15 years, about 96 cm. The largest fish reported by Alt (1969) was a 19+ of 119 cm from the Kobuk River. The oldest specimen reported by Alt, a 20+ from the Selawik area, was 112 cm long.

The inconnu is known to hybridize with other coregonids, doubtless due more to the broadcasting of eggs and sperm than to pairing between species or genera. Known hybrids include combinations with *Coregonus nelsoni* (Alt, 1971c), *C. autumnalis* (Kuznetsov, 1932; Dymond, 1943) and *C. muksun* (Kuznetsov, 1932).

As with most fishes, the food of the inconnu changes with the age and size of the individual as well as with the time of year. The very young postlarvae feed almost exclusively on plankton of various sorts, but soon graduate to insect larvae and larger zooplankton. In the upper Yukon River and in the Ob River of Siberia, inconnu begin to feed on fish in their first year (Vork, 1948; Alt, 1965) but in Great Slave Lake they apparently do not do so until they are about 4 (Fuller, 1955).

Adults feed mostly on fish, especially on the least cisco, *Coregonus sardinella.* Also important in the adults' diet are the isopod, *Mesidotea entomon,* and the mysid, *Mysis relicta.* Other foods include king salmon fingerlings, several species of coregonids, lampreys, charr, smelt, blackfish, suckers, burbot, chubs, sticklebacks, sculpins and the nymphs and larvae of several orders of insects. The last are eaten almost exclusively by the smaller fish (Fuller, 1955; Alt, 1965, 1969). Food habits vary with locality and time of year. In the early spring in Selawik Lake, *C. sardinella* was the major food item of large inconnu, while smaller fish fed heavily on small coregonids and invertebrates. In the latter part of June, *Mesidotea* and small coregonids became more important in inconnu of all sizes, as did the rainbow smelt, *Osmerus mordax* (Alt, 1969).

The inconnu of Alaska constitute five rather distinct populations that do not mix with each other to any appreciable extent. Two groups, the Minto Flats and the upper Yukon River groups, are year-round residents, wintering in the large rivers and moving relatively short distances to clear streams to spawn. The Minto Flats population spawns chiefly in the Tolovana and Chatanika rivers, with a few

*K. T. Alt, Alaska Department of Fish & Game: personal communication.

entering the Chena River and other clear streams. The fish of the upper Yukon apparently make use of almost every major tributary for spawning.

Two more groups, the fish of the Kuskokwim and lower Yukon rivers, winter in the delta areas of these streams. The spawning area of the Kuskokwim fish is probably in clear tributaries, but that is not known definitely. The fish of the lower Yukon travel 1,600 km to spawn in the Alatna River (Alt, 1971b, 1973a, 1977).

The fifth group, the Kobuk-Selawik population, spends the winter in the brackish waters of Selawik Lake and Hotham Inlet, but to spawn, may move as far as 670 km up the Kobuk River.

Upstream migration from the wintering areas begins at ice breakup. The early upstream movement appears to be associated with feeding, but this movement soon becomes a definite migration to the spawning area. Depending on the distance to be traveled, the true spawning migration may last only a few weeks or, as with the lower Yukon fish, may take as long as four months. During this spawning migration, the inconnu feed little if at all but, unlike salmon, they are still in good condition when they reach the spawning grounds in late September. They appear to use excess visceral fat during the migration (Alt, 1969).

Following spawning, there is a fairly rapid downstream migration to the wintering grounds, where the inconnu again commence to feed. It is not certain whether inconnu spawn annually or at longer intervals. Russian fish appear to spawn only every third or fourth year (Nikolskii, 1961). Alt (1969) found two stages of gonad development in mature fish at Selawik and suggested that this might indicate spawning every other year. On the other hand, he felt that all mature fish in the Kobuk River were spawners. It may be that nonspawners do not migrate very far upstream.

IMPORTANCE TO MAN

Wherever it is found the inconnu is prized for sport, subsistence or commercial purposes. It is an excellent sport fish and its fighting qualities and size make it a trophy worth any angler's best endeavors. As food it is likewise excellent. The flesh is white, sweet and slightly oily. It has not always enjoyed a high reputation, however, for Richardson (1823) wrote that it was "disagreeable when used as daily food."

Subsistence fisheries of considerable size exist along the Kobuk, Selawik, lower Yukon, Koyukuk and Kuskokwim rivers. In the early 1960s, the subsistence catch on the lower Yukon was on the order of 5,000 fish annually, while the Kuskokwim produced about 1,600 to 1,700. No data are available for the Koyukuk, but statements from residents of Hughes, a village on the river, suggest that the subsistence take on that river is in excess of 2,000 fish a year. The greatest subsistence fishery is in the Kobuk-Selawik area, where Alt (1969) estimated a catch of 19,240 to 22,000 fish in 1965. This represents something like 50,000 kg, of which about 900 kg were sold commercially.

The only commercial fishery for Alaskan inconnu is in the Kotzebue area. This fishery has produced up to 45,000 kg per year (Wigutoff and Carlson, 1950). The total catch, including fish for both subsistence and commercial uses, from the northwestern part of Alaska in 1965 was estimated at 34,200 to 37,000 fish, or nearly 90,000 kg.

Commercial fisheries for inconnu also exist in Great Slave Lake, with annual yields on the order of 144,000 kg (Sinclair et al., 1967), and in the rivers of Siberia, where the annual catch between 1936 and 1940 was reported as about 4.15 million kg per year (Nikolskii, 1961).

LEAST CISCO

Coregonus sardinella Valenciennes

DISTINCTIVE CHARACTERS

Adults of the least cisco are easily distinguished from other adult ciscoes of Alaska by the lower jaw, which protrudes slightly beyond the upper jaw when the mouth is closed, and by the pelvic fins, which are dusky to black in color. The latter characteristic, however, does not appear until the fish are about 15 cm long, so identification of the young is sometimes difficult (Figure 13, page 28).

DESCRIPTION

Body slightly to moderately compressed, its greatest depth 19% to 24% of total length. Head rather short, less than 25% of total length. Snout about 25% of head length. Eye round, large, 26% to 32% of head length. Nostrils have a double flap between the openings. Mouth moderate, lower jaw protruding slightly beyond upper when mouth is closed. Maxilla reaches backward to below anterior half of eye. No teeth on jaws, vomer or palatines, but a patch of small teeth present on tongue. Gill rakers long and slender: 42 to 53 on first arch. Branchiostegals: 8 or 9. Lateral line has 78 to 98 pored scales. Pyloric caeca: 74 to 111. Vertebrae: 58 to 64.

FINS. Dorsal, which is rather high and falcate, has 12 to 14 rays. Adipose fin present. Anal has 11 to 13 rays; pectorals, which are narrow, 14 to 17; pelvics, 8 to 12, with a distinct axillary process present. Caudal forked.

SCALES. Moderately large, cycloid. Statements that "spawning males probably develop tubercles

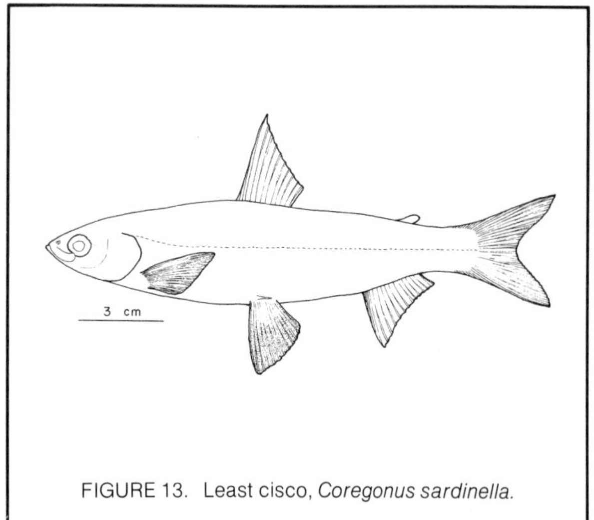

FIGURE 13. Least cisco, *Coregonus sardinella*.

along the sides'' (McPhail and Lindsey, 1970) are in error. In interior Alaska at least, spawning tubercles are not developed by either sex.

COLOR. Brownish to dark greenish above, silvery below. Pelvic fins dark in adults (photograph, page 84; Plate 21, page 132).

SIZE. The least cisco is known to reach fork length of at least 41.3 cm in interior Alaska (Kepler, 1973). Scott and Crossman (1973) gave 41.9 cm for Canadian fish, while Nikolskii (1961) indicated a maximum size of 42 cm and .5 kg for fish from Siberia. (In neither of these cases is there any indication whether the length is total length or fork length.)

RANGE AND ABUNDANCE

The least cisco is present in most streams and lakes of Alaska north of the Alaska Range, and from Bristol Bay to the arctic coast. It is also present throughout the Kuskokwim and Yukon drainages, and ranges south in the Mackenzie River to Fort Simpson and eastward along the arctic coast of Canada to Bathurst Inlet and Cambridge Bay. McPhail and Lindsey (1970) noted its presence on Victoria and Banks islands in the Arctic Ocean. Westward, the range extends across the Bering Strait and Siberia as far as the White Sea.

The least cisco is one of the more abundant freshwater fishes of Alaska, but because of its migratory habits the abundance is seasonal.

HABITS

The least cisco spawns in late September and early October. Spawning takes place at night, with peak activity between 8 p.m. and midnight. The spawning ground in the Chatanika River, near Fairbanks, is confined to a stretch of river from 16 km below to 12 km above the Elliott Highway Bridge. Individual spawning areas vary in size from 100 to 800 m in length and 15 to 22 m in width. Water depth ranges between 1.3 and 2.6 m, with average velocity of about .5 m per second. Surface temperatures during the spawning period are between 0° and 3°C (Kepler, 1973). The stream bottom in the spawning areas is composed of gravel with a little sand.

In the spawning act, a female swims almost vertically upward, with her ventral side upstream. She is joined by as many as five males (but usually only one or two) who swim vertically and close to her. As the spawners approach the surface, eggs and milt are released. A small cloud of milt can sometimes be seen as the fish enter the upper 20 to 30 cm of water. The fish break the surface, fall over backward, and swim back to the bottom of the pool. It is not known whether a female deposits all her eggs in one night or whether more nights are required.

The eggs, somewhat less than .1 cm in diameter and cream to yellow in color, sink to the bottom, where they lodge in crevices in the gravel. They are not adhesive. Fecundity varies between 9,800 to 93,500 eggs, the average per female being about 54,350. The number of eggs is more closely related to age than to size of the individual (Kepler, 1973). Chatanika River ciscoes are more fecund than those of Siberia, for Nikolskii (1961) gave only 23,600 as the maximum egg count for fish from the Yenisei River.

The eggs winter in the gravel and hatch early in the spring. By mid-June large numbers of young-of-the-year, which may be up to 4 cm long, are moving downstream to deeper slower water (Townsend and Kepler, 1974).

Males can become sexually mature at age 2+, with the majority maturing at 3+. Females begin to mature at 3+ (in rare cases, at 2+), but most mature at 4+. A large mature female can weigh as much as 2.5 kg (Alt, 1971a).

Occasional hybrids between the least cisco and the Alaska whitefish occur (UAFC #2173), but such hybrids are rare despite the fact that the two species spawn more or less simultaneously in the same areas and have similar breeding behavior.

The maximum age attained in most populations seems to be between 8 and 11 years (Cohen, 1954; Nikolskii, 1961; Kepler, 1973), although Scott and Crossman (1973) mentioned that ages approaching 26 years have been recorded in specimens from Victoria Island, Northwest Territories.

Growth rates vary widely from place to place, even within the same habitat. Although stream-dwelling, migratory populations are generally stated to grow faster and live longer than lake-dwelling, non-migratory fish (McPhail and Lindsey, 1970; Scott and Crossman, 1973), Cohen (1954) found that the anadromous fish at Point Barrow grew slower and were thinner than a nonmigratory population in Ikroavik Lake. To further confound the situation, a second population in Ikroavik Lake was slower-growing and shorter-lived than the first two.

Kepler's (1973) data on various numbers of spawning females from the Chatanika River yield the following average fork lengths at ages from 2+ to 8+: 2+, 31.1 cm (2 fish); 3+, 31.6 cm (4); 4+, 33.3 cm (15); 5+, 37 cm (12); 6+, 38.3 cm (5); 7+, 41.3 cm (1); 8+, 40.5 cm (2). Alt (1971a), on the basis of back-calculating from scales, gave the following fork lengths at the end of each year of life for Chatanika River fish: 1, 12 cm; 2, 20.8 cm; 3, 26.1 cm; 4, 30.4 cm; 5, 33.7 cm; 6, 36.4 cm; 7, 38.7 cm; and 8, 41 cm.

Although lake-dwelling populations appear to be nonmigratory, those least ciscoes living in streams or reaching brackish water go to considerable effort to reach or leave their spawning grounds. As already noted, young-of-the-year move off the spawning grounds shortly after spring breakup. The upstream spawning migration of adults begins in early July in the Chatanika River and is completed by late September.

Least ciscoes feed primarily on various types of zooplankton, including various small copepods, cladocerans, mysids and the adults and larvae of a variety of insects. They may also eat plant material. The ciscoes normally do not feed during the spawning run (Nikolskii, 1961; Furniss, 1974; Morrow et al., 1977).

The least cisco is sought by many predators including the eagle, hawk, kingfisher, pike, inconnu, lake trout, burbot, man and, no doubt, any others capable of catching it. The eggs may be eaten by grayling and Alaska whitefish during spawning (Morrow et al., 1977).

IMPORTANCE TO MAN

In North America the least cisco is relatively unimportant. It is taken by subsistence fisheries in Alaska and northern Canada, usually as an incidental in nets set primarily for other whitefishes or for pike or grayling. Spearfishing for least cisco has developed as a sport of small proportions in the Chatanika River in interior Alaska. The least cisco is an important commercial fish in Siberia. Annual landings in the late 1930s were in excess of 1 million kg (Nikolskii, 1961).

As a food fish, the least cisco is generally considered somewhat inferior to the humpback whitefishes. Nevertheless, it is a very good fish for eating, with firm, tasty meat.

BERING CISCO

Coregonus laurettae Bean

DISTINCTIVE CHARACTERS

The pale, almost colorless pelvic and pectoral fins distinguish the Bering cisco from the least cisco, and the smaller number of gill rakers (18 to 25) on the lower portion of the first gill arch distinguish it from the arctic cisco, which has 26 to 31 gill rakers (Figure 14).

DESCRIPTION

Body rather elongate, slightly compressed; depth about 20% of total length. Head moderate, 22% to 25% of total length. Snout 20% to 25% of head length. Eye about equal to snout, round. Two nostrils on each side of head with a double flap between openings of each pair. Mouth moderate, terminal; upper and lower jaws equal. Maxilla reaches backward to middle of eye. Usually no teeth on jaws, but weak teeth are present on maxilla in young and in rare cases a few small teeth are present on lower jaw of adults. Small patch of teeth present on tongue. From 18 to 25 gill rakers on lower portion of first gill arch; total gill rakers on first arch: 35 to 39. Branchiostegals: 8 to 9. Lateral line has 76 to 95 pored scales. Pyloric caeca: 71 to 123. Vertebrae: 62 to 65.

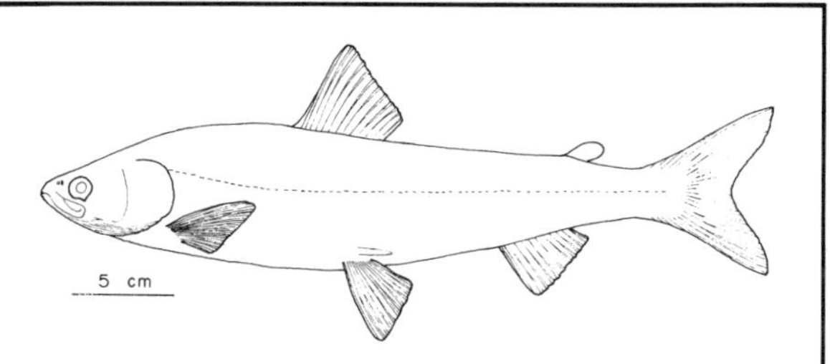

FIGURE 14. Bering cisco, *Coregonus laurettae*. The arctic cisco, *Coregonus autumnalis*, appears identical with this species but has more gill rakers.

FINS: Dorsal, which is rather high and falcate, has 11 to 13 rays. Adipose fin present. Anal has 12 to 14 rays; pectorals, 14 to 17; pelvics, 10 to 12, axillary process present. Caudal forked.

SCALES. Cycloid, fairly large.

COLOR. Generally brownish to dark green on back; silvery on lower sides and belly. Anal, pelvic and pectoral fins pale; caudal and dorsal fins dusky (photographs, page 85; Plate 22, page 133).

SIZE: The largest known Bering cisco, recorded by Alt (1973), was a female of 48 cm fork length from the lower 500 m of Hess Creek, Alaska. The average size of adults is about 30 cm.

RANGE AND ABUNDANCE

The Bering cisco is found from Bristol Bay north and east to Oliktok Point on the arctic coast of

Alaska. It is present in the Yukon River as far upstream as Fort Yukon, and also in the Porcupine River. It has been found at the mouth of Ship Creek, Knik Arm, at Anchorage (SUFC #41858, now in the Ichthyological Collection of the California Academy of Sciences) (McPhail, 1966), in Tolugak Lake in Anaktuvuk Pass in the Brooks Range (UAFC #617, #618), and was found in 1972 in the Kenai River on the Kenai Peninsula.*

Throughout its range the Bering cisco is fairly abundant, at least seasonally; Alt (1973c) reported up to 18 a day taken in a fish wheel at Rampart, on the Yukon River, in September, 1972.

HABITS

Very little is known of the biology of the Bering cisco. Most of the following is derived from Alt (1973c).

Spawning runs begin in the spring. Most Bering ciscoes apparently winter in salt or brackish water near river mouths, but the presence of potential spawners well up the Yukon and Kuskokwim rivers suggests that some populations may spend the winter in fresh water, far from the sea. Bering cisco were first observed well inland in 1968 and 1969, when one (UAFC #2176) was taken in the Chatanika River near Fairbanks and seven (UAFC #632) at Rampart, on the Yukon River. Two more specimens (UAFC #617, #618) are from Tolugak Lake in Anaktuvuk Pass. Subsequently, Alt (1973c) found Bering cisco in the Yukon River at Fort Yukon; in the Porcupine River, 1,400 km from the mouth of the Yukon; and in the South Fork of the Kuskokwim River, 840 km from the ocean.

Spawning probably takes place in the fall, but spawning behavior and the location of the spawning grounds are unknown.* From the distribution of the fish in June it may be presumed that the spawning grounds are in clear-water streams tributary to major rivers. Dymond (1943) mentioned hybrids between *C. laurettae* and *Stenodus leucichthys,* but the location from which the specimens came, the Mackenzie River Delta, strongly suggests that they were actually hybrids between the arctic cisco, *C. autumnalis,* and the inconnu.

Alt (1973) stated that the majority of his specimens from Hess Creek were 4+ to 6+ and were mature. His fish from Port Clarence and Grantley Harbor were mostly 2+ and 3+ immatures, but included a few adults. These adults showed slower growth than the Hess Creek fish, possibly because of a shorter growing season. Mean fork lengths at age, were for the Hess Creek fish: 4+, 34.4 cm; 5+, 35.4 cm; 6+, 37.3 cm; 7+, 40.5 cm; 8+, 44.6; and for the Port Clarence-Grantley Harbor fish: 3+, 24.1 cm; 4+, 26.3 cm; 5+, 28.5 cm; 6+, 31.3 cm; 7+, 35 cm.

As noted above, Bering cisco undertake extensive spawning migrations. Presumably they move downstream after spawning. However, the precise extent of the migrations is unknown.

The Bering cisco, like other ciscoes, apparently does not feed during its spawning runs. All the fish examined from the Yukon and Kuskokwim rivers in June through September had empty stomachs. By contrast, fish taken at Port Clarence-Grantley Harbor had fed on invertebrates and small cottids (Alt, 1973). McPhail and Lindsey (1970) listed amphipods as food of the Bering cisco.

IMPORTANCE TO MAN

The Bering cisco is little used. Small numbers are taken for subsistence use by gill net and by fish wheel in the Yukon and Kuskokwim rivers. Similar use probably exists wherever subsistence fishing and the Bering cisco coincide.

ARCTIC CISCO

Coregonus autumnalis (Pallas)

DISTINCTIVE CHARACTERS

Pale or colorless pelvic fins, a terminal mouth and the presence of 41 to 48 gill rakers on the first gill arch serve to distinguish the arctic cisco (Figure 14, page 29).

DESCRIPTION

Body elongate, slightly compressed. Depth 20% to 23% of total length. Head moderate, somewhat less than 25% of total length. Snout about 25% of head, a little longer than eye diameter. Eye round, 20% to 24% of head. Nostrils have a double flap between the openings. Mouth moderate, jaws toothless in adults (a few weak teeth may be present in very small young), a patch of teeth on tongue. Maxilla extends backward to about middle of eye. Gill rakers: 41 to 48 on first arch. Branchiostegals: 8 to 9. Lateral line has 82 to 110 pored scales. Pyloric caeca: 113 to 183. Vertebrae: 64 to 67.

FINS. Dorsal, which is fairly high and slightly falcate, has 10 to 12 rays. Adipose fin present. Anal has 12 to 14 rays; pectorals, 14 to 17; pelvics, 11 to 12, axillary process present. Caudal forked.

SCALES. Moderately large, cycloid; 82 to 110 pored scales in lateral line.

COLOR. Brown to dark greenish above fading to silvery on sides and belly. Fins pale.

SIZE. Specimens up to 64 cm in total length and up to 2.68 kg in weight have been reported from the Lena River in Siberia (Berg, 1948). However, North American specimens generally are much smaller, averaging somewhere in the neighborhood of 35 to 40 cm long (Roguski and Komarek, 1971) and perhaps 1 kg in weight.

*K.T. Alt: personal communication.

RANGE AND ABUNDANCE

In North America, the arctic cisco is found along the arctic coast of Canada and Alaska from the southeastern end of Victoria Island, Northwest Territories, westward to Point Barrow and in the Mackenzie River as far south as the Liard River. It ranges westward across arctic Siberia to the White Sea. Due to its migratory habits, it is abundant seasonally.

HABITS

The arctic cisco is truly anadromous. It seems to be much more tolerant of salt water than most coregonids, for it has been taken in water with a salinity content of up to 22 parts per thousand (Roguski and Komarek, 1971). The upstream spawning run takes place in the summer and may cover as much as 1,000 km (Nikolskii, 1961). Spawning occurs over gravel in fairly swift water, the eggs being broadcast and left to fend for themselves. Mature females may produce as many as 90,000 eggs (Berg, 1948). After spawning, the adults return downstream. The arctic cisco occasionally hybridizes with the inconnu (Kuznetsov, 1932; Dymond, 1943).

The young probably hatch in the spring and descend the rivers to estuaries, as do other ciscoes.

Little is known of growth rates in North America. Roguski and Komarek (1971) and Kogl (1971) have provided the following data regarding the fork length of 65 specimens from the Beaufort Sea and the Colville River Delta: age I, 11.4 to 11.5 cm; II, 13.6 cm; III, 23.3 cm; IV, 29.7 cm; VI, 31.7 cm; VI, 32.5 cm; VII, 37.3 cm; and VIII, 41.4 cm. This is somewhat faster growth than was listed by Berg (1948) for Yenisei River ciscoes. The fish become mature at about 6 years of age and apparently do not breed every year (Nikolskii, 1961; Roguski and Komarek, 1971).

The arctic cisco shows a wide range in its feeding and has been found to eat mysids, copepods, amphipods, isopods, chironomids and other insects and a variety of small fishes (Nikolskii, 1961; Kogl, 1971).

IMPORTANCE TO MAN

In North America the arctic cisco is used primarily in subsistence fisheries, and these may be of considerable magnitude. The fish are caught "in abundance" during August at Barter Island, where they are preferred over charr (Furniss, 1974). A small commerical fishery on the Colville River Delta takes about 11,000 kg per year, about 60% of the total catch of all species there (Winslow and Roguski, 1970). The arctic cisco is an important component of the fisheries along the Mackenzie River (Wynne-Edwards, 1952) and is an important commercial fish in Siberia and the eastern parts of northern U.S.S.R. (Nikolskii, 1961).

PYGMY WHITEFISH

Prosopium coulteri (Eigenmann and Eigenmann)

DISTINCTIVE CHARACTERS

The pygmy whitefish is distinguished by a bluntly rounded snout, the presence of 70 or fewer pored scales in the lateral line, and 13 to 33 pyloric caeca (Figure 15).

DESCRIPTION

Body elongate, round in cross-section; depth about 17% of fork length. Head moderate, its length about 22% of fork length. Snout short, broadly rounded when seen from above. Eye large, round, the diameter usually greater than snout length; a notch present in lower posterior portion of adipose lid. Nostrils have a single flap between the openings. Mouth small, subterminal; maxilla reaches to anterior portion of eye. No teeth on jaws, vomer or palatines, but a small patch of fine teeth present on tongue. Gill rakers short, the longest 6.5% to 9% of head length; 12 to 21 on first arch. Branchiostegals: 6 to 9. Lateral line has 50 to 70 pored scales. Pyloric caeca: 13 to 33. Vertebrae: 49 to 55.

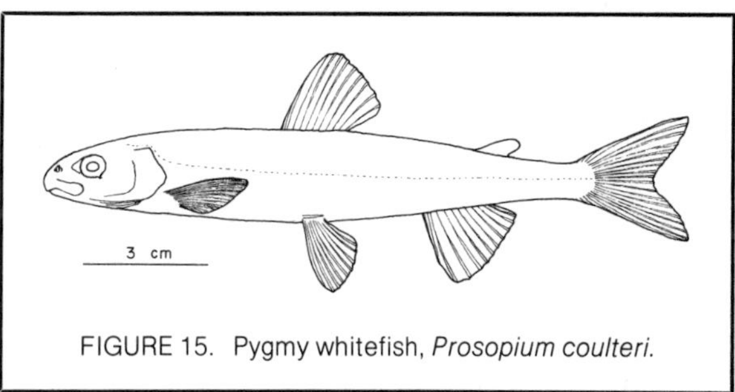

FIGURE 15. Pygmy whitefish, *Prosopium coulteri.*

FINS. Dorsal has 10 to 13 rays. Small adipose fin present. Anal has 10 to 14 rays; pectorals, 13 to 18; pelvics, 9 to 11. Axillary process present. Caudal forked.

SCALES. Large, round, cycloid.

COLOR. Brownish, often with somewhat green tints, above; sides silvery; belly white. A row of about 11 large round parr marks present along sides of young, persisting in all dut the largest adults (photograph, page 86).

SIZE. This is the smallest of the Alaskan coregonids. The largest specimens recorded were only 27.1 cm fork length (McCart, 1965) and most are scarcely half that size.

RANGE AND ABUNDANCE

The pygmy whitefish has a remarkably discontinuous distribution. It is known from Lake Superior; from parts of the Columbia, Fraser, Skeena, Alsek, Peace, Liard and upper Yukon systems in Washington, Montana, British Columbia and the Yukon Territory; and from the Chignik, Naknek and Wood river systems in southwestern Alaska. It is not known outside of North America. Wherever it is found, it seems to be quite abundant.

HABITS

Details of breeding behavior of the pygmy whitefish are unknown. Spawning takes place at night in late fall and early winter (November to January) at water temperatures of about 4°C or colder. Spawning grounds appear to be on gravel in lake shallows and in streams. Presumably the eggs are broadcast; then they settle into interstices in the gravel and hatch the following spring. In the Bristol Bay region, the eggs are about .24 cm in diameter (Heard and Hartman, 1966), somewhat larger than the .2 cm reported for Lake Superior fish (Eschmeyer and Bailey, 1955). Egg number varies between 103 and 1,153 per female in Bristol Bay fish, a greater average number than in Lake Superior fish. Males may become sexually mature at as early an age as a year; females, a year later (Weisel et al., 1973).

Growth of the pygmy whitefish is very slow and shows considerable variation from one population to another. In general, females grow faster than males, although in some populations the males grow faster than females during the first year (Eschmeyer and Bailey, 1955). In Brooks Lake, Alaska, the average 3-year-old fish was about 7 cm in fork length, while in South Bay, Naknek Lake, fish of the same age averaged about 11.6 cm. The maximum age recorded for fish in the Naknek system was 5+ (Heard and Hartman, 1966), but ages up to 9+ have been noted in Maclure Lake, British Columbia (McCart, 1965).

The pygmy whitefish does not make extended migrations. However, it does move on to the spawning areas in the early winter and presumably back into deeper water after spawning.

Food of the pygmy whitefish includes a rather wide variety of items. Listed as most important in the Naknek system were cladocerans, dipteran (chiefly Chironomidae) larvae and pupae, adult Diptera and nymphs of Plecoptera. Other food included diatoms and other algae, pelecypods, nematodes, arachnids and fish eggs (Kendall, 1921; Heard and Hartman, 1966). In Lake Superior, ostracods and amphipods were the principal foods (Eschmeyer and Bailey, 1955). The pygmy whitefish feeds almost exclusively during daylight hours, making "short distinct jabs or darts, apparently at specific food items, such as insect larvae, when picking up mouthfuls of bottom material." They may also rise off the bottom and take specific items from the current (Heard and Hartman, 1966).

There is a distinct positive correlation between the diet and the average size of individuals in a population. Fish belonging to groups in which insects are the dietary mainstay are, on the average, much larger than those in which zooplankton is the chief food (Heard and Hartman, 1966). McCart (1970) found forms with high and low gill raker counts in Aleknagik, Naknek and Chignik lakes in Alaska and suggested that these represented sibling species. The high-count form, which was found almost exclusively in deep water, fed on plankton and grew more slowly. By contrast, the low-count form was found in both shallow and deep water, ate mostly insects and grew faster. However, the difference in growth rates through age IV in Chignik Lake does not appear to be significant. More careful analyses of larger samples are needed.

As noted above, the pygmy whitefish is found in both deep and shallow water. In Lake Superior, it was reported as most abundant at depths of 46 to 71 m (Eschmeyer and Bailey, 1955; Dryer, 1966). In the Naknek system, the species was found at depths to 168 m but was also abundant in the shallows (Heard and Hartman, 1966). McCart (1970) found that in Chignik Lake beach seine samples were composed entirely of the form with the low gill raker count, while in gill nets set at 30 m or deeper, the high-count form accounted for 36.2% of the fish taken.

IMPORTANCE TO MAN

The pygmy whitefish is of no direct importance to man. It is too small and scarce and of too limited distribution to be profitable for any kind of fishery. However, it is undoubtedly fed upon by predatory fishes such as charr, pike and burbot and may contribute to the overall scheme of competition for food. In this respect, it is interesting to note that the pygmy whitefish attains its greatest size in waters where there is no competition from other coregonids (McCart, 1965).

ROUND WHITEFISH

Prosopium cylindraceum (Pallas)

DISTINCTIVE CHARACTERS

The narrow, rather pointed snout, the 74 or more pored scales in the lateral line, and the 50 or more pyloric caeca distinguish the round whitefish (Figure 16).

DESCRIPTION

Body elongate, cylindrical, slender; depth 15% to 20% of fork length. Head relatively short, its length averaging 20% of fork length. Snout short, about 22% of head, pointed when seen from above. Eye round, diameter equal to or less than snout length; notch present in membrane below posterior edge of pupil. Nostrils have a single flap separating the openings on each side. Mouth small, upper jaw overhanging lower; maxilla reaches about to anterior margin of eye in adults, a little farther back in young. Teeth restricted to a small patch of embedded teeth on tongue; also present on bases of gill rakers. Gill rakers, which are short: 14 to 21. Branchiostegals: 6 to 9. Lateral line has 74 to 108 pored scales. Pyloric caeca: 50 to 130. Vertebrae: 58 to 65.

FINS. Dorsal has 11 to 15 rays. Adipose fin present. Anal has 10 to 13 rays; pectorals, 14 to 17; pelvics, 9 to 11, axillary process present. Caudal forked.

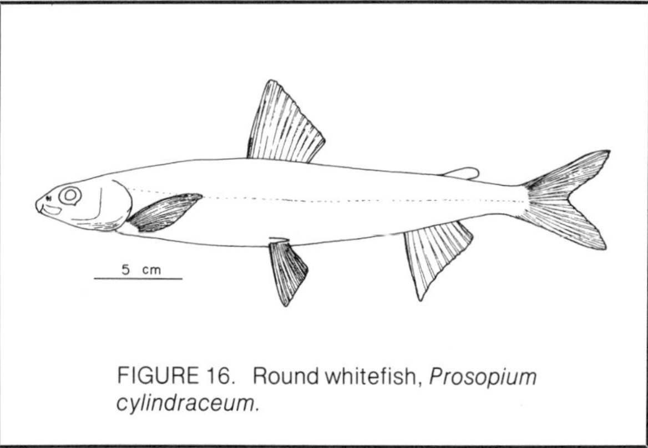

FIGURE 16. Round whitefish, *Prosopium cylindraceum.*

SCALES. Cycloid, fairly large; nuptial tubercles prominent on lateral scales of breeding males, but only feebly developed in females.

COLOR. Bronze on back, sometimes with a greenish tinge. Sides silvery, belly silvery white. Fins of most Alaskan specimens are more or less colorless or slightly dusky. Scott and Crossman (1973) reported the pectoral, pelvic and anal fins to be an amber color, becoming orange at spawning time. The young are marked with 3 rows of fairly well-defined parr marks, the first row lying along the lateral line, a second row (sometimes not well defined) just above the first, and a third row just below the midline of the back. The spots of this third row often coalesce across the middorsal line (photographs, page 86 and 87).

SIZE. The largest round whitefish on record was a specimen of 56.1 cm total length from Great Slave Lake (Scott and Crossman, 1973). The round whitefish is known to reach a weight of 2 kg (Keleher, 1961) and has been reported as reaching "about 5 pounds" (2.27 kg) in Lake Superior (Koelz, 1929).

RANGE AND ABUNDANCE

The round whitefish is found throughout mainland Alaska from the Taku River, near Juneau, north to the arctic coast. It ranges eastward across Canada to the western shores of Hudson Bay. A discontinuity in range exists in Manitoba and northern Ontario, and the species is again present in the Great Lakes (except Lake Erie), eastward to New Hampshire and Maine, south to Connecticut and north to Labrador's arctic coast. In Asia the round whitefish ranges west to the Yenisei River and south to Kamchatka.

The round whitefish is fairly abundant wherever it is present, although it usually does not occur in such large numbers as some of its relatives.

HABITS

Spawning occurs in late September through October in interior Alaska, but not until November or December in more southern parts of the range. Spawning appears to be an annual affair, with many fish breeding in successive years, even in the Arctic (McCart et al., 1972). Spawning beds are located on gravelly shallows of rivers and the inshore areas of lakes. Inshore and upstream migrations have been observed (Harper, 1948; Normandeau, 1969) at spawning time and are probably characteristic. However, fish in interior Alaska do not seem to show the concentrated migrations characteristic of ciscoes and humpback whitefish. According to Normandeau (1969), the fish swim in pairs during spawning, a single male with each female. Details of spawning behavior have not been described, but probably resemble those of the mountain whitefish, *Prosopium williamsoni.* In that species, the fish contact each other and rest on the bottom for 2 to 4 seconds, emitting eggs and milt, then separate (Brown, 1952). The eggs of the round whitefish are known to be broadcast and to receive no parental care. Females produce between 1,000 and 12,000 eggs, with the average between 5,000 and 6,000 (Bailey, 1963; Normandeau, 1969; Furniss, 1974). The size of ovarian eggs varies with locality. In New Hampshire unfertilized eggs averaged .27 cm, in diameter (Normandeau, 1969), but Furniss (1974) found ovarian eggs of Alaskan fish to be only .1 to .18 cm in diameter. The eggs absorb water after fertilization and may reach diameters of .3 cm to almost .5 cm in a few hours. The eggs, which are yellow to orange and demersal but not sticky, settle into crevices in the rocks and gravel of the bottom. Time of development has been reported as about 140 days at 2.2°C in New Hampshire (Normandeau, 1969) and presumably is not much different in Alaska. The young hatch out as sac fry. In two to three weeks, the yolk has been absorbed and the young have left the spawning grounds.

Growth rates vary from one locality to another. Lake Michigan fish grow very rapidly, reaching a total length of about 50 cm in 7 years (Mraz, 1964a). By contrast, in Elusive Lake, in the Brooks Range of Alaska, this length is not achieved until age 12. The oldest known round whitefish is one of 16+ from Shainin Lake, Alaska (Furniss, 1974). Sexual maturity is reached in about 5 years in the southern parts of the range, but not until age 7 in the Brooks Range of Alaska (Furniss, 1974).

Except for the spawning movements already mentioned, the round whitefish apparently does not migrate.

Food of the round whitefish is primarily the immature stages of various insects, especially Diptera and Trichoptera. Adult Trichoptera are also important, as well as gastropods, *Daphnia* and fish eggs (Martin, 1957; Loftus, 1958; Normandeau, 1969; Furniss, 1974). In some areas the round whitefish is considerd a serious predator on the eggs of lake trout (Martin, 1957; Loftus, 1958).

IMPORTANCE TO MAN

The round whitefish was formerly taken in considerable quantities in the Great Lakes. In the late 1920s annual catches from northern Lake Michigan were on the order of 90,900 to 163,200 kg (Mraz, 1964a), but present-day catches are much smaller, primarily because of the relatively small size of the fish and an uncertain supply. In Alaska the round whitefish is of some importance in freshwater subsistence fisheries. It is occasionally smoked in strips and sold as "squaw candy."

BROAD WHITEFISH

Coregonus nasus (Pallas)

DISTINCTIVE CHARACTERS

The broad whitefish is set off by its short gill rakers, which are less than one-fifth as long as the interorbital width, and the rounded to flat profile of the head (Figure 17).

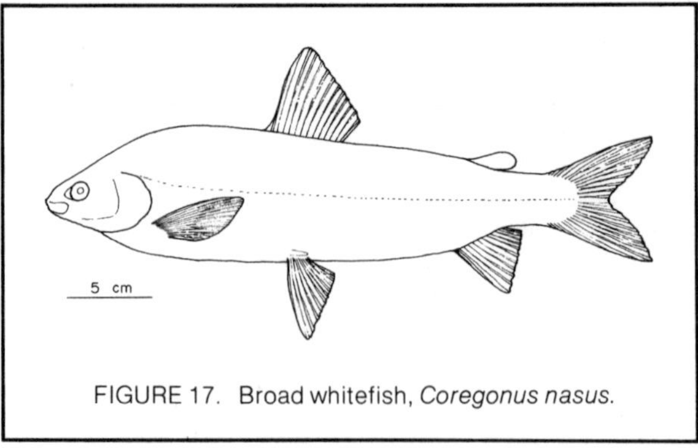

FIGURE 17. Broad whitefish, *Coregonus nasus.*

DESCRIPTION

Body elongate and compressed, especially in large specimens; sides a bit flatter than in most other whitefishes. Depth of body 23% to 31% of fork length in adults, less in young. Head short, 15% to 20% of fork length. Dorsal profile rounded to flat (may be slightly concave in large specimens). Snout blunt, short, rounded, sheep-nosed in profile, its length equal to or less than diameter of eye. Eye small, 12% to 16% of head length. No notch in adipose lid. Nostrils have a double flap between openings. Mouth small, upper jaw overhanging lower, maxilla reaching rearward approximately to below anterior edge of eye. No teeth except for a small patch of weak teeth on base of tongue. The 18 to 25 gill rakers are blunt and short, longest 13% to 19% of interorbital width. Branchiostegals: 8 or 9. Lateral line has 84 to 102 pored scales. Pyloric caeca: about 140 to more than 150. Vertebrae: 60 to 65.

FINS. Dorsal has 10 to 13 rays. Adipose fin present and fairly large. Anal, 11 to 14 rays; pectorals, 16 to 17; pelvics, 11 to 12, axillary process present. Caudal forked.

SCALES. Large, cycloid. Males develop prominent breeding tubercles on lateral scales at spawning time, but these are only weakly developed in females.

COLOR. Olive-brown to nearly black on back; sides silvery, often with a gray cast; belly white to yellowish. Fins usually rather gray in adults, pale in young (photograph, page 87).

SIZE. This species is the largest of the Alaskan whitefishes. It is reported to reach weights up to 16 kg in the Kolyma River of Siberia (Berg, 1948), but most mature fish run around 2 to 5 kg. One of 71.5 cm weighing 5.7 kg from the Yenisei River is mentioned by Berg (1948). The largest Alaskan specimen known was a fish of 67 cm fork length from the Colville River at Umiat (Alt and Kogl, 1973).

RANGE AND ABUNDANCE

The broad whitefish is found throughout Alaska from the Kuskokwim River north to the arctic coast. It is present in the Yukon River from the mouth to the headwaters. In the Tanana River drainage it is known from Minto Flats and the Tolovana, Chatanika and Chena rivers and probably occurs farther upstream as well. It is present in most, if not all, of the rivers draining into the Bering, Chukchi and Beaufort seas. The range extends eastward to the Perry River, Northwest Territories, westward across Siberia to the Pechora River, south to the Bay of Korf and to the Penzhina River on the Sea of Okhotsk. It is fairly abundant seasonally, though apparently not in as large numbers as some of its relatives.

HABITS

Little is known of the biology of the broad whitefish. Although the adults are more or less anadromous, those reaching the sea apparently do not venture far from brackish water. Upstream spawning runs begin as early as June and may extend into September or even later (Kogl, 1971; Alt and

Kogl, 1973; Kepler, 1973; Townsend and Kepler, 1974). Spawning actually takes place from September through October, possibly even into November. Wynne-Edwards's (1952) statement that "The broad whitefish spawns in the rivers in August . . ." is probably based on a misinterpretation of the timing of the spawning runs. Except for our knowledge that spawning takes place in streams with gravel bottoms, nothing is known of the breeding habits. Presumably they are similar to those of other coregonids. The ovarian eggs are pale yellow to milky white in color and up to .4 cm in diameter (Berg, 1948; Nikolskii, 1961). Young hatch in the spring and move downstream. Adults apparently move downstream after spawning and overwinter in deep parts of the rivers or in estuaries.

Growth is relatively slow, especially in the arctic. Berg (1948) mentioned lengths of 50 to 53 cm at 8+ for fish from the Kara and Kolyma regions of Russia, but in the Colville River, Alaska, the average length of 8+ fish was under 40 cm (Kogl, 1971). Broad whitefish from the Minto Flats area grow at about the same rate as the Siberian fish (Alt and Kogl, 1973). Maximum age recorded is 15 years (Alt and Kogl, 1973), although Nikolskii (1961) stated that "The age limit of this fish exceeds 15 years."

The broad whitefish appears to be mainly a bottom feeder. It is known to eat chironomids, snails, bivalve mollusks (Kogl, 1971), mosquito larvae (Berg, 1948) and crustaceans (Scott and Crossman, 1973).

IMPORTANCE TO MAN

The broad whitefish is taken commercially in Siberia, but it is not of great importance. Pre-World War II catches in Siberia averaged 40,000 kg per year. In North America the broad whitefish is used almost exclusively in subsistence fisheries, although a commercial fishery in the Colville River Delta takes about 7,000 kg per year. Despite its lack of popularity the broad whitefish is an excellent food fish.

THE HUMPBACK WHITEFISHES

Coregonus clupeaformis complex

This group of three closely related species forms a most confusing assemblage because almost the only means by which they can be distinguished from one another seems to be the modal number of gill rakers in large samples (the mode is the most frequent number to appear in a count). The form here called *Coregonus pidschian* has average gill raker counts of 21 to 23, with a range from about 17 to 24 or 25 in individual specimens. *Coregonus nelsoni* averages 24 or 25 (the mode is usually 25) with a range of 22 to 27, while *Coregonus clupeaformis* has modal counts of 26 or more, with individual counts ranging from 24 to 33. *C. pidschian* appears to have lower average vertebral counts than do *C. nelsoni* and *C. clupeaformis.* Fisheries biologists in Alaska have applied one or another of these names to humpback whitefish throughout the state, all too often without adequate samples for proper identification. Hence, distributional records are often of little value.

There appear to be some differences in ecological relationships among the three species. *C. clupeaformis* is primarily a lake-dwelling form. *C. nelsoni* is mostly a stream dweller, only rarely being encountered in lakes. It seems to be intolerant of salt water. *C. pidschian* apparently is truly anadromous, at least in some areas, and may winter in the sea near river mouths.

ALASKA WHITEFISH

Coregonus nelsoni

DISTINCTIVE CHARACTERS

The distinctive marks of the Alaska whitefish are gill rakers that are longer than 20% of the interorbital width, a total of 22 to 27 gill rakers on first arch (with modal counts of 24 or 25) and a pronounced hump behind the head in adults (Figure 18).

DESCRIPTION

Body moderately compressed, sides rather flat. Depth of body 25% to 33% of fork length in adults, the percentage increasing in larger fish. Head short, less than 25% of fork length. Dorsal profile of head distinctly concave behind eyes in adults due to the prominent nuchal hump. Snout 27% to 35% of head length. Eye small, its diameter 20% to 25% of head length; no notch present in lower posterior part of membrane. Nostrils have a double flap between openings. Mouth rather small with upper jaw over-

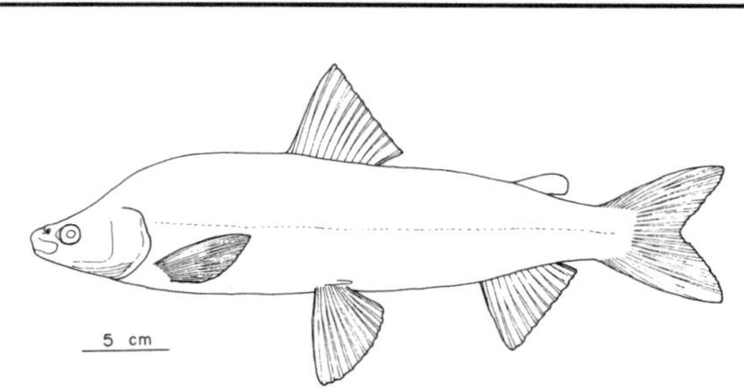

FIGURE 18. Alaska whitefish, *Coregonus nelsoni.* The humpback and lake whitefishes closely resemble this species but differ in number of gill rakers.

hanging lower and maxilla reaching backward to below front third of eye. A few weak teeth present on premaxilla in young, no teeth on jaws in adults. A few small teeth present on tongue. Gill rakers: 22 to 27, with total counts averaging around 24 or 25. Longest raker longer than 20% of interorbital space. Branchiostegals: 8 to 10. Lateral line has 77 to 95 pored scales. Vertebrae: 60 to 63.

FINS. Dorsal has 11 to 13 rays. Adipose fin well developed, often larger in males than in females. Anal has 10 to 14 rays; pectorals, 15 to 17; pelvics, 11 to 12, axillary process present. Caudal forked.

SCALES. Cycloid, fairly large. Well-developed nuptial tubercles on lateral scales of males, less developed in females.

COLOR. Dark brown to midnight blue above fading to silver on sides and white beneath. No parr marks in young (photograph, page 88).

SIZE. Up to at least 53.2 cm fork length in the Chatanika River (Alt, 1971a).

RANGE AND ABUNDANCE

The precise distribution of Alaska whitefish is uncertain, primarily because of the difficulty of identifying the three species of humpbacked coregonids which occur in Alaska. However, as far as can be determined, the Alaska whitefish seems to be pretty well confined to the Yukon and its tributary drainages, where it is to be found all the way from Nulato to the Canadian border. It is present in the Tanana River and the Koyukuk River and their tributaries and in Lake Minchumina. Specimens that may be of this species have been reported from the Unalakleet and Wulik rivers. Possible *C. nelsoni* are known from the Alsek, Copper and Susitna systems, the upper parts of the Yukon River in Canada, the lower reaches of the Mackenzie River and several lakes in western Canada (Lindsey, 1963a, b; Lindsey et al., 1970; McPhail and Lindsey, 1970).

The Alaska whitefish is locally and seasonally abundant during the summer and fall. Throughout the rest of the year the fish apparently disperse widely.

HABITS

The Alaska whitefish spawns from late September through October in interior Alaska. Spawning areas are in clear, moderately swift streams with fairly clean gravel bottoms. In the Chatanika River, these areas are from 100 to 800 m long, 15 to 22 m wide, and 1.3 to 2.6 m deep, with water velocities of about 0.5 m per second. Water temperatures at spawning are between 0° and 3°C (Kepler, 1973). Average fecundity of 20 mature females 5 to 10 years old and 39.5 to 52 cm fork length was about 50,000 eggs. Fecundity was not closely related to age or size of the fish (Townsend and Kepler, 1974).

The spawning act is similar to that of the least cisco. A female begins to swim vertically toward the surface, belly upstream. She is joined by a male (sometimes two, rarely three). Eggs and milt are extruded as the fish approach the surface of the water. The fish break the surface, fall away from each other and return to the bottom of the pool. In contrast to the least cisco, the Alaska whitefish spawns actively both at night and in the daytime. The yellow to orange eggs, with an average diameter of .21 to .23 cm, drift down to the bottom where they lodge in crevices in the gravel. The exact time of incubation is unknown. However, young-of-the-year have been taken in June and July, so presumably the young fish hatch in late winter or early spring.

The Alaska whitefish of the Chatanika River grow rapidly during their early years. A year-old fish averages about 12 cm fork length. By the age of 5, the fish average between 35 and 40 cm fork length, and at 10 years about 48.5 cm. The oldest so far recorded was a 12+ of 53.2 cm fork length. Sexual maturity is reached between 3 and 5 years (Alt, 1971a; Townsend and Kepler, 1974).

The Alaska whitefish of the interior undertakes fairly extensive upstream and downstream movements. Upstream migration, apparently the beginning of the spawning run, may start as early as late June. The migration seems to be rather indefinite at first but it becomes marked as the season progresses and more and more fish approach breeding condition. By September schools of up to several hundred fish are on or close to the spawning areas. Following the completion of spawning, the majority of the fish move downstream but a few may winter in deep pools near the spawning grounds. The young-of-the-year move downstream in their first year and as a rule do not return to the spawning areas until they are sexually mature.

Alaska whitefish generally return to the same spawning grounds year after year. Townsend and Kepler (1974) found that five fish tagged in 1972 were present on the same grounds in 1973. On the other hand, these same investigators noted far fewer tag returns than were expected and suggested that this might indicate either increased mortality of tagged fish or nonconsecutive (nonannual) spawning. The October, 1975, recovery at Nenana of an Alaska whitefish tagged in the Chatanika River in 1974* suggests that some fish may wander far from their natal streams. Apparently not all fish return each year to the same spawning areas.

Hybrids of Alaska whitefish and inconnu are known to exist (Alt, 1971c). The two species spawn at

*A.H. Townsend: personal communication.

the same time and in the same places. Because of the differences in breeding behavior, hybridization is probably not the result of pairing between genera but due rather to simultaneous broadcasting of reproductive products in the same area. Occasional hybridization occurs also between the Alaska whitefish and the least cisco (UAFC #2173).

Alaska whitefish feed primarily on immature stages of insects, notably Diptera and Trichoptera. Although they generally do not feed during the latter part of the spawning run, this is not always so. On occasion they will feed heavily on eggs of the least cisco (Morrow et al., 1977).

IMPORTANCE TO MAN

The Alaska whitefish is an excellent food fish but is virtually never eaten. Its major importance is in the subsistence fisheries, but even here it falls far behind the various salmons. Spearfishing for sport has resulted in a small fishery in the Chatanika River; this fishery, which takes place at night, is estimated to take up to 500 fish yearly (Kepler, 1973) and similar spear fisheries, also small, exist at other locations in Alaska. Commercial fisheries have operated in some of the lakes of the Copper River drainage, but the take has not been large (Williams, 1968, 1969). The young are consumed by predatory fishes such as pike and burbot (Alt, 1968) and by other predators such as kingfishers, mink and otter.

HUMPBACK WHITEFISH

Coregonus pidschian

DISTINCTIVE CHARACTERS

The humpback whitefish is distinguished by gill rakers that are longer than 20% of the interorbital width, 19 to 25 gill rakers (with modal counts of 22 or 23), and a pronounced hump behind the head in adults.

DESCRIPTION

See description of *C. nelsoni* (page 35). Except for the gill raker counts, there are no known morphological differences of any significance. It is my impression, as well as that of several fisheries biologists in the Fairbanks office of the Alaska Department of Fish & Game, that pearl organs are far fewer in number and are less well developed in *C. pidschian* than in *C. nelsoni*. Specimens from the Kobuk River that I have seen myself, and specimens from Highpower Creek and the Kalitna River in the Kuskokwim system,* all taken in early October, had few pearl organs. Vertebrae (in Siberian fish): 58 to 63.

*K.T. Alt: personal communication.

RANGE AND ABUNDANCE

The humpback whitefish is to be found in most of the Alaskan rivers that empty into the Bering, Chukchi and Beaufort seas. It ranges throughout the Kuskokwim River drainage and well above Umiat in the Colville. Alt and Kogl (1973) found it at Umiat in July; thus it is presumed that the spawning grounds in the Colville must be much farther upstream. In the Yukon, on the other hand, it apparently is confined to the lower reaches, where it has been recorded from Marshall. Its range extends eastward along the arctic coast at least to the Sagavanirktok River, Alaska, westward across Siberia to the Kara Sea. Throughout its range it is quite abundant during the spawning concentrations, but the fish apparently disperse at other times of the year.

HABITS

Humpback whitefish appear to be truly anadromous, but it is not known how far the wintering fish move from the river mouths. They have been taken in the Beaufort Sea several miles offshore of the Colville and Sagavanirktok rivers as well as in Kotzebue Sound, off Nome, and around the mouths of the Yukon and Kuskokwim rivers. In the Kara Sea of western Siberia they have been taken well out in the northern parts "which are characterized by high salinities" (Berg, 1948). Upstream spawning migrations may be extensive. Fish tagged in the Kuskokwim River below Bethel have been recovered on the North Fork at Medfra and Telida, the latter representing a migration of not less than 1,280 km. Possible *C. pidschian* have been found in the Yukon River at Fort Yukon and in the Porcupine River,* but their origin remains unknown. Other populations seldom venture far upstream and still others may never go to sea at all (Berg, 1948).

The spawning run generally begins in June and spawning usually occurs in October. However, humpback whitefish have been found spawning under the ice in the Kuskokwim River near Bethel as late as November 15* and similar phenomena have been recorded in Siberia (Berg, 1948). Spawning behavior has not been described, but presumably is similar to that of the Alaska whitefish. Sexual maturity is attained at 4 to 6 years. Ovarian eggs are reported as .12 cm in diameter in Siberian fish (Nikolskii, 1961). Fecundity of females varies from one population to another and with the size of the fish. The general range is from about 8,000 to nearly 50,000 eggs per female. It is assumed that the young hatch in the late winter and spring, subsequently moving downstream, to return as mature adults 4 to 6 years later.

The young feed mainly on zooplankton, but adults feed mostly on mollusks, crustaceans and chironomid larvae (Nikolskii, 1961).

Growth rates vary greatly from place to place and even in different sections of the same river (Nikolskii, 1961). In Alaska, fish in arctic rivers such as the Colville, Kobuk and Agiakpuk grow much more slowly than do those in the Kuskokwim and lower Yukon drainages. Humpback whitefish from the first three rivers average about 26.7 cm fork length at 5+ and 40.5 cm at 10+ while those from the latter areas average 34.7 cm and 44.5 cm at the same ages (Alt, 1973b).

IMPORTANCE TO MAN

The humpback whitefish of Alaska is of little direct importance except in local subsistence fisheries. A commercial operation on the Colville River Delta takes about 1,000 fish annually (Alt and Kogl, 1973). However, this fish is an important commercial species in Siberia (Berg, 1948; Nikolskii, 1961).

LAKE WHITEFISH

Coregonus clupeaformis (Mitchill)

DISTINCTIVE CHARACTERS

The lake whitefish is differentiated from the other two humpback whitefishes of Alaska by its higher gill raker count, which ranges from 26 to 33.

DESCRIPTION

See description of *C. nelsoni* (page 35). Except for the gill raker counts, there are no known differences in appearance of any significance. Pyloric caeca: 140 to 222. Vertebrae: 55 to 64.

RANGE AND ABUNDANCE

The lake whitefish is widely distributed across Canada and the northern United States, from the upper Yukon and Northwest Territories south to Montana, Minnesota and the Great Lakes, and east to New England, Quebec and Labrador. Records of its distribution in Alaska are not completely reliable due to the confusion with closely related species. However, the lake whitefish has been recorded with reasonable certainty from Paxson and Crosswind lakes in the Copper River drainage and from Lake Louise and the Tyone Lakes in the Susitna drainage (Williams, 1968; Van Wyhe and Peck, 1969). Lindsey et al., (1970) show a possible record of lake whitefish from Old John Lake at the head of the Sheenjek River, but the record is based on only two specimens.* Wherever it is found, the lake whitefish is quite abundant, especially when schooled up for spawning.

*C. Lindsey: personal communication.

HABITS

Breeding behavior of the lake whitefish is similar to that of the Alaska whitefish except that spawning generally takes place in the inshore regions of lakes. Stream populations, of course, use the rivers and creeks. Spawning takes place over rocky or gravelly bottom in depths of 1 to 3 m. A female and one or more males rise to the surface, extrude eggs and milt, then descend separately toward the bottom. Spawning occurs at night (Bean, 1903; Hart, 1930; Everhart, 1958). Adults breed annually in the southern parts of the range, but apparently only every other year or even every third year in the arctic and sub-arctic (Kennedy, 1953).

Fecundity varies greatly from one population to another, averaging around 50,000 eggs per female, with a reported range of less than 6,000 to more than 150,000. Spawning occurs from October to December, depending on locality, and seems to be associated with water temperatures of about 6°C or less. Hatching normally occurs in late April. Development of the eggs takes 140 days at .5°C, which seems to be the optimum temperature for the eggs. In laboratory studies, no eggs survived at 0° or at 12°C. Mortalities through hatching increased from 27% at .5° to 41% or 42% at 2° to 6°, 81% at 8° and 99% at 10°C. Abnormalities also increased from none at .5° to 2°C to 50% at 10°C (Price, 1940).

The larvae are 1.1 to 1.4 cm long at hatching and grow rapidly during the summer. In Lake Huron the larvae are close inshore from soon after breakup to the end of the summer (Faber, 1970), their location often being associated with emergent vegetation. They stay at or near areas with temperatures of 17°C (Reckahn, 1970), descending with it to the metalimnion. Van Wyhe and Peck (1969) found similar movements of young-of-the-year that were believed to be lake whitefish in Paxson Lake, Alaska.

Growth slows abruptly in September so that by the end of October the larvae are about 12 cm long. This slowing of growth is associated with descent into the colder water of the hypolimnion.

Growth rates vary with locality and population. Average total lengths at age, covering a wide variety of localities in the U.S. and southern Canada, are: 1+, 13 cm; 2+, 21.6 cm; 5+, 38.6 cm; 10+, 51.1 cm; 15+, 62.7 cm (Carlander, 1969). By contrast, lake whitefish in Paxson Lake, Alaska, had the following age-length relationships: 1+, 4 cm; 2+,

7.7 cm; 5+, 20.2 cm; 10+, 37.3 cm; 15+, 46 cm (Van Wyhe and Peck, 1969). Maximum age reported was that of a fish of 28 years from Great Slave Lake (Kennedy, 1953), while the largest size was of a fish of 19 kg taken in Lake Superior in 1918 (Van Oosten, 1946). If the length-weight relationship given by Dryer (1963) for Lake Superior whitefish can be applied to this second specimen, then the fish must have been on the order of 135 cm total length. The next largest known weighed just over half as much, 10.9 kg (Keleher, 1961).

The lake whitefish appears to be a rather sedentary fish, at least in the Great Lakes. Tagging studies (Budd, 1957; Dryer, 1964) indicate that the majority of fish stay within 16 km of their spawning ground, although one fish in Lake Huron was recaptured 240 km from the point of release. There seems also to be a tendency toward movement in definite directions, although no well-defined routes have been determined (Budd, 1957). In general, movement of lake whitefish in large lakes consists of four stages: travel from deep to shallow water in the spring; movement back into deep water during the summer as the shoal water warms; migration back to the shallow-water spawning areas in the fall and early winter; and post-spawning movement back to deeper water.

Within each of the Great Lakes, and probably in most large lakes, the lake whitefish form more or less separate populations. These are usually characterized by different growth rates rather than by morphological differences (Budd, 1957; Roelofs, 1958; Dryer, 1963, 1964; Mraz, 1964b). It is not known whether these populations are genetically distinct or are produced by environmental factors. In any case, the lack of migratory habits probably tends to keep them separate.

Food of the lake whitefish varies with size and age of the fish, location, and the type of food available. The initial food of the young consists of copepods, later on of cladocerans. By early summer they begin to feed on bottom organisms, but Cladocera, especially *Bosmina,* remain a dominant food item for some time (Reckahn, 1970). Adults feed mainly on benthic organisms, but pelagic and semipelagic forms also are important. Kliewer (1970) found a significant negative correlation between gill raker length and the proportion of benthic food, and a strong positive correlation between the number of gill rakers and the amount of benthic food. He listed the following food items for lake whitefish from the Cranberry Portage area in northern Manitoba: Pelecypods, gastropods, amphipods, Diptera (tendepedid larvae and pupae, culicid and ceratopogonid larvae), Ephemeroptera, Trichoptera, Megaloptera, plant material, fish eggs, Hirudinea, Cladocera, Copepoda, mysids, Hemiptera (Corixidae), Hymenoptera and fishes. In Paxson Lake, Alaska, adult whitefish were seen to prey upon young sockeye salmon until the fry grew too big for the whitefish (Van Wyhe and Peck, 1969).

Although extensive hatchery programs for the propagation of lake whitefish have been carried on for years on the Great Lakes and other places, there is no evidence to show that these programs have ever influenced the strength of year classes (Koelz, 1929; Christie, 1963). Weather seems to be the most important factor. Cold water temperatures at spawning time—below 6 °C—followed by a steady nonfluctuating decrease to .5 °C and by warm temperatures at hatching time, produce the strongest year classes (Christie, 1963; Lawler, 1965a).

IMPORTANCE TO MAN

The lake whitefish has long been one of the most valuable freshwater species in North America. Deterioration of its environment, depletion of the stocks and other factors led to a decline in yield from the 5.5 million kg per year of the 1880s to the 700,000 kg per year of the 1920s (Koelz, 1929), but in the late 1960s the catch was increasing. In 1970 the U.S. and Canadian landings from the Great Lakes and the International Lakes between Minnesota and Ontario amounted to about 1.69 million kg (Anonymous, 1973). In addition, there are considerable Canadian fisheries in the northern lakes such as Lake Winnipeg and Great Slave Lake. In Alaska, however, the lake whitefish is virtually unused. Attempts at commercial fishing for lake whitefish have been made in Crosswind Lake in the upper Copper River drainage and in Lake Louise and Tyone Lake in the upper Susitna. These have not, however, been especially successful (Williams, 1968, 1969).

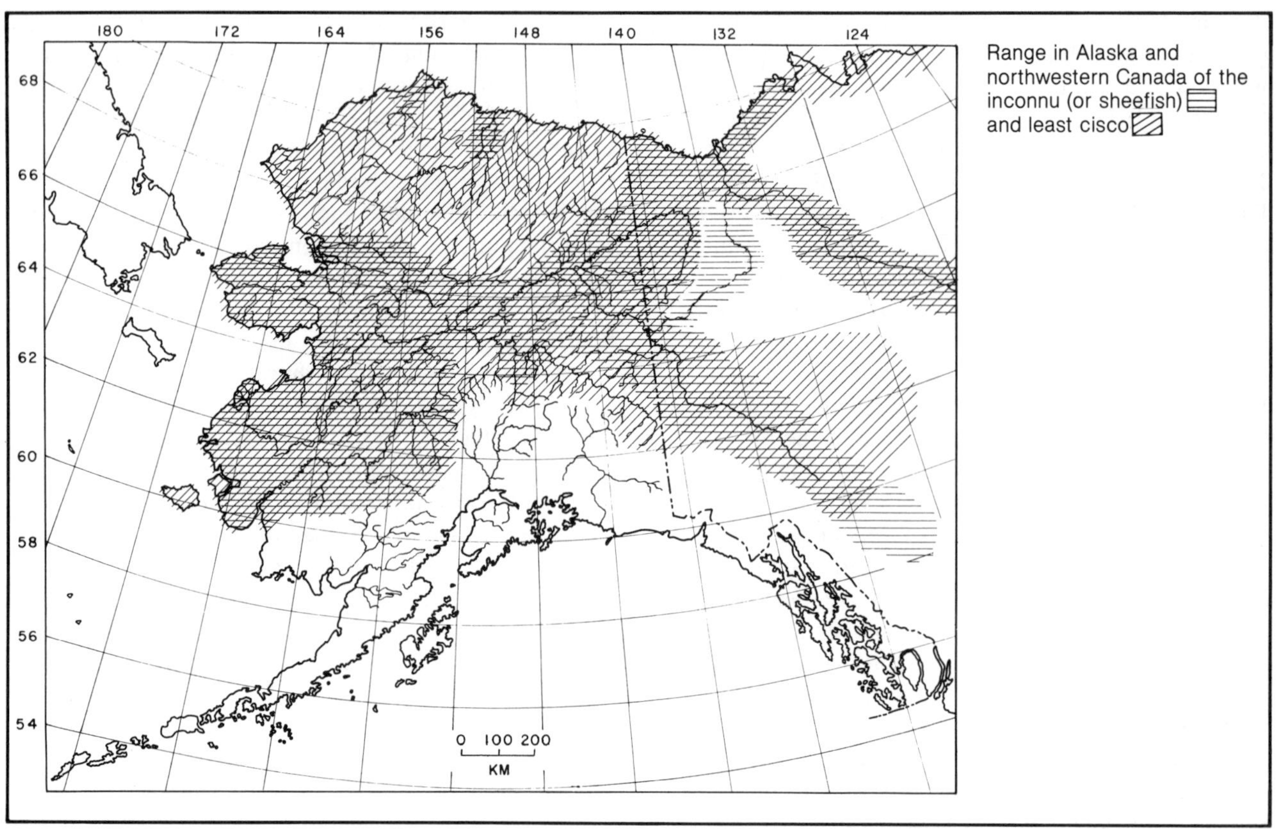

Range in Alaska and northwestern Canada of the inconnu (or sheefish) ▤ and least cisco ▨

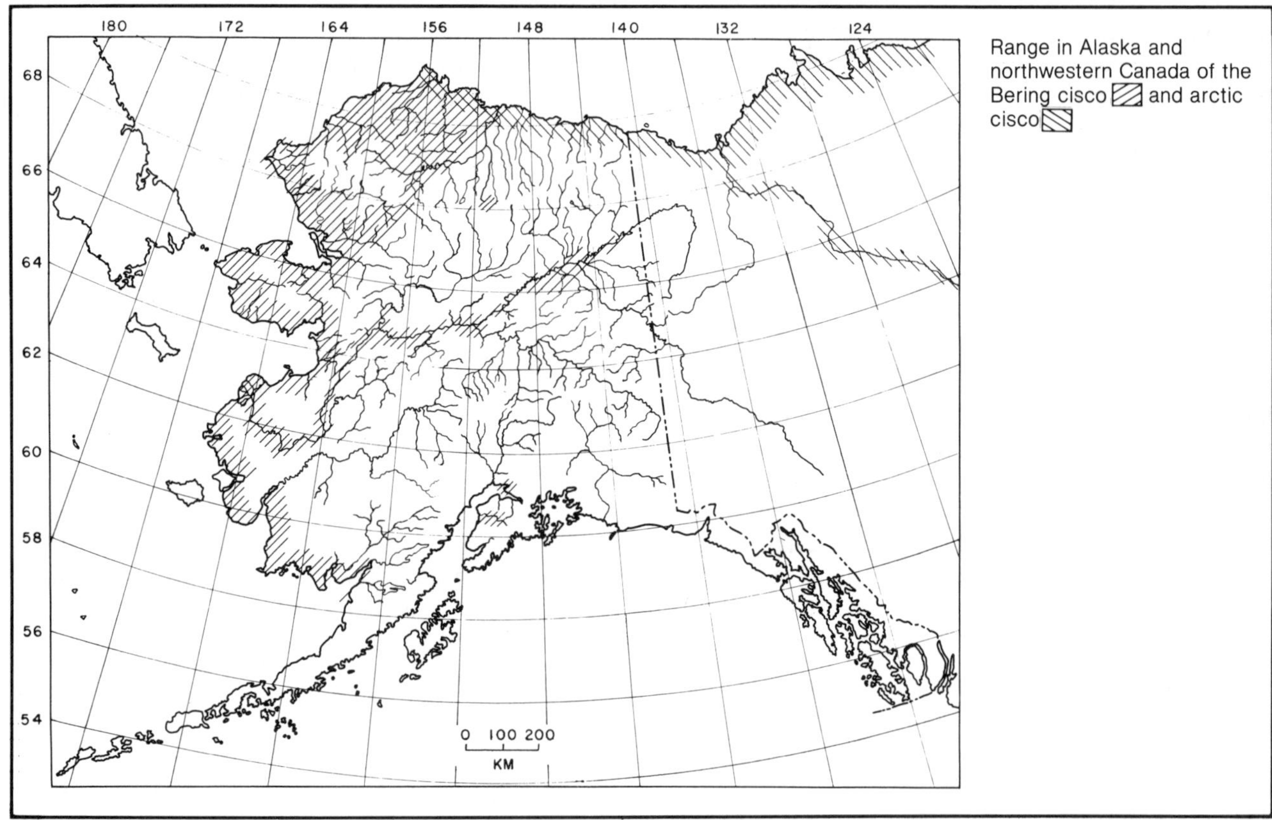

Range in Alaska and northwestern Canada of the Bering cisco ▨ and arctic cisco ▧

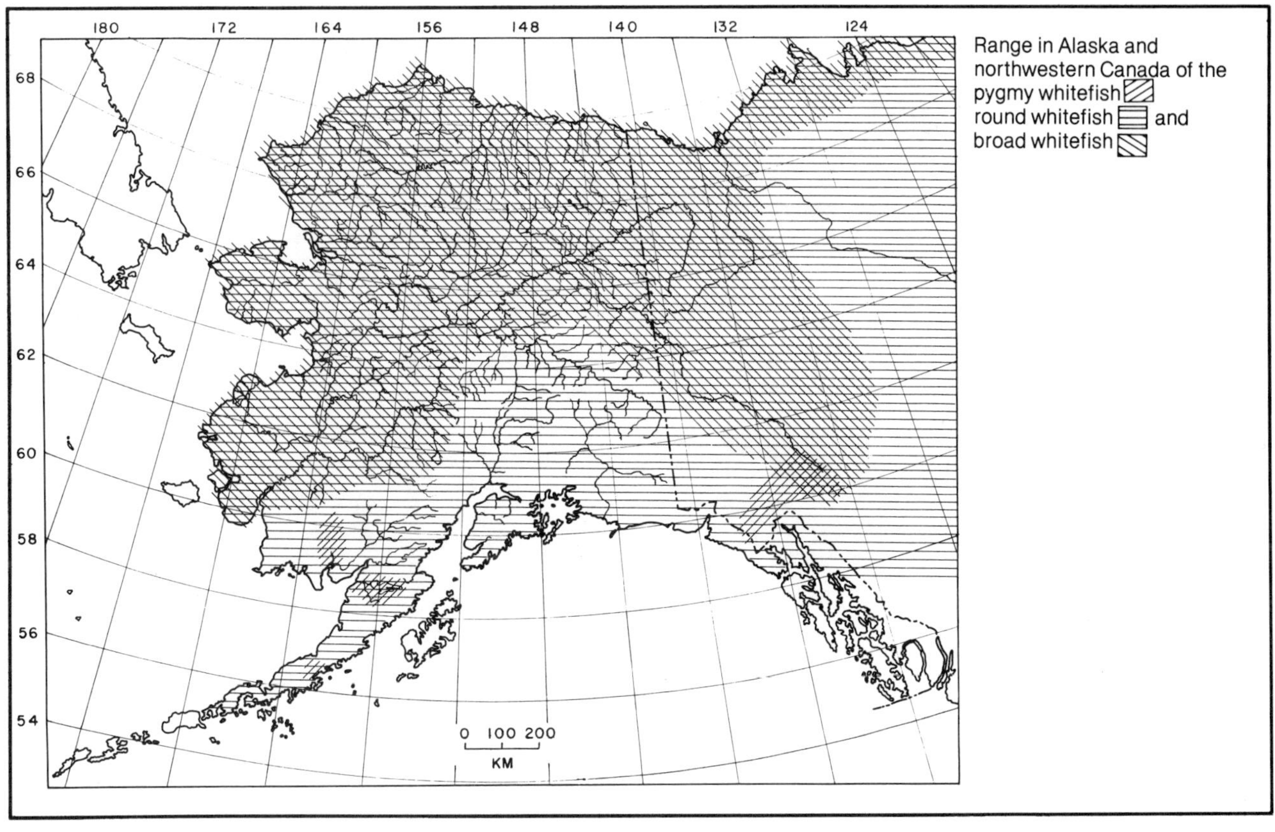

Range in Alaska and northwestern Canada of the pygmy whitefish, round whitefish and broad whitefish

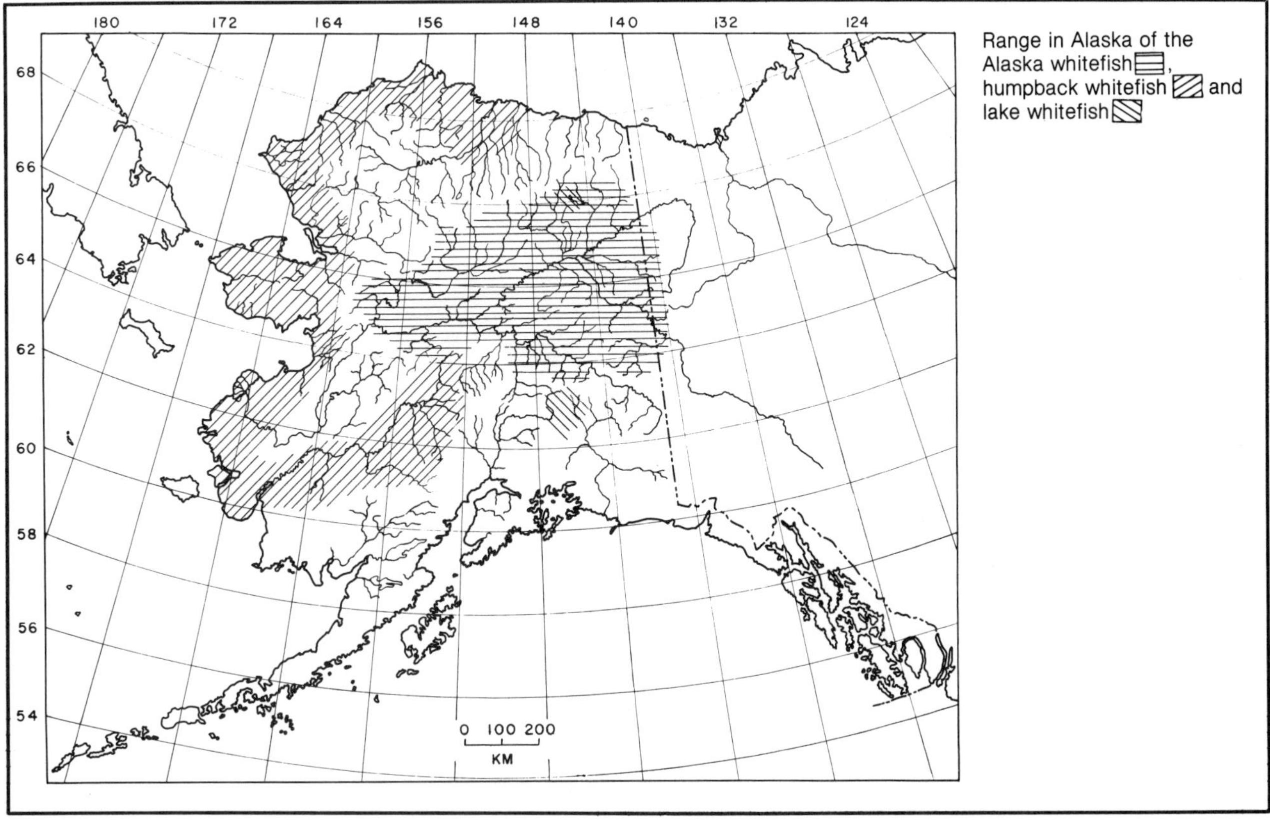

Range in Alaska of the Alaska whitefish, humpback whitefish and lake whitefish

Chapter Five

TROUTS AND SALMONS

SUBFAMILY SALMONINAE OF THE FAMILY SALMONIDAE

The Salmoninae characteristically have small scales—115 to 200 along the lateral line; well-developed teeth on the jaws and vomer; a truncate caudal fin (which is forked in the lake trout); and prominent parr marks on the young except for the pink salmon, which has no parr marks. (For description of the family see page 23.)

KEY TO THE ALASKAN SPECIES

SECTION	DESCRIPTION	THE FISH IS	PROCEED IN THIS KEY TO SECTION
1 a.	Anal rays: 8 to 12.		**2**
b.	Anal rays: 13 to 19 (in rare cases 12).		**8**
2 a.	Teeth present on both head and shaft of vomer (Figure 4, page 3). Spots on body dark brown or black.		**3**
b.	Teeth present on head of vomer, absent on shaft. Spots on body pale or red, never brown or black.		**4**
3 a.	Small teeth, which are hard to see, present on floor of mouth behind tongue. Red slash present under lower jaw (usually pale in sea-run fish and missing in some populations). No red band on sides. Upper jaw reaches well behind eye in adults.	Cutthroat trout, *Salmo clarki* Richardson, page 48.	
b.	No teeth on floor of mouth behind tongue. Generally no red slash under jaws (although slash is present in some Bristol Bay populations). A reddish band on sides, most prominent in spawning males, absent on individuals fresh from the sea. Upper jaw reaches little, if at all, behind eye in adults.	Rainbow trout, *Salmo gairdneri* Richardson, page 50.	
4 a.	Dark green wavy marks on back and on dorsal fin.	Brook trout, *Salvelinus fontinalis* (Mitchill), page 53.	
b.	No dark green marbling on back or dorsal fin.		**5**
5 a.	Caudal fin deeply forked. Body color dark green to grayish, with numerous oval or irregular whitish to yellow spots on sides and back. Pyloric caeca: 90 to 200.	Lake trout, *Salvelinus namaycush* (Walbaum), page 55.	
b.	Caudal fin only slightly forked. Spots on body are round, may be red, pink or yellowish in live specimens. Pyloric caeca: 13 to 74.		**6**

KEY TO THE ALASKAN SPECIES (CONT.)

SECTION	DESCRIPTION	THE FISH IS	PROCEED IN THIS KEY TO SECTION
6 a.	Pyloric caeca: 30 to 74. Lake spawners.	Arctic charr, *Salvelinus alpinus* (Linnaeus), page 58.	
b.	Pyloric caeca: 13 to 35. Stream spawners.		**7**
7 a.	Body color velvety black in adults, often brownish in juveniles, with fiery red spots. Pelvic rays: usually 10. A dwarf form, not known to exceed about 28 cm fork length.	Angayukaksurak charr, *Salvelinus anaktuvukensis* Morrow, page 63.	
b.	Body color not black, but may be very dark with a greenish tinge. Pelvic rays: usually 9. Sea-run fish may reach large size.	Dolly Varden, *Salvelinus malma* (Walbaum), page 60.	
8 a.	Distinct black spots present on back and tail.		**9**
b.	No distinct black spots on back or tail, although fine, dark speckling may be present.		**12**
9 a.	Spots large, more or less oval; longest as long as diameter of eye. Scales small, with 170 or more in first row above lateral line.	Pink salmon, *Oncorhynchus gorbuscha* (Walbaum), page 64.	
b.	Spots small and irregular, the largest smaller than the eye diameter. Scales larger, 155 or less in first row above lateral line.		**10**
10 a.	Gill rakers: 30 to 40.	Sockeye salmon, *Onchorhynchus nerka* (Walbaum), page 75.	
b.	Gill rakers: less than 25.		**11**
11 a.	Tail fin has small black spots on both upper and lower lobes. Gumline of lower jaw black. Anal rays: 15 to 17.	Chinook salmon, *Oncorhynchus tshawytscha* (Walbaum), page 67.	
b.	Tail fin without spots or spotted only on the upper lobe. Gumline of lower jaw not black. Anal rays: 13 to 15.	Coho salmon, *Oncorhynchus kisutch* (Walbaum), page 72.	
12 a.	Gill rakers: 18 to 28; short, stout, smooth and widely spaced. Pyloric caeca: 163 to 249.	Chum salmon, *Oncorhynchus keta* (Walbaum), page 69.	
b.	Gill rakers: 30 to 40; long, fine, serrated and closely spaced. Pyloric caeca: 45 to 115.	Sockeye salmon *Oncorhynchus nerka* (Walbaum), page 75.	

KEY TO YOUNG SALMONS AND TROUTS LESS THAN 13 CM LONG
(FIGURES FOLLOW KEY)

SECTION	DESCRIPTION	THE FISH IS	PROCEED IN THIS KEY TO SECTION
1 a.	Anal rays: 8 to 12.		**2**
b.	Anal rays: 13 or more (in rare cases 12).		**6**
2 a.	Dorsal fin has distinct dark spots or first dorsal ray is black.		**3**
b.	Dorsal fin has no dark spots and first dorsal ray is not black (although lake trout may have faint dark bars).		**5**
3 a.	Red or yellow spots present along lateral line. Combined width of dark parr marks along lateral line equal to or greater than combined width of intervening light areas (Figure 19, page 46).	Brook trout, page 53.	
b.	No red or yellow spots along lateral line. Combined width of dark parr marks along lateral line less than combined width of intervening light areas.		**4**
4 a.	Usually 5 to 10 dark marks along middle of back in front of dorsal fin. Black border of adipose fin unbroken or with only one break (Figure 20, page 46).	Rainbow trout, page 50.	
b.	No more than 5 (usually 4 or less) dark marks on back in front of dorsal fin. Black border of adipose fin usually has several breaks (Figure 21, page 47).	Cutthroat trout, page 48.	
5 a.	Parr marks in form of vertical bars. Width of light areas along lateral line equal to or greater than width of dark areas. Distance from snout to front of dorsal fin about half the distance from snout to base of tail (Figure 22, page 47).	Lake trout, page 55.	
b.	Parr marks are irregular, often rectangular, blotches. Width of dark areas greater than width of light areas along lateral line. Distance from snout to front of dorsal fin less than half the distance from snout to base of tail (Figure 23, page 47).	Dolly Varden and Arctic charr, pages 63 and 58.	
6 a.	No parr marks. Maximum length in fresh water about 5 cm (Figure 24, page 47).	Pink salmon, page 64.	
b.	Parr marks present. Maximum length in fresh water up to 12.5 cm or even more.		**7**

KEY TO YOUNG SALMONS AND TROUTS (CONT.)

SECTION	DESCRIPTION	THE FISH IS	PROCEED IN THIS KEY TO SECTION
7 a.	Parr marks elliptical or oval and short, not much longer than vertical diameter of eye, reaching barely if at all below lateral line.		**8**
b.	Parr marks are tall vertical bars almost bisected by lateral line; highest parr mark is much longer than vertical diameter of eye.		**9**
8 a.	Gill rakers: about 11 on upper arch, 18 on lower. A row of definite black spots on back (Figure 25).	Sockeye salmon, page 75.	
b.	Gill rakers: about 10 on upper arch, 14 on lower. Black spots on back, if present, are irregular in position (Figure 26).	Chum salmon, page 69.	
9 a.	First anal ray elongate, producing a concave outer margin on anal fin. Usually some pigment behind white leading edge of anal fin. Adipose fin uniformly dark (Figure 27).	Coho salmon, page 72.	
b.	First anal ray not elongate. Anal fin usually without dark pigment behind leading edge. Adipose fin pigmented only around edge (Figure 28).	Chinook salmon, page 67.	

YOUNG SALMON AND TROUT LESS THAN 13 CM LONG

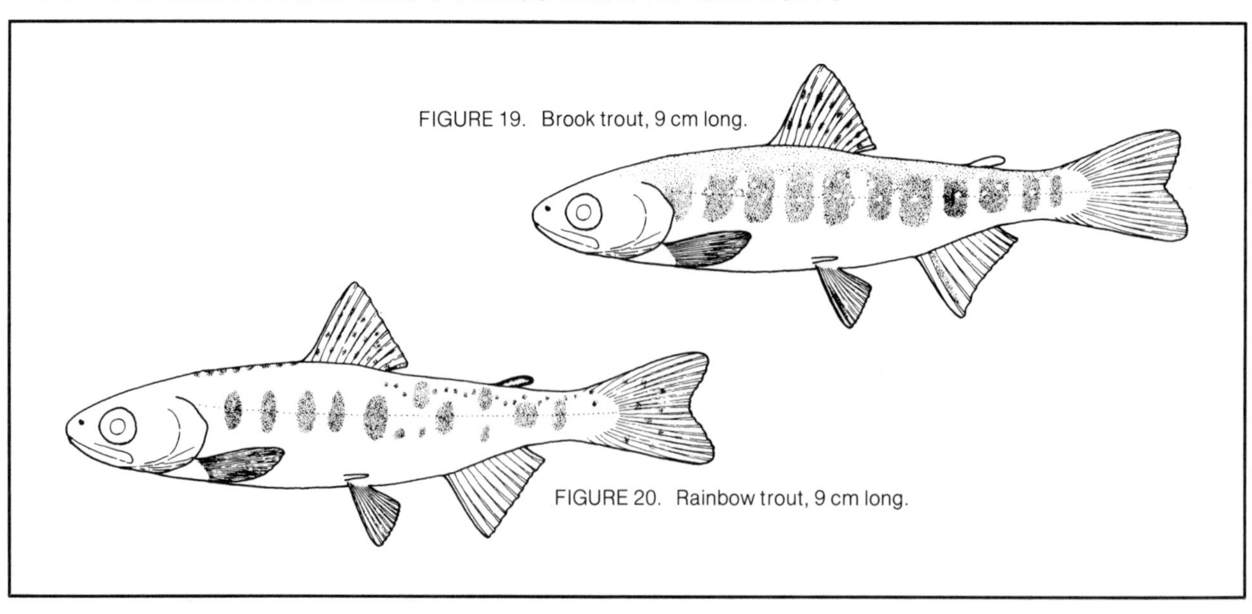

FIGURE 19. Brook trout, 9 cm long.

FIGURE 20. Rainbow trout, 9 cm long.

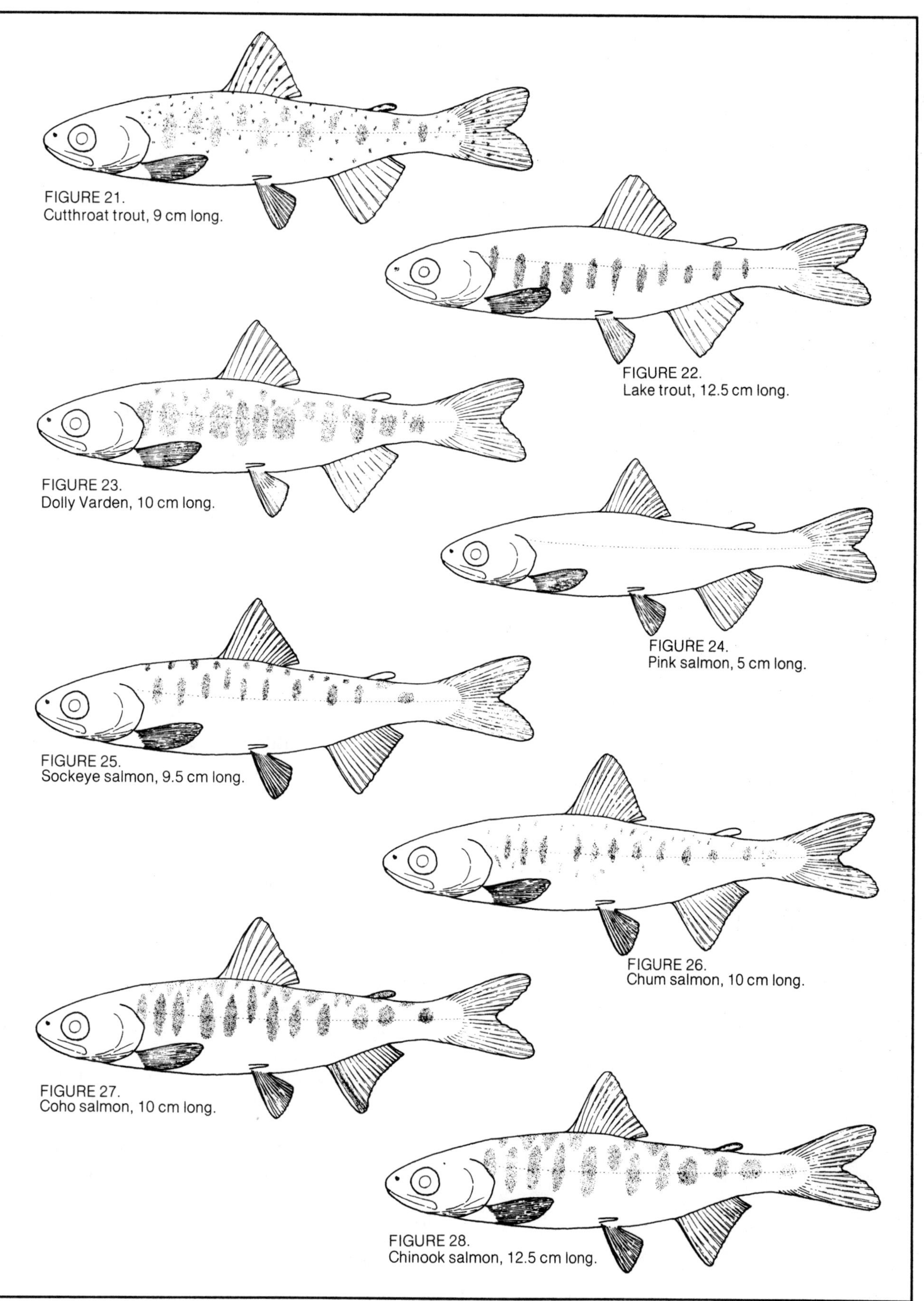

FIGURE 21.
Cutthroat trout, 9 cm long.

FIGURE 22.
Lake trout, 12.5 cm long.

FIGURE 23.
Dolly Varden, 10 cm long.

FIGURE 24.
Pink salmon, 5 cm long.

FIGURE 25.
Sockeye salmon, 9.5 cm long.

FIGURE 26.
Chum salmon, 10 cm long.

FIGURE 27.
Coho salmon, 10 cm long.

FIGURE 28.
Chinook salmon, 12.5 cm long.

CUTTHROAT TROUT

Salmo clarki Richardson

DISTINCTIVE CHARACTERS

The cutthroat trout is distinguished by a red to orange mark on the underside of each lower jaw, numerous small black spots over most of the body, and a patch of small basibranchial teeth behind the tongue between the gills (Figure 29).

DESCRIPTION

Body elongate, terete, little to moderately compressed. Greatest depth of body about 25% of fork length although this may be greater in large specimens. Head length about equal to body depth. Snout rounded to slightly pointed, longer than eye diameter, especially in spawning males. Eye round, its diameter about 22% of head length. Mouth terminal, large; upper jaw reaching well behind eye in adults. Teeth caniniform, well developed, present on both upper and lower jaws and on tongue, head and shaft of vomer, and palatines. A patch of minute teeth usually present between gills behind base of tongue. Gill rakers: 14 to 22. Branchiostegals: 10 to 12. The lateral line curves slightly downward from the head. Pyloric caeca: 27 to 57. Vertebrae: 60 to 64.

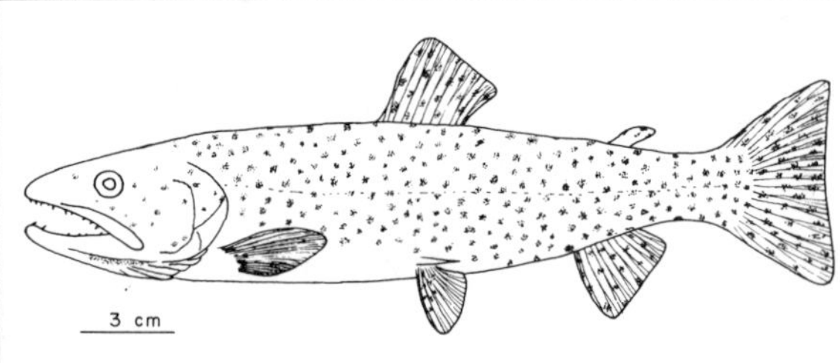

FIGURE 29. Cutthroat trout, *Salmo clarki*. In Alaska, most freshwater populations are heavily spotted, as shown, but in more southerly populations the spots are generally not so numerous. Spots are missing on freshly sea-run cutthroats.

FINS. Dorsal has 8 to 11 rays. Adipose fin present. Anal, 11 to 13 rays; pectorals, 12 to 15; pelvics, 9 to 10, with a distinct axillary process present. Caudal slightly forked.

SCALES. Cycloid, small; 116 to 230 (usually 120 to 180) along lateral line.

COLOR. Dark greenish on back and upper sides, olivaceous on middle sides fading to silvery below. Often a pinkish sheen on gill covers. Numerous small black spots on back and sides extending to or almost to the belly. Spots also present on dorsal, anal and caudal fins. Usually several spots on adipose fin, edge of adipose having an incomplete black border. Fins of a uniform ground color, with no white or colored borders. Underside of lower jaw has a yellow to red (usually red) slash in the skin folds of each side. Fish fresh from the sea are usually more bluish, with silvery sides, inconspicuous spots and the red jaw marks inconspicuous or absent (photograph, page 88).

SIZE. The largest cutthroat known was a fish of the interior subspecies *(S. clarki lewisi)* taken in Pyramid Lake, Nevada, in 1925. This specimen was 99.1 cm long (probably total length) and weighed 18.6 kg. However, the average coastal cutthroat *(S. clarki clarki)* of 5 or 6 years will be only 25 to 38 cm long.

RANGE AND ABUNDANCE

The coastal cutthroat ranges from the northern parts of Prince William Sound, Alaska, south to the Eel River in northern California and is found in most of the streams emptying into the Pacific within those limits. It has been widely introduced into various streams and lakes within its natural range, as well as into a few lakes in eastern North America.

The abundance of the cutthroat trout is irregular. In some streams it may be the most numerous sport fish present, while other streams support only small populations. Its willingness to strike a lure, coupled with its generally small populations and low fecundity, leads to adverse response to heavy fishing pressure. It may well be said that the relatively untouched streams of Alaska constitute the last stronghold of this species.

HABITS

Coastal cutthroat spawn from April to mid-May in southeastern Alaska (Baade, 1957). In some parts of its range, the cutthroat may spawn as early as February (Scott and Crossman, 1973).

Spawning as a rule takes place in small, gravel-bottomed streams, (Sumner, 1953, 1962; Dewitt, 1954; Baade, 1957; Lowry, 1965), but may go on in the mainstream of small drainages (Jones, 1975). At spawning time the male courts the female by nudging her and coming to rest beside her and quivering. Having chosen the site for her redd or nest, the female begins to dig out the egg pit in typical salmonid fashion; heading upstream she turns on her side, presses her tail against the bottom and gives five to eight vigorous upward flaps of the tail. This sucks silt, debris and pebbles out of the bottom whence they are carried downstream by the current. Digging in this fashion continues every few minutes, with occasional interruptions, until the pit is deep and clean enough for egg-laying. Such a pit is usually 10 to 15 cm deep and not quite as long as the fish. Two to four hours seems to be the usual time required to dig the redd.

Meanwhile, the male takes no part in the digging. He is very attentive to the female, however, courting her and driving away intruders.

When the pit begins to take shape, the female tests it frequently by sinking down into it and feeling around the stones with the tip of her anal fin. Finally, she settles into the pit, with her anal fin pushed into the gravel and her head and tail arched upward. The male joins her at once, both fish open their mouths and become rigid, they quiver slightly, and eggs and milt are extruded.

The fish now leave the pit and the female moves to its upstream end and begins to dig again. The gravel she disturbs is carried down into the pit, covering the eggs. She continues digging until the entire pit is filled and the eggs well covered, a process requiring 40 minutes to an hour (Smith, 1941). The new pit, upstream of the first, may also be used for spawning, or the female may seek out a new spot and repeat the entire process. Both male and female cutthroat may spawn with one or more members of the opposite sex. Spawning goes on both in daylight and at night.

Fecundity varies with the size of the individual and with locality. Egg numbers up to 6,500 have been reported from Wyoming, but Alaskan fish average something less than 1,000 eggs per female (Baade, 1957; Jones, 1975).

The eggs, .43 to .51 cm in diameter, hatch in six to seven weeks and the fry remain in the redd for one or two weeks longer before they become free-swimming. The young are only about 1.5 cm long at hatching, but they grow quite rapidly. Growth rate varies tremendously with stock and locality but, overall, the young average 5 to 7.5 cm long by the end of September. By the end of the first year, most of the fish are around 10 to 15 cm long. At age 3, Alaskan fish average about 17.9 cm; 4, 21 cm; 5, 25.4 cm; 6, 30.9 cm; 7, 33.2 cm; and 8, 38 cm (Jones, 1973, 1975). Farther south, growth rates are faster. About 90% of a year's growth occurs between April and September (Cooper, 1970). Most young cutthroat do not go to sea until they are 2 or 3 years old. Most populations of coastal cutthroat are dominated by fish 4 to 7 years old. Two thousand adult fish in an Alaskan stream constitute a large population. Sexual maturity is reached in the second or third year, with males generally maturing earlier than females. The young fish usually stay in the stream for a year or two before going to sea, but some populations may never go to sea at all. In sea-going populations, the freshwater life may be as long as 8 years for rare individuals (Sumner, 1962; Jones, 1975).

The outmigration to the sea takes place in late spring and summer (mid-April to July), the peak movement being in late May and early June (Baade, 1957; Jones, 1973, 1975), but in the southern part of the range the migration may be several months earlier (Lowry, 1965). Most movement goes on at night on moderate stream flows. Extreme high or low water inhibits migration. In general, the larger fish migrate to sea earlier in the season than the smaller ones. Cutthroats stay in the sea for 12 to 150 days in southeastern Alaska, those migrating earliest staying out the longest. It is possible that some individuals may stay at sea for a year or more, as seems to be true of some southern populations. However, most of the Alaskan cutthroats seem to go to sea annually and to stay there a relatively short time (Baade, 1957; Armstrong, 1971; Jones, 1973, 1975). Most of the fish seem to stay fairly close to the home stream, but tagged fish have been recovered as far as 70 km from the mouth of the home stream (Jones, 1973).

Mortality of smolts—fish going to sea for the first time—is extremely high: 98% or more between the beginning of the outmigration and return (Sumner, 1953, 1962).

The return migration from the sea to fresh water takes place in the summer and fall, with peak movement in September (Armstrong, 1971; Jones, 1973, 1975). In Alaskan waters, this inmigration takes place mostly at night on moderate stream flows, but in Oregon streams the cutthroat appear to move most actively during periods of high water and later in the year (Sumner, 1953; Lowry, 1965). It is apparent that this migration pattern is not firmly associated with spawning, for in Petersburg Creek, Alaska, over half the incoming fish are immature (Jones, 1973).

Post-spawning mortality in northern Oregon averaged 68.4% over a four-year period and ranged from a low of 54% to a high of 89%. Of the upstream migrants, 68.4% had not spawned previously, 26.6% had spawned once, 4.5% twice and only .5% had spawned three times (Sumner, 1962). In Blue Lake, in northern California, only 5% to 10% survived to a second spawning, and these fish produced significantly fewer eggs than did first-time spawners (Calhoun, 1944). Post-spawning mortality has not been studied in Alaskan cutthroats.

The food of the cutthroat varies with locality and time of year. Fish from Lake Eva on Baranof Island, Alaska, had fed chiefly on insects and young salmon during the late summer; on sticklebacks, insects and gastropods in winter; mainly on insects during the outmigration; and on amphipods and young salmon while at sea. Near Ketchikan, cutthroats fed on salmon eggs and fry, insect larvae and sculpin eggs in the spring; on insects, sculpins, coho fry and leeches in summer; and chiefly on salmon eggs in the fall. Oregon fish were reported to eat aquatic and terrestrial arthropods, frogs, earthworms, crayfish, small fishes and fish eggs (Baade, 1957; Lowry, 1966; Armstrong, 1971).

Cutthroat trout prefer relatively small streams

(draining an area of less than 13 square km), with gravel bottoms and gentle gradients (Hartman and Gill, 1968). However, they may also be present in the sea, estuaries, lakes and alpine lakes and streams to over 4,375 m in altitude. The residents of these high-altitude habitats, however, belong to the inland subspecies.

IMPORTANCE TO MAN

The cutthroat trout is an important sport fish wherever it occurs. Although it does not jump as much as the rainbow trout and is generally considered inferior to the rainbow, it is nevertheless a hard fighter. The cutthroat will take a wide variety of lures—spinners, spoons, wet and dry flies and small plugs. Cutthroats are raised commercially in the southwestern United States, mainly for introduction into private ponds. The flesh is orange-red and of excellent flavor. Because of the small populations and rather low growth rates and fecundity, cutthroat trout often do not stand up well to fishing.

RAINBOW TROUT AND STEELHEAD

Salmo gairdneri Richardson

DISTINCTIVE CHARACTERS

Black spots on the sides, back and dorsal and anal fins, a reddish band along the side, and a lack of basibranchial teeth serve to distinguish the rainbow trout. Steelhead, which are sea-run rainbows, do not have the red band on the side until they have been back in fresh water for some time (Figure 30).

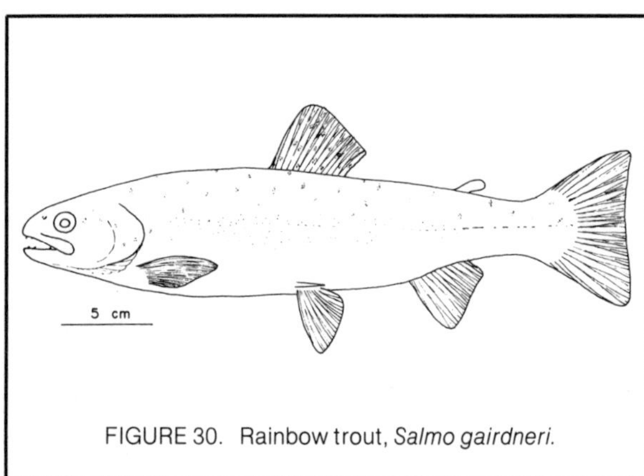

FIGURE 30. Rainbow trout, *Salmo gairdneri.*

DESCRIPTION

Body elongate, moderately compressed, its greatest depth varying, according to locality and size of fish, from about 19% to 28% of fork length. Head about 20% of fork length but larger in breeding males, especially steelhead. Snout round, a little longer than eye diameter, but much extended in breeding males. Eye round, about 20% of head length in females and nonbreeding males. Mouth large, terminal, slightly oblique, maxilla reaching to or well behind posterior edge of eye. Teeth caniniform and well developed on both jaws, on head and shaft of vomer, on palatines and on tongue. No teeth on basibranchials at base of tongue. Gill rakers: 15 to 22. Branchiostegals: 8 to 13. Lateral line has 100 to 150 pored scales; slightly curved behind the head but is straight on most of sides and tail. Pyloric caeca: 27 to 80. Vertebrae: 60 to 66.

FINS. Dorsal has 10 to 12 rays. Adipose fin present. Anal has 8 to 12 rays; pectorals, 11 to 17; pelvics, 9 or 10, with axillary process. Caudal broad, slightly indented in small fish but quite square-edged in large specimens.

SCALES. Small, cycloid, the size and number variable in different populations.

COLOR. Extremely variable according to locality, sexual condition and size of fish. In general, top of head, back and upper sides are dark blue to greenish or brownish. Lower sides silvery, somewhat white or pale yellow. Belly silvery white to grayish. Cheek and gill cover rather pink; sides have a band of bluish pink to rose red. This band is reddest in spawning or recently spawned-out fish, especially males, but is not present at all in fish fresh from the sea (steelhead). Back and upper sides of fish have many small black spots that may extend well down on lower sides. Dorsal and caudal fins profusely spotted with black. Adipose fin with black spots and a black border. Other fins have few spots or are dusky or unmarked. In some populations inhabiting Bristol Bay drainages, red to orange marks are present on lower jaw, as on cutthroat trout. Stream-dwelling fish may retain parr marks as adults (photograph, page 89; Plate 2, page 113).

SIZE. Although in most areas a rainbow of 1 or 2 kg is considered a very good fish, rainbow trout are known to reach much greater size. The largest taken by angling was a steelhead of 19.1 kg from Bell Island, near Ketchikan, in June, 1970. Another of the same weight was recorded from Corbett, Oregon (*Field and Stream Magazine*, March, 1960) and one of 23.6 kg was recorded from Jewel Lake, British Columbia (McPhail and Lindsey, 1970).

RANGE AND ABUNDANCE

The original native range of the rainbow is from northern Mexico near Ciudad Durango north to the Kuskokwim River in Alaska and westward to Port Moller on the Alaska Peninsula. The entire range is west of the continental divide except for the headwaters of the Peace River in British Columbia and the Athabasca River in Alberta.

Rainbow and steelhead have been introduced into every continent and most major islands of the world. Rainbow trout have been planted virtually all over North America, with the result that the species is now present in every state of the U.S. except Louisiana,

Mississippi and Florida, and in every province and territory of Canada except the Northwest Territories (MacCrimmon, 1971).

The rainbow is not native to interior Alaska but has been planted in a number of lakes, ponds and gravel pits in the Fairbanks area and near Big Delta, as well as in Summit Lake. Lost Lake, about 48 km from Big Delta, was rehabilitated in 1951 and received its first plant of young rainbows in 1952, making Alaska the last state to practice planting rainbow trout. These first plants were made with fish raised from eggs imported from Idaho and Montana as this was, surprisingly, less expensive than taking eggs of native fish (Marvich, 1952; Marvich and McRea, 1953; Marvich et al., 1954).

HABITS

The rainbow trout is basically a spring spawner, with the majority breeding between mid-April and late June. (Lindsey et al., 1959; Hartman, 1959; Hartman et al., 1962). However, various populations may spawn as early as November or December (Dodge and MacCrimmon, 1970) or as late as August, and fish have been bred in Idaho hatcheries to spawn in the fall. When these latter were transplanted to warm temperatures (up to 17 °C) in California, they were able to spawn twice a year, both in summer and winter (Hume, 1955).

Spawning takes place in streams, usually on a riffle above a pool. Most spawning occurs at temperatures between 10° and 13 °C but early spawners in the north may encounter temperatures as low as 5.5 °C, while southern fish have been known to spawn when the water temperature was 17 °C. Breeding behavior is typically salmonid. The male courts the female by coming in contact with her, sliding over her back, rubbing her with his snout, vibrating beside her and pressing against her. When the female has selected a site for the redd, she turns on her side and gives several strong, upward flips of her tail. This displaces sand and gravel which is washed downstream by the current. Repeated digging soon results in a pit somewhat longer and deeper than the female's body. Meanwhile, the attendant male has been courting her and driving off rival males, although a subordinate male may also be in attendance. These processes may go on both in daylight and at night.

When the redd is finished, the female drops down into the pit. The dominant male joins her, the bodies of the two parallel and close together. Both fish open their mouths, quiver and extrude eggs and milt for a few seconds. The subordinate male often participates in the spawning also. The eggs fall into the interstices in the gravel, where they are fertilized. From 100 to as many as 1,000 eggs may be dropped in a single nest. Fecundity per female ranges from as low as 200 (Needham, 1938) to a high as 12,749 eggs, the latter from specially selected stock (Buss, 1960). Average fecundity is on the order of 3,250 eggs per female, with young, small fish producing fewer eggs than large, older fish. The number of eggs produced depends in part on adequate nutrition. Insufficient food, which can be the result of large populations and excessive competition for food within the species, leads to follicular degeneration of the eggs, although the eggs that survive are of normal size (Scott, 1962). As soon as the spawning act is completed, the female moves to the upstream edge of the redd and digs again. The displaced gravel is carried downstream and covers the eggs. The whole process is repeated, either with the same or other males, until the female's egg supply is exhausted.

The eggs average between .3 and .5 cm in diameter and are pink to orange in color. Time of development, which varies with temperature, ranges from as little as 18 days at 15.5 °C to 101 days at 3.2 °C (Embody, 1934; Wales, 1941; Knight, 1963). Under most natural conditions, development to hatching takes 4 to 7 weeks. The sac fry require 3 days to more than 2 weeks to absorb the yolk sac completely, but normally begin to feed about 15 or 16 days after hatching, even though some yolk may still be unabsorbed. The young emerge from the redds in mid-June to mid-August if spawning was in April or May. Oddly enough, the eggs and early alevins are much more resistant to certain toxic substances, such as ammonia, than are fry or adults (Rice and Stokes, 1975).

Survival of eggs is directly related to the velocity of ground-water passage through the redd and to the amount of dissolved oxygen in this ground water (Coble, 1961). It has been found that wood fibers in the water do not affect the survival of eggs but have pronounced adverse effects on growth and survival of young fish (Kramer and Smith, 1965).

Subsequent life history varies greatly according to environmental conditions and the genetic makeup of the population. Stream-dwelling fish generally stay in the natal stream. By contrast, the young of lake-resident fish usually move upstream or downstream to the lake, taking a few days to several months for their migration. However, rainbows introduced into the Finger Lakes of New York State have been found to stay as long as four years (usually one or two) in the streams before moving down to the lake (Hartman, 1959). Movement of the young appears to be associated with water temperature. In cold water—water less than 13 °C—the fry rarely contact the bottom during the hours of darkness and are carried downstream. By contrast, in waters over

14 °C, the young fish make frequent contact with the bottom and tend to stay more or less in one area. Upstream movements are associated with rapid increases in water temperature (Northcote, 1962).

Growth rates and growth patterns vary tremendously. Genetic composition, water temperature, type and availability of food, type of habitat, and geographical area all come into play. Sexual maturity is usually reached at two years or more (in rare cases in the first year by some males) or as late as six years in some females. In general age at maturity is between 3 and 5 years, with males usually maturing a year earlier than females. The size at sexual maturity is equally variable. Mature individuals from small streams may be only about 15 cm long, while steelhead or fish in large lakes may be as long as 40 cm. Maximum age seems to be about 9 years (Sumner, 1948).

Many rainbow trout spawn more than once. If environmental conditions are good, rainbows may spawn annually for up to five successive years (Hartman, 1959). The percentage of repeat spawners in a population varies widely, from 5% to 57%. In general, large, older females are less likely to survive spawning than small, younger ones, and males are less likely to survive than females (Hartman, 1959; Hartman et al., 1962; Withler, 1965). Survival to subsequent spawning seems to be inversely related to the number of spawners entering a stream (Hartman, 1959).

Although the rainbow is generally considered a cold-water fish, preferring a temperature of about 13 °C (Garside and Tait, 1958), it can tolerate fairly warm water and indeed seems to grow best at about 21 °C. The upper lethal temperature is 24 °C. Temperature and population density appear to be major factors affecting growth and food conversion (Black, 1953; Murai and Andrews, 1972).

The migratory patterns of rainbows are as varied as the populations and the areas in which they are found. In general, stream-dwelling rainbows tend to be nonmigratory and to spend their entire lives in relatively short sections of a stream. Lake-dwelling fish migrate into the spawning streams in the spring. Those going to outlet streams generally migrate early in the spring; those going to inlet streams go a month or more later. Both groups move back into the lake three to six weeks after leaving it. This return seems to be triggered by rising temperature. In Loon Lake, British Columbia, the return to the lake occurred when the water temperature reached 10 °C (Hartman, et al., 1962).

Steelhead undertake the greatest movements of any form of rainbow trout. After one to four years (usually about two) of stream life, the steelhead run downstream in the spring and summer and enter the sea. Here they may stay for only a few months or for as much as four years before returning to the natal stream to spawn.

Once in the sea, steelhead can be found throughout most of the North Pacific above 42 °N. They are most abundant in the Gulf of Alaska and the eastern part of the North Pacific, least abundant in the western North Pacific and the western Aleutian area. This distribution conforms closely to the 5 °C isotherm in the north and the 15 °C isotherm in the south. Shifts in abundance of steelhead in the ocean are correlated with temperature changes. The fish move north and west in late winter and early spring and are most extensively distributed in the summer. In late summer, fall and early winter there is a reverse movement to the south and east (Sutherland, 1973).

Most of the freshwater movement of rainbow trout, both upstream and downstream, goes on at night (French and Wahle, 1959). At the time of the first downstream migration, the young fish lose their parr marks and become silvery, reaching the smolt stage. This change in color is the result of increased activity of the thyroid gland (Robertson, 1949). The younger fish adapt readily to sea water, but the longer the period of previous freshwater life, the longer the period of adaptation required (Houston, 1961). The return migration may take place in spring or summer—from May through August—or in the winter, from December through March. Fish in the latter group are nearly ripe and spawn that same spring. By contrast, the spring-summer fish stay almost a year in fresh water and spawn the following spring. At spawning, these fish are typical rainbows, having the usual red band along the side and a well-developed kype appearing on the males. By contrast, winter fish show little, if any, sexual dimorphism (Smith, 1960). Spring-run fish in California have been reported to spawn in the late autumn (Briggs, 1953; Shapovalov and Taft, 1954). This division into spring-summer runs and winter runs appears to be genetically controlled. It is probable that the evolution of the two types has come about in response to stream barriers which are passable only during periods of high water (Withler, 1965).

Rainbows resident in fresh water generally do not migrate very far. Stream-dwelling fish in particular may spend their entire lives within a few kilometers of the places where they were hatched. Lake residents generally do not move about much in the lake, but may move up to 60 to 70 km in streams, especially up inlet streams. Steelhead, however, move extensively, undertaking upstream migrations of hundreds of kilometers in large rivers such as the Columbia. Steelhead introduced into Great Lakes drainages of

Michigan have been known to travel as much as 1,320 km in 8 months through the lakes. Regardless of strain, rainbows exhibit a high degree of homing instinct. Better than 90% of surviving migrants return to the home stream (Taft and Shapovalov, 1938; Lindsey, et al., 1959).

Food habits of rainbow and steelhead seem to depend as much on size and availability of food as on any preference on the part of the fish. In general, fish in fresh water feed on various invertebrates, especially the larvae and adults of dipteran insects, and crustaceans such as *Gammarus,* but plankton, various insects, snails and leeches also may be eaten. Other fishes may be eaten by adult rainbows, and the availability of such fishes may even be necessary for the rainbows to reach maximum size. Steelhead in the sea are known to feed heavily on squid and fishes (Reimers et al., 1955; Le Brasseur, 1965; Scott and Crossman, 1973).

Because of its popularity as a sport fish, the rainbow has been widely introduced, and many populations are maintained at levels suitable to anglers only by continued stocking. Planted hatchery fish, especially in fast-moving streams, have a regrettable tendency to die off in a relatively short time, yielding but poor returns to the angler (Randle and Cramer, 1941; Burns and Calhoun, 1966). At least some, and perhaps a major, part of the die-off results from the inability of the fish to cope with the continued vigorous swimming necessary in fast water. As a result, glycogen reserves are used up faster than they can be replaced, blood lactate reaches very high levels (four or more times above the level found in surviving fish), the blood becomes slightly acidic and death ensues (Black et al., 1962; Hochachka and Sinclair, 1962; Jonas et al., 1962; Miller and Miller, 1962).

Rainbow trout have been experimentally crossed with other salmonids, but survival of the fry is generally low (Mighell and Dangel, 1975).

IMPORTANCE TO MAN

It is safe to say that *Salmo gairdneri* is one of the most sought-after sport fishes in North America, and probably the most important of all sport fishes west of the Rockies. It takes both flies and lures, fights hard and leaps frequently. The flesh is of high quality, both in texture and flavor. Rainbows are raised for eating purposes in a number of hatcheries in the U.S. as well as in Europe and Japan, and a few thousand cases of steelhead are canned annually from fish taken by commercial salmon fishermen. The economic value of the sport fishery is not to be sneezed at. Anglers spend vast sums for tackle, bait, lodging and transportation in order to fish for rainbows and steelhead. In the Copper River (tributary to Lake Iliamna) sport fishermen in 1972 spent $125,552.00 to catch 3,621 rainbows—an average cost of $35.50 per trout (Siedelman et al., 1973).

BROOK TROUT

Salvelinus fontinalis (Mitchill)

DISTINCTIVE CHARACTERS

The brook trout is distinguished by the combination of dark green marbling on its back and dorsal fin and by the red spots with blue halos on its sides (Figure 31).

DESCRIPTION

Body elongate, only slightly compressed, its greatest depth 20% to 28% of total length, generally deeper in large, sexually mature individuals. Head longer than in most other members of the genus: 22% to 28% of total length. Snout more or less rounded, longer than eye diameter, 25% to 38% of head length. Eye round, its diameter 15% to 22% of head length. Mouth large, terminal, with maxilla reaching well behind eye in adults, only to posterior edge of eye in young. Breeding males often develop a kype. Teeth caniniform and well developed on upper and lower jaws, on head but not on shaft of vomer and on palatines and tongue. Gill rakers: 14 to 22. Branchiostegals: 9 to 13, usually with 1 less on right side than on left. Lateral line present with 110 to 130 pored scales. Pyloric caeca: 23 to 55. Vertebrae: 58 to 62.

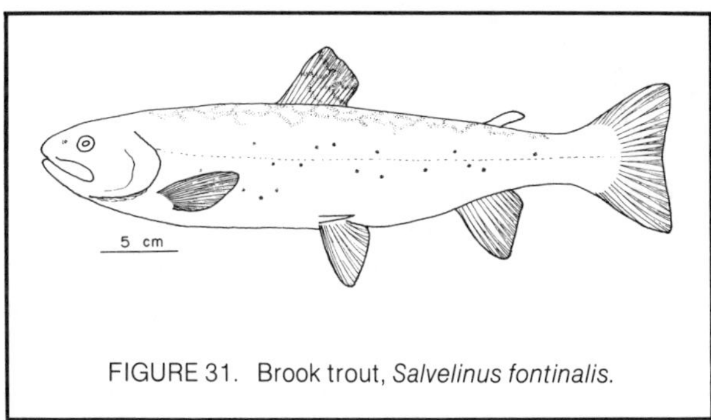

FIGURE 31. Brook trout, *Salvelinus fontinalis.*

FINS. Dorsal has 10 to 14 rays. Adipose fin present. Anal has 9 to 13 rays; pectorals, 11 to 14; pelvics, 8 to 10, with an axillary process present. Caudal nearly straight (hence the old popular name squaretail) or with a shallow indentation.

SCALES. Cycloid, minute, in about 230 rows in a midlateral series.

COLOR. Varies, but generally more or less as follows: back rather green to brownish, marked with paler vermiculations or marbling that extend onto the dorsal fin and sometimes the caudal. Sides lighter than back, marked with numerous pale spots and some red spots, each of the latter surrounded by a blue halo. Anal, pelvic and pectoral fins with a white leading edge followed by a dark stripe, the rest of fins reddish. In spawning fish the lower sides and fins become red. Sea-run fish are dark green above with silvery sides, white bellies and very pale pink spots (photograph, page 89).

SIZE. The largest known was a fish of 6.6 kg and 70 cm long, taken in the Nipigon River, Ontario, in 1916. In most areas fish as large as 1 to 1.5 kg are considered large. Occasionally fish over 7 kg have been reported, but these have invariably turned out to be arctic charr.

RANGE AND ABUNDANCE

The native range of the brook trout is from Ungava Bay in northern Quebec to New Jersey and southern Pennsylvania in the lowlands and still farther south to northern Georgia in the Appalachian highlands; from the easternmost tip of Newfoundland west to eastern Minnesota and Manitoba, and north along the west coast of Hudson Bay to the Churchill River, Manitoba. The brook trout has been widely introduced into the western states and provinces as well as other parts of the world such as South America, New Zealand, Asia and Europe. In Alaska, brook trout were introduced into southeastern in 1920 (MacCrimmon and Campbell, 1969), with plantings continuing into the 1950s (Anonymous, 1953a). Unfortunately, it hybridizes readily with the native Dolly Varden and the resultant hybrid is inferior to both the parent species (Baade, 1962). The brook trout also has a distressing tendency to overpopulate in some situations, resulting in large numbers of stunted fish which are of no interest to anglers.

HABITS

The brook trout spawns from late August in the far north to as late as December in the southern part of the range, at water temperatures between about 3° and 9°C. Maturation of sex products appears to be stimulated by lessening day length and falling temperatures (Henderson, 1963). Artificial manipulation of day length, beginning in mid-January, in hatchery situations has resulted in fish becoming ripe as early as the first week of August. Fish subjected to this treatment produced smaller than normal, but more numerous, eggs. The treatment was highly successful with two-year-old fish, less so with older ones (Corson, 1955).

Spawning takes place over a gravelly bottom, most often in fairly shallow streams but sometimes also in lakes at locations where there is an upwelling of ground water. The presence of springs seems to be essential and may be the most important factor in the choice of a spawning site (White, 1930; Hazzard, 1932; Webster, 1962). Gravel size on spawning beds has been noted to vary from coarse sand to stones 7.5 to 10 cm in diameter, and apparently is unimportant as long as ground water seepage is present.

Courtship begins with a male attempting to guide or drive a female towards suitable spawning gravel. A ripe, receptive female makes close visual inspection of the gravel and, having chosen a spot, begins to dig the redd. She turns on her side and lifts gravel and silt from the bottom with powerful thrusts of her tail. The smaller and lighter particles are swept away by the stream current, but the larger ones settle at once to the bottom, building a mound just downstream from the pit. Repeated digging forms a depression from 10 to 15 cm deep. The female tests the pit from time to time with her anal, caudal and pelvic fins. Meanwhile the male continues his courtship activities, darting alongside the female and quivering, swimming over and under her and rubbing her with his fins. He spends most of his time, however, in driving off other males, in which the female assists.

When the pit suits the female, she drops her anal fin deeply into it and arches her tail. The male comes beside her, both fish open their mouths and quiver, and eggs and milt are deposited in the pit. This process takes about one second, and up to 800 eggs may be dropped at one time (Greeley, 1932). Due to the depth of the pit, quiet water and gentle eddies are present at the bottom, and these hold the eggs and the cloud of sperm in place or spread the sperm upstream and sideways (Smith, 1941; Needham, 1961).

After spawning, the female at once begins to cover her eggs, but the method is very different from that used by most salmonids. She goes to the mound of gravel which has formed at the downstream edge of the redd and begins a sinuous movement, using the tips of her anal and caudal fins to sweep small pebbles upstream into the nest. The eggs are quickly covered, after which the female circles the pit, continuing to sweep in this manner for about half an hour. Only after the eggs are well covered does she go to the upstream end of the nest and begin again the characteristic salmonid digging of a new redd (Smith, 1941; Needham, 1961).

In Alaska the brook trout may hybridize with the native Dolly Varden. The brook trout has been experimentally crossed with kokanee and with brown, rainbow and lake trout. Survival of offspring is virtually nil in the first three crosses. Brook trout crossed with lake trout produce viable offspring called splake, but survival and fertility are lower than for either parent species (Buss and Wright, 1956, 1958; Crossman and Buss, 1966). It is not known whether the brook trout-Dolly Varden hybrids are fertile.

The eggs of the brook trout are large, .35 to .5 cm in diameter after spawning. The number of eggs produced is directly related to the size of the female. The average number varies from 100 eggs for a fish of about 15 cm to 5,000 for a fish of 56.5 cm (Vladykov, 1956; Wydoski and Cooper, 1966).

Hatching time varies with temperature, but usually occurs in late winter. At 5°C 100 days are required, but normal, though slower, development occurs at temperatures as low as 1.7°C. The upper limit appears to be about 11.7°C (Embody, 1934; Bigelow, 1963).

The young fish remain in the gravel until the yolk sac has been absorbed. They emerge in April or May when they are about 3.8 cm long. They stay on the redd for a few days and may burrow into the gravel if frightened, but soon disperse. Scales begin to form at a length of about 5 cm. Survival to this stage is good, ranging from 3.6% to 42.4% in one series of observations (Smith, 1947).

Growth is rapid during the first summer. By the end of September the young may be as much as 10 cm long and weigh about 10 g. Subsequent growth rates vary with locality, temperature, food supply and the genetic compositon of the population. The most rapid growth takes place in May, slows through the summer and goes on at a minimal level from September until spring (Cooper, 1951).

Sexual maturity may be reached as early as at 1 year of age but is usually achieved in the second year. All fish are mature at 3 years (Wydoski and Cooper, 1966).

The brook trout is a relatively short-lived fish. Few wild individuals survive past age 5, although there are reports of introduced fish reaching 15 years of age in California (McAfee, 1966).

Most brook trout are more or less stable residents in streams or lakes, where they prefer temperatures below 20°C. On the east coast of North America general upstream movements have been observed in early spring, summer and late fall; downstream movements, in late spring and fall (White, 1941, 1942; Smith and Saunders, 1958, 1967). Some fish, popularly known as salters, run to sea in the spring as stream temperatures rise. They stay at sea for up to three months, feeding and growing but never venturing more than a few kilometers from the river mouths. Their return to fresh water apparently is related to freshets in the main river and there is a definite homing tendency to the tributaries of origin within the drainage (White, 1941, 1942; Bigelow, 1963).

Brook trout eat an amazing variety of food organisms ranging from copepods, eaten by the young, to small mammals (mice, voles and shrews) consumed by large adults. The most important food items are insects of all sorts, both aquatic and terrestrial. Other foods include Cladocera, spiders, worms, leeches, crustaceans, mollusks, fishes, amphibians and mammals (Clemens, 1928; Ricker, 1930, 1932; Wadman, 1962). The most intensive feeding and best growth occur at temperatures of about 13°C (Baldwin, 1957).

IMPORTANCE TO MAN

The brook trout is one of the most important sport fishes in North America. It is angled for with all types of sport gear by people from all walks of life. In addition, it is amenable to pond culture and large numbers are raised in private ponds for commercial sale, either for food or for stocking.

Lake Trout

Salvelinus namaycush (Walbaum)

DISTINCTIVE CHARACTERS

The lake trout is easily distinguished by its color, white or yellowish spots on a dark green to grayish background, its deeply forked tail and its numerous (93 to 208) pyloric caeca (Figure 32).

DESCRIPTION

Body elongate, more or less terete. Depth usually 18% to 26% of total length but much deeper in some populations, especially those that feed largely on mollusks. Head fairly long, 21% to 28% of total length. Snout long, 26% to 36% of head length. Eye rather small in adults, 12% to 20% of head length.

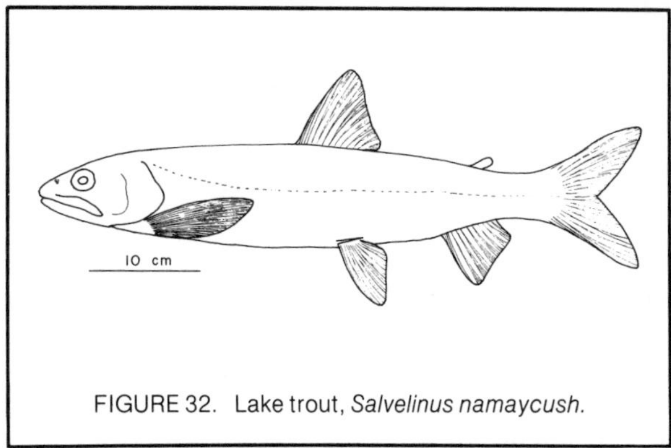

FIGURE 32. Lake trout, *Salvelinus namaycush*.

Mouth terminal, large, with maxilla reaching well behind eye in adults, snout protruding beyond lower jaw when mouth is closed. Teeth caniniform, present on both jaws, on head but not shaft of vomer, on palatines, tongue and basibranchials. Gill rakers: 16 to 26. Populations of lake trout that feed mostly on plankton tend to have more gill rakers than those that are mainly piscivorous. Branchiostegals: 10 to 14, usually more on left than on right. Lateral line, which is slightly curved anteriorly, has

116 to 138 pores. Pyloric caeca numerous: 93 to 208, mostly 120 to 180, the number increasing with size. Vertebrae: 61 to 69.

FINS. Dorsal has 8 to 10 rays. Adipose fin present. Anal has 8 to 10 rays; pectorals, 12 to 17; pelvics, 8 to 11, with small axillary process present. Caudal deeply forked.

SCALES. Small, cycloid. Breeding tubercles present on at least some scales during the spawning season but disappearing rapidly thereafter (Vladykov, 1954).

COLOR. Back and sides usually dark green liberally sprinkled with whitish to yellowish (never pink or red) spots. Overall color varies from light green to gray, brown, dark green or nearly black. Belly white. Pale spots present on dorsal, adipose and caudal fins and usually on base of anal. Sometimes orange-red on paired fins and on anal, especially in northern populations. Anterior edge of paired and anal fins sometimes with a white border (photograph, page 89). At spawning time the males develop a dark lateral stripe and become paler on the back (Royce, 1951).

SIZE. The lake trout is the largest member of the genus *Salvelinus*. Mitchill (1818) reported a specimen of 54.5 kg from the Michilimackinac area of Lake Michigan. Although the validity of this record is doubted by some, it is within the bounds of possibility, for the next largest on record is a fish of 46.4 kg, only 8.1 kg less, from Lake Athabasca, Alberta (Canadian Dept. Fisheries, 1961). The angling record is a fish of 29.5 kg from Great Bear Lake, Northwest Territories, but a report of a 39.5 kg fish from Lake Bennett appears to be well authenticated (Anonymous, 1953b).

RANGE AND ABUNDANCE

The lake trout is widely distributed in northern North America and has been introduced into other parts of the world including Scandinavia, South America and New Zealand. Its natural range in North America corresponds closely with the limits of Pleistocene glaciation (Lindsey, 1964). It is generally absent from lowland regions such as the Yukon-Kuskokwim valleys in Alaska and the Hudson Bay-James Bay lowlands of Canada. The range extends from the Alaska Peninsula east to Nova Scotia, south to northern New York and Pennsylvania and the Great Lakes, and north to the islands of the Canadian arctic. The species is intolerant of salt water (Boulva and Simard, 1968) and has made its way across only narrow stretches of the marine environment. However, in the Canadian arctic it has been found on Southampton Island (Manning, 1942), and Baffin, King William, Victoria and Banks islands (Scott and Crossman, 1973).

In the more isolated parts of its range the lake trout is abundant, but in many other areas, especially the Great Lakes, it has become rather scarce except where maintained by artificial propagation and careful management.

HABITS

Like most charrs the lake trout spawns in the fall, the exact time varying with latitude and temperature. Over the entire range spawning activity occurs as early as late August and early September in the far north, for example in Great Bear Lake and certain lakes in northern Alaska (Miller and Kennedy, 1948a; McCart et al., 1972), to as late as December in the southern parts of the range (Royce, 1951).

Spawning takes place over clean, rocky bottom in depths from a meter or even less (Merriman, 1935; Martin, 1957, Rawson, 1961) to as deep as 36 m (Eschmeyer, 1955). Virtually all lake trout spawn in lakes, but a few populations are known to spawn in streams tributary to Lake Superior (Loftus, 1958). Conversations with residents of Kobuk, Alaska, suggest that a few lake trout may spawn in the Kobuk River. However, this has not been verified.

During the spawning season the males reach the spawning beds first and spend some time cleaning the rocks. This they do by twisting their tails and bodies over the bottom and rubbing the rocks with their snouts. This activity by a group of males cleans an area of several dozen square meters. When the females arrive, a few days after the males, they are courted by the males. A male butts the side of the female, follows her, and may swim beneath her, brushing her vent with his dorsal fin. At this time the males become pale on their backs and develop a dark stripe on each side and dark areas around the head (Royce, 1951; Martin, 1957).

Spawning takes place mostly at night, with peak activity between dusk and 9 or 10 p.m. (Royce, 1951; Martin, 1957). During the day the fish are more or less dispersed away from the spawning beds but they return in considerable numbers in the late afternoon.

During and following courtship, the males attempt to spawn with the females. One or two males approach a female, press against her sides with vents close to hers and then quiver. Both sexes have their mouths open and the male's dorsal fin is erect. On occasion as many as seven males and three females may engage in a mass spawning act (Royce, 1951). The spawning act lasts only a few seconds and is probably repeated many times before a female has voided all her eggs. Fecundity varies from a few hundred to more than 17,000 eggs per female, the number of eggs increasing with the size of the fish (Eschmeyer, 1955).

Spawning is an annual affair in southern areas, but evidence indicates that it occurs only every other year in Great Slave Lake, Northwest Territories, and only every third year in Great Bear and some other lakes of the high arctic (Miller and Kennedy, 1948a; Kennedy, 1954; Furniss, 1974).

The large eggs, .5 to .6 cm in diameter, fall to the bottom and lodge in crevices and crannies among the rocks. Incubation requires 15 to 21 weeks or more, depending on temperature, and hatching normally occurs between mid-February and late March (Eschmeyer, 1955; Martin, 1957). The newly hatched young are about 1.6 cm long, with an exceptionally large yolk sac. Buds of the pelvic fins and elements of the anal and caudal are already present (Fish, 1932). Growth is usually good during the summer and by September or October the young fish are about 6 to 7 cm long. Subsequent growth rates vary widely from place to place according to water temperature, altitude, type and amount of food available, and the genetics of the fish. Most growth occurs during the summer, with some northern populations growing only from June to September (Kennedy, 1954). Overall, age I fish average about 20 cm total length; age V, 45 cm and .87 kg; age X, 72.8 cm and 3.24 kg; age XV, 96.4 cm and 7.63 kg. The slowest-growing lake trout are those of Great Bear Lake, Northwest Territories, and of Itkillik and Campsite lakes in Alaska. Ten-year-olds from Great Bear Lake average only 40.6 cm total length; at age XV, 52.8 cm; and age XX, 67.8 cm. A 37-year-old fish was 104.6 cm total length and weighed 15.4 kg (Miller and Kennedy, 1948). Fish from Itkillik and Campsite lakes in Alaska had even slower growth rates when calculations were based on otoliths. However, when calculations were based on scales, growth rates of Itkillik Lake fish were comparable to those from Great Bear Lake (McCart et al., 1972). Growth of lake trout in other Alaskan lakes is generally better than in Great Bear Lake but below the general average (Roguski and Spetz, 1968; Van Wyhe and Peck, 1969; Furniss, 1974). What appears to be the oldest known lake trout was a fish of 92.7 cm and 12.5 kg estimated to be 42+ taken in Chandler Lake, Alaska, in July, 1973 (Furniss, 1974). Another, reckoned to be 41+, was reported from the west coast of Hudson Bay (Sprules, 1952).

Sexual maturity is generally reached around the seventh year but may be achieved as early as age 5 or as late as 13. Males usually mature a year earlier than females.

The lake trout can hardly be called migratory, since whole populations do not undertake movements in definite directions, but it is definitely a solitary wanderer. Tagged fish in Lake Superior have been recovered up to 408 km from the point of release. In other areas lake trout wander throughout the lake, the extent of their movements apparently limited chiefly by the size of the body of water. Small fish tend to move shorter distances than larger fish (Eschmeyer et al., 1953; DeRoche and Bond, 1957; Rawson, 1961). Dispersal begins shortly after spawning. By spring, the fish are widespread, and as the water warms to above 10°C, they tend to go into deeper water and to congregate below the thermocline during the summer (Martin, 1952; Rawson, 1961; Dryer, 1966). With the approach of fall the fish return to the spawning beds. They show a marked tendency to return to their natural spawning areas, although stocked fish may make use of artificial spawning beds (Eschmeyer, 1955; Hacker, 1957; Loftus, 1958; Martin, 1960). The newly hatched fish move off the spawning areas and into deep water a month or so after hatching, and apparently stay there for some time.

As with most fishes, food habits of lake trout vary with the age and size of the fish, locality and the food available. Total diet includes a wide variety of such items as zooplankton of various sorts, insects, spiders, clams, snails, many kinds of fishes, plant material such as algae, sponges, amphibians, worms, shrews and mice. The very young fish subsist almost entirely on small crustaceans of various sorts. As size increases, larger organisms such as mysids, *Pontoporeia* and insect larvae are of major importance. Later, ninespine sticklebacks may become a major food. Mature lake trout in most areas feed almost exclusively on fishes (Hildebrand and Towers, 1927; Dunbar and Hildebrand, 1952; Hacker, 1957; Kimsey, 1960; Rawson, 1961; Martin, 1970; Griswold and Smith, 1973). Coregonids appear to be a particularly important food item in most places and to provide superior nourishment for the lake trout. In Lake Opeongo, Ontario, a shift to consumption of coregonids from other kinds of fish resulted in faster growth, greater weight, older age at maturity and larger and more numerous eggs (Martin, 1970).

Some populations of lake trout feed on plankton throughout their lives. This may be due to unavailability of forage fish or perhaps to a genetic characteristic of the particular trout population. Such fish tend to have more numerous and longer gill rakers, and often develop accessory rakers on the median side of the gill arch (Martin and Sandercock, 1967). Plankton-feeding lake trout grow more slowly, mature earlier and at smaller size, die sooner, and attain smaller maximum size than do their fish-eating counterparts (Martin, 1966). Seasonal changes in the food habits of the lake trout, probably in response to availability, have been observed in several areas. In Lake Superior coregonids made up the major food in fall and early winter but were replaced by smelt in February and March, with cottids, mysids and insects most common in late summer (Dryer et al., 1965). A similar situation prevailed in certain lakes in Ontario where, again, fishes were eaten more commonly in winter (Martin, 1954).

Lake trout are not known to produce natural hybrids with other species of *Salvelinus,* perhaps because of their unique spawning habits. However, artificial crossing of female lake trout and male brook trout yields viable offspring called splake. These grow more rapidly than either parent species, are fertile and are known to reproduce naturally (Martin and Baldwin, 1960).

Lake trout are highly susceptible to pollution, especially from insecticides such as DDT. This substance accumulates in the yolk and fatty tissues, and concentrations of less than three parts per million produce mass mortalities of the alevins following yolk-sac absorption (Burdick et al., 1964).

IMPORTANCE TO MAN

The lake trout was formerly one of the mainstays of the Great Lakes fisheries, with landings up to nearly 7 million kg in 1940 (Fiedler, 1943). However, with the entrance of the sea lamprey, *Petromyzon marinus,* into these waters, and the extensive use of insecticides such as DDT, the stocks declined drastically and annual catches now amount only to about 190,000 kg (Anonymous, 1975). It is still an important commercial species in Canada, however, especially in the Northwest Territories, but even there, where the lake trout is free of the lamprey, landings have declined by a third in recent years (Scott and Crossman, 1970).

As a sport fish, the lake trout is well regarded. It fights hard, though not spectacularly, and the large size attained makes it a trophy worthy of any angler's skill. The flesh is usually of a yellow or creamy color but may be anything from white to orange, depending, at least in part, on diet. Regardless of color, lake trout is excellent as human food.

ARCTIC CHARR

Salvelinus alpinus (Linnaeus)

DISTINCTIVE CHARACTERS

The arctic charr is distinguished by the presence of 23 to 32 gill rakers, 37 to 75 pyloric caeca and, on the sides and back, pink to red spots, the largest of which are usually larger than the pupil of the eye.

DESCRIPTION

Body elongate, more or less terete, compressed toward the tail. Depth about 20% of total length but highly variable, depending on time of year, sex, size and state of maturity. Head moderate, 22% to 25% of total length. Snout rounded, its length usually equal to or longer than eye diameter. Eye more or less round, large, its diameter averaging about 23% of head length, but highly variable. Mouth large, terminal, the maxilla reaching nearly to posterior margin of eye in small specimens, to well behind eye in large fish, especially in spawning males. Teeth caniniform, in an irregular single row on each jaw and on palatines. Patch of teeth present on head of vomer. Ten to 24 teeth on tongue in 2 rows. Gill rakers: 23 to 32 on first arch. Branchiostegal rays: 10 to 13. Lateral line, which curves slightly downward from the head, has 123 to 152 pored scales. Pyloric caeca: 35 to 75. Vertebrae: 63 to 68.

FINS. Dorsal has 12 to 16 rays, 10 to 12 major rays. Adipose fin present. Anal has 11 to 15 rays; pectorals, 14 to 16; pelvics, 9 to 11, with axillary process present. Caudal emarginate.

SCALES. Small, cycloid.

COLOR. Highly variable, depending on location, time of year and degree of sexual development. In general, the back is dark, usually rather brown but sometimes with a green cast. The sides are lighter, belly pale. Sides and back are liberally sprinkled with pink to red spots, the largest spots along the lateral line usually being larger than the pupil of the eye. Forward edges of pectoral, pelvic and anal fins, and sometimes the caudal, have a narrow white margin. Fins pale in young fish; dorsal and caudal fins dark in adults, but other fins light. Spawning adults, especially males, are brilliant orange-red to bright red on the ventral side and on pectoral, pelvic and anal fins. Young arctic charr have about 11 dark parr marks on each side (Plate 14, page 125).

SIZE. The largest arctic charr known is one of 13.5 kg from the Arctic Red River, Northwest Territories. However, average size is much less than this. Arctic charr in Lake Aleknagik, Alaska, run about 1 to 2 kg. Fourteen fish taken in a small gill net in Campsite Lake at the head of the Kuparuk River, Alaska, in August 1973, averaged less than 1 kg, but others, taken on hook and line in the same lake, ran up to 5 kg. Thirty-four charr from Chandler Lake, Alaska, taken by gill net in July, 1973, ranged in weight from .56 to 2.19 kg (Furniss, 1974).

RANGE AND ABUNDANCE

Distribution of the arctic charr is circumpolar in arctic and subarctic regions, with isolated relict populations in cold lakes south of the normal range. In North America the species ranges from the Aleutian Islands, the Alaska Peninsula and Kodiak Island north to the Arctic Ocean as far as Discovery Harbor, Ellesmere Island, Northwest Territories (82°34' N according to Günther, 1877, but more recently listed as 81°42' N, 65°20' W in the *Gazeteer of Canada* 1971). Thus the arctic charr is the most northerly of all salmonids. The general distribution is circumpolar, reaching south to New England, the British Isles, isolated locations in the Alps and Siberia, and the islands of Japan. In most areas where it is present, the arctic charr is abundant, though this abundance is often highly localized. Arctic charr in Alaska seem to be confined to lakes, although in the eastern Canadian arctic anadromous populations are present.

HABITS

Spawning occurs in the fall of the year, usually over gravel shoals in lakes but sometimes in quiet pools in streams close to a lake. In lakes of the North Slope of the Brooks Range, Alaska, spawning may begin as early as late August or early September, while farther south it may not take place until November or December. Water temperatures range from about 3° to nearly 13°C. In the high arctic, on Baffin Island, arctic charr have been found spawning at water temperatures as low as 0.5°C (Moore, 1975).

The male fish are territorial, guarding their areas and driving off intruding males with considerable vigor (photograph A, page 142). However, as soon as the females begin to show spawning behavior, the males pair with the females and lose interest in their territories. The female invades the male's territory and at first may be attacked by the male. She persists, however, and makes visual examination of the bottom. With head and tail bent downward and eyes directed toward the bottom, she swims slowly about until she finds a suitable spot for a redd (photograph B, page 142). During this period, she may attack nearby fish of either sex. When a suitable spot has been found, the female begins to dig the redd. This may start with powerful swimming movements that push water backward and result in sand and loose debris being carried away. More often, however, digging begins in the typical salmonid fashion. The female turns on her side and gives a few strong upward flaps of her tail, thus displacing lighter particles of sediment as well as sand and small gravel (photograph C, page 142). After each spell of digging, the female swims forward, circles the area and returns to approximately the same spot to dig again. Digging occurs about once a minute. Depending largely on the size of the bottom particles, the completed redd varies from a fairly deep pit to a clean spot on large stones.

While the female digs the redd, the male courts her by circling around her and then gliding along her side and quivering. In intensive courtship, the vertical and pelvic fins are erected and the male opens his mouth. During the courtship period the male develops a dark band along the side and across the top of the head, while the back becomes pale.

When the redd is completed the female tests it with her erected anal fin, bends head and tail upward, opens her mouth and quivers. The male joins her, assuming a like position, and eggs and sperm are ejected. The fish then swim forward out of the nest, often still ejecting sex products. This act may be repeated up to five times before the female begins to cover the eggs. She does this by swimming about the redd, sweeping the gravel with her anal and caudal fins. This activity pushes the eggs into the nooks and crannies of the gravel. The female then digs at the edge of the pit, covering the eggs and beginning the next redd.

Spawning apparently takes place at almost any time of the day or night, although most apparently occurs during the day. Males often mate with more than one female, taking the second mate after the first has exhausted her eggs. Occasionally a female will mate successively with two or more males (Fabricius, 1953; Fabricius and Gustafson, 1954).

Several days are usually required for a female to deposit all her eggs. Depending upon her size, a female may produce as few as a couple of hundred to as many as 5,000 or 6,000. The eggs are fairly large, .35 to .55 cm in diameter, yellowish to orange in color. Larger fish produce more and larger eggs than do small fish (Moore, 1975). Time of development seems to vary widely according to conditions and stock. Under hatchery conditions at 4.4°C, hatching may occur in 60 to 70 days (Bigelow, 1963); in the northwestern part of the Hudson Bay area, however, "eggs are still visible at breakup in the following spring, probably hatching soon after open water appears" (Sprules, 1952). The situation in Alaskan waters is not known.

The young are about 1.7 cm long at hatching. Subsequent growth rates depend largely on temperature and the abundance of food. In Swedish hatcheries, average lengths of 9.7 cm at the end of the first year, 12.3 cm at the end of the second, and 13.7 to 21.6 cm at the end of the third have been reported (Bigelow, 1963). Growth under wild conditions is much slower. In the eastern Canadian arctic, 5+ fish averaged from 13 to 38.2 cm fork length; 10+, from 36.3 to 58.4 cm; and 15+, from 55.3 to 67.1 cm (Sprules, 1952; Grainger, 1953; Andrews and Lear, 1956). In Chandler Lake in Alaska's Brooks Range, 10+ fish averaged 42.4 cm fork length; 14+, 53.7 cm (Furniss, 1974). The arctic charr is thus an especially slow-growing fish. It is known to achieve an age of at least 24 (Grainger, 1953).

Some populations of arctic charr, particularly in Europe, Siberia and eastern Canada, are anadromous, running to sea shortly after breakup in the spring and returning to fresh water in late summer and early fall. Other populations, especially lake-dwelling fish, remain in fresh water all their lives and do not migrate. In Alaska it appears that all arctic charr are of the freshwater, lake-dwelling type. The species has been reported as being anadromous in most rivers from Bristol Bay to Barter Island.

However, examination of numerous specimens and published data shows that these anadromous fish are the northern form of the Dolly Varden, *Salvelinus malma* (Morrow, 1980).

The food of the arctic charr is varied, mostly according to what is available. In Chandler Lake, Alaska, insects, especially Diptera, were most important. Arctic charr feed heavily on young sockeye salmon in the Karluk Lake and Wood River Lakes systems in Alaska. Indeed, it has been estimated that 27% of the sockeye smolts produced in the Wood River system in 1971 were eaten by charr. Other foods consumed in various parts of the world, some of which I have observed personally, include fishes, crustaceans, mollusks, nereid worms and the charr's own young (DeLacy and Morton, 1943; Thompson, 1959; Rogers, 1972; Moore and Moore, 1974).

IMPORTANCE TO MAN

The arctic charr is an important sport fish in the Canadian arctic and in Scandinavia, as well as in the Wood River Lakes of Alaska. Canadian Eskimos rely heavily on it for food in some regions. It is fished commercially in various locations in northern Canada, Greenland, the Scandinavian countries and Siberia. The flesh is of excellent quality and commands a good price. The red-meated fish are preferred over those with pink or white meat and are priced accordingly. Frozen arctic charr are shipped to gourmet restaurants in most of the large cities of the world. Canned charr is another high-priced delicacy. However, because the arctic charr is slow-growing, there is some doubt as to whether many populations can withstand heavy exploitation. There are a number of examples of serious depletion in only a couple of years (Andrews and Lear, 1956).

DOLLY VARDEN

Salvelinus malma (Walbaum)

DISTINCTIVE CHARACTERS

The Dolly Varden is identified by the lack of wormlike marbling on the back, the presence of pink or red spots on the sides, the number of gill rakers—11 to 26—and the presence of 13 to 35 (in rare cases up to 40) pyloric caeca (Figure 33).

DESCRIPTION

Body elongate, rounded. Depth about 20% of fork length. Head moderate to fairly long, 15% to 28% of fork length, longest in breeding males. Snout rounded, about equal to eye in small fish, longer in adults, especially breeding males. Eye round or nearly so, about 20% of head length. Mouth large, terminal, upper jaw reaching about to a point below hind margin of eye in small fish, well behind it in large ones. Well-developed caniniform teeth present on both jaws, on head but not shaft of vomer, on palatines and tongue. From 0 to 44 small teeth on base of tongue. Gill rakers: 11 to 26, average number 15 to 19 in the southern form, 21 to 23 in the northern. Branchiostegals: 10 to 15, usually 1 more on left than on right. Lateral line present with 105 to 142 pored scales. Pyloric caeca: 13 to 35, rarely up to 40. Vertebrae: 61 to 67 in the southern form, 63 to 71 in the northern.

FINS. Dorsal has 13 to 16 rays (10 to 12 major rays). Adipose fin present. Anal has 11 to 15 rays (9 to 12 major rays). Pectorals, 14 to 16 rays; pelvics, 8 to 11, usually 9, with an axillary process present. Caudal emarginate.

SCALES. Small, cycloid.

COLOR. Extremely variable according to locality, size of fish and degree of sexual maturity. Very young parr are usually brownish with 8 to 12 dark parr marks, the sides and back showing small red spots, the fins pale to dusky. Fish in salt water or just entering fresh water may be dark above, with silvery sides sprinkled with pale or pink spots. Breeding fish become dark greenish black above and on the upper sides. Males in breeding condition turn bright orange to red on the lower sides and belly; females take on the same colors but are less brilliant. Pectoral, pelvic and anal fins usually have white or creamy leading edges followed by a black or red line. Dorsal and caudal fins usually dusky or rather brown. Largest spots on sides usually smaller than pupil of eye (photographs, page 90).

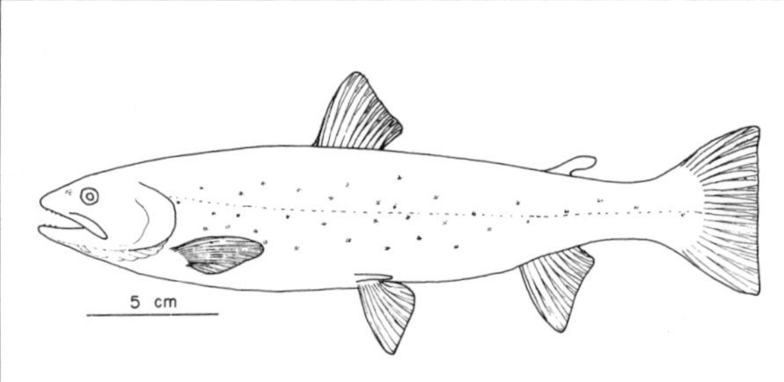

FIGURE 33. Dolly Varden, *Salvelinus malma*. The arctic charr and angayukaksurak charr look very much like the Dolly Varden, but the angayukaksurak charr is black and the arctic charr has more gill rakers and pyloric caeca.

SIZE. The angling record for Dolly Varden is a fish 103 cm long and weighing 14.5 kg taken in Lake Pend Oreille, Idaho. The largest known weighed 18.3 kg and was taken in the Lardeau River, British Columbia (Hart, 1973). In the light of recent, as yet unpublished, studies by Dr. Ted Cavender of Ohio State University, it is probable that both these fish were actually specimens of a similar and closely related species, the bull trout, *Salvelinus confluentus*. Alaskan Dolly Varden do not, as a rule, reach great size. Adult fish rarely exceed 3 kg, although around Kotzebue they are sometimes twice that weight.

RANGE AND ABUNDANCE

Definition of the range of the Dolly Varden is difficult because it has, in the past, been confused with the arctic charr, *Salvelinus alpinus,* and the bull trout, *S. confluentus.* The anadromous charr of arctic Alaska and extreme northwestern Canada were formerly considered as *S. alpinus,* (McPhail, 1961), but Morrow (1980) has shown that all the stream-dwelling charr in this area are the northern form of the Dolly Varden. Conversely, the so-called Dolly Varden of the Columbia River Basin and possibly of other southern drainages as well are *S. confluentus.* At present, then, the certain range of the Dolly Varden in North America extends from the arctic coast of Alaska south to southern British Columbia. Within this area, both anadromous and nonanadromous populations are to be found in clear-water streams. The northern form is present in Alaska and northern Canada north and east of the Alaska Range, while the southern form is to be found south of the range and along the Aleutian Island Chain. The presence of northern-type Dolly Varden in the lower Susitna drainage and of the southern type in the upper Tanana has undoubtedly been brought about by exchange of headwaters between the Nenana and Susitna rivers in the one case, the Slana and the Little Tok rivers in the other (Morrow, 1980). On the western side of the Pacific, Dolly Varden are found from the Chukhotsk Peninsula of Russia south to Japan and Korea.

Wherever present, the Dolly Varden is usually abundant, although, because of its migration patterns, the abundance may be seasonal.

HABITS

An account of the life history of the Dolly Varden is not simplified by the fact that the fish occupies at least five different types of habitat, with behavioral and biological modifications in each one. The present account will deal only with the major, most general life histories. Readers wanting greater detail and additional references should consult Armstrong and Morrow (1980).

Six isolated populations of Dolly Varden have been found in springs in Beaufort Sea drainages in Alaska and Canada. These fish characteristically mature at an early age, grow slowly and do not reach large size. Spawning occurs annually, usually late in the fall—November or later. Major food items are insects.

Three populations that are confined to lakes are known: two in Kamchatka and one in arctic Alaska. In these groups, spawning is not annual and takes place in late summer or early fall. Like the stream-resident fish, these Dolly Varden grow slowly, and maximum size tends to be small, although fish in Lake Azabach'ye, Kamchatka, may reach 75 cm.

The remaining life histories are for anadromous, stream-dwelling northern and southern forms; nonanadromous, stream-dwelling northern and southern forms; and anadromous dwellers of a stream-lake system, southern form only.

Spawning takes place from late August to the end of November, most activity being in September and October. Spawning is a yearly event for southern fish but normally occurs only every second or third year in the Arctic. Spawning behavior is similar to that of other members of the genus. The male courts the female by swimming around and beside her, pressing against her and quivering. The female selects the nest site on clean gravel, the stones being from .6 to 5 cm in diameter. The redd is located in fairly strong current, usually near the center of the stream in water at least .3 m deep. Preferred water temperature in southeastern Alaska seems to be around 5.5° to 6.5 °C. The female digs the redd in typical salmonid fashion, turning on her side and giving several strong upward flips of her tail, thus dislodging the gravel and debris, which are carried downstream. While the female is preparing the redd, the male continues to court her and to drive off intruding males. When the redd is finished, both fish drop into it, press against each other with arched backs and open mouths, quiver and expel the sex products. This procedure lasts about five seconds and may be repeated several times before the female begins to cover the eggs. This is accomplished by the female swimming along the edge of the redd and sweeping small pebbles and other particles into it with her tail and anal fin. Later she may dig again in typical salmonid fashion and further cover the eggs while preparing a new nest (Needham and Vaughn, 1952; Blackett, 1968). Sexual dimorphism is apparent at this time. Females develop an extended and swollen ovipositor. Males, at least of anadromous populations, develop a pronounced kype which begins to return to normal sometime in November.

The mature eggs of anadromous females are .45 to .6 cm in diameter, but those of nonanadromous fish are much smaller, rarely exceeding .4 cm. Egg number per female varies with stock and location. Anadromous fish in southeastern Alaska produce from 739 to 5,968 eggs. Fish in the streams of the arctic coast may surpass 6,000 eggs, while the maximum number recorded from the small non-anadromous stream residents is only 346 (Nagata, 1967; Blackett, 1968; Yoshihara, 1973; Savvaitova, 1973).

Development to hatching requires 129 to 136 days at 8.5 °C (Blackett, 1968), but as long as eight months along Alaska's North Slope (Yoshihara, 1973). The newly hatched young, about 1.5 to 2 cm long, remain in the gravel until the yolk sac has been absorbed, a period of 60 to 70 days. On emergence, they are about 2.5 cm long.

The young begin to feed actively as soon as they emerge from the redd. The major foods are various winged insects and the larvae of mayflies and midges, but other insects and various small crustaceans are also consumed (Karzanovskii, 1962). These newly emerged fry tend to stay on the bottom in pools or eddies, relatively inactive except when feeding. Growth rates vary tremendously from area to area and population to population. Thus in Eva Creek, in southeastern Alaska, young fish reach only about 6.3 cm at 1 year; 7.8 cm at 2; and 10 cm at 3 (Heiser, 1966; Blackett, 1968). By contrast, young fish at nearby Hood Bay, on Admiralty Island, and fish on Prince of Wales Island achieve 9 cm at 1 year; 15 to 18.2 cm at 2; and over 20 cm at 3 years (Reed, 1967b; Armstrong, 1967). Dolly Varden in rivers of the North Slope grow at intermediate rates (Roguski and Komarek, 1971; Yoshihara, 1973). The young Dolly Varden usually spend three or four years in the creek before going to sea. These young fish going to sea are typical smolts. The parr marks have disappeared and the fish are silvery. Nothing is known of the growth rates of nonanadromous stream-resident fish.

Greatest annual growth takes place between May and September each year. Anadromous fish in the sea may double their weight in this short time (Revet, 1962; Heiser, 1966). The Dolly Varden of southeastern Alaska appear to grow more slowly than those of arctic rivers. At 6+, arctic fish run about 5 cm longer than those from southeastern areas, and at 10+ the difference is nearly 8 cm. Typical lengths at various ages for northern fish are: 3+, 16.4 cm; 5+, 32.9 cm; 8+, 47 cm; 10+, 51.7 cm (Reed, 1967b; Armstrong, 1967; Roguski and Komarek, 1971; Kogl, 1971; Yoshihara, 1973). Whether this difference reflects food conditions or a genetic difference between the northern and southern forms of Dolly Varden is not known.

Sexual maturity is reached at 4 to 6 years in the southern form, but not until 7 to 9 in the northern. Spawning is annual in the southern form, but most fish of the northern populations spawn only every second or third year (Blackett, 1968; Roguski and Komarek, 1971; Kogl, 1971; Yoshihara, 1973; Furniss, 1974).

The migration patterns of the Dolly Varden are rather complex. In southeastern Alaska, a migration of smolts and adults out of the lakes where they wintered begins in the early spring and continues into July. In some streams there may be a second outmigration of smolts in the fall; these fish probably had not achieved migratory size in the spring but have done so by the end of the summer. After a stay of as little as a couple of weeks or as long as seven months, the fish return to spawn in the stream and winter in the lake. Thus, some fish are still moving out while others are already returning to fresh water. Some may enter nonlake streams to spawn, then leave and enter a lake-stream system to winter. Immature fish often enter several streams after their migration to the sea. About 40% to 50% of the fish wintering in a lake are fish that originated there; the remaining wintering fish are of unknown origin. Homing of adult spawners to their natal stream is very high (Revet, 1962; Armstrong, 1965a).

Smolts, mostly 3 or 4 years old, and adults of the northern anadromous populations go to sea immediately after breakup. In arctic rivers adults winter in large springs and spring-fed areas of the streams, while the young appear to winter in smaller springs farther upstream. The return from the sea begins in August, with nonspawners tending to return later than spawners. For mature spawners, there is a high degree of homing to the natal stream. Nonspawners, by contrast, are not so specific. In the Wulik River, on the west coast of Alaska north of Kotzebue Sound, almost the entire wintering population, estimated at about 200,000 fish, seems to be composed of nonspawners from other drainages (Winslow, 1968, 1969a).

It is a peculiarity of these Arctic populations that the vast majority of the male fish never go to sea and remain small, seldom exceeding 22 cm in length. They mature early, as early as age 2. In contrast to the alternate-year spawning of the large anadromous individuals, these residual males breed annually.

The migratory patterns of the stream-resident fish are not at all well known. These fish are most often found well up toward the headwaters. There is some evidence to suggest that during the summer they may spread out and occupy larger parts of the stream. They probably spend the winter in deep pools or move downstream toward the lower reaches for this purpose. As far as is known, these small stream residents never enter the major rivers.

Movement of anadromous fish in salt water is usually more or less along the coast. In southeastern Alaska, this may well be due to the arrangement of islands and channels in the area. Within these confines tagged Dolly Varden have been recovered as much as 115 km from the point of release. In the arctic, tagged fish have been recovered as much as 350 km from the tagging point. Northern Dolly Varden of unknown origin have been taken in the Bering Sea at least as far west as 170°W (Hanavan and Tanonaka, 1959; Armstrong, 1965a; Craig, 1977).

The Dolly Varden is known to hybridize with the brook trout in some lakes in southeastern Alaska where the latter species has been introduced. The hybrids are said to be inferior to both parent species.

Dolly Varden in southeastern Alaska reach 10+ to 12+ years, although there is a rapid reduction in numbers after age 5+, perhaps because of post-spawning mortality (Heiser, 1966). Northern fish, especially along the arctic coast, live longer. The majority of spawners are fish of 8+ or 9+, although one of 18+ has been recorded (Yoshihara, 1973). A hatchery fish in California was reported to have reached its 20th year (Shebly, 1931).

The diet of the Dolly Varden varies with the size and age of the fish, location, time of year and local availability of food. As already noted, the young fry feed chiefly on insects and small crustacea. Stream food of both young fish and adults consists largely of various insects, spiders and annelids as well as snails, clams, fish eggs and various small fishes. However, mature spawners feed little, if at all, when wintering in fresh water. In estuaries and in the sea, the food of the adults consists largely of small fishes and invertebrates, including smelts, herring, young salmon, sand lance, greenlings, sculpins, flounder larvae and cods as well as amphipods, decapods, mysids, euphausiids, brachipods, polychaetes, megalopids and isopods. In the high arctic, mysids seem to be the most important food, with fish second (Townsend, 1942; Roos, 1959; Lagler and Wright, 1962; Narver and Dahlberg, 1965; Armstrong, 1965b, 1967, 1971b; Yoshihara, 1973).

IMPORTANCE TO MAN

The Dolly Varden has long been reviled by salmon fishermen, canners and others (some of whom should have known better) as an eater of salmon spawn and a most serious predator on young salmon, especially sockeye (see, for example, Ohmer 1929a, b; Rounsefell, 1958). Despite the fact that a few bold biologists began to refute this shortly after the turn of the century (Chamberlain, 1907), it was not until the 1940s that it became apparent that the Dolly Varden did not deserve its bad reputation and that, at least in some areas, the real culprit was the closely related arctic charr (DeLacy and Morton, 1943). Dolly Varden do eat salmon eggs and young salmon on occasion; however, the eggs are drifters washed out of the redd or dug up by later spawners, which would not survive anyhow (Chamberlain, 1907; Reed, 1967a; Armstrong, 1967). With respect to young salmon, especially sockeye, other predators appear to make much greater inroads on the population than Dolly Varden. Removal of more than 20,000 predaceous fishes from Cultus Lake, British Columbia, led to a 33% increase in sockeye survival (Foerster and Ricker, 1941). However, the Dolly Varden made up less than 5% of the predators, so its removal could scarcely have accounted for much of the increase. In other places, such species as coho salmon, rainbow and cutthroat trout, squawfish and sculpins have been shown to be much more serious predators on salmons than the Dolly Varden (Chamberlain, 1907; Pritchard, 1936b; Ricker, 1941; Armstrong, 1965b; Reed, 1967a). Dolly Varden certainly will eat young salmon when they are abundant and concentrated (Bower and Fassett, 1914; Pritchard, 1936; Ricker, 1941; Hartman et al., 1962; Armstrong, 1965b; Thompson and Tufts, 1967; McCart, 1967), but in most places the damage has been grossly exaggerated.

For many years a bounty was paid in Alaska for Dolly Varden tails in the hope of decreasing the Dolly Varden population and thus assisting the survival of young salmon. While this practice may have served as a welcome addition to the income of local fishermen, it did little, if anything, toward accomplishing its stated purpose. The bounty was finally eliminated in 1941.

As a sport fish, the Dolly Varden will take many artificial lures, especially shiny spoons and spinners, and also flies. Dolly Varden fight gamely, though not spectacularly, seldom jumping, and are not as strong as rainbow trout of comparable size. However, Dollies generally are quite a satisfactory sport fish.

For many years, Dolly Varden were taken incidental to the salmon fisheries of southeastern and western Alaska and in some years as much as 91,528 kg were marketed fresh, frozen, canned or pickled (Bower, 1919). In recent years, however, landings have been miniscule, only 2,000 or 3,000 kg a year (Anonymous, 1975). The Dolly Varden is an important part of the subsistence fishery in many areas of Northern Alaska.

ANGAYUKAKSURAK CHARR

Salvelinus anaktuvukensis

DISTINCTIVE CHARACTERS

The angayukaksurak charr is distinguished from its closest relative, the Dolly Varden, by the more numerous rays in the dorsal, anal, pectoral and pelvic fins, and by the larger number of lateral line pores and parr marks. The angayukaksurak is easily distinguished from the arctic charr by the smaller number of gill rakers and pyloric caeca in the angayukaksurak.

DESCRIPTION

Body elongate, subcylindrical toward the head, somewhat compressed toward the tail. Depth 18% to 24% of standard length. Head moderately large, its length 20% to 29% of standard length. Snout longer than eye diameter, 24% to 31% of head length. Eyes nearly round, the horizontal axis a little longer than the vertical; 16% to 23% of head. Nostrils double, the anterior nostril having a flap around its posterior margin. Mouth large, upper jaw reaching nearly to posterior margin of eye in young, well behind eye in adults. Teeth small, caniniform, in a single irregular row on each jaw and palatine. Teeth in a V-shaped patch on head of vomer, ends of patch usually separated by a wide toothless space from anterior palatine teeth. Tongue teeth: 4 to 13, in two widely separated rows. Gill rakers: 18 to 23. Branchiostegals: 9 to 12 on left, 9 to 11 on right, usually one more on left than on right. Straight lateral line present, with 127 to 152 pores. Pyloric caeca: 24 to 32. Vertebrae: 65 to 69.

FINS. Dorsal has 14 to 17 rays. Adipose fin present. Anal has 13 to 15 rays; pectorals, 13 to 15; pelvics, 10, in rare cases, 9, with small axillary process present. Caudal only slightly indented, with 19 principal rays.

SCALES. Small, cycloid.

COLOR. Deep velvet black on back and sides, paler below. Small bright red spots on back and sides, spots smallest and most numerous on back. Largest spots smaller than pupil of eye. Some or all spots may be surrounded by a blue to pale halo. Leading edges of dorsal, anal and pelvic fins cream to yellow. All rayed fins dark, without spots or marks. Adipose fin paler than rayed fins, with a dark posterior margin.

SIZE. The angayukaksurak does not reach a large size. The largest known is the holotype, only 27.8 cm fork length.

RANGE AND ABUNDANCE

Known only from headwaters situations in the Brooks Range of Alaska, where it is distributed somewhat discontinuously from Howard Pass eastward to the Romanzof Mountains. Specifically, distribution is in the western part of Howard Pass; Killik River; Ikiakpuk (Ekokpuk) Creek, Giant Creek, Contact Creek, Loon Lake Creek, all in the John River drainage; Tolugak Lake, Kanayut (Shainin) Lake, Willow Creek in the Anaktuvuk River drainage; Chandler River; north fork, Koyukuk River; Hulahula River; Aichilik River (Walters, 1955*; personal observations).

HABITS

Virtually nothing is known of the biology of the angayukaksurak. It is found only in small headwaters streams. In the winter it congregates in springs where there is a constant flow of water, and it is reported to spawn in the springtime.† This report is borne out by the appearance of the gonads of the topotype series, which was taken in December. The angayukaksurak is extremely slow-growing. Five specimens taken in October, 1968, were 23 to 27.5 cm fork length and were six to nine years old. Dolly Varden of the same age and from the same general area are about twice that size (Winslow, 1969b).

IMPORTANCE TO MAN

At present the angayukaksurak is important only as a rare species—a zoological curiosity. In the old days, however, it was important to the inland Eskimos as an emergency source of winter food.†

PINK SALMON
ALSO KNOWN AS HUMPBACK SALMON OR HUMPY
Oncorhynchus gorbuscha (Walbaum)

DISTINCTIVE CHARACTERS

The pink salmon is distinguished from its relatives by the presence of large black spots on the back and on both lobes of the caudal fin. The young have no parr marks (Figure 34).

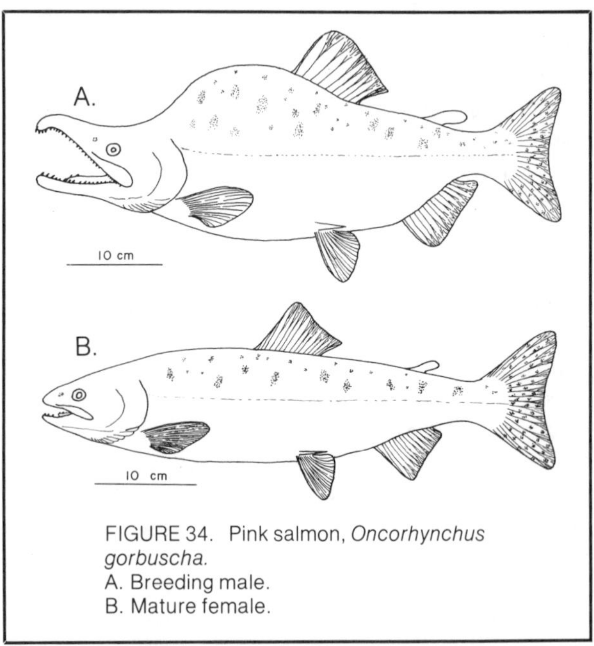

FIGURE 34. Pink salmon, *Oncorhynchus gorbuscha*.
A. Breeding male.
B. Mature female.

DESCRIPTION

Body elongate, fusiform, slightly compressed. Depth about 22% of fork length in females and non-breeding males. Breeding males develop a great hump behind the head, so that body depth at that time is about 33% of fork length. Head moderate,

*Also, Simon Paneak, Anaktuvuk Village: personal communication.
†Simon Paneak: personal communication.

about 20% of fork length, but much longer in breeding males, which develop an elongate, hooked snout. Snout about 30% of head in females, nearly 50% in breeding males. Eyes rather small, round, in front of posterior end of maxilla. Mouth terminal, slightly oblique; breeding males have a pronounced kype. Teeth caniniform, well developed on both jaws, on head and shaft of vomer, on palatines and on tongue. No teeth on basibranchials. Gill rakers moderate: 24 to 35 on first arch. Branchiostegals: 9 to 15. Lateral line has 147 to 205 pored scales. Pyloric caeca: 95 to 224. Vertebrae: 63 to 72.

FINS. Dorsal has 10 to 15 rays. Large adipose fin present. Anal has 13 to 19 rays; pectorals, 14 to 17; pelvics, 9 to 11, with axillary process present.

SCALES. Cycloid, small.

COLOR. Pink salmon in the sea are steel blue to blue green on the back, silver on the sides and white on the belly. Large oval black spots present on back, adipose fin and both lobes of caudal fin. Breeding males become dark on the back, red with brownish green blotches on the sides; breeding females are similar but less distinctly colored (photographs, page 91; Plate 3, page 114; Plate 4, page 115).

SIZE. The pink is the smallest of the Pacific salmons. The greatest size achieved is about 76 cm and 6.4 kg, but most run from 1 to 3 kg, with the average a bit less than 2.

RANGE AND ABUNDANCE

The pink salmon is found from La Jolla, California (Miller and Lea, 1972), north to the Arctic Ocean. The range extends eastward to Kidluit Bay in the Mackenzie River Delta, westward across northern Siberia to the Lena River, and south along the Asian coast to Korea and Kyushu, Japan. The fish is most abundant in the central parts of the north-south range.

Pink salmon have been introduced along the Atlantic coast from Maryland north to Newfoundland. These transplants apparently survived for some years but seem to have disappeared recently (Hart, 1973). An accidental introduction into a tributary of Thunder Bay, Lake Superior, in 1956 seems to have survived. Introductions have been made into several European areas and one stock is said to have survived (Scott and Crossman, 1973). Pink salmon are present in the lower Yukon River in June and early July and are known to spawn as far upstream as Grayling (62°57'N, 160°03'W).

HABITS

Adult pink salmon move from the sea into streams any time from June to late September, depending largely on location. As a rule they do not go far upstream and in many areas spawning occurs in the lower tidal areas. Even though the eggs and alevins are unable to adapt to salt water (salinity 31.8 parts per thousand) they can withstand exposure to it for a day or more without serious harm (Weisbart, 1968). This, of course, is much longer than the periods of high tide during which intertidal redds are exposed to sea water. However, some spawning pinks may ascend rivers such as the Kuskokwim and Yukon for as much as 160 km; in Siberia pink salmon ascend the Amur River as much as 600 km. Spawning takes place in mid-July in the lower Yukon but generally not until late August to October in areas to the south.

Spawning behavior is typically salmonid. The female prepares the redd by turning on her side, pressing her caudal fin against the bottom and giving several strong flaps with her tail. This dislodges silt, debris and small gravel, which are carried downstream by the current. Repeated digging results in a pit somewhat longer than the female and perhaps as deep as the depth of her body, but the redd can be as long as 91.5 cm and up to 45.7 cm deep. The male takes no part in the digging, spending most of his time driving off intruding males. When the redd is finished, male and female drop into it, erect their fins, open their mouths, vibrate and release eggs and sperm. Pairing is usually on a one-to-one basis, but up to six males have been seen to spawn with a single female (Wickett, 1959). All pink salmon die after spawning.

The large—.6 cm—orange-red eggs fall into the interstices of the gravel and are fertilized by the milt. The eggs are covered with gravel as the female subsequently digs a new nest at the upstream edge of the previous one. Each female may produce as few as 800 or as many as 2,000 eggs. In general, larger fish have more eggs, but fish from small runs are said to be more fecund than those of the same size from large populations (Nikolskii, 1952). Development requires 61 to about 130 days, depending largely on temperature. Initial temperatures above 4.5°C are needed for normal development. Lower temperatures lead to deformities and high mortality (Bailey and Evans, 1971). The young hatch out from late December through February and remain in the gravel until spring. Mortality within the redd occurs chiefly before the eyed stage, and survival from spawning to emergence from the gravel shows a strong inverse correlation with the number of adult spawners (Hanavan, 1954; Hunter, 1959). The alevins have large yolk sacs, the yolks sustaining the alevins while they remain buried in the gravel through the winter. Usually in April or early May the yolk is fully absorbed and the young fry, now 3 to 4.5 cm long, wriggle up through the gravel. Almost immediately they begin to move downstream to the sea. Most of the fry swim downstream at night, staying at or close to the surface of the water. Migrations of up to 16 km may be accomplished in a single night. In short streams, or from spawning areas near a river mouth, the migration to the sea may be accomplished in a single night. If not, the fry hide in the gravel during the day and resume their downstream movement the next night (Neave, 1955). Sometimes the fry become daylight-adapted, in which case they school and no longer hide during the day. This is particularly apparent in fry that have been migrating for several days (Hoar, 1956). In southeastern Alaska, this out-migration begins in March, peaks in mid-May and ends by mid-June. The young fish are about 3 cm long at this time. They stay in the estuary for about a month, growing to a length of about 4 cm, then follow the salinity gradient within the estuary (Thorsteinson, 1962; McInerney, 1964) and move off, generally staying fairly close to shore. Larger fry tend to migrate first, so schools farthest from the river mouth tend to be made up of larger individuals than schools close to the river. Within a school the larger fry are usually found on the offshore side of the school. When the fry have reached a length of 6 to 8 cm they move offshore (Le Brasseur and Parker, 1964).

The life cycle normally takes two years, though rare 3-year-old fish have been found (Anas, 1959; Turner and Bilton, 1968). It is probable that these fish are sterile.

Mortality during early sea life is fairly high, 2% to 4% per day for the first 40 days. Predation by birds, fishes and various invertebrates may be an important factor in mortality at this time. In the subsequent 410 days this mortality rate changes, resulting in an average sea mortality of .4% to .8% per day. These rates are highly variable, however, with sea survival computed at about 2% to 22% and probably averaging about 5% (Neave, 1953; Parker, 1966; Novotny and Mahnken, 1971).

During their oceanic life, pink salmon from the southern part of the range tend to remain in a broad band of ocean more or less parallel to the coast. Alaskan pinks, on the other hand, may be found in most of the northeast Pacific, from the Bering Strait southwestward to about Kiska Island in the Aleutians, and from there more or less southeasterly to the California coast (Hart, 1973).

In the sea the young feed chiefly on copepods and larvacean tunicates *(Oikopleura)*. As the fish grow there is a shift towards amphipods, euphausiids and fishes. Other items include ostracods, decapod larvae, cirripeds and tunicates (Levanidov and Levanidova, 1957; Le Brasseur, 1966a; Manzer, 1969; Bailey et al., 1975).

After spending about 18 months in the sea, the adults return to spawn in their natal streams. The pink salmon is less certain in its homing than the other Pacific salmons, and there is a certain degree of wandering. Pink salmon have been found spawning in streams as much as 640 km from the natal streams.

In general the upstream run seems to be triggered by high water. A significant correlation has been found between the number of fish entering a stream each day, the daily water level in the stream and the daily rainfall in the area. But if water levels are too high and the current too strong, the fish stay in eddies and wait for a drop to suitable current strength (Pritchard, 1936a).

The males are usually larger than the females and tend to precede the females in entering fresh water. Early-running females tend to be larger than late arrivals (Skud, 1955). Due to the two-year life cycle, the runs in odd-numbered and even-numbered years are genetically separated, often with observable, though minor, morphological differences. Thus, in British Columbia, the adults of the odd-year cycle are consistently larger than those of the even-year runs (Godfrey, 1959).

The pink salmon occasionally hybridizes in nature with the chum. Artificially produced hybrids show characteristics of both parent species rather than being intermediate between the two. The hybrids exhibit the size of the chum, but have the short (two- or three-year) life cycle of the pink. Most of the hybrids return as two-year-olds, a group in which males have been known to outnumber females by as much as 4.2:1. In those returning as three-year-olds, the sex ratio was reversed. The pink-chum hybrid is fertile, but data are not available to indicate whether or not self-sustaining populations could be established (Simon and Noble, 1968).

IMPORTANCE TO MAN

Until World War I the pink salmon was of negligible importance in North America either for subsistence or commercial use. Demands for food during the war, however, led to rapid growth of the fishery. The pink salmon is the most numerous of the Pacific salmons and the annual pack in North America runs from several million to tens of millions of kilograms annually. The U.S. catch in recent years has ranged from a low of 23 million kg in 1967 to a high of 53 million kg in 1970. Alaska's share of these catches has run between 88.1% and 99.96%, but the price per pound paid to Alaskan fishermen is usually somewhat less than the U.S. average, which has ranged from $.30 to $.40 per pound in recent years. The pink salmon is considered only slightly better than the chum and is priced accordingly. Thus, while pinks since 1967 have made up from 23.9% to 41.9% of the total pack, they have accounted for only 12.9% to 26.8% of the total value. Virtually all the catch is canned.

About 20 years ago it was discovered that pink salmon in the sea will take a trolled lure. Since that time a small sport fishery for pinks has developed (Scott and Crossman, 1973).

CHINOOK SALMON
ALSO KNOWN AS KING SALMON
Oncorhynchus tshawytscha (Walbaum)

DISTINCTIVE CHARACTERS

The small black spots on the back and on the upper and lower lobes of the caudal fin, and the black gums of the lower jaw serve to distinguish the chinook salmon (Figure 35).

DESCRIPTION

Body elongate, fusiform, laterally compressed in adults; depth about 25% of fork length. Head moderate, its length about 20% of fork length but longer in breeding males. Snout blunt, less than 33% of head in females and immature males, but elongate and turned down in breeding males. Eye small, nearly round. Mouth terminal, slightly oblique, upper jaw reaching well behind eye. In breeding males both jaws elongated and curved, forming a kype. Teeth caniniform, present on both jaws, on head and shaft of vomer, on tongue and on palatines; anterior jaw teeth notably enlarged in breeding males. Gill rakers: 16 to 30, wide-spaced and rough. Branchiostegals: 13 to 19. Lateral line has 130 to 165 pored scales. Pyloric caeca numerous: 90 to 240, usually 140 to 180. Vertebrae: 67 to 75.

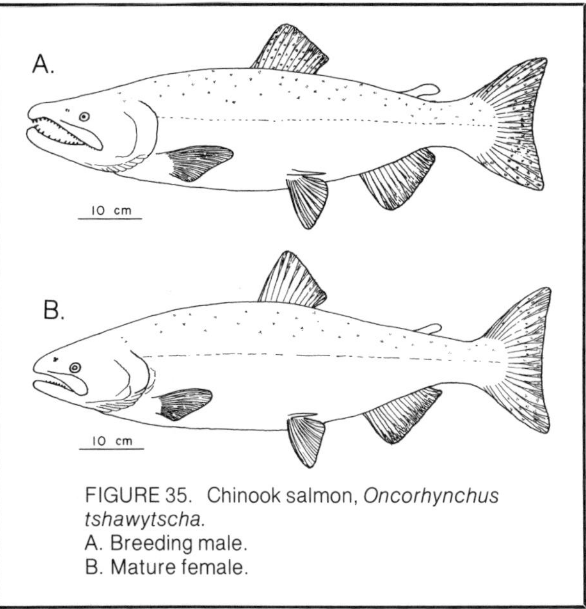

FIGURE 35. Chinook salmon, *Oncorhynchus tshawytscha*.
A. Breeding male.
B. Mature female.

FINS. Dorsal has 10 to 14 rays. Adipose fin present. Anal has 13 to 19; pectorals, 14 to 17; pelvics, 10 or 11, with axillary process present. Caudal emarginate.

SCALES. Cycloid, small.

COLOR. Fish in the sea are dark greenish to blue black on top of head and back, silvery to white on the lower sides and belly. Numerous small, dark spots present along back and upper sides and on both lobes of caudal fin. Gum line of lower jaw black. In fresh water, with the approach of breeding condition, the fish change to olive brown, red or purplish, the color change being more marked in males than in females (photographs, page 92; Plate 5, page 116; Plate 6, page 117).

SIZE. This is the largest of the Pacific salmons. The largest officially recorded came from Petersburg, Alaska, and weighed 57.3 kg, but another has been reported at 61.4 kg. In most areas, however, 90 to 104 cm and 12 to 18 kg would be the maximum size range. The average length for Cook Inlet chinook is about 75 cm for males, 85.5 cm for females, and average weight is about 7 to 9 kg (Yancey and Thorsteinson, 1963).

RANGE AND ABUNDANCE

Spawning populations of chinook salmon are to be found all the way from the Ventura River in southern California north to Point Hope, Alaska. The chinook is rare in streams south of San Francisco Bay, but it has been taken in the sea, as a stray, as far south as La Jolla (Hubbs, 1946). At the northern end of the range strays have been reported from the Coppermine River, which empties into the Arctic Ocean at about 115°W. The marine adults range all across the northern Pacific Ocean and through the Bering Sea. Along the coast of Asia chinooks are known from the Anadyr River of northern Siberia south to Hokkaido in northern Japan (Shmidt, 1950). Asian populations are much smaller than those of North America (Nikolskii, 1961). Within its North American range the chinook is most abundant from the Sacramento River to the Yukon River. However, because of its anadromous habits, this abundance is highly seasonal.

Chinook have been introduced into many areas outside their normal range including the Great Lakes, eastern United States and Canada, Central and South America, Hawaii, northern Europe, Australia, Tasmania and New Zealand. Some of the Great Lakes transplants seemed to thrive at first, but sooner or later died out. Of all the introductions attempted, only those to New Zealand have resulted in self-sustaining populations (Davidson and Hutchinson, 1938).

HABITS

Adult chinook salmon return from the sea and move into freshwater streams to breed. The time of arrival at the main river mouth varies with geographic location and stock. In many streams in the southern part of the range, for example the Columbia River and the Fraser River, there are fairly well-defined early and late (spring and fall) runs, while farther north, for example in the Yukon River, there is only a single run, although it may be spread over a period of several months. The chinooks enter the Yukon in June and reach the Canadian border by mid- to late July. In Cook Inlet, chinooks may appear in the Susitna River as early as May, but most appear in late June and July (Yancey and Thorsteinson, 1963). As a rule the fish entering fresh water earliest are those that will travel farthest upstream. Spawning takes place from July to early September in the Yukon drainage, but the season may continue into November or even December in the southern part of the range (Briggs, 1953; Scott and Crossman, 1973). Chinook use remarkably few streams for major spawning areas. In British Columbia 50% of the spawning occurs in only 14 streams. In the United States, chinook spawn in some 380 streams from California to Alaska, although this figure does not include the numerous tributaries of the Yukon and Kuskokwim rivers (Aro and Shepard, 1967; Atkinson et al., 1967).

On reaching the spawning area in the natal stream, the female selects the spot for her nest. She turns on her side and gives several powerful thrusts, up and down, with her tail. The gravel, sand and debris thus loosened from the bottom are carried downstream by the current. Repeated digging at the same spot at intervals of five to ten minutes produces a pit, the redd, which may be more than 3.5 m long and 35 cm deep, although usually it is only about 1.3 m long. The female drives off other females during the period of nest digging, but pays little if any attention to males. She is usually accompanied by a dominant male and one or more subordinate males. The dominant male, in particular, drives off intruding males, although subordinates may undertake this activity if a new intruder arrives while the dominant male is engaged. During nest digging, the male may court the female by coming to rest beside her and quivering; by swimming about over her, touching her dorsal fin with his body and fins; and occasionally by nudging her side gently with his snout (Schultz, 1938).

When the pit is finished, the female drops into it, pushing her vent well down toward the bottom of the pit. She is immediately joined by the dominant male, sometimes by one or more subordinate males as well. The fish open their mouths, quiver and eject the eggs and sperm. The female at once swims to the upstream edge of the nest and digs. The eggs are quickly covered with the gravel displaced from the new pit, and the whole process is repeated until the female has voided all her eggs, a process which may take several days. The male then leaves and may mate with another female. The female continues to dig for a week or more, the digging becoming haphazard and aimless as she weakens. She finally dies, as do the males.

Fecundity of females varies with the population and the size of the individuals. Average number of eggs per female varies from about 2,600 to 8,500, with northern fish generally producing more eggs than southern. In Alaska, egg numbers range from 4,242 to 13,619 (Rounsefell, 1957; Yancey and Thorsteinson, 1963).

The eggs are large, .6 to .7 cm in diameter, orange-red in color and demersal. They hatch in 7 to 9 weeks in the southern part of the range, probably taking up to 12 weeks or perhaps a little longer in interior Alaska. The alevins remain in the gravel until the yolk sac has been absorbed, usually about 2 to 3 weeks after hatching, then work their way up through the gravel to become free-swimming, feeding fry. The young fish do well in cool, clear streams; warm, shallow lakes apparently are not suitable for them (Higley and Bond, 1973).

The fry may go to sea after only three months in fresh water, as is the case with fall-run fish in the Puget Sound area (Mason, 1965), or may stay in fresh water for as long as two (in rare cases three) years, as happens in the Yukon River. Most chinooks stay a year in the stream before migrating. During this period they feed chiefly on terrestrial insects, chironomids, corixids, caddis flies, mites, spiders, aphids, small crustaceans—virtually anything available to them, although they do not appear to eat fishes during their freshwater life. Growth is moderate during the freshwater existence. By the end of the first year, the young chinooks are 10 to 15 cm long, and by the end of the second year they may exceed 20 cm.

As the time for migration to the sea approaches, the young fish smolt up, losing their parr marks and becoming silvery. They tend to seek deeper water and avoid light. In the sea the young fish remain for a time near shore, where they feed mostly on herring, sand lance, terrestrial insects, crustaceans and mollusks (Foskett, 1951). In some areas there are seasonal changes in the diet, with euphausiids important in early spring and a shift to fishes in the summer (Prakash, 1962).

Some of the chinooks may remain close inshore throughout their lives (Milne and Ball, 1958), but others undertake extensive migrations. Fish from California to British Columbia reach the outer waters of southeastern Alaska. Others from the same populations and from Alaskan streams go even farther, entering the Gulf of Alaska gyre and moving extensively across the northern Pacific. In the spring of the year they seem to be scattered across the northern Pacific and in the Bering Sea, while during the summer their numbers increase in the area of the Aleutian Islands and in the western Gulf of Alaska (Manzer et al., 1965). However, many of the inshore fish in waters off southeastern Alaska appear to be of local origin (Parker and Kirkness, 1951; Mason, 1965; Royce et al., 1968). During ocean life growth is rapid, often averaging .5 kg per month. The chinooks feed largely on herring and sand lance, as well as on pilchards, walleye pollock, Pacific cod, tomcod, smelts, sand fish, rockfishes, sticklebacks, shiner perch, wolffish, anchovies, squid, euphausiids, amphipods and crab larvae (Pritchard and Tester, 1939, 1940, 1942). Sexual maturity is reached from age 2+ to 7+. Fall-run fish from the Columbia River are mostly 3+ and 4+ fish, but the spring run is dominted by those of 5+. In the Yukon River 6+ fish predominate.

The return to fresh water from the sea begins in the winter so that the first fish are near the river mouths by spring. Just how this oceanic movement is accomplished is not understood, but it may well be on the basis of inherited responses to electromagnetic cues (Royce et al., 1968). The final year in the ocean is very important for the chinook to attain full growth, so much so that maximum harvest can be achieved only by harvesting mature fish (Parker, 1960).

Once a chinook is in fresh water, the home stream is picked out through olfactory stimuli (Hasler, 1966). Despite the amazingly acute sense of smell, chinooks apparently do not respond to a wide variety of pollutants and are not deterred by them. On the other hand, minute amounts of extracts from mammalian skin (human hands, bear paws, deer feet, dog paws and sea lion meat) produce an immediate alarm reaction and a temporary halt to upstream migration (Brett and MacKinnon, 1952, 1954).

IMPORTANCE TO MAN

The chinook is a most important part of the Native subsistence fisheries of Alaska and British Columbia, and in former times held a similar position in Washington, Oregon and Northern California.

Commercially, most of the chinook catch is taken by trolling and is sold fresh or frozen. Some chinook are taken by purse seines and gill nets, and most of these go to canneries. In terms of poundage, the chinook, along with the coho, is a relatively small part of the Alaskan salmon catch. In recent years Alaska has produced an average catch of about 5.3 million kg of chinook per year, representing between 3.3% and 5.5% of the total Alaskan salmon catch. However, chinook is the highest-priced of the salmons so the value of the catch is on the order of 10% of the total.

Chinooks usually have red meat but some have white. Flesh color is probably genetically controlled. About 70% of the chinook of southeastern Alaska are of the red-meated form, the remaining 30% white (Finger and Armstrong, 1965). The red chinooks command a higher price.

As a sport fish, the chinook is highly regarded wherever it is found. Its large size, fighting ability and eating qualities all make it a much-sought-after species. In the Strait of Georgia region of southern British Columbia, as many as 93,000 adult chinooks have been taken by anglers in a single year (Scott and Crossman, 1973). In southeastern Alaska the sport catches from the Juneau and Ketchikan areas account for 2,000 to 2,500 fish a year. Herring is the most popular bait in those regions, the strip cut being the most successful followed by plug-cut and whole herring. Various artificial lures are also quite popular. Spinning from drifting or anchored boats is the most successful method (Finger and Armstrong, 1965).

The viscera of chinook salmon, normally discarded, have quite a high vitamin A content and have been used successfully as food for hatchery fish and, for this particular use, are said to be superior to beef liver (Butler and Miyauchi, 1947; Burrows and Karrick, 1947).

CHUM SALMON
ALSO KNOWN AS DOG SALMON
Oncorhynchus keta (Walbaum)

DISTINCTIVE CHARACTERS

Chum salmon are distinguished by the lack of distinct black spots on the back and tail and by the presence of 18 to 28 short, stout, smooth gill rakers on the first arch (Figure 36, page 70).

DESCRIPTION

Body elongate, fusiform, slightly compressed. Depth about 25% of fork length, usually slightly deeper in mature males than in females. Head about 22% of fork length, but much longer in breeding males due to elongation of snout and lower jaw. Snout usually blunt, moderately long, about 35% of head length in females, but much longer in breeding males. Eye round, rather small. Mouth large, terminal. Jaws of breeding male develop a noticeable hook or kype. Teeth caniniform, well developed on both jaws, on head and shaft of vomer, and on palatines and tongue. Gill rakers short, stout, smooth, rather widely spaced, with 18 to 28 on first arch. Branchiostegals: 12 to 16. Lateral line has 124 to 153 pored scales. Pyloric caeca numerous: 163 to 249. Vertebrae: 59 to 71.

FINS. Dorsal has 10 to 14 rays. Adipose fin present. Anal has 13 to 17 rays; pectorals, 14 to 16;

pelvics, 10 or 11, with an axillary process present. Caudal truncate to slightly emarginate.

SCALES. Small, cycloid.

COLOR. Large fish in the sea are dark metallic blue dorsally, becoming silvery on sides and belly. Fine dark speckling may be present but there are no definite large dark spots. At spawning the fish become dirty red on the sides and dusky below, with greenish bars or mottling on the sides. Females are less brightly colored than males (photographs, page 93; Plate 7, page 118; Plate 8, page 119).

SIZE. Known to reach 102 cm and 15 kg, but average size of mature fish in most places is about 60 to 70 cm and 4.5 to 6 kg.

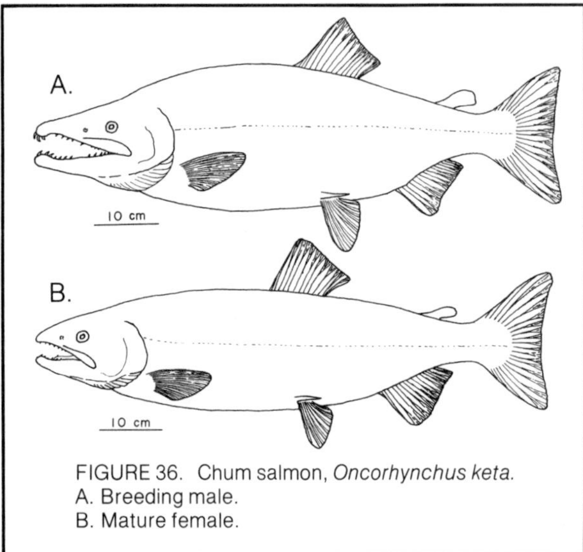

FIGURE 36. Chum salmon, *Oncorhynchus keta*.
A. Breeding male.
B. Mature female.

RANGE AND ABUNDANCE

The chum salmon ranges from the Sacramento River in California (and as a stray as far south as Del Mar, about 50 km north of the Mexican border) north to the arctic, east at least as far as the Mackenzie and Anderson rivers, west along the arctic coast of Siberia to the Lena River, and south on the coast of Asia to Korea and Japan. In North America it is most abundant from the Columbia River to Kotzebue Sound. The Yukon River is the greatest producer of chum salmon, although the catch is relatively small. The Noatak and Kobuk rivers support runs estimated at about 1 million fish each (Smith et al., 1966), but north of those rivers the runs are too small to be of more than incidental value.

HABITS

The chum salmon is typically a fall spawner, with the greatest spawning activity generally occurring in September and October. However, a ripe male was found near Fairbanks in February, 1962, and April spawning on Vancouver Island has been recorded by Wickett (1964), but these occurrences seem to be anomalies. In interior Alaska the first spawners appear in the Chena River, near Fairbanks, in late July and the run is at its height about a month later. Along the upper Yukon River, the major portion of the run passes the village of Eagle in August and early September.

In most areas there is a single run of fish and the fish do not travel far, seldom going more than 160 km or so upstream. However, in the Yukon River there are two distinct runs known as the summer chums and the fall chums. The summer fish average about 3 kg in weight and enter the river in June, although they sometimes arrive as early as late May. They spawn in run-off streams tributary to the lower Yukon, almost all of these streams being downstream from the mouth of the Koyukuk River.

The fall chums average about .5 kg more than the summer chums and do not enter the river until late June or July. The fish of this run, in addition to being larger, are also fatter and their flesh maintains its quality much longer. Their spawning grounds are in spring-fed streams (usually in the springs and ground-water seeps), mostly upstream from the Kantishna River. Some of these fish travel all the way to the headwaters of the Yukon in Teslin Lake, Yukon Territory, and British Columbia, some 3,200 km from the sea.

Quite early in the upstream migration the fall chum begin to segregate according to their destinations. By the time the fish reach the mouth of the Koyukuk River, about 800 km from the sea, fish bound for the Tanana River drainage are to be found along the south bank of the Yukon while those that will go farther upstream hold close to the north bank. It has not yet been possible to make more detailed analyses of the Yukon River populations.*

Similar summer and fall runs are present in the Amur River of Siberia. Again, the fall fish are larger (averaging about 73 cm as opposed to the 60 cm of the summer fish) and are more fecund (averaging 3,366 eggs per female against 2,468) (Nikolskii, 1961). Fish from other areas in Asia, as well as those in the streams of southeastern Alaska and farther south in North America, all appear to be summer chum (Lovetskaya, 1948).

Spawning usually occurs over gravel 2 to 3 cm in diameter, but chums have also been seen to use coarser stones, even bedrock covered with small boulders. In the upper Yukon drainage and also in the Amur River in Siberia, at least some of the fish select spawning sites in springs or ground-water seepages, presumably to protect the redds against freezing (Birman, 1953; Kogl, 1965). In preparing the

*F. Anderson, Alaska Dept. Fish & Game, Fairbanks: personal communication.

nest, the female faces upstream, turns on her side and gives several powerful flaps of her tail, thus displacing the smaller particles of the bottom, which are carried downstream by the current. Continued digging at the same spot produces a long pit—somewhat longer than the fish herself—up to about 40 cm deep. The female drifts into the pit, which apparently stimulates the attending males. She is joined by the dominant male and both fish open their mouths, quiver and extrude the sex products into the nest. The female may then proceed to dig a new pit at the upstream end of the first one, covering the newly laid eggs as she does so. The process is repeated until all her eggs are shed. The males take no part in nest digging, but are aggressive toward each other. One male usually dominates the rest, driving them away from the nest site. However, a female may spawn with several males, and a male may mate with more than one female. After the spawning is completed, the female remains near the nest and may continue digging, although in a haphazard, unorganized way. Fish of both sexes die a few days after spawning.

The eggs are large, up to .7 cm in diameter before fertilization (McPhail and Lindsey, 1970), and they swell from .8 to .95 cm after being fertilized (Mahon and Hoar, 1956). Major mortality of eggs seems to occur between fertilization and the eyed stage (Hunter, 1959). Hatching occurs from December to February in the more southerly parts of the range, depending largely on temperature. Time of hatching in interior and northern Alaska is not definitely known, as it must take place while the streams are still ice-covered. However, in an experiment, eggs fertilized on September 30 were placed in artificial redds in the Chena River and were observed to hatch between November 17 and December 31 (Kogl, 1965). The alevins remain in the gravel until the yolk sac is absorbed, 60 to 90 days after hatching (Nikolskii, 1961). They then make their way up through the gravel and begin migration to the sea. The young chums can stand temperatures up to about 23.8 °C but, along with the pinks, are the least resistant of the Pacific salmons to prolonged exposure to high temperatures (Brett, 1952). Young chum with only a short distance to travel probably do not feed until they reach the ocean. However, those that must spend several days to weeks on their journey feed actively on chironomid larvae and cladocerans (water fleas) such as daphnids and bosminids, and may grow significantly before reaching the sea (Sparrow, 1968). Most of this seaward movement is accomplished at night, the young fish hiding in the stream bottom during the day (Neave, 1955; Hoar, 1956; Meehan and Siniff, 1962). However, when the migrations are long, the fish may travel in daylight as well. The young chum may form schools while still in fresh water and always do so upon reaching the estuaries.

Once in the sea, the young chum, now up to 7 cm long, remain close to shore for several months before dispersing into the open ocean. Alaskan chum salmon occupy the Chukchi and Bering seas and are found westward along the Aleutian chain to about 178 °E, southward in the Gulf of Alaska to about 43 °N, and eastward to the North American coast. Chums from the southern part of the North American range tend to stay in the Gulf of Alaska and regions along the coast to the south, while Asian chums may spread out through virtually the entire north Pacific Ocean. The fish are found from close to the surface down to at least 61 m. There is some indication of vertical movement according to the time of day, with the fish tending to go toward the surface of the water at night and deeper during the day (Manzer, 1964). This is probably a response to movements of food organisms.

Growth is fairly rapid in the sea and the chums attain weights of 3.6 to 5.5 kg in three or four years. A large portion of this growth is accomplished during the final year in the sea, so much so that it has been estimated that high-seas fishing for chum results in more than a 50% loss of total yield (Ricker, 1964). After three or four years in the sea, the adult chums return to spawn in the natal streams. The average time spent in the sea varies to some extent with geographical location. In general, fish from the southern part of the range return to the streams during their third or fourth years, while those from the Yukon (and probably other far northern rivers as well) return mostly in their fourth and fifth years (Gilbert, 1924; Chatwin, 1953). Fish that have only a short freshwater journey ahead of them may begin to show pale flesh, less oil, sexual dimorphism and spawning colors even before they enter the river. By contrast, fish facing long freshwater trips are still silvery when they enter rivers, their flesh still red and oily, and the males have not yet developed a kype. The closer to the spawning grounds the fish are, the more pronounced are the secondary sex characteristics, spawning colors and loss of fats.

Upon reaching the sea, the young chum salmon feed largely on many varieties of small crustaceans, on terrestrial insects and young herring (Foskett, 1951). In an experimental situation, copepods between .16 and .45 cm long were the preferred food, to the almost total exclusion of other items (Le Brasseur, 1966b). Farther at sea the diet consists largely of copepods and tunicates (Larvaceae) (Manzer, 1969) as well as euphausiids, pteropod mollusks, squids and a variety of fishes. Upon reaching fresh water on the spawning run, the adults cease feeding. The digestive tract may undergo considerable shrinkage and degeneration at this time.

IMPORTANCE TO MAN

Although generally regarded as one of the less desirable species of salmon, the chum has always been an important source of food for native peoples as well as for their dogs. (The alternative name, dog salmon, comes from its long-standing use as dog food.) Large numbers of chums are still taken with gill nets and fish wheels and are smoked and/or dried for winter subsistence. The commercial fishery for chum began about 1893 on the Columbia River when a scarcity of other species made the chum profitable (Craig and Hacker, 1940). However, the yellowish color and low fat content of the flesh make for a product less desirable than sockeye. The price for chums is scarcely higher than that for pinks. Still, the species is abundant and Alaskan landings in recent years have ranged between 10 and 25 million kg, with values to the fisherman on the order of $.10 to $.13 per pound (Anonymous, 1971, 1972, 1973, 1974). In 1976 chum salmon brought Cook Inlet's commercial fishermen $.50 per pound.* Fluctuations in landings are the result of several factors including abundance, price and abundance of higher-priced species. The chum salmon is not considered a sport fish. Nevertheless, chums will often take small spinners and the angler who is equipped for Dolly Varden or grayling and who hangs a chum will find that he or she has tangled with a worthy opponent.

COHO SALMON
ALSO KNOWN AS SILVER SALMON
Oncorhynchus kisutch (Walbaum)

DISTINCTIVE CHARACTERS

The coho is characterized by the presence of small black spots on the back and on the upper lobe of the caudal fin, and by the lack of dark pigment along the gum line of the lower jaw (Figure 37).

DESCRIPTION

Body elongate, streamlined, somewhat compressed. Depth 22% to 25% of fork length, deepest in adult males. Head about equal to body depth, but longer in breeding males. Snout bluntly pointed, about 33% of head in adult females, about 40% of head in breeding males. Eye small, round. Mouth terminal, gape reaching well behind eye; upper and lower jaws of breeding males hooked. Teeth sharp, well developed, present on both jaws, on head and shaft of vomer, on palatines and on tongue, but not on basibranchials. Gill rakers: 18 to 25 on first arch; rough, widely spaced. Branchiostegals: 11 to 15. Nearly straight lateral line has 112 to 148 pored scales. Pyloric caeca: 45 to 114. Vertebrae: 61 to 69.

FINS. Dorsal has 9 to 13 rays. Slender adipose fin present. Anal has 12 to 17 rays; in young fish first ray is longest, resulting in a curved outer margin. Pectorals, 13 to 16 rays; pelvics, 9 to 11, with axillary process present.

SCALES. Cycloid, small.

COLOR. Fish in or fresh from the sea are dark metallic blue or greenish on the back and upper sides, a brilliant silver color on middle and lower sides, and white below. Small black spots present on back and upper sides and on upper lobe of caudal fin. Fish in breeding condition turn dark to bright green on the head and back, bright red on the sides, and often dark on the belly. Females are less brightly colored than males (photographs, page 94; Plate 9, page 120; Plate 10, page 121).

SIZE. The record for size was long held by a fish of 14.1 kg caught in 1947 in Cowichan Bay, British Columbia. However, a fish of 15 kg was later taken in the Manistee River, Michigan (Scott and Crossman, 1973). Usual weights of adults are between 2.7 and 5.4 kg. Such fish are usually between 63 and 90 cm long.

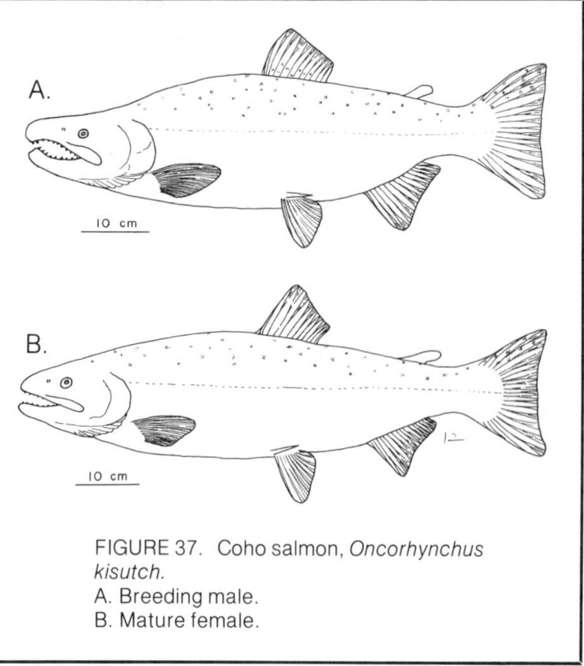

FIGURE 37. Coho salmon, *Oncorhynchus kisutch*.
A. Breeding male.
B. Mature female.

RANGE AND ABUNDANCE

The natural range of the coho is from Monterey Bay, California (although it apparently strays in the sea as far south as Chamalu Bay, Baja California), north to Point Hope, Alaska, westward across the Bering Sea to the Anadyr River in Siberia and south along the coast of Asia to Japan. In addition to introductions in the Great Lakes, cohos have also been planted in east coast waters from Maine to

*J. Rearden: personal communication.

Maryland. A few populations apparently have survived in New Hampshire. California, Oregon, Washington, Alaska and Alberta have planted cohos in lakes to provide sport fishing. These plants are strictly "put and take," for the planted fish do not spawn and the stocks must be renewed periodically. Despite the fact that the catches represent but a small percentage of the young fish planted, the cohos nevertheless provide a significant portion of the sport catch in these waters.

Nowhere are cohos as numerous as chums, pinks and sockeyes. Nevertheless, in most areas the coho probably should be considered as at least moderately abundant. Abundance is, of course, seasonal, depending on the arrival of the spawning run. When spawning is not taking place, adult anadromous coho are scarce or absent in fresh water.

HABITS

Coho salmon may enter fresh water on their spawning run any time from midsummer to winter. As a rule the winter (December and January) entries occur in the southern parts of the range, with appearance in fresh water becoming progressively earlier to the north. Entry of the fish into fresh water seems to be triggered by a rise in water level and possibly also by a rise in water temperature (Briggs, 1953; Shapovalov and Taft, 1954; McHenry, 1973).

The preferred streams are usually short coastal streams, but coho salmon are known to spawn in spring-fed tributaries of the Yukon system from the Bonasila River at least as far upstream as the Tanana. Within the Tanana drainage, virtually all spawning takes place in north-flowing streams draining the north side of the Alaska Range. Clearwater Creek, near Big Delta, is probably the greatest producer of coho salmon in this group of rivers. Reports of coho in streams above the Tanana, for example in the Chandalar River and various tributaries of the Porcupine River, may be valid. However, both the coho and chum are known as silver salmon in interior Alaska. Since the chum is one of the most abundant fish in the area, these reports of silver salmon far up the Yukon should be viewed with some skepticism until they can be verified.

On arrival at the spawning area, the female coho selects a suitable spot and begins to dig the redd. She turns on her side, facing upstream, and gives several powerful flips of her tail. The currents and suction so generated raise debris, silt, sand and pebbles off the bottom to be carried downstream by the current. Repeated digging in the same spot at intervals of two to five minutes produces a pit somewhat longer than the fish and usually 20 to 25 cm deep. The female is agressive toward other females, driving them away vigorously. The attendant male takes no part in nest digging, but usually stays slightly downstream and to one side of the female. He courts her by occasionally swimming close to her side, sometimes coming to rest beside her and quivering; by swimming over her and touching her dorsal fin with his body and fins; and by gently nudging her side with his snout (Schultz, 1938). The male drives other males away from the nest site.

When the pit is finished to the satisfaction of the female, she drops into its deepest part. The male joins her at once. The two fish, side by side in the pit, open their mouths, quiver, and expel the eggs and sperm. The eggs drop to the bottom of the pit, lodging in crevices between the stones, and are fertilized by the cloud of milt. The female immediately moves to the upstream edge of the nest and starts digging a new pit. The gravel so removed is carried downstream and covers the eggs just deposited.

Nest digging and spawning continue at intervals during the next several days to a week, until the female has deposited all her eggs. The male then leaves and may seek another female. The spent female usually continues to dig, but weakly and irregularly, until she dies.

The number of eggs a female deposits varies with the size of the fish, the stock and, sometimes, the year. Numbers have been reported from 1,440 to 5,700; the average is probably between 2,500 and 3,000.

The eggs are fairly large, .45 to .6 cm in diameter, and orange-red in color. Development time varies with temperature, usually taking six or seven weeks. Development periods up to 115 days have been reported from Asia (Nikolskii, 1961). The young remain in the gravel until the yolk sac has been absorbed (two or three weeks or more), then emerge as free-swimming fry and begin feeding.

At first the alevins are negatively phototropic, avoiding light. They begin to emerge from the gravel about 25 days after hatching and by this time, instead of avoiding light, they tend to swim toward it and also tend to swim upstream, 69% to 82% of the alevins exhibiting this behavior. The peak of emergence from the gravel, during which up to 94% of the alevins become free-swimming, is usually within the median 10 days of the emergence period (Mason, 1976).

The fry begin to feed as soon as they have left the redd. The major foods are terrestrial insects, especially Diptera and Hymenoptera. Aphids and thrips may also be important. The diet can also include mites, beetles, collembola, spiders and a little zooplankton. Feeding at this period involves shore-oriented cruising, both by individuals and by schools, at least when the fish are in a lake (Mason, 1974a). In streams in the summer young coho feed mostly on adult Diptera, Trichoptera and Coleoptera. These insects are taken near and at the surface; young coho feed but little on bottom-dwelling organisms. As the young fish grow, they consume larger food items and often become serious predators of young sockeye salmon. In Chignik Lake, Alaska, young coho have been found to eat seven times as many sockeyes as do Dolly Varden, and in other localities coho may be equally serious predators (Pritchard, 1936b; Ricker, 1941; Roos, 1960; Reed, 1967a).

The young coho normally spend a year in fresh water before going to sea, although some may go to sea at the end of the first summer and others, as in the Karluk River of Alaska, may stay two, three or even four years in fresh water. The longer stay in fresh water yields fewer but larger smolts that apparently survive better in the ocean (Drucker, 1972). Some fish that stay more than two years in fresh water—residuals—may become sexually mature without ever going to sea. However, residuals never spawn, so all residuals are the offspring of anadromous parents. Early migration may be the result of overcrowding (Mason, 1974b). Summer carrying capacity of a stream can be greatly increased by supplemental feeding, but this benefit is lost if winter capacity cannot be increased as well (Mason, 1974c).

During their life in freshwater streams the young coho stay almost entirely in pools, avoiding riffle areas. They soon become strongly territorial, defending their space against other coho and against other salmonids (Hartman, 1965).

After a year or two in fresh water the young begin to turn silvery (smolt up), avoid light and seek deeper water. They move downstream, usually at night (Meehan and Siniff, 1962), and reach the sea in the spring or early summer.

When the young fish reach the sea they tend to stay fairly close to shore at first, feeding chiefly on various planktonic crustacea. As they grow larger, the fish move farther and farther from the home river and feed on larger organisms. Most coho in the sea feed chiefly on herring, with sand lance second in importance. Fishes make up 70% to 80% of the cohos' food, the remainder of the diet being invertebrates (Pritchard and Tester, 1943; Prakash, 1962). Some populations, however, remain on the crustacean diet, such fish generally not growing as big as those that eat fish (Prakash and Milne, 1958).

The oceanic movements of coho in the southern part of the range seem to be chiefly along the coast, with some fish apparently never venturing far from land (Milne and Ball, 1958; Allen, 1965). By contrast northern fish, particularly those from Alaskan streams, spread out all across the north Pacific and into the Bering Sea. It has been shown that these fish travel "downstream" in the Alaskan gyre and other major current systems, making one complete circuit per year (Manzer et al., 1965; Royce et al., 1968).

Having spent two or three years in the ocean and having reached full adulthood, the coho now return to their natal streams to spawn. As a rule 85% or more of the returning fish return to the proper stream, but only about 1% of the fish that originally left the stream as smolts survive to adulthood (Vreeland et al., 1975). The mechanism by which they make the return journey through the open ocean is not known, but it has been suggested that inherited responses to electromagnetic cues are involved (Royce et al., 1968). Once in the river, the fish home, apparently on the basis of olfactory cues, to the tributary from which they migrated (Dizon et al., 1973a, b). The place to which they will return apparently is impressed on the fish at the time of smoltation, so that fish transplanted as yearlings will return to the transplant location rather than to the place where they were reared (Donaldson and Allen, 1958).

IMPORTANCE TO MAN

Although the coho does not rival the sockeye, pink or chum in terms of numbers, it is nevertheless an important part of the fisheries of the Pacific coast of North America. In recent years Alaskan landings alone have averaged about 4.8 million kg per year, with an annual value to the fishermen of about $2.7 million. The fish are taken by purse seine, gill net or trolling and are sold fresh, frozen, canned, mild-cured or smoked. Frozen coho is a luxury item on the east coast.

In addition to its commercial value the coho is highly regarded as a sport fish. It is taken in the sea by anglers using a variety of trolling lures and is taken in fresh water on large flies, spoons, spinners and several kinds of bait.

In the spring of 1966 the coho was introduced into the waters of the Great Lakes that border Michigan. In the fall of the same year commercial fishermen from Michigan started catching coho of up to 1 kg or heavier, and an angler caught a coho of 3.2 kg. The fish spread rapidly and successfully, aided by further introductions in other lakes. In the first nine months of 1970, U.S. anglers in the Great Lakes took 320,000 kg of coho salmon. The coho of the Great Lakes grow rapidly, having enormous populations of smelt and alewife for food, and by the time they are three-year-old adults the coho average about 2.5 kg in weight (Scott and Crossman, 1973).

SOCKEYE SALMON AND KOKANEE

ALSO KNOWN AS RED OR BLUEBACK SALMON

Oncorhynchus nerka (Walbaum)

DISTINCTIVE CHARACTERS

The sockeye—as well as the kokanee, which is the landlocked form of the sockeye—is distinguished by its 30 to 40 long, fine, serrated, closely spaced gill rakers on the first arch and by its lack of definite spots on the back and tail (Figure 38).

DESCRIPTION

Body elongate, fusiform, somewhat compressed laterally. Depth of body about 20% of fork length, somewhat deeper (about 25% of fork length) in spawning males. Head about 22% of fork length, longer in breeding males due to elongation of the jaws and development of the kype. Snout rather long, about 40% of head in females and immature males, considerably longer in breeding males. Eye round, small, 8% to 16% of head length. Mouth large, terminal, reaching well behind eye. Teeth caniniform, well developed, and present on both jaws, palatines, head and shaft of vomer and on tongue. Gill rakers long, slender, serrated and close-set: 30 to 40 on first arch. Branchiostegals: 11 to 16. Straight lateral line has 120 to 150 pored scales. Pyloric caeca: 45 to 115. Vertebrae: 56 to 67.

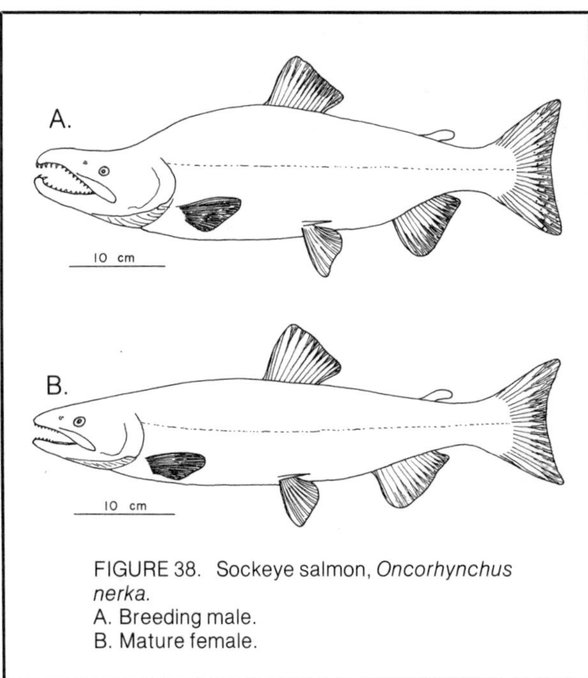

FIGURE 38. Sockeye salmon, *Oncorhynchus nerka*.
A. Breeding male.
B. Mature female.

FINS. Dorsal has 11 to 16 rays. Adipose fin present. Anal has 13 to 18 rays; pectorals, 11 to 21; pelvics, 9 to 11, with axillary process present. Caudal emarginate.

SCALES. Small, cycloid, the margins often resorbed in spawning fish.

COLOR. Prespawning fish are dark steel blue to greenish blue on the top of the head and back, silvery on the sides and white to silvery on the belly. There are no definite spots on the back, although some fish may have dark speckling and irregular marks on the dorsal fin. At spawning, the head of the males becomes a bright to olive green, with black on the snout and upper jaw; the lower jaw becomes whitish and the whole body turns brilliant red. The adipose and anal fins turn red and the paired fins and tail generally become grayish to green or dark. Various populations may show less brilliant colors, and a few turn dull green to yellowish, with little if any red. Females are generally less brilliantly colored than males (photographs, page 95; Plate 11, page 122; Plate 12, page 123; Plate 13, page 124).

SIZE. The sockeye is known to reach at least 84 cm and 7 kg, but the average fish in most areas will be in the neighborhood of 65 cm and 3 to 5 kg. The kokanee is much smaller, averaging about 35 cm and .5 kg or less.

RANGE AND ABUNDANCE

The sockeye salmon ranges from the Klamath River in California and Oregon north to Point Hope, Alaska. Stragglers have been reported from Bathurst Inlet in the Canadian Arctic Ocean. The most northerly population of any size is that of Salmon Lake on Alaska's Seward Peninsula. Sockeye have been taken in the Yukon River as far upstream as Rampart (UAFC #2023). On the Asian side of the Pacific sockeye are known from the Anadyr River in Siberia south to Hokkaido, Japan. The abundance of sockeye varies tremendously from place to place, the most populous areas being in the Fraser River system in British Columbia and in the Bristol Bay system of Alaska: the Kvichak, Naknek, Ugashik, Egegik and Nushagak rivers. In good years the runs to these areas may be in the tens of millions of fish.

The kokanee is known from Japan and Siberia on the Asian side and in North America from the Kenai Peninsula south to the Deschutes River in Oregon. It has been introduced widely into the Great Lakes, New England, various western and midwestern states and California. Kokanee may be extremely abundant in some lakes while in others the populations are small. There seems to be no particular explanation for the variation in population sizes.

HABITS

The adult sockeyes return to their natal streams during the summer and fall—from July to October in most areas—but as late as December in the southern part of the range. Spawning occurs almost exclusively in streams that connect with lakes, although some populations spawn in lakes and a few in streams with no lake. It is estimated that in the Copper River of Alaska about 20% of the run spawns in the delta. Lake spawners tend to breed later in the year than do stream spawners, but this is by no means universal.

As with other salmons, the female selects the nest site and makes the nest. Nest digging is accomplished by the female facing upstream, turning on her side on the stream bottom and giving several powerful strokes with her tail. This disturbs debris, sand and gravel, which are carried downstream by the current. Repeated digging at the same spot produces a pit somewhat longer than the fish and as much as 40 cm deep (Hanamura, 1966). The nest is usually constructed where the bottom is of fine gravel, but may be over large pebbles of 5 to 10 cm in diameter or even among large rocks. In the last case, no proper nest is dug (Ricker, 1966). Preferred sites have less than 10% of the gravel larger than 7.5 cm in diameter, about 50% of the gravel between 2.5 and 7.5 cm in diameter and the remainder smaller than 2.5 cm (Hoopes, 1962, 1972). During preparation of the nest, the female is attended by a dominant male and often by several subordinate males as well. The female is agressive toward other females and sometimes toward the subordinate males. The male is aggressive toward other males.

Between digging acts, the female often rests over the pit. The dominant male courts her by approaching her from behind, gently nudging her side with his snout, then coming to rest beside her and quivering. He may also swim over her, brushing her dorsal fin with his body and fins.

When the nest is completed, the female drops into it with her vent and anal fin well down in the deepest part of the pit. The male at once comes close beside her, both fish arch their bodies, open their mouths, quiver and extrude the eggs and sperm. One or more subordinate males may come to the other side of the female and join in the spawning.

The eggs, which are bright orange-red in color and .45 to .5 cm in diameter, fall into crevices in the gravel at the bottom of the nest, where they are fertilized by the male's milt. A female may deposit 500 to 1,000 eggs in a single nest. Having done so, she moves to the upstream edge of the nest and digs again. The gravel so disturbed is carried into the first nest, covering the eggs, and a new nest is dug just upstream from the previous one. The female usually produces between 2,500 to 4,300 eggs and will occupy three to five nests. Three to five days are normally required for a female to deposit all her eggs. She may spawn with several dominant males, and a male may breed with several females. All adult sockeye die after spawning.

Development of the eggs takes six to nine weeks in most areas but may require as long as five months, the time depending largely on water temperature (Hart, 1973). Hatching usually occurs from midwinter to early spring and the young emerge from the gravel sometime from April to June. There is strong positive correlation between intragravel water flow and egg survival. Deposition of silt in the redd, reducing water flow, may result in heavy mortality of the eggs. Oxygen consumption by the alevins in the nest is considerably higher than by eggs, further increasing the need for adequate flow (Cooper, 1965).

Upon emerging from the gravel, the fry at first tend to avoid light, hiding in the stones and gravel of the stream bottom during the day and emerging at night. In a few populations the fry go to sea during their first summer, but the vast majority spend one or two years in a lake before migrating and in rare cases spend three or even four years in fresh water (Margolis et al., 1966). The young sockeye in inlet streams go downstream to the lake, while those hatched in outlets swim upstream. The mechanisms of these different responses are unknown but they appear to be genetically controlled. In a few streams of the Copper River drainage young sockeye stay in the stream rather than going to a lake.

Once in the lake the young fish spend the first few weeks close to shore, feeding largely on ostracods, cladocerans (water fleas) such as *Bosmina,* and insect larvae. Subsequently, the fish become pelagic and move offshore, where they feed on plankton in the upper 20 m or so. The major food items during the summer are the copepod, *Calanus,* and *Bosmina,* with the latter preferred by the younger fish (Hoag, 1972).

Young sockeye eat many of the same foods as do threespine sticklebacks, so there may be competition for food between the two species. In some areas it is possible that this competition may be a limiting factor in sockeye production. As a rule, however, there is sufficient difference in the diets, and the overall food supply is large enough, so that this competition is not serious. However, when the ratio of available food to fish is unfavorable, as may happen when sockeye broods are extraordinarily successful, then the potential competition becomes actual. The result is poor growth of both sockeye and sticklebacks and—probably—reduced survival of sockeye (Rogers, 1968; Manzer, 1976).

The abundance of the sockeye fry is positively correlated with the abundance of adult spawners, and the growth of the fry through June is correlated with water temperature and an abundant food supply (Nelson, 1964; Narver, 1966; Rogers, 1973). Experimental fertilization of lakes to increase the standing crop of plankton has resulted in up to 30% greater size of under-yearling sockeyes. However, the increase in plankton was much greater. Apparently the upper layers of water are too warm for the young sockeye in July and August, leading to underutilization of the food (Le Brasseur and Kennedy, 1972; Barraclough and Robinson, 1972).

After a year in the lake (often two years in many Bristol Bay areas), the young sockeye lose their parr marks, turn silvery (smolt up) and migrate downstream to the sea. Smoltification is largely dependent on size, rather than age, and the threshold size seems to be determined by the genetics of the particular stock. Early-spawning adults tend to produce a greater percentage of age I smolts than do late spawners (Narver, 1966). In the Wood River system of Alaska the first smolts to migrate each year are age II, so they are probably late migrants from the upper lakes that encountered a temperature block and were forced to spend a second year in the lake (Nelson, 1964). In other systems, however, age II smolts seem to be the usual thing. Peak outmigration in the Bristol Bay region occurs in June, beginning when water temperatures reach about 4°C. Most of the migrants move at night, especially between 10 and 11 p.m. (Nelson, 1964), but schools of smolt leave Alaska's Agulowak River for Lake Aleknagik all day long in mid-July. In Babine Lake, British Columbia, the main movements are at dawn and dusk (Groot, 1965). The migrating smolts show well-directed orientation toward the lake outlet and travel 5 to 8 km each day in the lake, going farther on bright days than on cloudy ones. During the course of the migration, the fish reorient themselves according to the bodies of water to be traversed. Various mechanisms, including responses to celestial phenomena, polarized light and the immediate surroundings seem to be involved (Groot, 1965).

Once in the sea the young sockeye stay fairly close to shore at first, feeding mainly on various zooplankters (about 60% copepods) but also on small fishes and insects (Manzer, 1969; Carlson, 1974). As the young sockeye get bigger and stronger, they head out to sea. Fishes, especially sand lance, become more important in the diet. Sockeye from areas south of the Alaska Peninsula head out into the Alaska Gyre in the Gulf of Alaska. Those from Bristol Bay move westward along the north shore of the Alaska Peninsula and go through the eastern and central Aleutian passes into the Gulf. Salinity gradients are an important directive cue in this seaward migration. By late winter the sockeyes are spread in a band across the north Pacific south of 50°N. In late spring the young fish move north to between 50°N and the Aleutians, from about 160°W to 170° or 165°E. This appears to be an important feeding area, the major foods of the sockeye being amphipods, copepods and squid (Le Brasseur, 1966). When winter comes the fish separate into those that will mature in the coming spring and those that will spend another year or more in the sea. The early-maturing fish stay north of 50°N, while the others repeat the previous year's journey. In spring the mature fish head back to their natal streams, while the immatures continue to repeat the oceanic circuit (Thorsteinson and Merrell, 1964; Manzer et al., 1965; Margolis et al., 1966; Royce et al., 1968; French and Bakkala, 1974; Straty, 1974).

Most sockeye from British Columbia spend one year in fresh water and two in the sea, returning to spawn in their fourth year. Farther north, however, two years in fresh water and two or three in the sea are common. Therefore many Alaskan sockeye return in their fifth or sixth years. However, the four-year cycle is generally prevalent.

Growth of the sockeye in the ocean is rapid, especially in the final year. Because of this growth pattern, the inshore fishing practiced along the North American coast is the most efficient harvesting of the resource. Catching the fish at sea in the year before they mature results in loss of yield of 50% to 65% (Ricker, 1962).

The landlocked form of the sockeye, the kokanee, differs from the anadromous sockeye chiefly in spending its entire life in fresh water and in reaching a much smaller maximum size.

Kokanee, wherever they are native, have been derived from anadromous sockeye populations, and each kokanee population apparently has evolved independently from a particular sockeye run (Ricker, 1940; Nelson, 1968a). Offspring of kokanee occasionally become anadromous, and sockeye offspring sometimes will not go to sea. The lifespan of the kokanee varies from two to seven years in different stocks. The fish is confined to lake-stream systems and most of its life is spent in the lake, paralleling the sea life of the sockeye. In size the kokanee averages about 30 cm long in most locations although fish of over 60 cm have been recorded (Kimsey, 1951). Spawning time and behavior of the kokanee are like those of the sockeye (Schultz and students, 1935; Schultz, 1938). Fecundity, however, is related to the small size and is much lower than that of the sockeye, being on the order of 300 to 500 eggs per female.

Kokanee are either weak swimmers or, more likely, lack the strong urge to swim upstream that is so characteristic of the salmons. At any rate, small barriers effectively stop kokanee migrations (Seeley and McCammon, 1966). Spawning usually takes place in inlet or outlet streams, and sometimes in lakes near shore. All kokanee die after spawning.

Kokanee are mainly plankton feeders throughout their lives. In some lakes, however, there is seasonal variation in the type and quantity of food eaten. In Nicola Lake, British Columbia, the kokanee are known to feed most heavily in June and October, and less through the summer. Copepods of the genus *Diaptomus* dominated the food in the spring, chironomids in the summer and *Daphnia* in the fall (Northcote and Lorz, 1966).

IMPORTANCE TO MAN

The sockeye salmon is one of the most important of the Pacific salmons. Its flesh is of the highest quality, and although the sockeye is not as abundant as the pink and chum, the higher price it commands makes it the real "money fish" in the salmon industry. The kokanee is primarily a sport fish, generally well accepted by anglers despite its small size. Like the sockeye, the kokanee is excellent as food. It has been fished commercially in Lake Pend Oreille, Idaho. It is also well regarded in some areas as food for large trout, but in other places is looked upon as a competitor with the trout.

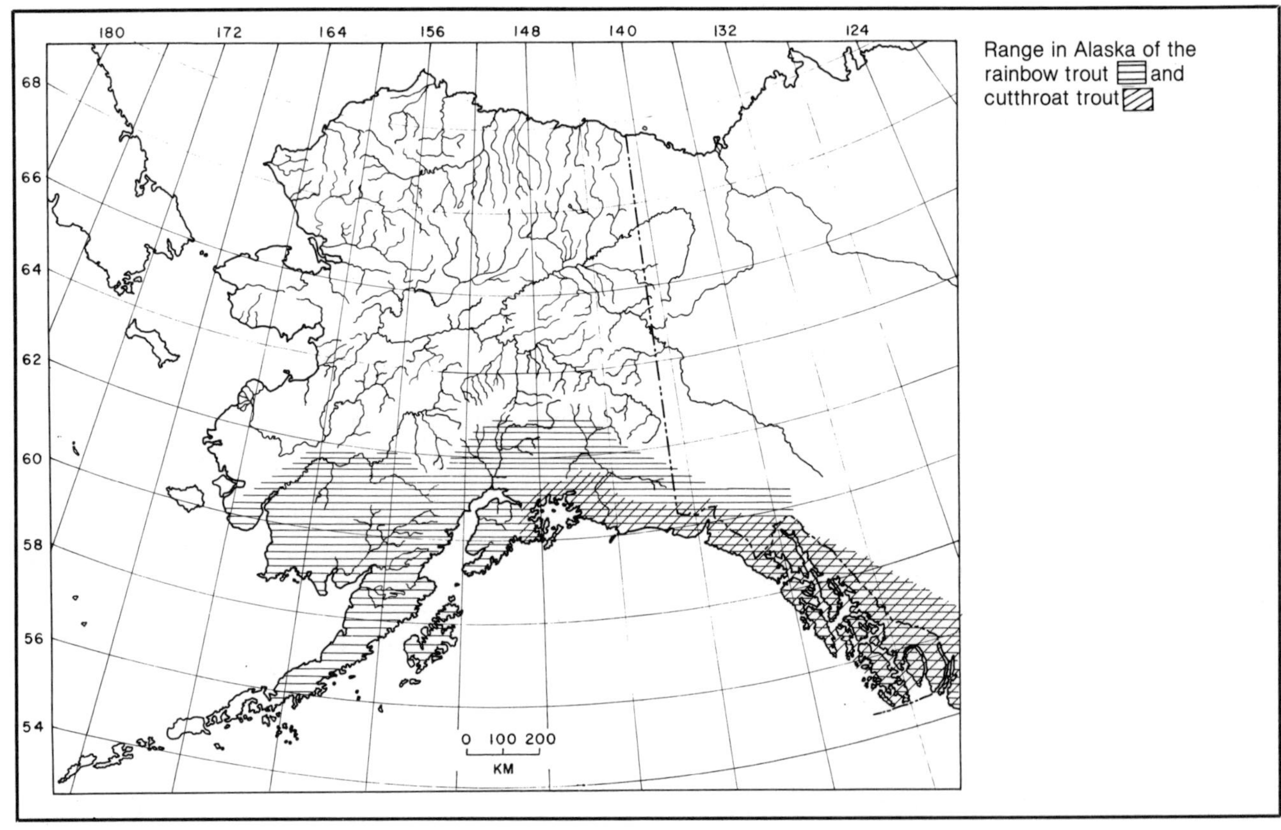

Range in Alaska of the rainbow trout ▤ and cutthroat trout ▨

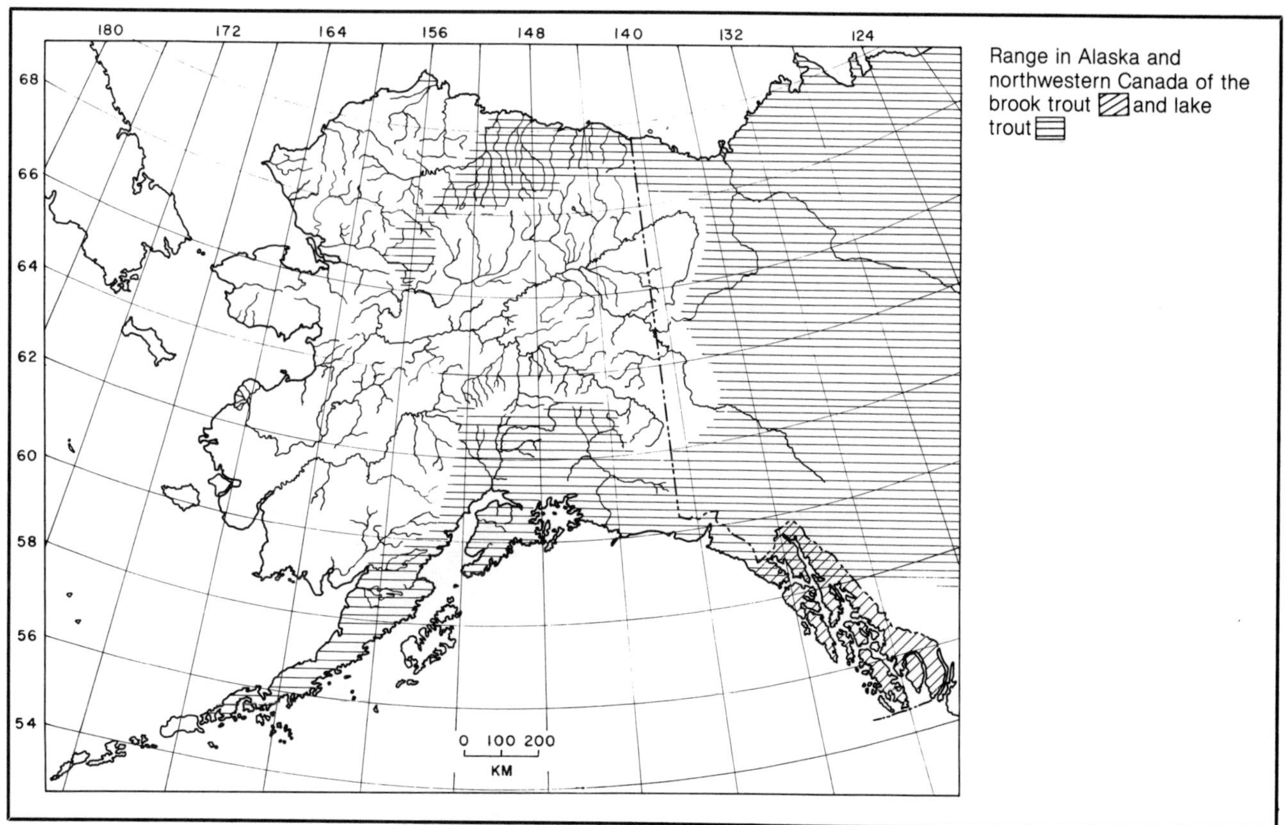

Range in Alaska and northwestern Canada of the brook trout ▨ and lake trout ▤

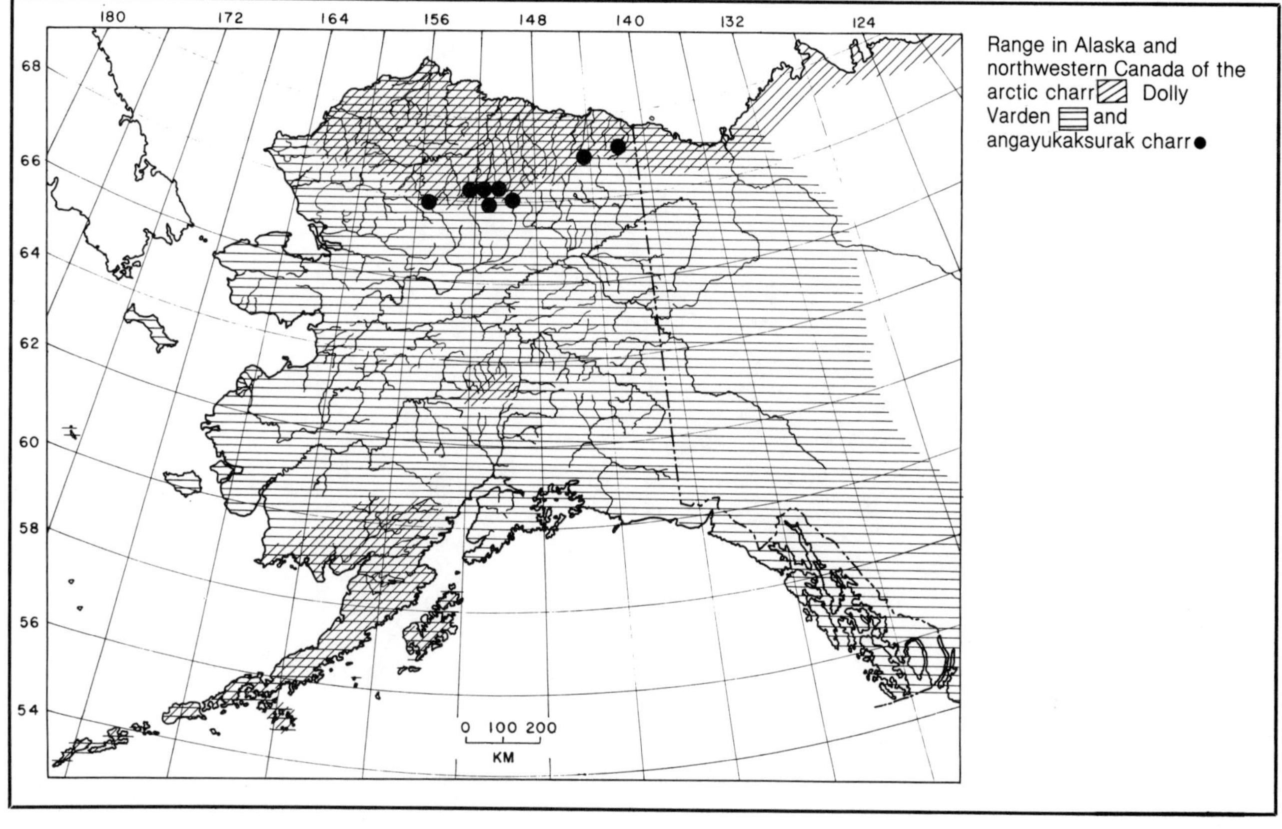

Range in Alaska and northwestern Canada of the arctic charr ▨ Dolly Varden ▤ and angayukaksurak charr ●

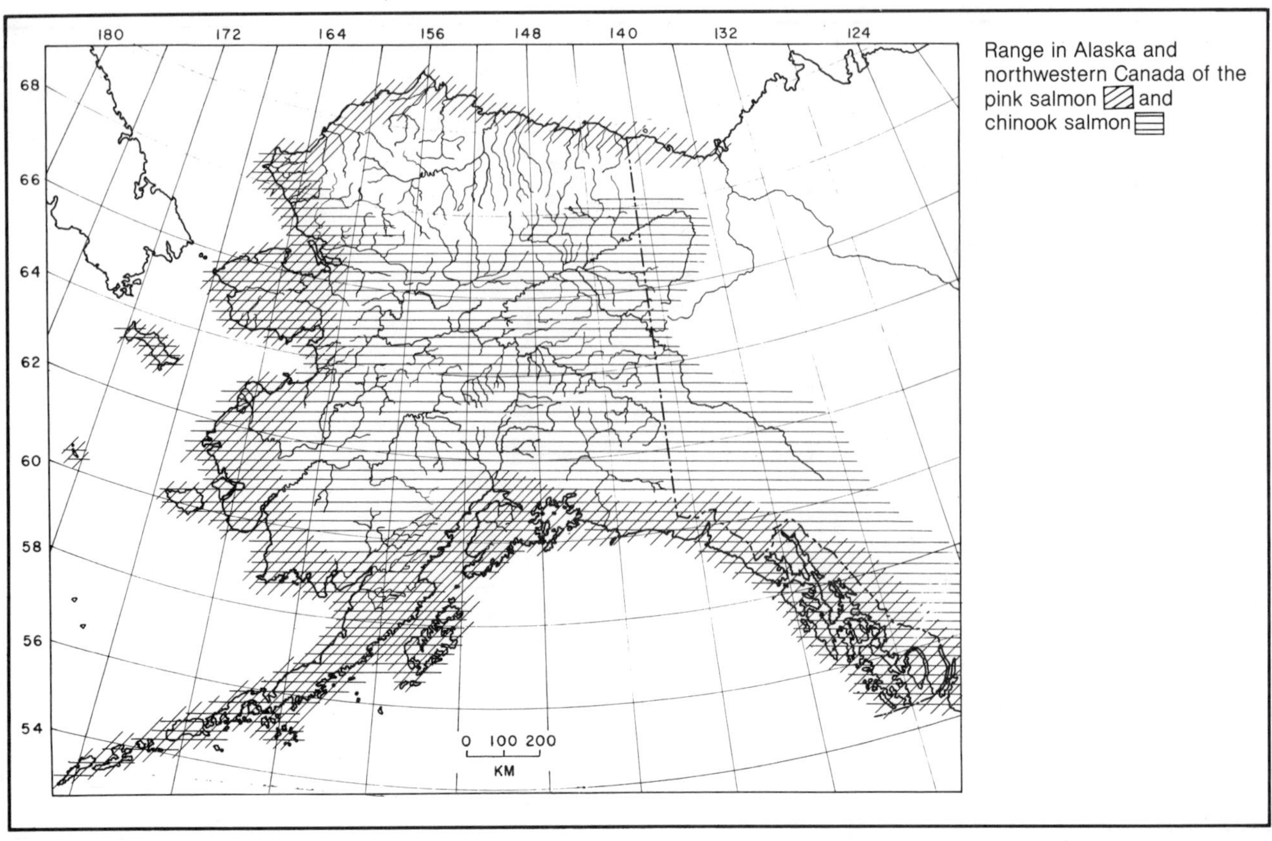

Range in Alaska and northwestern Canada of the pink salmon ▨ and chinook salmon ▤

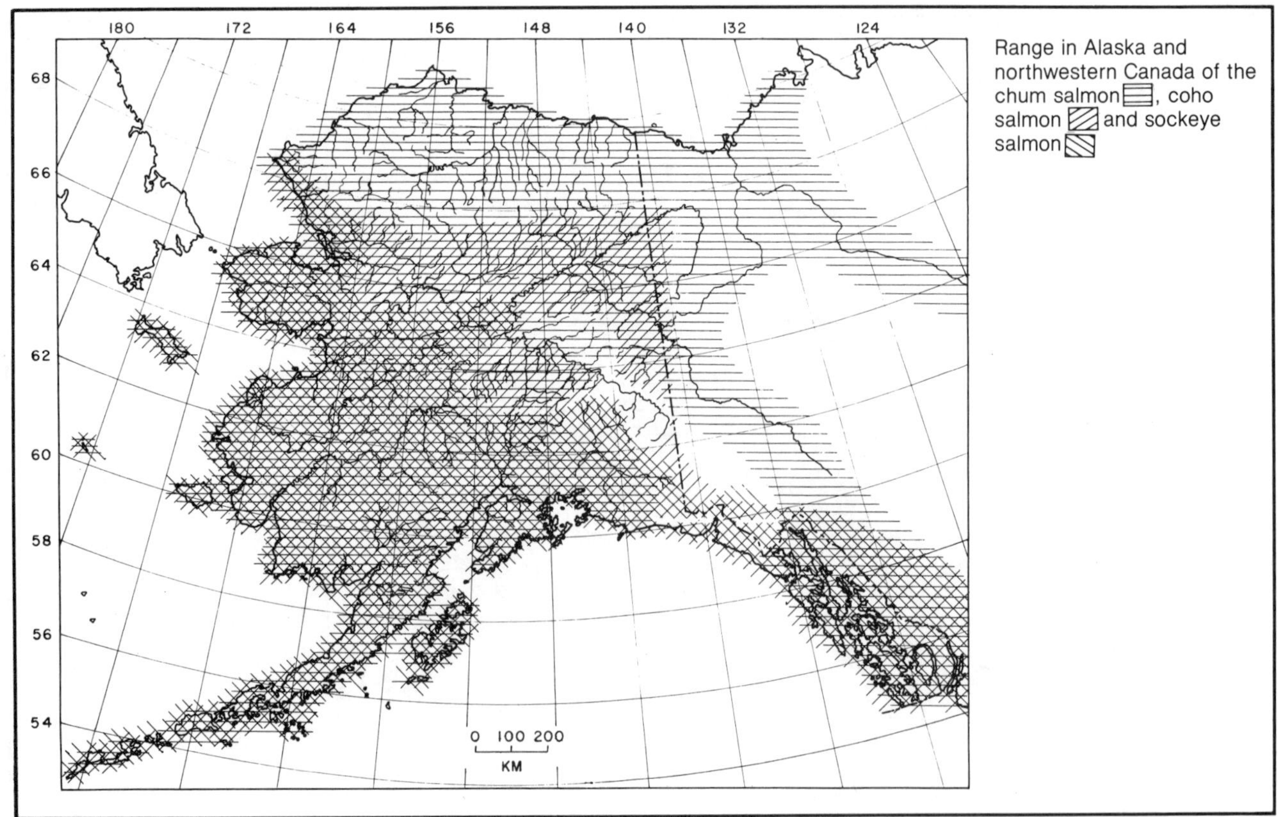

Range in Alaska and northwestern Canada of the chum salmon ▤, coho salmon ▨ and sockeye salmon ▧

IDENTIFICATION PHOTOGRAPHS

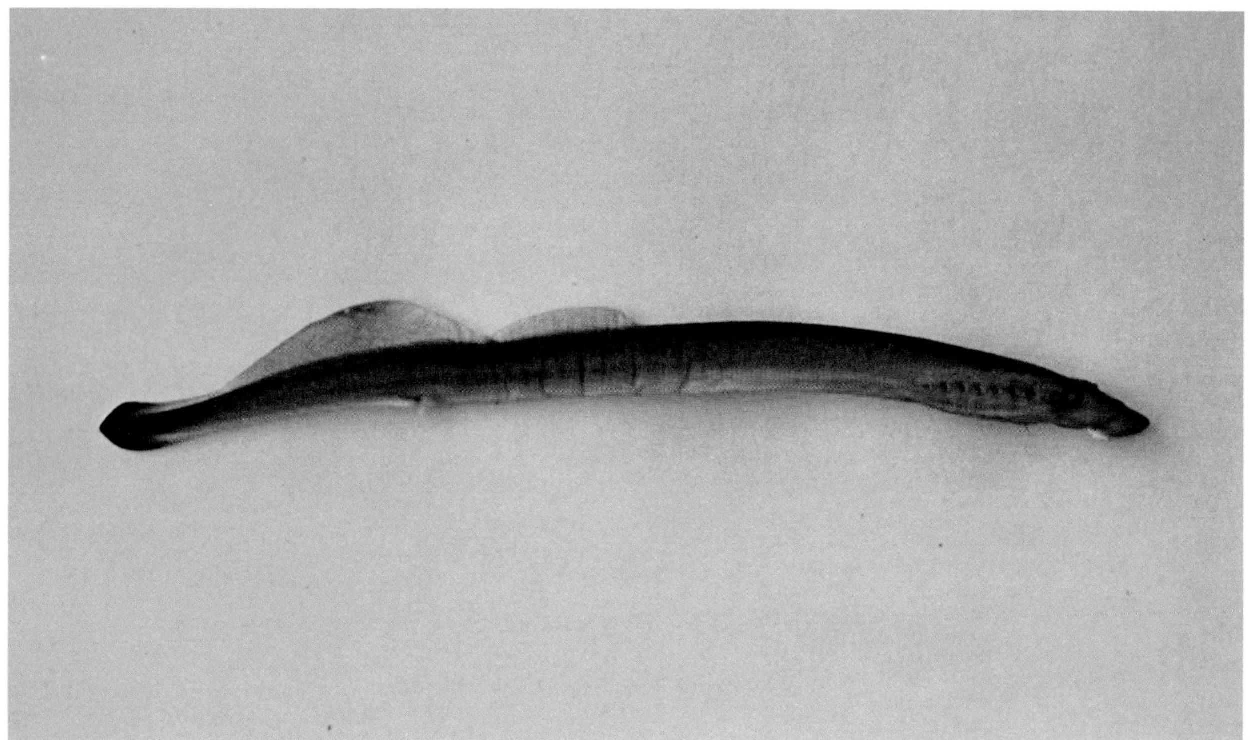

Arctic lamprey, *Lampetra japonica*

Green sturgeon, *Acipenser medirostris*

Richard R. Whitney, USFWS, UW

White sturgeon,
Acipenser transmontanus

Kenneth E. Lucas

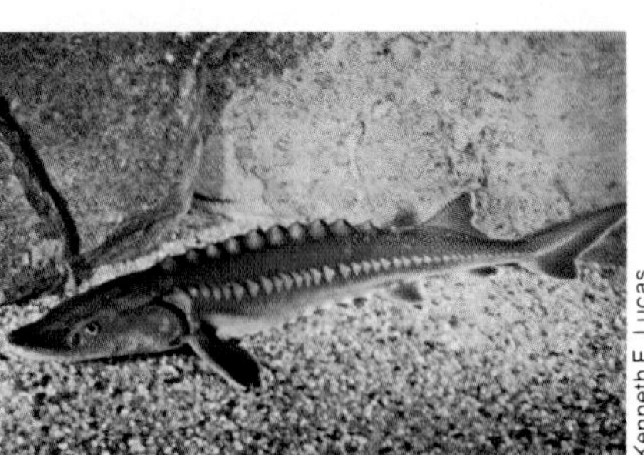

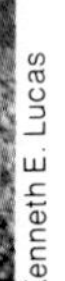

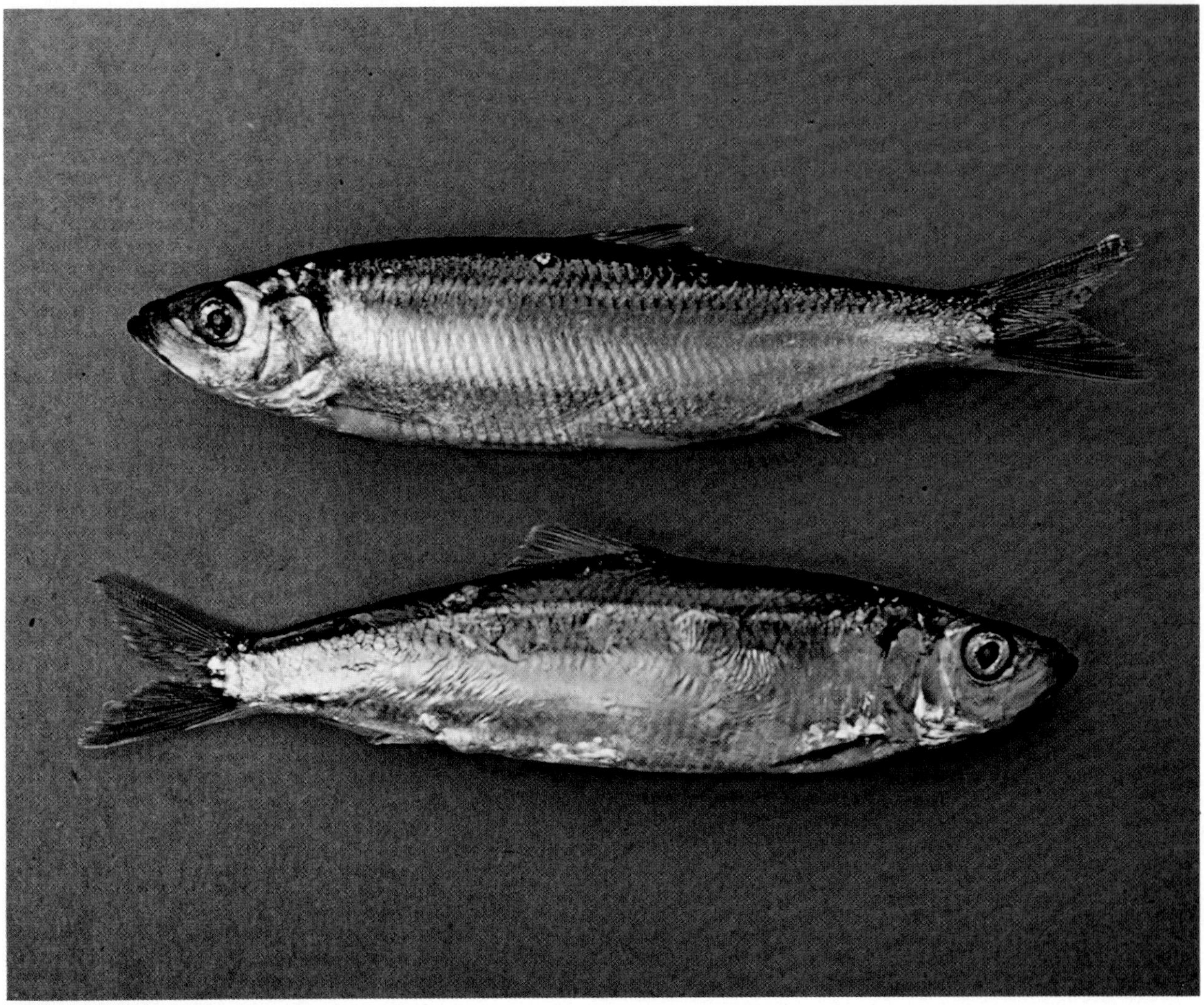

Pacific herring, *Clupea harengus*

Pacific herring spawning

John Helle

American shad, *Alosa sapidissima*

NMFS, reprinted from *Fisheries of the North Pacific*

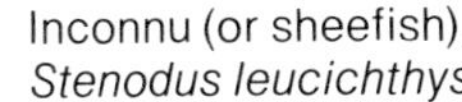

Inconnu (or sheefish),
Stenodus leucichthys

Kenneth T. Alt

Least cisco, *Coregonus sardinella*

Bering cisco, *Coregonus laurettae*

Rob Wolotira, NMFS

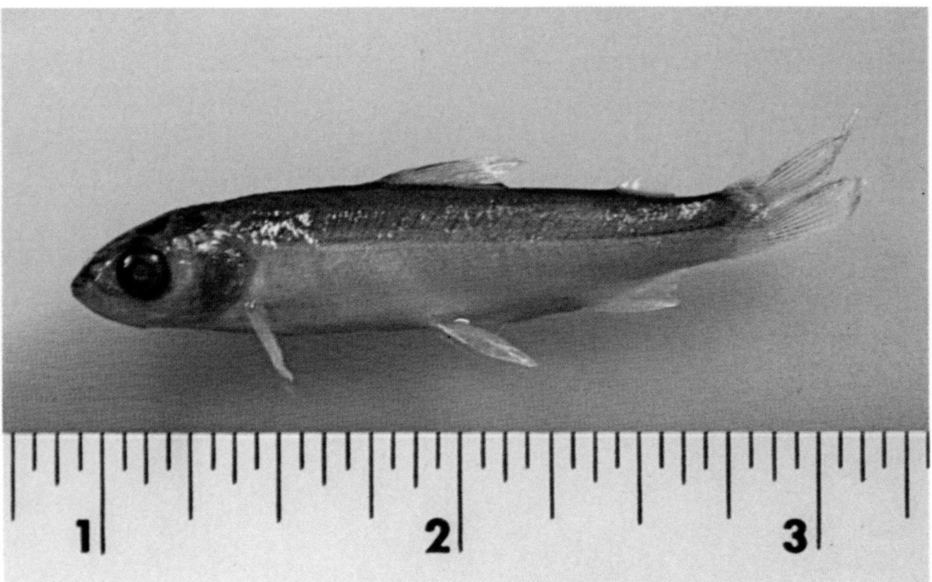

Bering cisco, juvenile

Pygmy whitefish, *Prosopium coulteri*

Round whitefish, *Prosopium cylindraceum*

Round whitefish, juvenile. Note round parr marks.

C.C. Lindsey, UM

Broad whitefish, *Coregonus nasus* (top); lake whitefish, *Coregonus clupeaformis* (bottom)

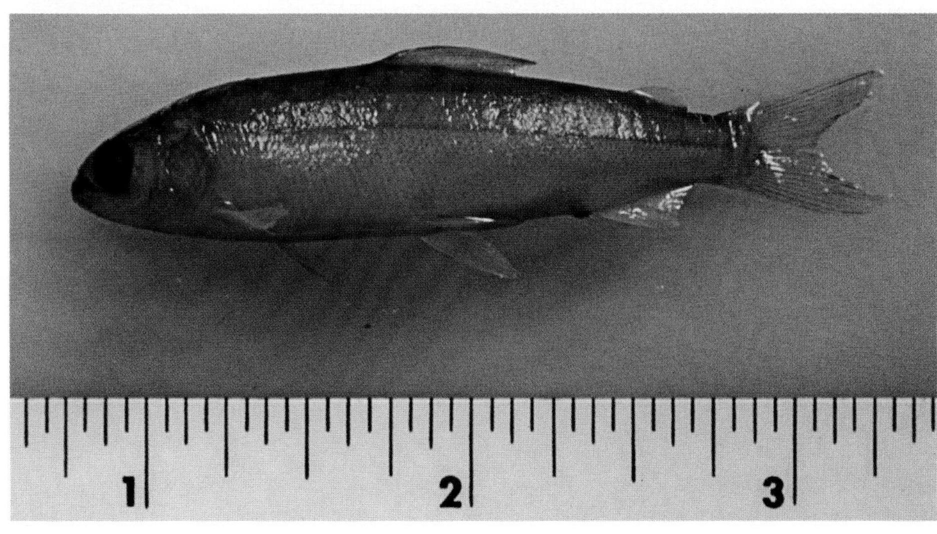

Broad whitefish, juvenile.

Alaska whitefish, *Coregonus nelsoni*

R.L. Wallace, OSU

Cutthroat trout, *Salmo clarki*

Tom Walker

Rainbow trout, *Salmo gairdneri*

Swedberg photo, MDFG

Brook trout, *Salvelinus fontinalis*

Lake trout, *Salvelinus namaycush*

Dolly Varden, *Salvelinus malma,* fresh from the sea

ADFG

Dolly Varden, spawning colors

Pink (or humpback) salmon, *Oncorhynchus gorbuscha*, fresh from the sea; female (top), male (bottom)

Kenneth T. Alt, reprinted from *ALASKA®* magazine

R. Redick, ADFG

Pink salmon, spawning colors; male (top), female (bottom)

Female chinook (or king) salmon,
Oncorhynchus tshawytscha, fresh from the sea

WSDF

Chinook salmon, spawning colors; male (top), female (bottom)

Chinook salmon,
young-of-the-year

WSDF, reprinted from *Fisheries of the North Pacific*

Chum (or dog) salmon, *Oncorhynchus keta*

John Helle

Chum salmon, spawning colors; male (top), female (bottom)

R. Redick, ADFG

Coho (or silver) salmon, *Oncorhynchus kisutch,* fresh from the sea; female (top), male (bottom)

WSDF

Coho salmon, spawning colors; female (top), male (bottom)

Coho salmon, juveniles

Female sockeye (or red or blueback) salmon, *Oncorhynchus nerka,* fresh from the sea

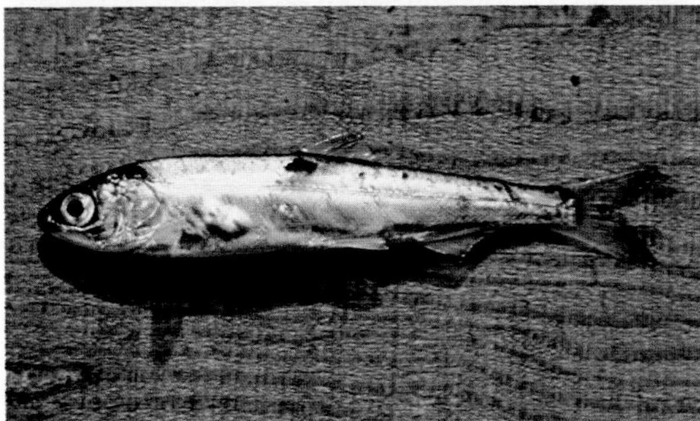

Sockeye salmon smolt

Rick Furniss

Sockeye salmon, spawning colors; male (top), female (bottom)

Arctic grayling, *Thymallus arcticus*

Rick Furniss

Arctic grayling, juvenile; note parr marks

L. L. Moulton,
Woodward-Clyde, Consultants

Longfin smelt, *Spirinchus thaleichthys;* male (top), spent female (bottom)

Pond smelt, *Hypomesus olidus*

Rob Wolotira, NMFS

Surf smelt, *Hypomesus pretiosus*

T. F. Pletcher

NMFS Auke Bay Lab

Eulachon, *Thaleichthys pacificus*

Rainbow smelt, *Osmerus mordax*

T. Bendock

J. Hout, reprinted from *ALASKA®* magazine

Alaska blackfish, *Dallia pectoralis;* the golden one is a rare albino.

Northern pike, *Esox lucius*

Northern pike, juvenile; note barred (rather than spotted) markings

Don McAllister, NMNS

Lake chub, *Couesius plumbeus*

C.C. Lindsey, UM

Longnose sucker, *Catostomus catostomus*

Longnose sucker, juvenile

Don McAllister, NMNS

Trout-perch,
Percopsis omiscomaycus

Burbot, *Lota lota*

L. L. Moulton, Woodward-Clyde, Consultants

Burbot, juvenile; 2.5 cm long

P.C. Craig

Arctic cod, *Boreogadus saida*

Pacific cod, *Gadus macrocephalus*

M. Dahlberg,
NMFS Auke Bay Lab

Rob Wolotira, NMFS

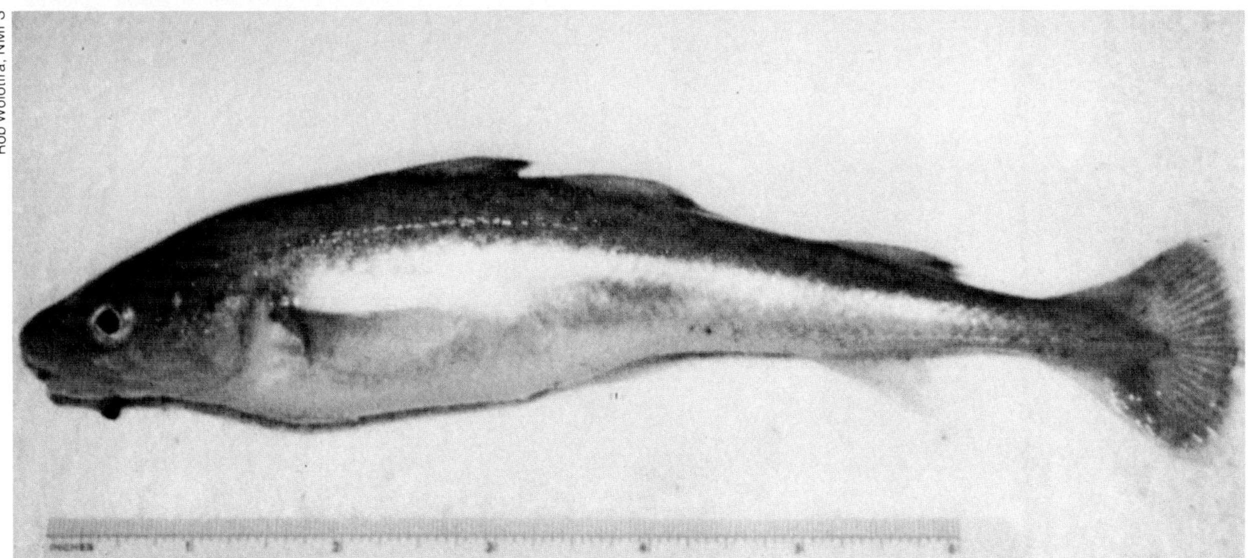

Saffron cod, *Eleginus gracilis*

Threespine stickleback, *Gasterosteus aculeatus*, breeding female

Don McAllister, NMNS

Ninespine stickleback, *Pungitius pungitius*

Norman Parks, NMFS

Shiner perch, *Cymatogaster aggregata*

Slimy sculpin, *Cottus cognatus*

H.F. Horton, OSU

Prickly sculpin, *Cottus asper*

Mike Chihuly, UA

Coastrange sculpin, *Cottus aleuticus*

Charles Simenstad, FRI, UW

Pacific staghorn sculpin, *Leptocottus armatus*

Fourhorn sculpin, *Myoxocephalus quadricornis*

Carl Bond, OSU

Sharpnose sculpin, *Clinocottus acuticeps*

Arctic flounder, *Liopsetta glacialis*

Starry flounder, *Platichthys stellatus*

Norman Parks, NMFS

WATERCOLOR AND CARBON DUST ILLUSTRATIONS by Marion J. Dalen

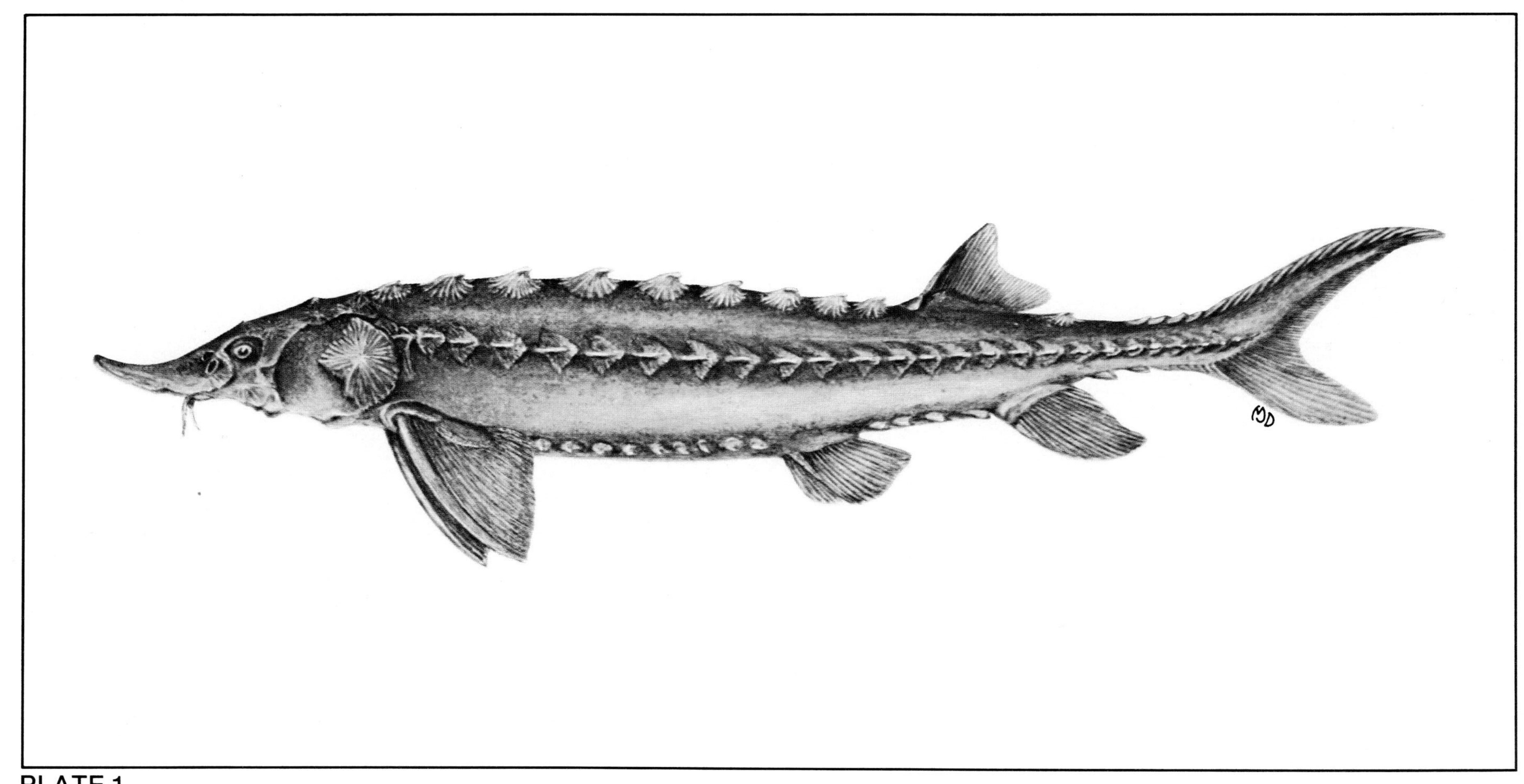

PLATE 1
Green sturgeon, *Acipenser medirostris*

PLATE 2
Rainbow trout, *Salmo gairdneri*

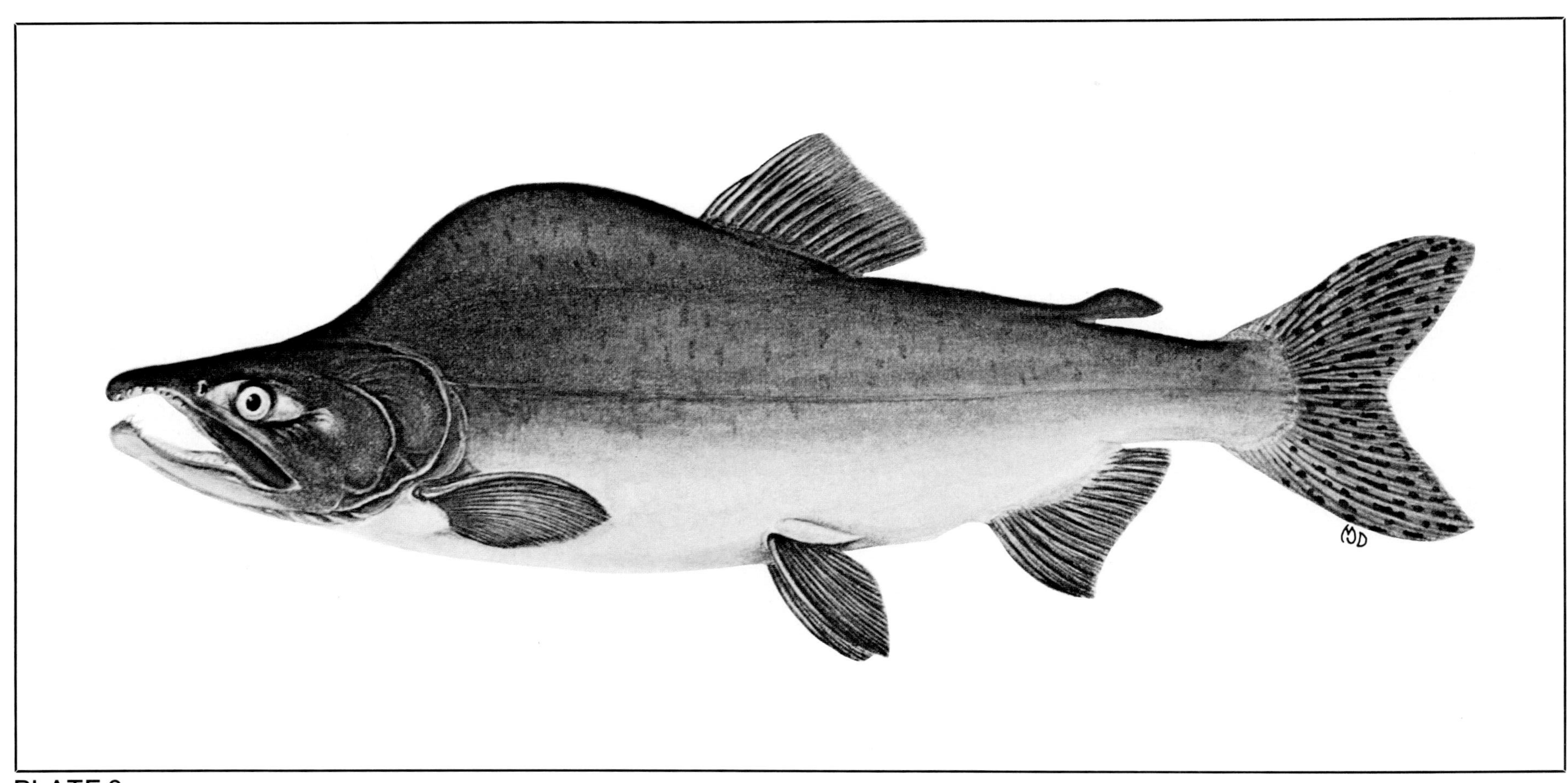

PLATE 3
Pink (or humpback) salmon, *Oncorhynchus gorbuscha;* spawning male

PLATE 4
Pink (or humpback) salmon, *Oncorhynchus gorbuscha;* spawning female

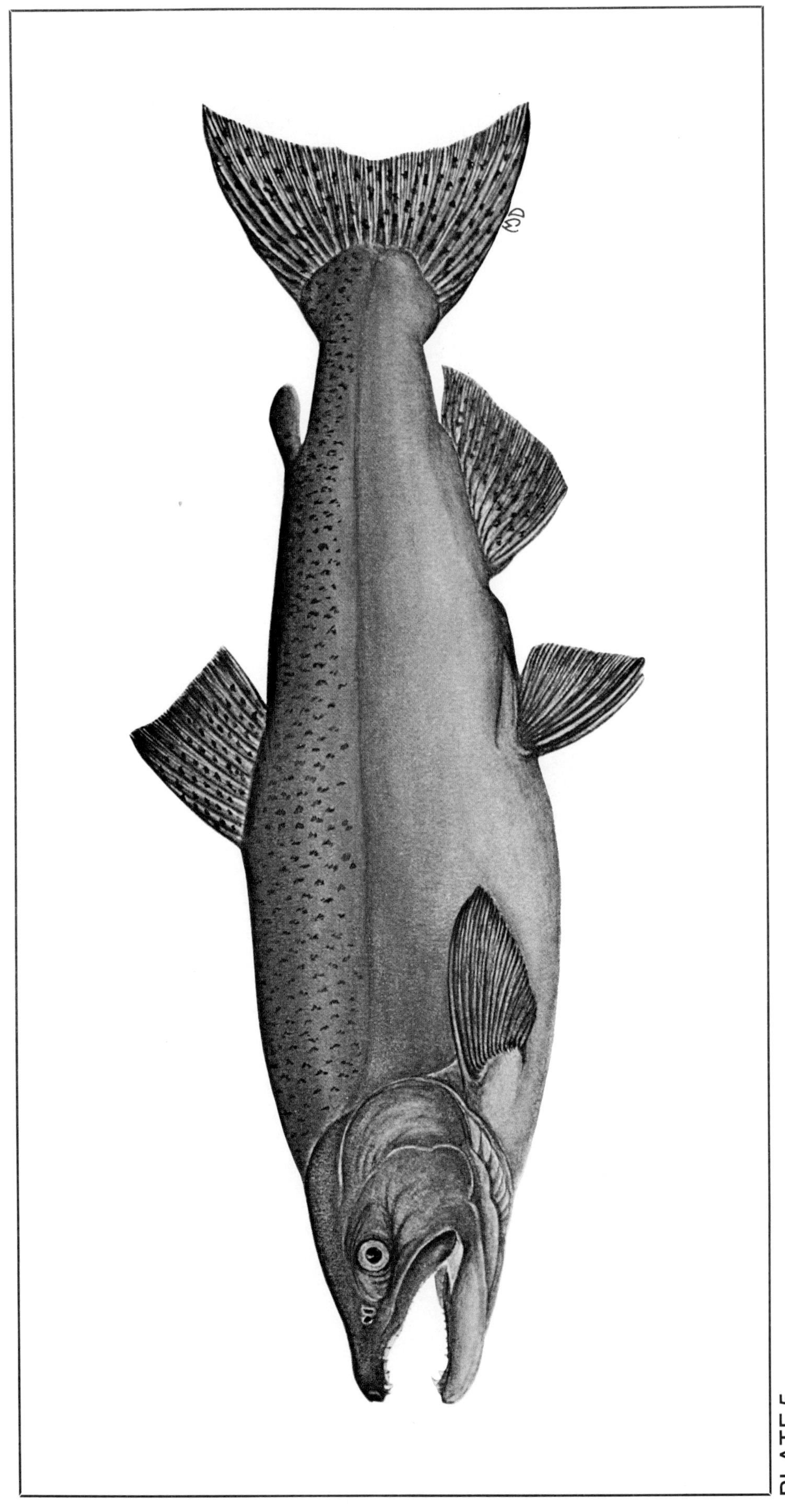

PLATE 5
Chinook (or king) salmon, *Oncorhynchus tshawytscha;* spawning male

PLATE 6
Chinook (or king) salmon, *Oncorhynchus tshawytscha;* spawning female

PLATE 7
Chum (or dog) salmon, *Oncorhynchus keta;* spawning male

PLATE 8
Chum (or dog) salmon, *Oncorhynchus keta;* spawning female

PLATE 9
Coho (or silver) salmon, *Oncorhynchus kisutch;* spawning male

PLATE 10
Coho (or silver) salmon, *Oncorhynchus kisutch;* spawning female

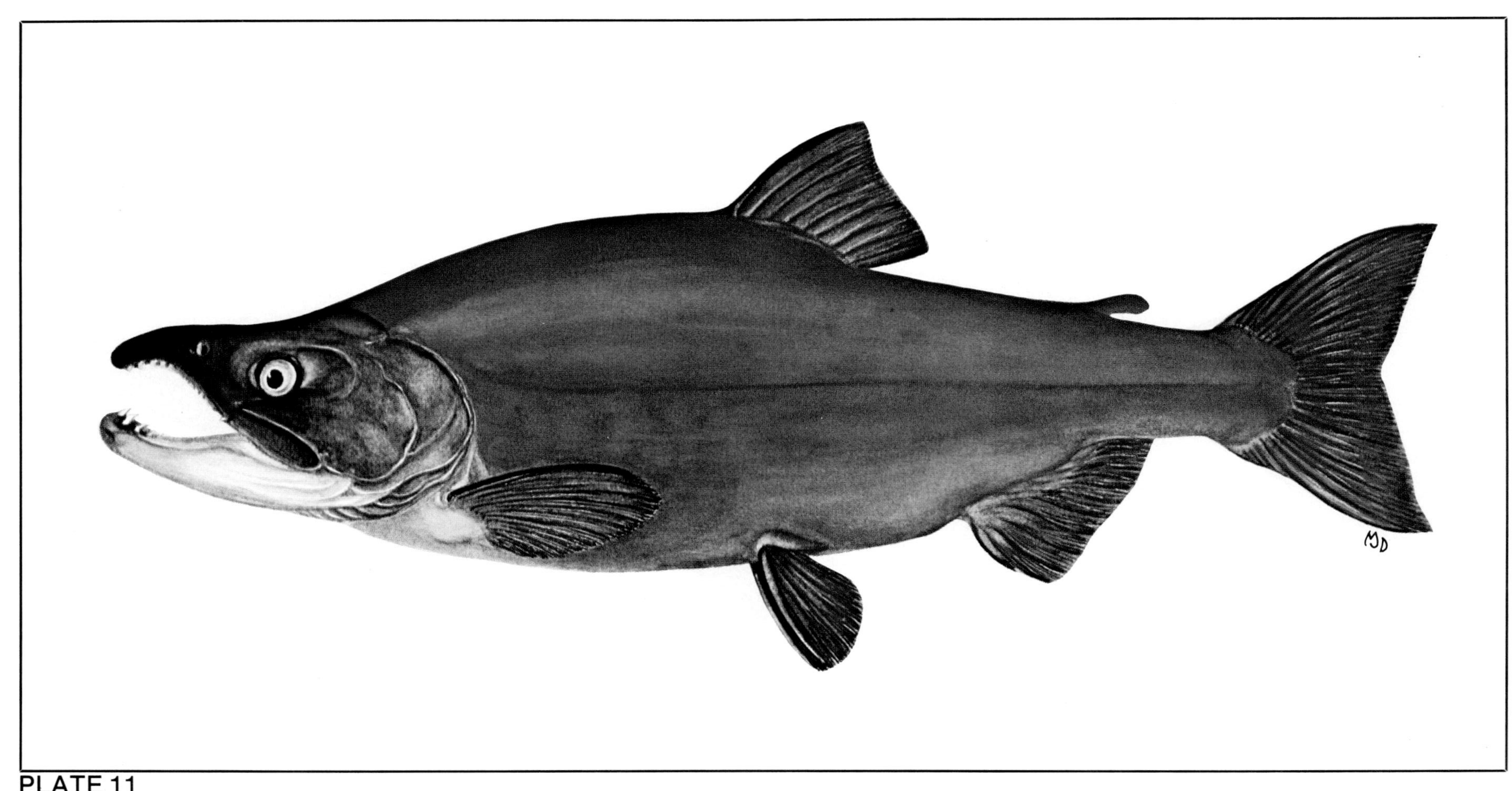

PLATE 11
Sockeye (or red or blueback) salmon, *Oncorhynchus nerka;* spawning male.

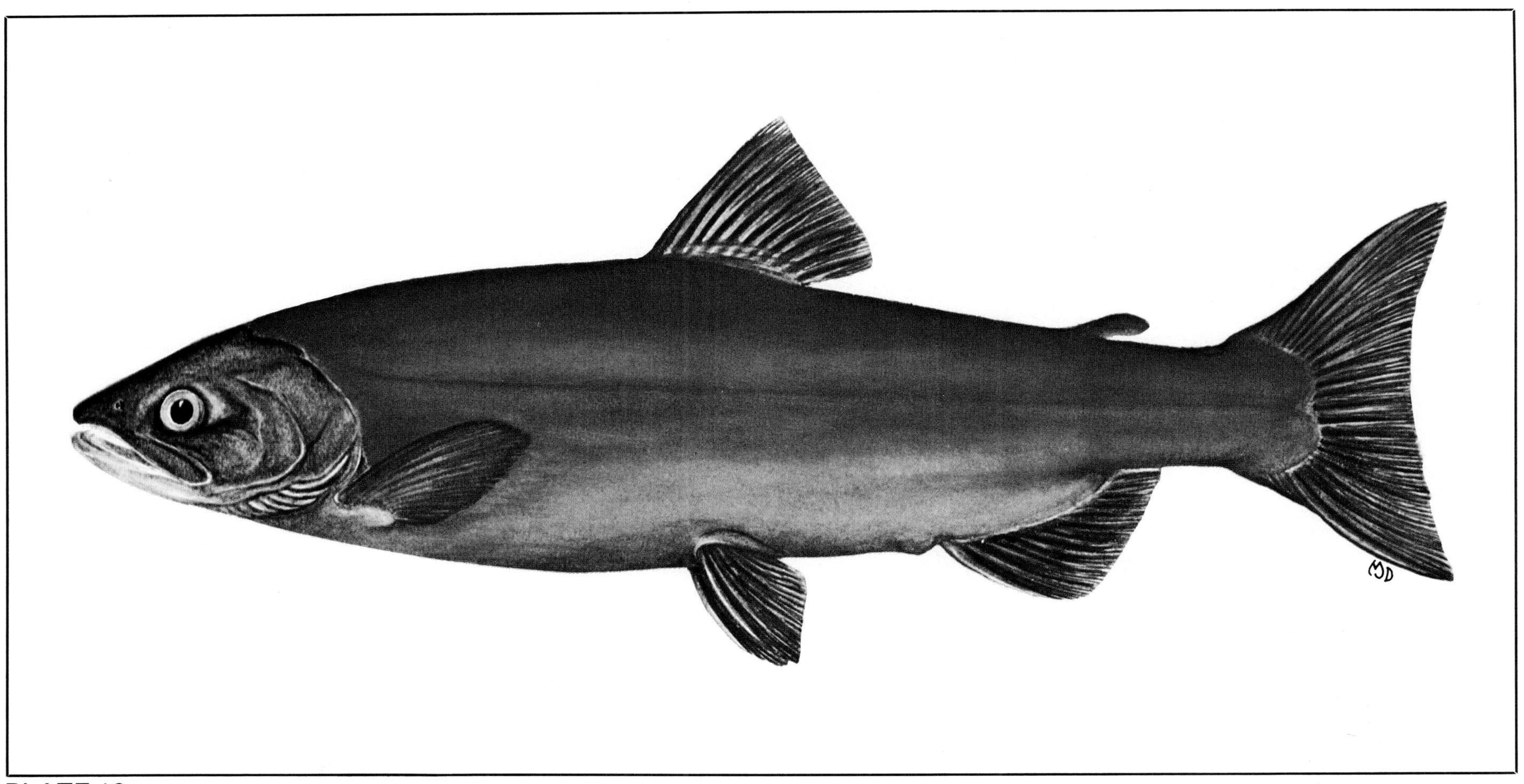

PLATE 12
Sockeye (or red or blueback) salmon, *Oncorhynchus nerka;* spawning female

PLATE 13
Kokanee salmon, *Oncorhynchus nerka;* spawning male

PLATE 14
Arctic charr, *Salvelinus alpinus*, spawning female

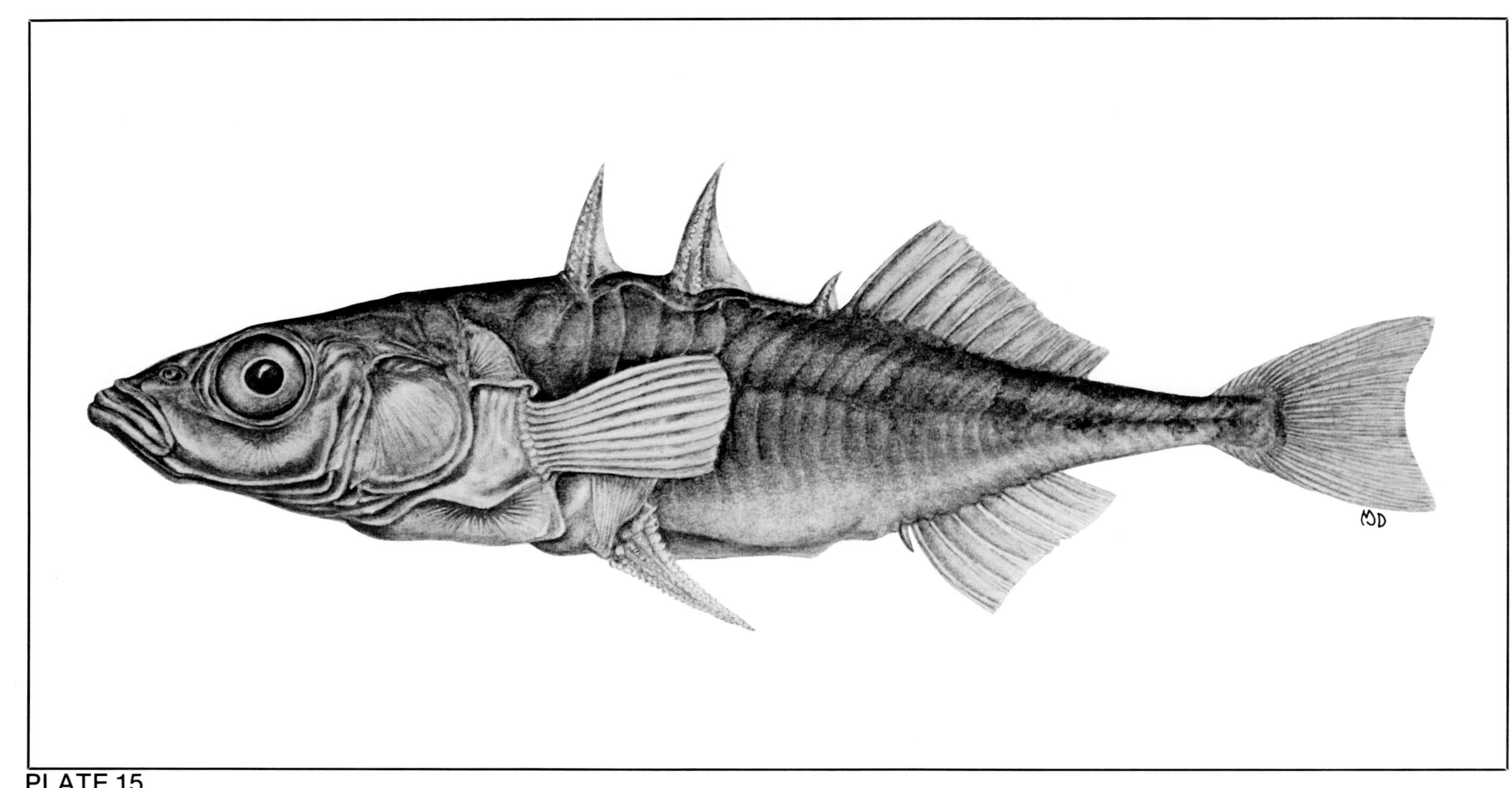

PLATE 15
Threespine stickleback, *Gasterosteus aculeatus;* spawning male

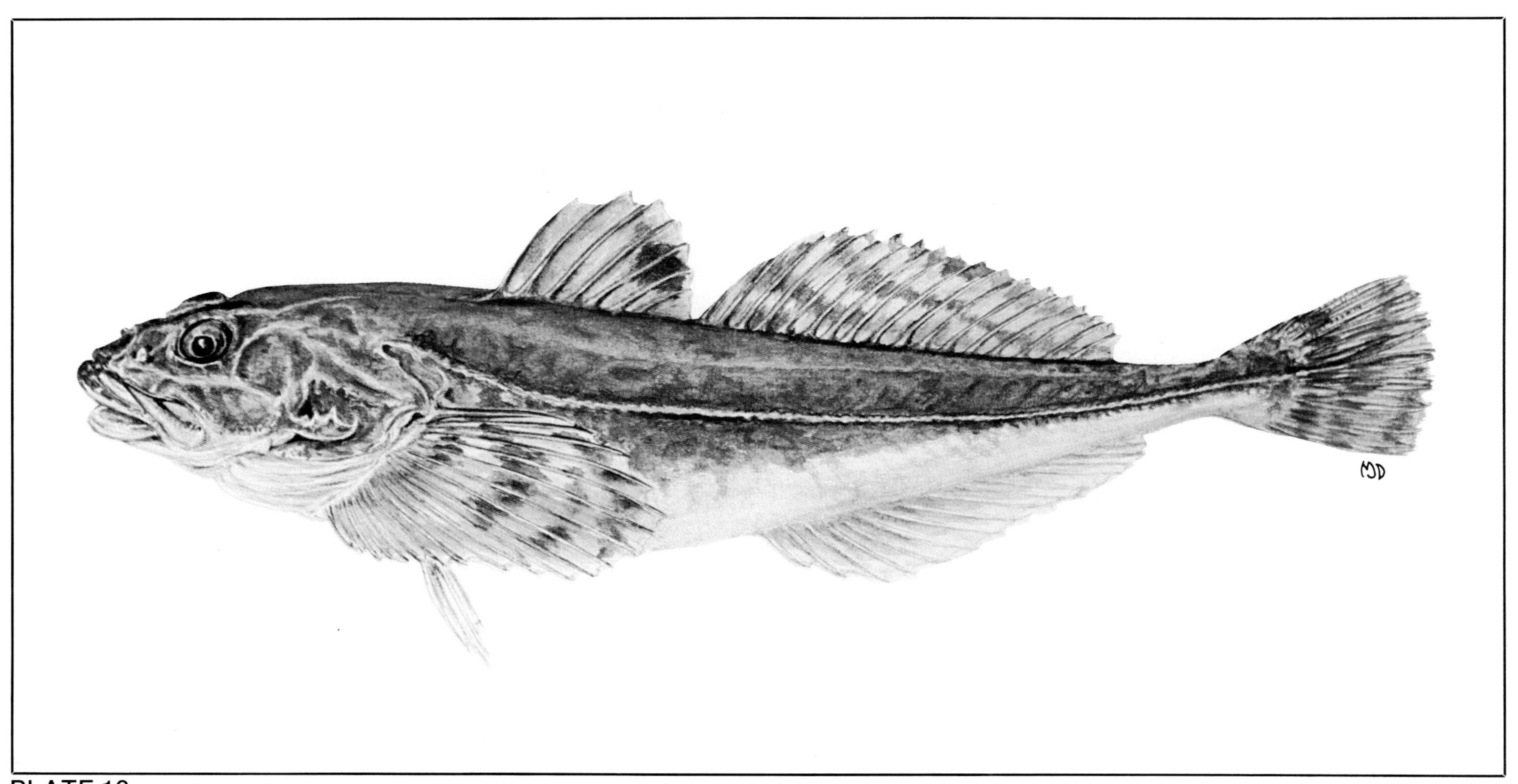

PLATE 16
Pacific staghorn sculpin, *Leptocottus armatus*

PLATE 17
Starry flounder, *Platichthys stellatus*

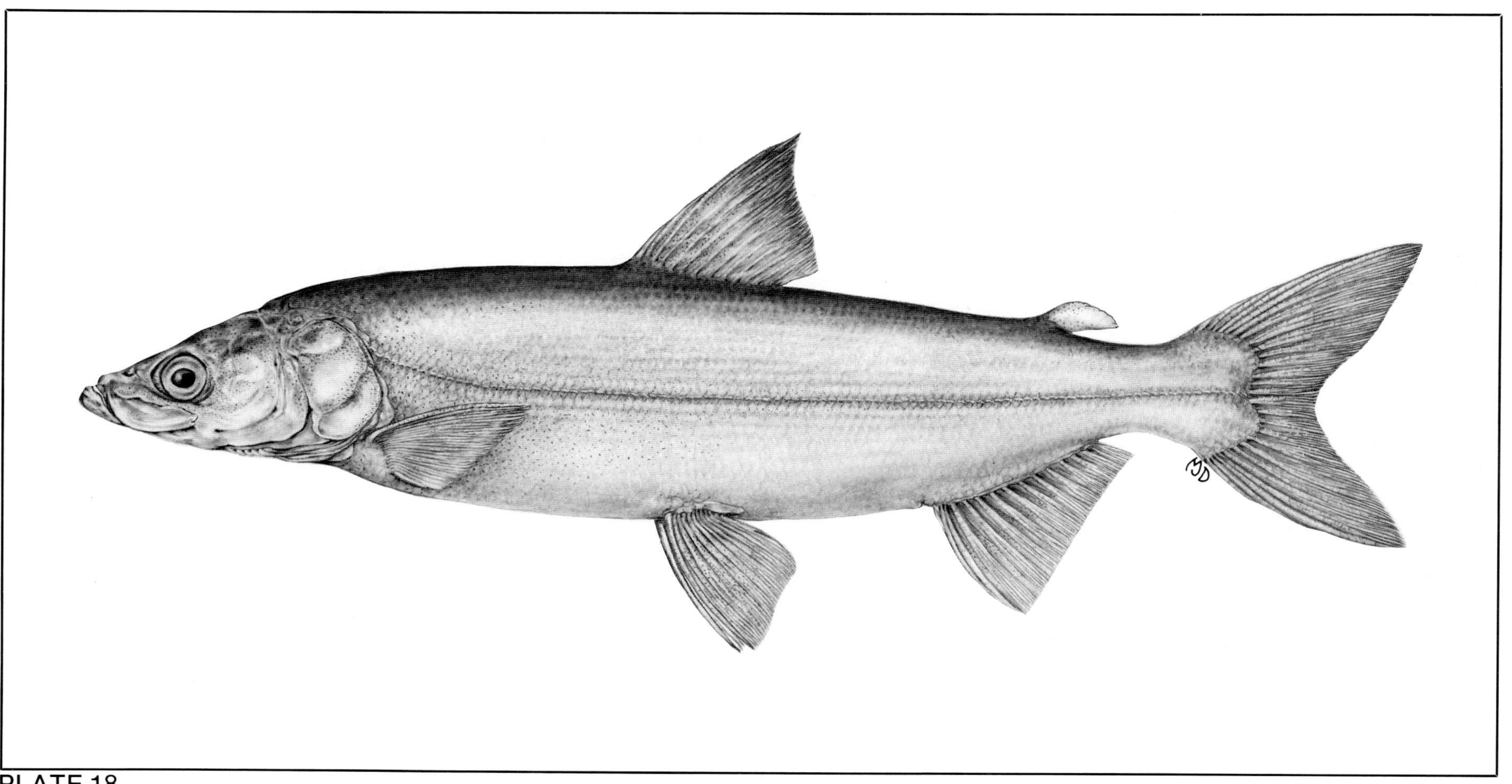

PLATE 18
Inconnu (or sheefish), *Stenodus leucichthys*

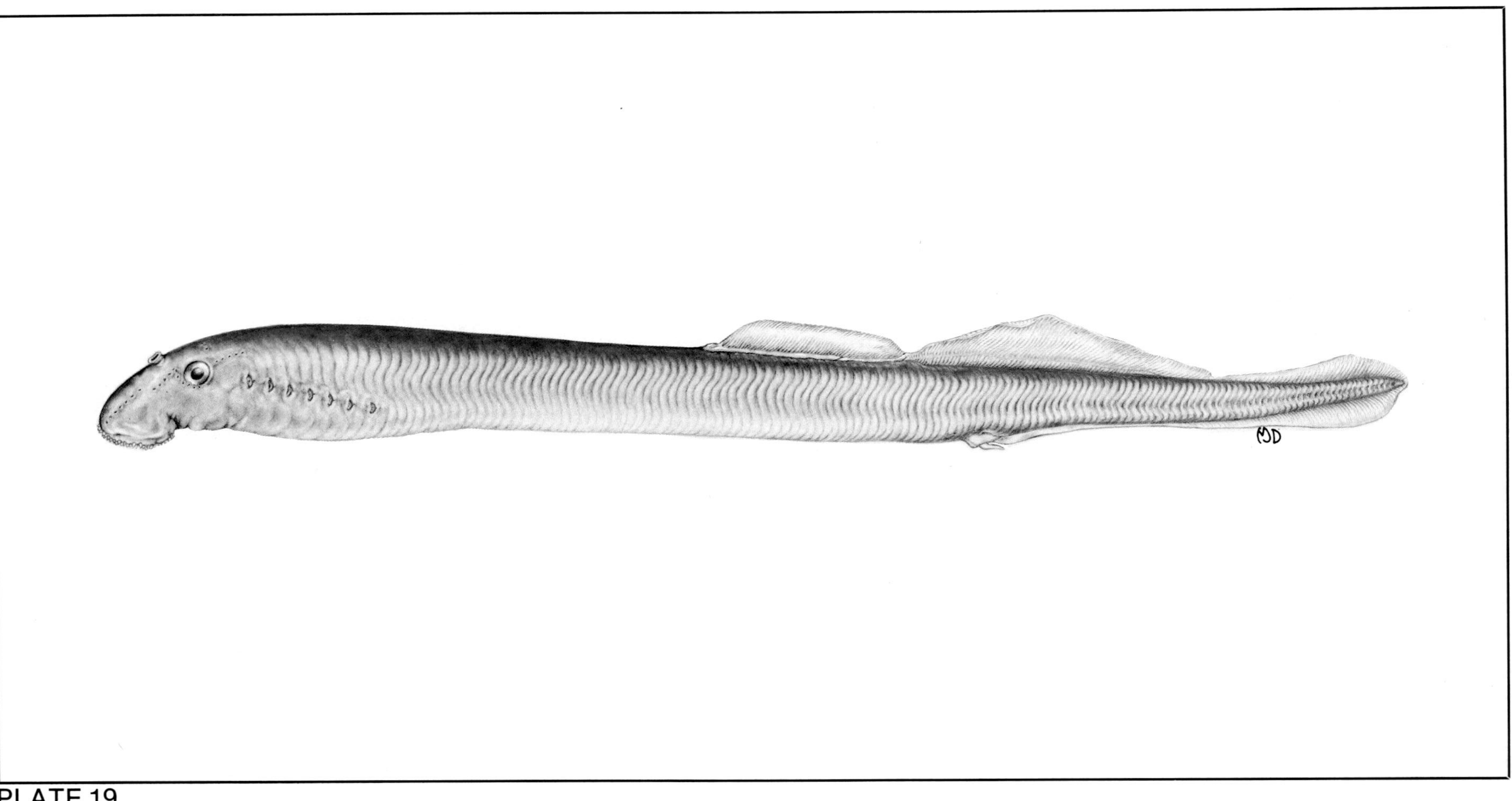

PLATE 19
Arctic lamprey, *Lampetra japonica*

A. Pacific lamprey,
Entosphenus tridentatus

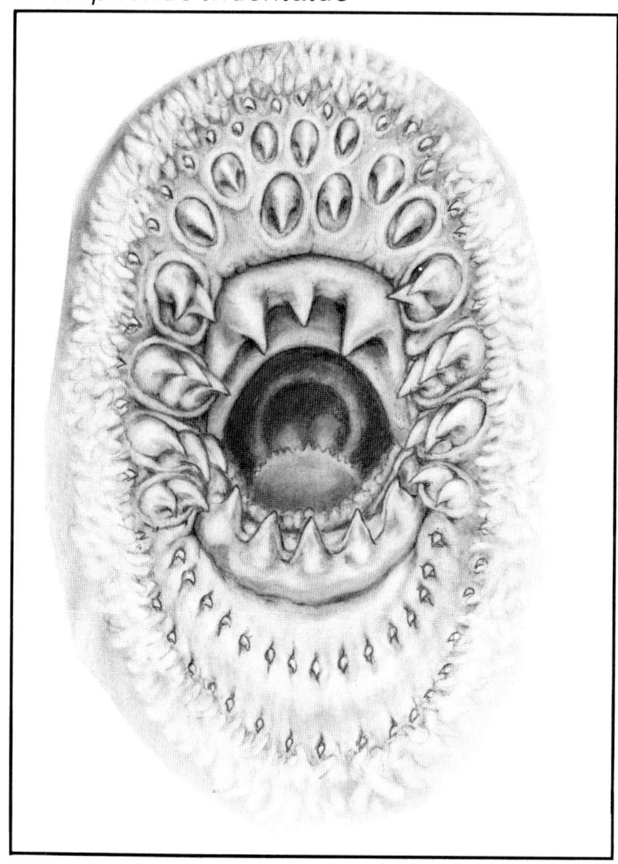

B. Arctic lamprey,
Lampetra japonica

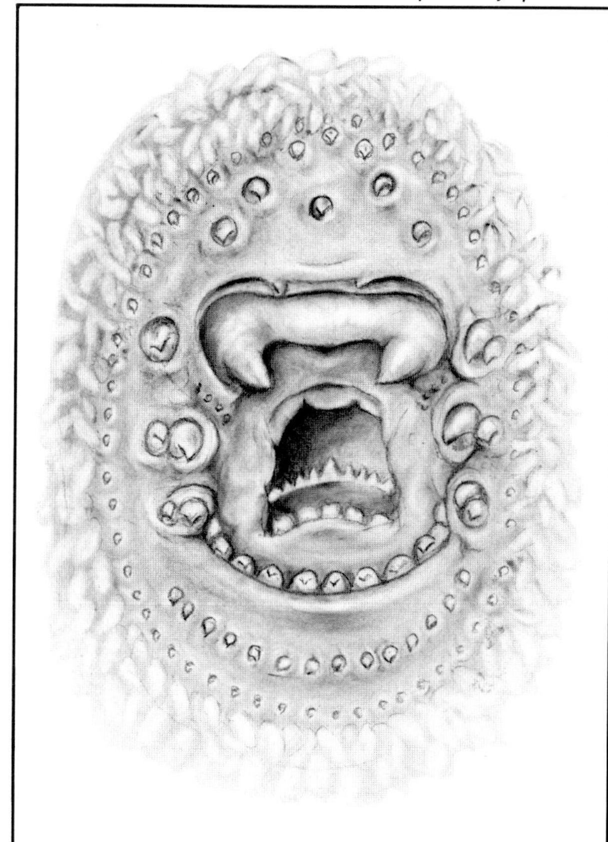

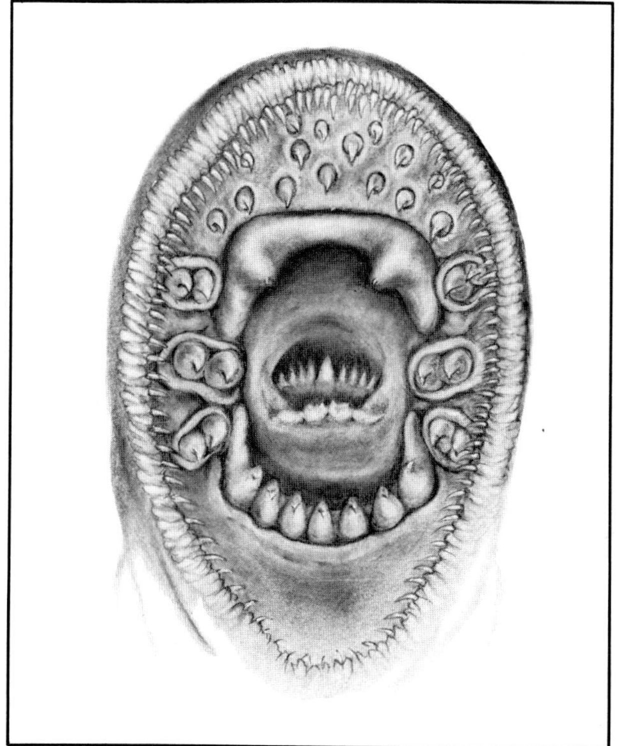

C. River lamprey,
Lampetra ayresi

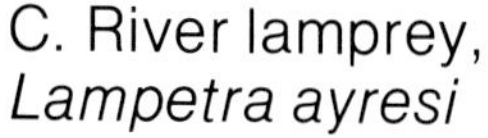

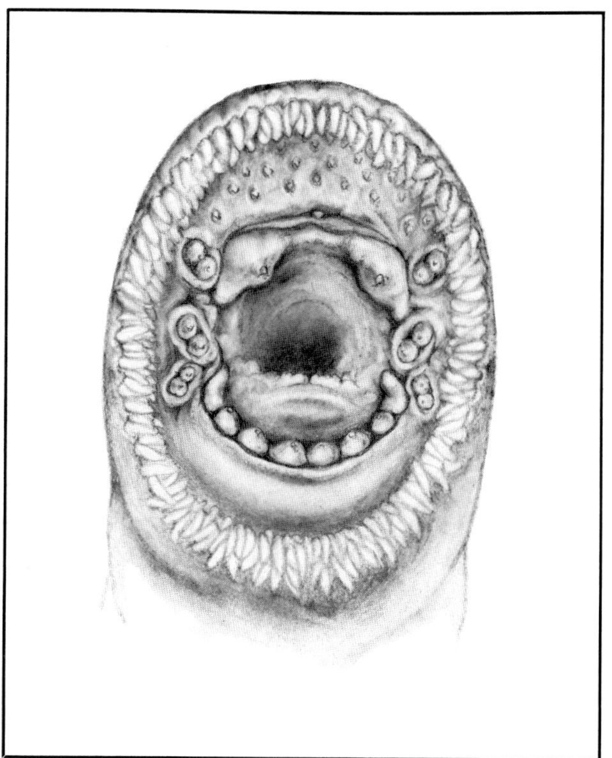

D. Western brook lamprey,
Lampetra richardsoni

PLATE 20
Tooth Patterns of the Alaskan Lampreys

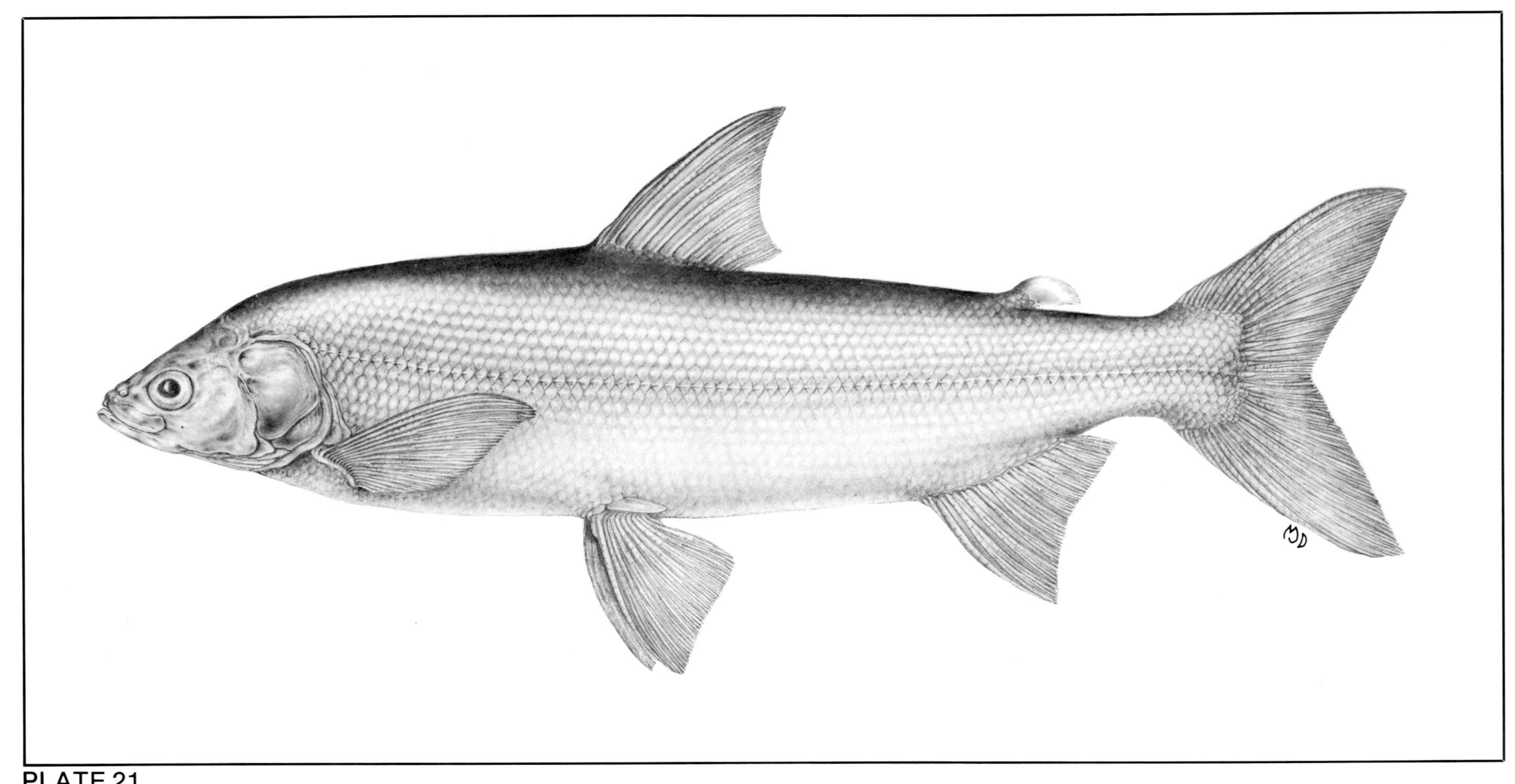

PLATE 21
Least cisco, *Coregonus sardinella*

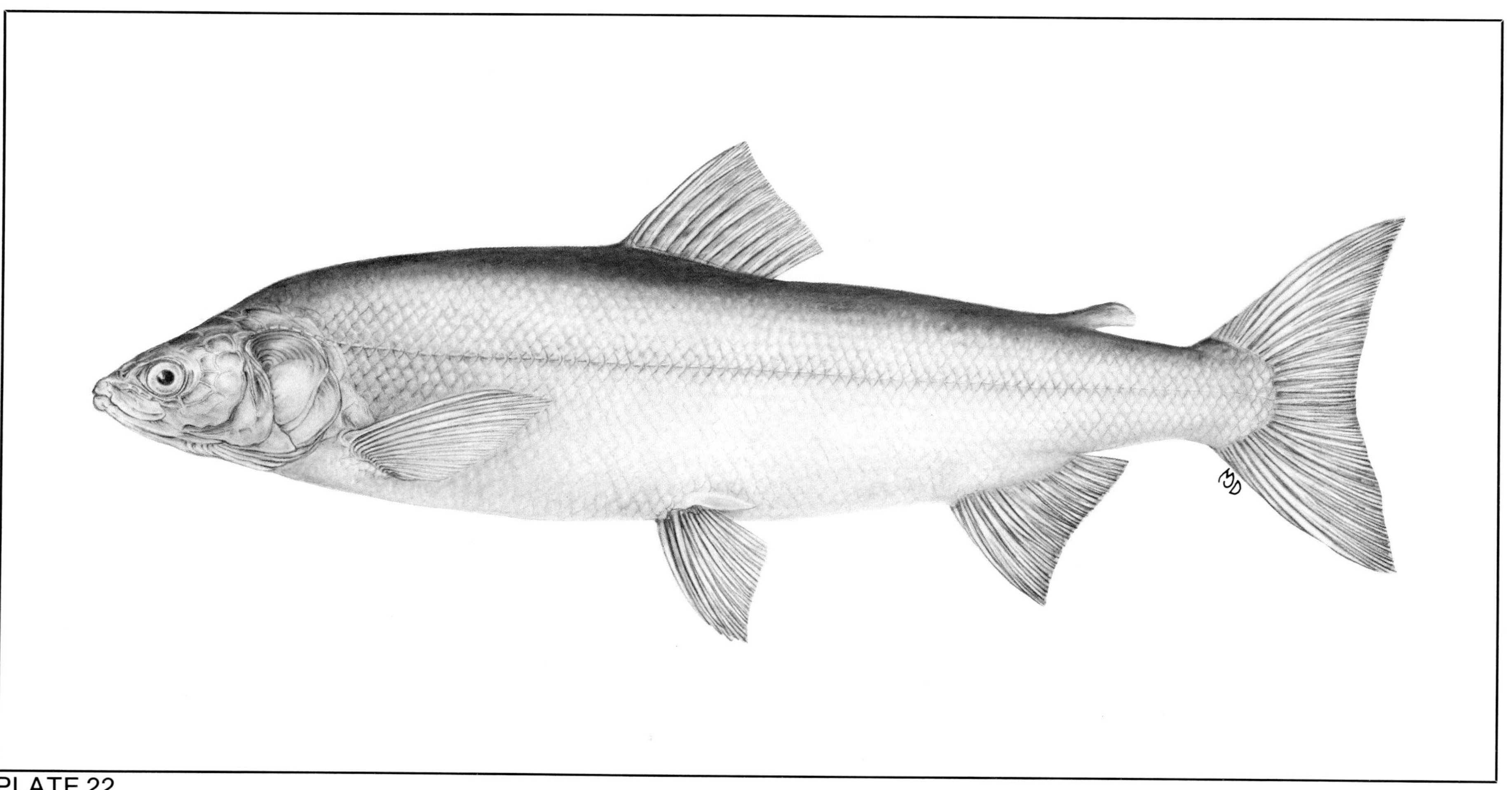

PLATE 22
Bering cisco, *Coregonus laurettae*

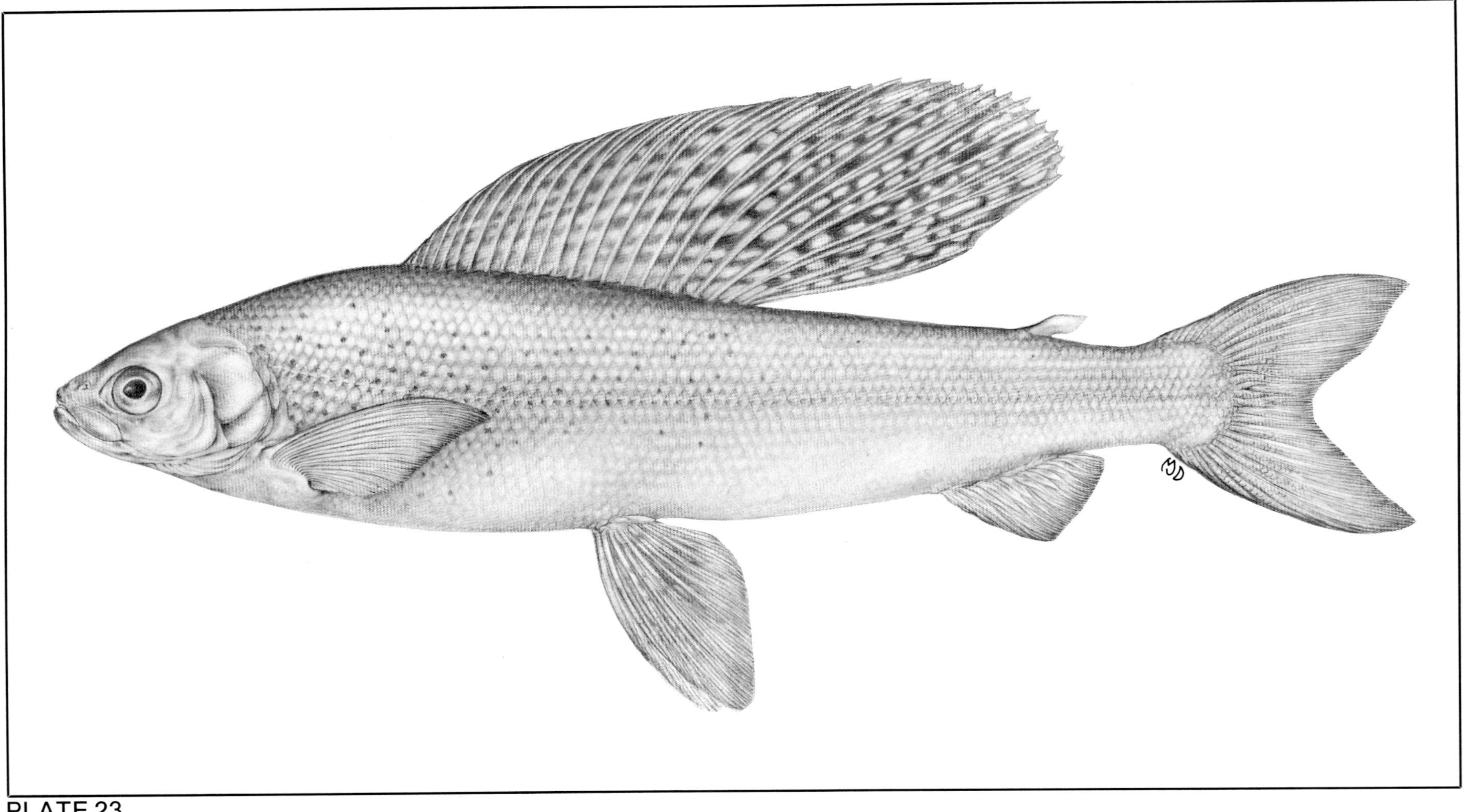

PLATE 23
Arctic grayling, *Thymallus arcticus*

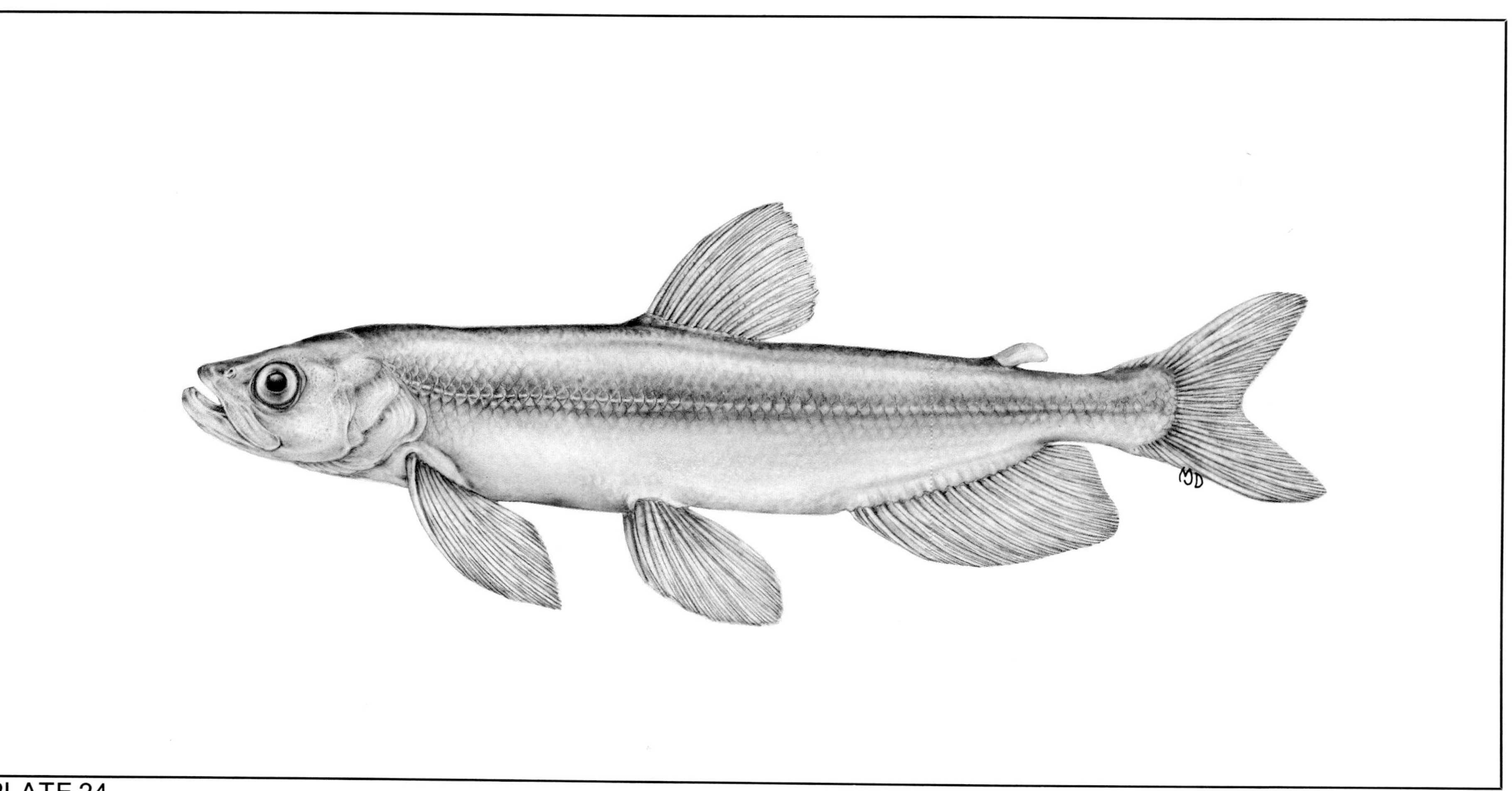

PLATE 24
Longfin smelt, *Spirinchus thaleichthys*

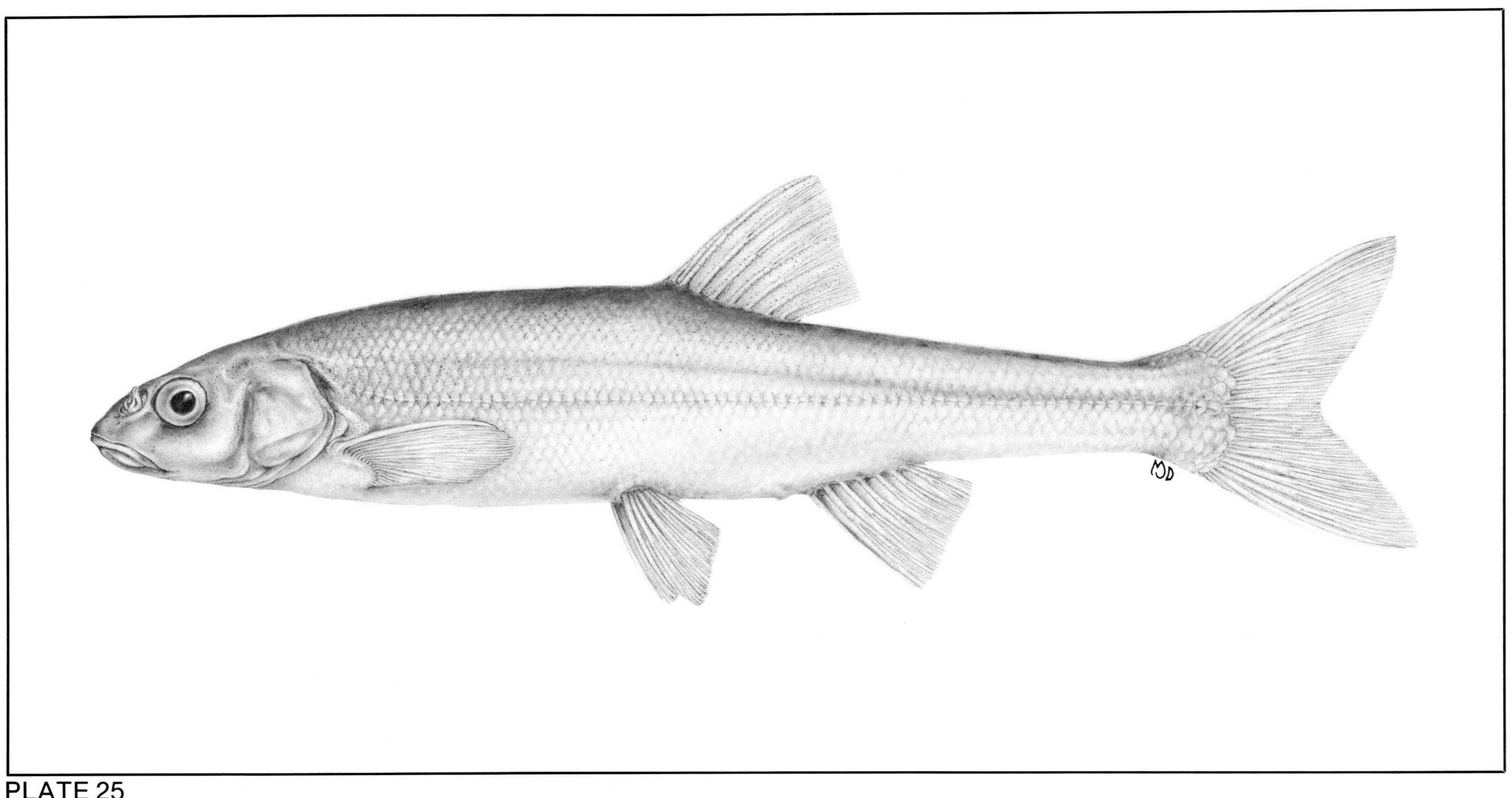

PLATE 25
Lake chub, *Couesius plumbeus*

PLATE 26
Longnose sucker, *Catostomus catostomus*

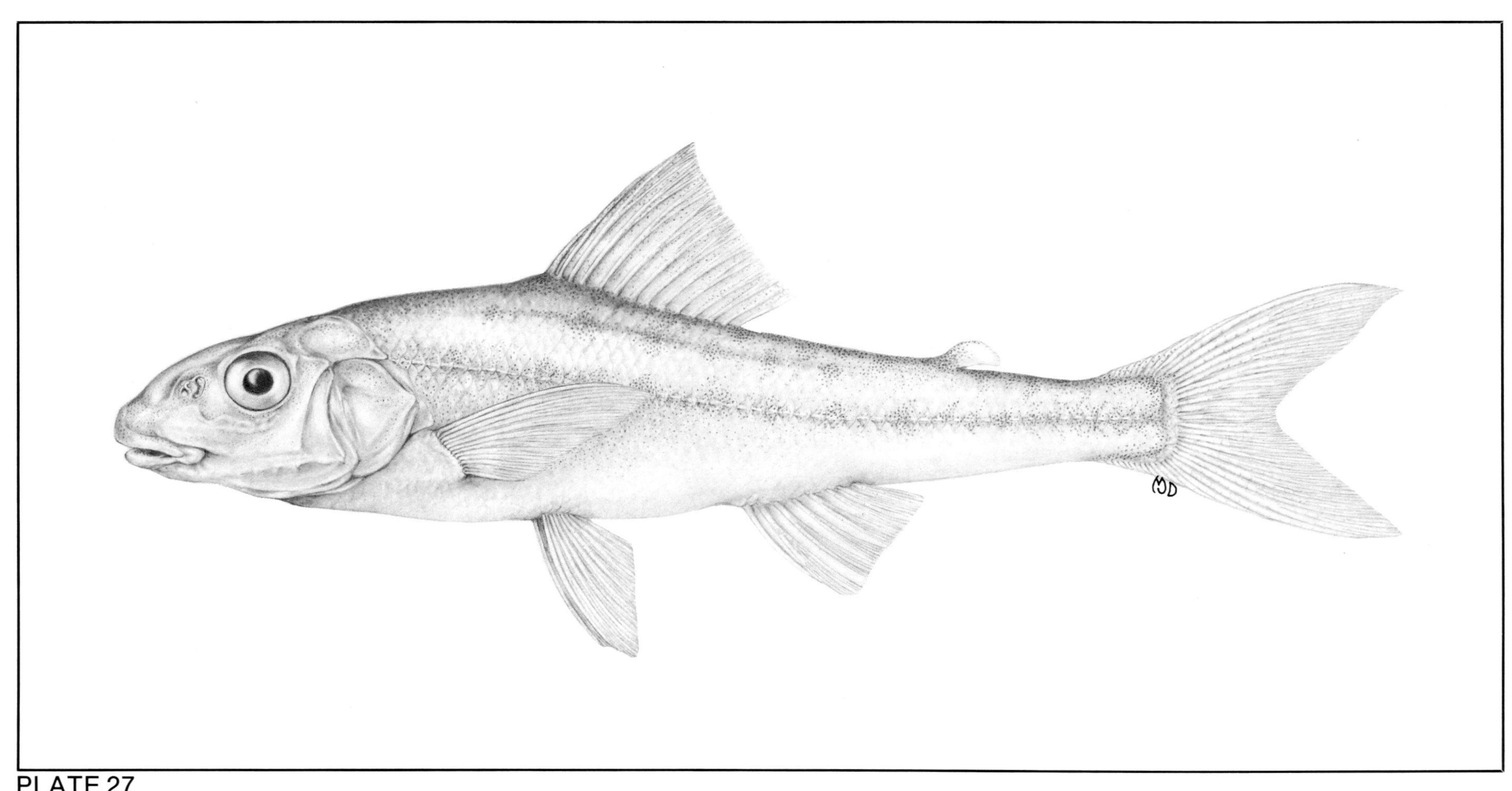

PLATE 27
Trout-perch, *Percopsis omiscomaycus*

PLATE 28
Saffron cod, *Eleginus gracilis*

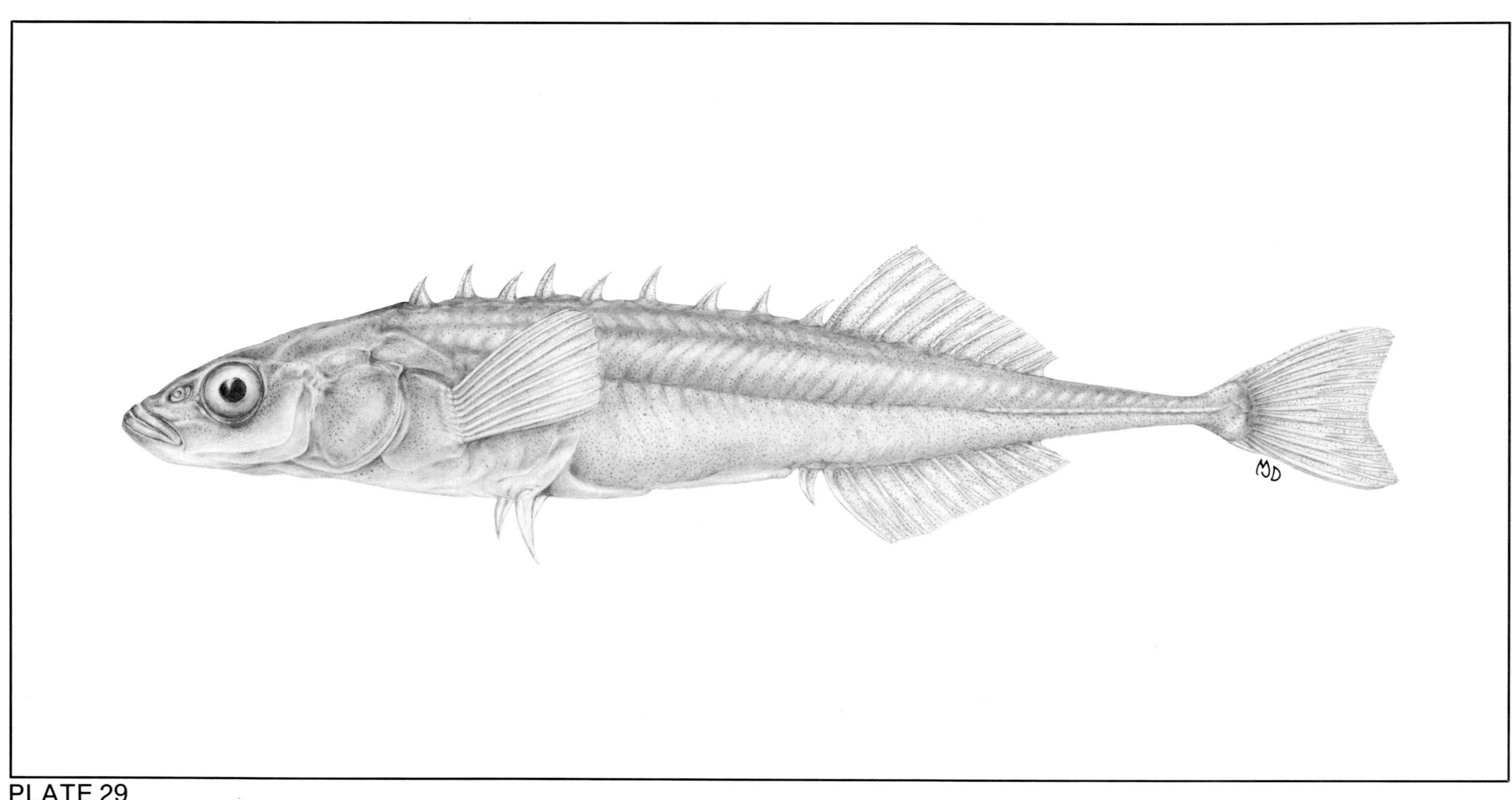

PLATE 29
Ninespine stickleback, *Pungitius pungitius*

A. Snout,
round whitefish, *Prosopium cylindraceum*

B. Snout,
Bering cisco, *Coregonus laurettae*

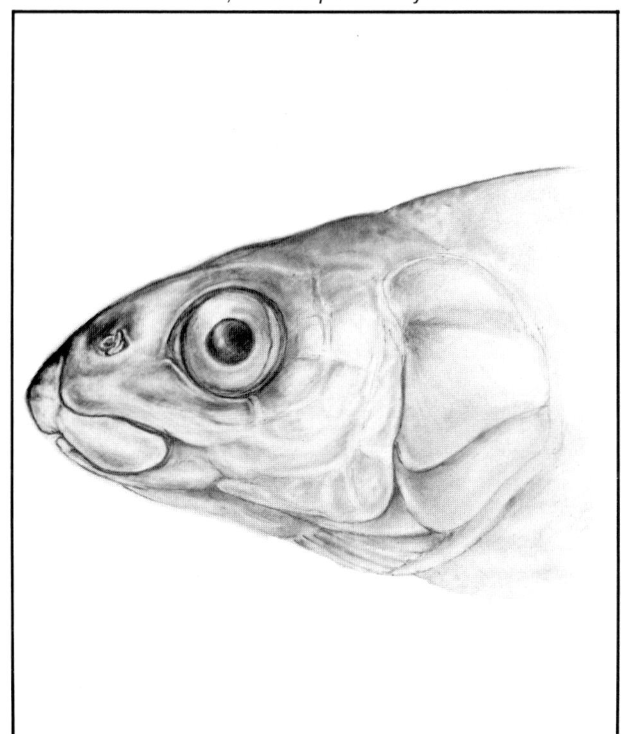

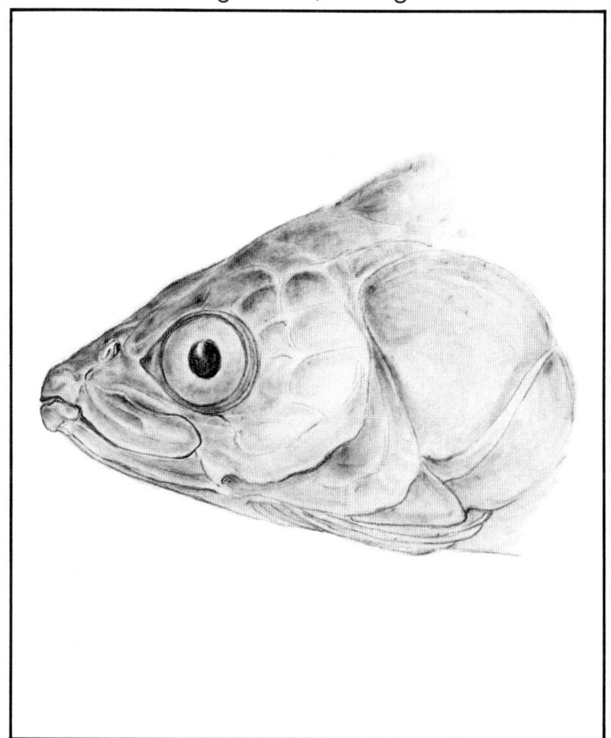

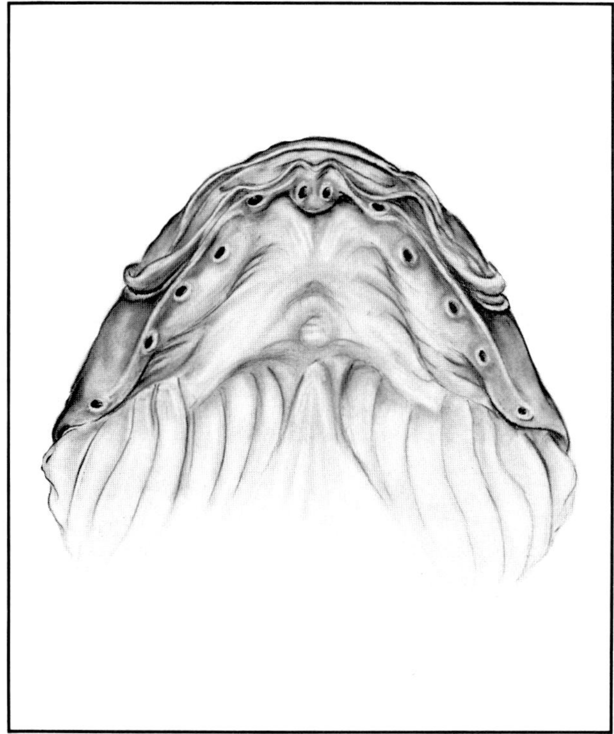

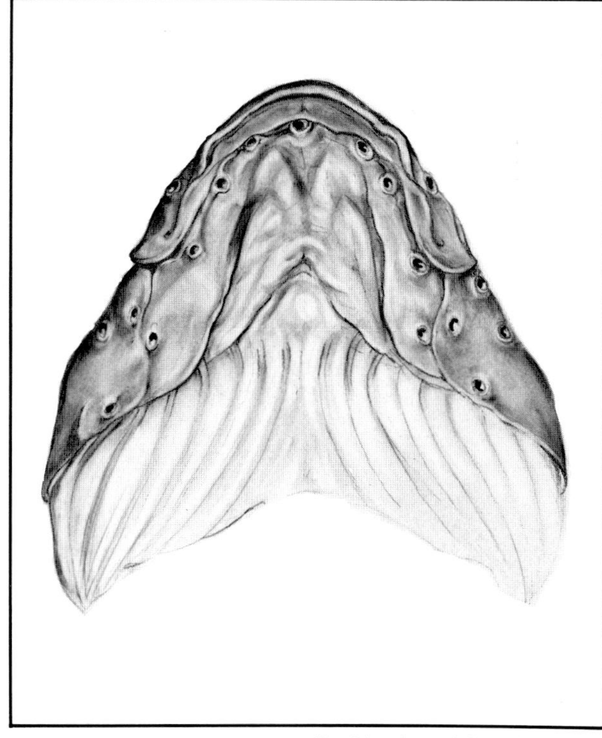

C. Underside of head,
slimy sculpin, *Cottus cognatus*

D. Underside of head,
coastrange sculpin, *Cottus aleuticus*

PHOTOGRAPHS OF BREEDING BEHAVIOR OF THE ARCTIC CHARR, NORTHERN PIKE AND FOURHORN SCULPIN

The breeding behavior of some fishes is well-known, but that of others still remains unobserved. The following photographs of some aspects of breeding behavior in the arctic charr, northern pike and fourhorn sculpin, are presented for the first time in a North American publication, through the courtesy of the Institute for Freshwater Research, Drottningholm, Sweden, and the respective photographers.

Breeding behavior in arctic charr.
A. Territorial male driving off an intruding male, while the female rests on the bottom.
B. Female inspecting the bottom preparatory to choosing a nesting site.
C. Female digging the nest; note small stone thrown up by the flaps.

A

Fabricius, 1953

B

Fabricius and Gustafson, 1954

C

Fabricius, 1953

A

B

C

D

Mating behavior in northern pike.
A. The mating thrust. The region of the male's genital opening hits the corresponding region of the female, causing a bending of the latter's body.
B. The female is thrown sidewards and upwards by the powerful mating thrust of the male.
C. A deep depression appears in the female's abdominal muscles and moves backward to the region of the genital opening, indicating ejection of eggs.
D. The mixing stroke. The caudal part of the male's body sweeps under the female's vent, where eggs can be distinctly seen.
All photographs, Fabricius and Gustafson, 1958

A

Male fourhorn sculpins guarding egg masses. The position of the egg mass by the pectoral fin is typical.
A. A nest on soft bottom free from algae; note the wall around the nest.
B. A nest dug in submersed wrack at a depth of 18 meters.
Both photographs, Westlin, 1970b

B

Chapter Six

GRAYLING

Subfamily Thymallinae of the Family Salmonidae

The Thymallinae, with only the arctic grayling, *Thymallus arcticus,* present in Alaska, externally resemble the Coregoninae (page 23) except that parr marks are present on the young and the dorsal fin of the adults is greatly enlarged, especially in mature males. (For description of the family see page 23).

ARCTIC GRAYLING

Thymallus arcticus (Pallas)

DISTINCTIVE CHARACTERS

The adult arctic grayling is distinguished by its greatly enlarged dorsal fin and its small mouth, which has fine teeth in both jaws. Juveniles may be differentiated from coregonids of similar size by the presence of narrow, vertically elongated parr marks, which are round or absent in coregonids (Figure 39).

DESCRIPTION

Body elongate, somewhat compressed. Greatest depth is at origin of dorsal fin; depth about 20% of fork length. Head short, about 17% of fork length. Snout about equal to or a little less than eye diameter, 21% to 25% of head length. Eye large, round, about equal to snout. Mouth terminal, small, with maxilla reaching about to middle of eye. Teeth small, present on both jaws, tongue (except in some large adults), on palatines and head of vomer. Gill rakers: 16 to 23 on first arch. Branchiostegals: 8 to 9. Straight lateral line has 77 to 103 pored scales. Pyloric caeca: 14 to 21. Vertebrae: 58 to 62.

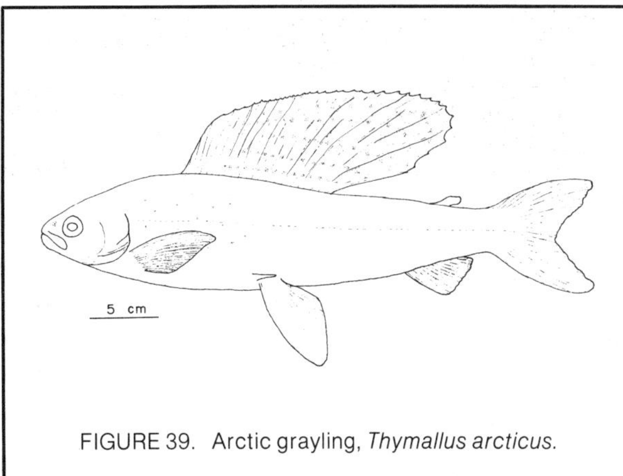

FIGURE 39. Arctic grayling, *Thymallus arcticus.*

FINS. Dorsal has 17 to 25 rays and is greatly enlarged in adults, especially in males. Adipose fin present. Dorsal fin of adult males reaches adipose fin when depressed, but is shorter in females. Anal has 11 to 15 rays; pectorals, 14 to 16; pelvics, 10 or 11. Pelvics are rather long, reach anal fin in adult males, but not in females. Small axillary process present. Caudal fin forked, lower lobe often longer than upper.

SCALES. Cycloid, fairly large; 77 to 103 pored scales in lateral line. It was once thought that the scales of grayling did not have breeding tubercles but work by Kratt and Smith (1978) has shown that these structures are present for a brief period during spawning on nearly all scales of the caudal region in both males and females.

COLOR. Back dark purple blue to blue gray; sides silvery gray to blue, sometimes with a pinkish wash; scattered dark spots on sides, these being more numerous in the young. A dark longitudinal stripe along lower sides between pectoral and pelvic fins. Dorsal fin dark with narrow purple edge; rows of reddish to orange and/or purple to green spots on body of fin. Pelvics dark with irregular diagonal orange-yellow stripes. Adipose, dorsal, anal, caudal and pectorals dusky to dark (photographs, page 96; Plate 23, page 134).

SIZE. The largest arctic grayling known was one 75.9 cm and 2.7 kg from the Katseyedie River, Northwest Territories. However, in most areas the average fish caught by an angler would be on the order of 30 to 35 cm long and would weigh 450 to 700 grams.

RANGE AND ABUNDANCE

The arctic grayling is common throughout Alaska and northern Canada and is found from the west side of Hudson Bay to the western shores of Alaska. It is present in the headwaters of the Missouri River above Great Falls, Montana, and ranges northward from central Alberta. To the west, it is present on Saint Lawrence Island, Alaska, and on the Asian mainland west to the Kara and Ob rivers of Siberia and south to the upper Yalu River.

The grayling has been introduced into a number of lakes in southeastern Alaska and on the Kenai Peninsula, as well as into mountainous areas of Colorado, Utah and Vermont.

HABITS

Grayling spawn early in the spring, immediately after breakup. In interior Alaska they begin to congregate at the mouths of clear-water tributaries in April and may start upstream through channels cut in the ice by surface runoff (Reed, 1964). As soon as the streams open the fish run upstream to the spawning grounds, a run sometimes being a matter of more than 160 km. Spawning takes place from mid-May to June. The grayling shows no particular preference for substrate when spawning, although sandy gravel seems to be used most often, perhaps because of its prevalence.

A male establishes a territory which he defends against intruding males by erecting his dorsal fin, opening his mouth and assuming a rigid posture. Persistent intruders may be rushed and driven off. Rarely, females may be attacked. At spawning, the male follows a female, courting her with displays of his dorsal fin. He then drifts over beside her and folds his dorsal fin over her back. Both fish arch, vibrate and release eggs and milt. They may or may not gape. No redd is constructed, but the vibrations of the tails during the spawning act stir up the substrate and produce a slight depression (Laird, 1928; Wojcik, 1955; Kruse, 1959; Reed, 1964; Bishop, 1971).

The eggs are orange in color and about .25 cm in diameter but they quickly swell to about .27 cm on hardening (Norden, 1959; Reed, 1964). During the next few days they continue to swell and after three or four days are about .35 cm in diameter (Ward, 1951). Egg number varies with size of the individual and the stock, with counts as low as 416 and as high as 12,946 (Brown, 1938b). Development to hatching requires from 11 to 21 days, depending on temperature (Lord, 1932; Brown, 1938b; Nelson, 1954; Bishop, 1971). The young, which have been described as resembling "two eyeballs on a thread" (Schallock, 1966), begin feeding the third or fourth day after hatching, and all are feeding actively by the eighth day (Lord, 1932; Brown and Buck, 1939). Growth is rapid during the ensuing summer. By September, the young-of-the-year are about 10 cm long. In general, growth is somewhat faster in the southern part of the range than in the northern, but rates may vary widely from tributary to tributary within a single drainage (Miller, 1946; Kruse, 1959; Reed, 1964). At age I, grayling of Interior Alaska average

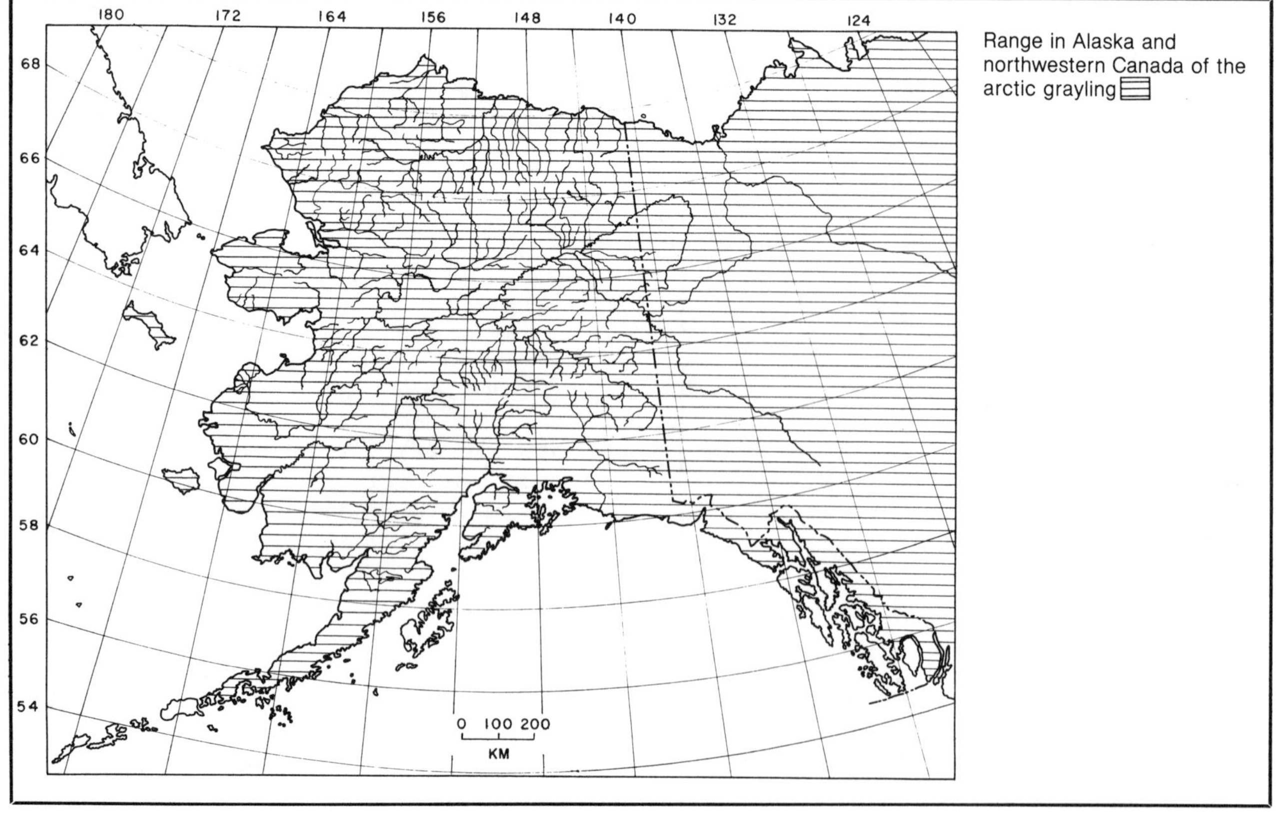

Range in Alaska and northwestern Canada of the arctic grayling

about 14.8 cm in fork length; at age II, 19.2 cm; age III, 22.8 cm; age IV, 26.5 cm; age V, 30.4 cm. A 30 cm grayling will weigh between .2 and .25 kg.

Following the spawning migration, the adult grayling move away from the spawning areas, generally but not always going farther upstream, to take up more or less permanent summer residence in pools (Schallock, 1966; Vascotto, 1970). Territoriality and social hierarchy develop quickly in each pool, with the largest and strongest fish occupying the most advantageous positions near the head of the pool, the smaller, subordinate fish farther downstream, and the smallest of all occupying the foot of the pool without any territories.

Territories are established and maintained through a series of ritualistic "challenge displays" involving seven distinct steps. First, an invader moves up parallel with a defender. Both fish then lie still, with dorsal fins folded. The invader drifts sideways toward the defender until they are less than 1 cm apart. One fish, usually the invader, moves forward about 15 cm and bends its body so that the inside of the curve is presented to the head of the defender. The invader drifts toward and beneath the defender. The invader rises toward the defender, who drifts back. Finally, the defender either keeps on retreating and leaves the territory or the defender moves around the invader and the pattern is repeated, with the roles reversed. Once territories and hierarchies have become firmly established in a pool, the ritual rarely goes beyond the stage in which the invader has come to within 1 cm from the defender. (Vascotto, 1970; Vascotto and Morrow, 1973).

The establishment and use of territories is related to the feeding habits of the grayling. Virtually the entire diet is composed of insects—larvae, pupae and adults—which are taken from the drift. The majority of these are aquatic forms that have been moved from the bottom by one means or another and thus become part of the benthic drift. The grayling is primarily a surface and middepth feeder and does not generally feed on the bottom except in the fall, when benthic drift is much reduced (Brown, 1938a; Reed, 1964; Vascotto, 1970; Vascotto and Morrow, 1973). Thus, establishment of a territory means access to the food supply within that area.

A downstream migration occurs in mid-September. The fish leave the smaller tributaries and the vast majority move downstream to overwinter in deep water. A few fish stay in the major clear-water streams and apparently overwinter in the deeper pools (Schallock, 1966).

IMPORTANCE TO MAN

The arctic grayling is one of the most important sport fishes of Alaska and northern Canada. It also makes a significant contribution to subsistence fishing in some remote areas.

Chapter Seven

SMELTS

Family Osmeridae

KEY TO THE ALASKAN SPECIES

SECTION	DESCRIPTION	THE FISH IS	PROCEED IN THIS KEY TO SECTION
1 a.	Teeth on vomer small and numerous, not caninelike.		**2**
b.	One or more large canine teeth present on each wing of vomer (but may be missing in spawning adults of the eulachon).		**4**
2 a.	Mouth small, upper jaw not reaching behind middle of pupil of eye. Two rows of teeth on both vomer and palatines.		**3**
b.	Mouth large, upper jaw reaching at least to middle of pupil of eye. A single row of teeth on vomer and palatines.	Longfin smelt, *Spirinchus thaleichthys* (Ayres), page 150.	
3 a.	Base of pelvic fin before or under anterior end of dorsal fin. Lateral line scales: 54 to 62.	Pond smelt, *Hypomesus olidus* (Pallas), page 151.	
b.	Base of pelvic fin behind anterior end of dorsal fin. Lateral line scales: 66 to 76.	Surf smelt, *Hypomesus pretiosus* (Girard), page 152.	
4 a.	Anal rays: 18 to 23. Front of dorsal fin behind bases of pelvic fins.	Eulachon, *Thaleichthys pacificus* (Richardson), page 154.	
b.	Anal rays: 11 to 16. Front of dorsal fin directly above or ahead of bases of pelvic fins.	Rainbow smelt, *Osmerus mordax* (Mitchill), page 155.	

The Osmeridae is a group of small fishes which rarely if ever exceed about 30 cm in length. They differ morphologically from salmonids chiefly in having no pelvic axillary process; having a lower jaw that is longer than the upper; a head that is, in general, proportionately smaller and a body that is more slender than the salmon's; and having few if any pyloric caeca.

The smelts are slender-bodied, silvery or dull, and have forked tails. Sexual dimorphism, usually in the form of nuptial tubercles, appears at spawning time.

Smelts may be entirely freshwater, anadromous or marine in their life history. Spawning usually takes place in fresh water or on beaches, although a few species spawn in the sea.

The smelts are generally quite abundant, at least during the spawning season, and are of considerable economic value.

LONGFIN SMELT

Spirinchus thaleichthys (Ayres)

DISTINCTIVE CHARACTERS

The longfin smelt is distinguished by the long upper jaw, which reaches at least to below the middle of the eye in adults; the fine teeth in a single row on the vomer and palatine bones; and the 38 to 47 gill rakers on the first arch (Figure 40).

DESCRIPTION

Body elongate, slender, compressed, its depth 14% to 20% of fork length. Head short, 20% to 25% of fork length. Snout, 22% to 28% of head. Eye fairly large, its diameter about equal to snout length. Mouth large, oblique, lower jaw projecting beyond upper when mouth is closed, upper jaw reaching backward at least to below middle of eye in adults, not as far in young. Teeth small, fine, present on both jaws and on tongue, vomer and palatines. Gill rakers long; 38 to 47 on first arch. Branchiostegal rays: 7 or 8. Lateral line is incomplete, with 14 to 21 pored scales, and reaching not quite to below dorsal fin. Pyloric caeca: 4 to 6. Vertebrae: 55 to 61.

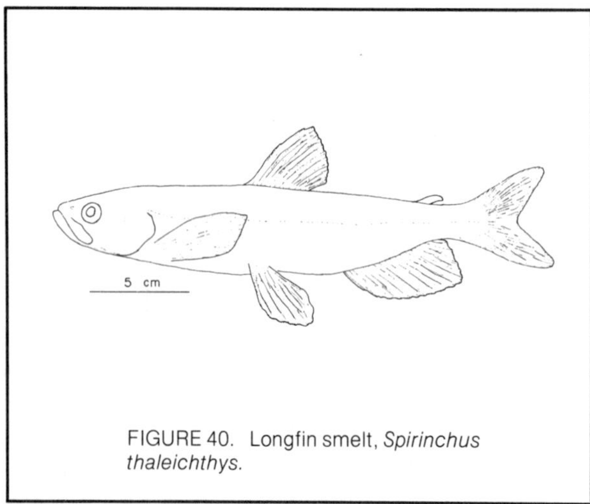

FIGURE 40. Longfin smelt, *Spirinchus thaleichthys.*

FINS. Dorsal fin is moderately high, originating near middle of body length; 8 to 10 rays. Adipose fin present. Anal fin, 15 to 19 rays. Pectorals have 10 to 12 rays, reach to origin of pelvic fins. Pelvics have 8 rays and originate under anterior edge of dorsal fin. In breeding males paired fins have tubercles on upper sides. Caudal fin forked.

SCALES. Moderately large, cycloid; 55 to 61 (in rare cases 62 or 63) in a midlateral row. Tubercles present in breeding males.

COLOR. Dusky to olive or olive brown above, sides and belly silver white. Fin rays usually dusky, membranes clear (photograph, page 97; Plate 24, page 135).

SIZE. Up to as much as 20 cm, but average adults are about 15 cm or a bit less.

RANGE AND ABUNDANCE

The longfin smelt is found along the coast of North America from San Francisco Bay (Rutter, 1908) north to Prince William Sound, Alaska, where it has been found near Hinchinbrook Island at 60°12'N, 146°15'W (Dryfoos, 1961). The record from the Nushagak River in the Bristol Bay area (Gilbert, 1895) is an error that has been unquestioningly accepted even by some modern authors, although Hubbs (1925) long ago pointed out that the specimens in question were pond smelt, *Hypomesus olidus.* Within its range, the longfin smelt is locally and seasonally abundant, appearing chiefly during the spawning runs.

HABITS

Extraordinarily little is known of the biology of the longfin smelt. The fish are anadromous, although a few landlocked populations are known. Spawning runs occur between October and December in most areas, with a few populations breeding as late as February. Details of spawning have not been recorded, but spawning is known to take place in streams not far from the sea. Fecundity varies from 535 eggs in small females of a landlocked stock to more than 23,600 for large anadromous fish. Average fecundity for anadromous females is said to be about 18,000 eggs. The eggs, about .12 cm in diameter, hatch in 40 days at 6.9°C. The newly hatched larvae are .7 to .8 cm long. They probably spend considerable time in fresh water, as young fish up to 7.2 cm long have been taken in the Fraser River (Hart and McHugh, 1944). Year-old fish average about 7.5 cm long , while 2-year-old males are about 10.6 cm, females about 11 cm. Sexual maturity is reached at the end of the second year. Most individuals die after spawning, although a few females apparently survive to age 3. It is not known whether or not these 3-year-olds spawned at the age of 2. Members of landlocked populations apparently do not reach as great a size as the sea-run fish.

In the sea, the longfin smelt apparently stay fairly close to shore. In the winter they are taken in shrimp trawls at depths to 41 m. Food of smelt in the sea consists of small crustaceans, especially euphausiids, copepods, and cumaceans, while in fresh water the young feed on a small shrimplike crustacean, *Neomysis mercedis* (Hart and McHugh, 1944), small, bottom-dwelling crustaceans and insect larvae (Hart, 1973).

IMPORTANCE TO MAN

This smelt is but little used. Fish from the sea are reported to have a good flavor, but the supply is limited and the species is lumped with other smelts on the market (Hart, 1973). The longfin smelt is often abundant during the spawning run, but at that time the flesh is soft and oily and spoils quickly (Scott and Crossman, 1973).

POND SMELT

Hypomesus olidus (Pallas)

DISTINCTIVE CHARACTERS

The small mouth, the two rows of teeth on the vomer and palatines, and the number of midlateral scales—51 to 62—distinguish the pond smelt (Figure 41).

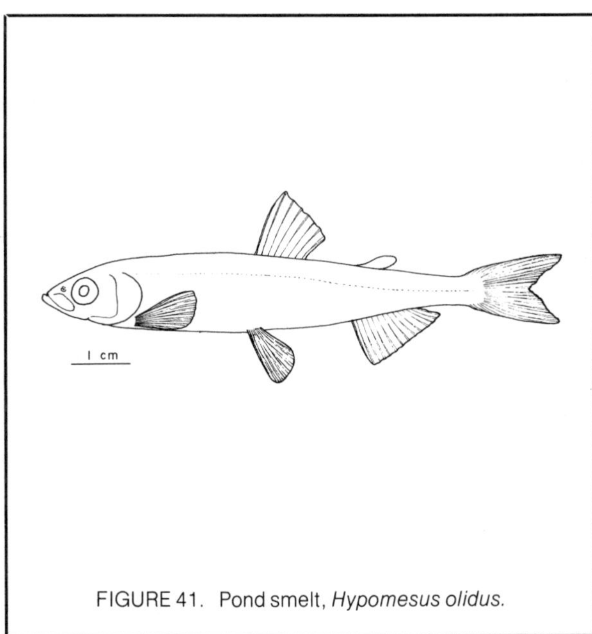

FIGURE 41. Pond smelt, *Hypomesus olidus*.

DESCRIPTION

Body elongate, somewhat compressed. Depth 16% to 24% of standard length. Head short, 20% to 25% of standard length. Snout short and blunt, length usually a little less than eye diameter. Eye round, moderate, diameter equal to 20% to 30% of head length. Mouth small and oblique, lower jaw protruding beyond upper when mouth is closed, maxilla reaching to below pupil. Small pointed teeth present on both jaws and on tongue, and in 2 rows on vomer and palatines. Gill rakers long and slender; 26 to 34 on first arch. Branchiostegals: 6 to 8. Lateral line is incomplete, with 7 to 16 pored scales, and reaching scarcely beyond tip of pectoral fin. Pyloric caeca: 0 to 3, usually 2 and in rare cases 4. Vertebrae: 51 to 62.

FINS. Dorsal fin originates slightly before middle in standard length; 7 to 9 rays. Adipose fin present. Anal fin, 12 to 18 rays, usually 12 to 16. Pectorals short; 10 to 12 rays, in rare cases, 13. Pelvics arise below or ahead of origin of dorsal fin; 8 rays. Caudal forked.

SCALES. Large cycloid; 51 to 62 in a midlateral row. Males develop breeding tubercles on scales as well as on fin rays and head.

COLOR. Light brown to olive green above, with a metallic silver band along middle of sides. Ventral regions silver white. Fins pale (photograph, page 97).

SIZE. Reported to reach 18.5 cm in the Anadyr River (Andriyashev, 1954). Most North American adults are 10 to 15 cm in total length.

RANGE AND ABUNDANCE

In Asia, the pond smelt is found from Wonsan, Korea, north to the Chukhotsk Peninsula, westward to the Alazaya River in Siberia. It is also present on Hokkaido Island, Japan, and on Sakhalin Island, U.S.S.R. An isolated population is present in Lake Krugloe, Siberia, in the Kara Sea drainage (Ivanova, 1952). In North America, the pond smelt is known from the Copper River north along coastal regions to the Kobuk River in Alaska, and from the Mackenzie drainage as far upstream as Great Bear Lake in northern Canada.

The pond smelt is often extremely abundant in suitable ponds and streams (Turner, 1886).

This species (or possibly the closely related *H. transpacificus japonicus*) was introduced into a number of reservoirs in California, but only one of the introductions, that in Freshwater Lagoon, Humboldt County, seems to have been at all successful (Wales, 1962).

HABITS

Spawning occurs in shallow water in streams or ponds, over pebbly bottoms in streams but often in littoral areas of ponds where the bottom is covered by organic debris (Jordan and Evermann, 1896; Nikolskii, 1956; Narver, 1966). Time of spawning is late April to May in Asia, but not until June in the Copper River and in certain lakes in Alaska. On the spawning grounds, there are about three females for every male. Each female produces 1,200 to nearly 4,000 eggs. The eggs are about .075 cm in diameter at fertilization, but quickly swell to about .095 cm on contact with the water. They are demersal and sticky, adhering to whatever they touch. Like other smelt eggs, those of the pond smelt form a short pedicle from the inverted outer coat. However, about two days after fertilization the egg breaks off the pedicle and thereafter develops pelagically (Nikolskii, 1956). This pelagic development has not been reported by other authors. Hatching occurs on the 11th day at temperatures between 11° and 15°C (Nikolskii, 1956) but not until the 18th to 24th day at 10°C (Narver, 1966).

The larvae are .4 to .5 cm long, with a well-developed yolk sac. They begin to feed almost immediately after hatching, even before the yolk sac is absorbed, feeding on minute crustaceans and rotifers (Sato, 1952). When they are about 1 cm long the young school up and move close to shore, where they tend to stay for most of the summer, moving into deeper water with the approach of fall. After a month of planktonic life, the young are about 2 cm long; they reach 3 to 4 cm by the end of the summer (Nikolskii, 1956). During this time, the larval population may decline drastically, but the cause of the decline is unknown (DeGraaf, 1974).

Pond smelt are about 6 cm long at the end of their first year, about 8 to 10 cm at the end of their second. Apparently only a few survive beyond age 3. Sexual maturity is reached at the end of the second year in most populations, although in some Japanese populations spawning occurs at age 1+, with virtually no survivors. Most pond smelt are 5 to 7 cm long by the end of the first year, 7 to 9 cm at 2, 9 to 11 cm at 3, and about 12 cm at 4. The last two age groups are extremely scarce.

A unique population of pond smelt is reported from an unnamed lake on the Arctic coastal plain of the Yukon Territory at 69°18'N, 138°57'W (DeGraaf, 1974). If the age determinations are correct, a few of these fish may survive to 9+. The growth rates given are extraordinarily slow, with 1+ fish smaller than young-of-the-year from other places; fish of 5+ no longer than 1+ fish from Black Lake, Alaska; and fish presumed to be 8+ and 9+ about the same length as Black Lake 2+ fish.

As a rule, pond smelt do not migrate. However, within a specific lake or pond the adult fish generally stay on the inshore spawning areas in spring and early summer, later moving offshore. Young-of-the-year follow the same pattern, while immature fish stay in the pelagic regions all summer. There may be outmigrations to other parts of the drainage system if populations are high in relation to the abundance of food (Narver, 1966).

Food of the pond smelt is virtually exclusively zooplankton. Very young fish feed largely on rotifers, while adults take larger zooplankton such as copepods and cladocera, as well as insects and, occasionally, algae (Sato, 1952; Nikolskii, 1956).

IMPORTANCE TO MAN

The pond smelt is of no direct importance to man, due chiefly to its limited distribution. Where it is present, it is of value in subsistence fisheries (Turner, 1886). Pond smelt are doubtless used locally in Asia as well as in Alaska.

It has been suggested (McPhail and Lindsey, 1970) that, since the adults feed mainly on zooplankton, they may sometimes be important competitors with young sockeye salmon.

SURF SMELT

Hypomesus pretiosus (Girard)

DISTINCTIVE CHARACTERS

The surf smelt is distinguishable from other species of *Hypomesus* by its midlateral scale count of 66 to 73 and the presence of 4 to 7 pyloric caeca (Figure 42).

DESCRIPTION

Body elongate, slender, slightly compressed. Depth 14% to 22% of fork length. Head rather short, 19% to 21% of fork length. Snout moderate, about 30% of head length and about equal to interorbital width. Eye round, its diameter about equal to snout length. Mouth rather small, maxilla reaching to below front half of eye. Teeth small, pointed, present on both jaws. Gill rakers: 31 to 36 on first arch. Branchiostegals: 7 to 8. Lateral line short and incomplete, reaching about to tip of pectoral fin. Pyloric caeca: 4 to 7. Vertebrae: 62 to 70, usually 64 to 68.

FINS. Dorsal fin, which originates above or slightly behind middle of body length, has 8 to 10 rays. Small, sickle-shaped adipose fin present. Anal has 12 to 16 rays; pectorals, which are slightly longer in males than in females, have 14 to 17 rays. Pelvics, with 8 rays, originate below or behind front of dorsal fin. Caudal forked.

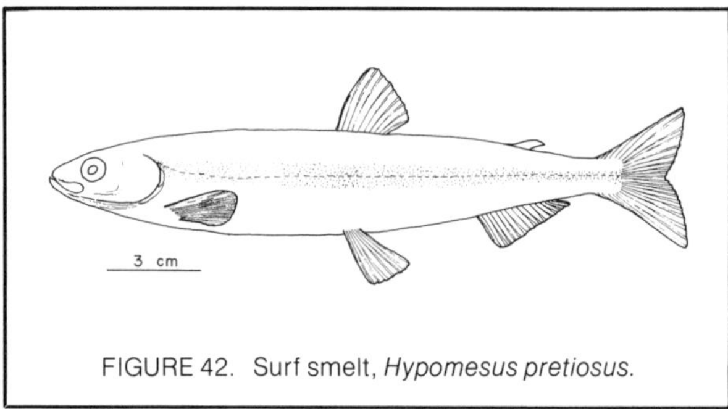

FIGURE 42. Surf smelt, *Hypomesus pretiosus*.

SCALES. Cycloid; 66 to 73 in a midlateral series. Scales are deciduous and easily removed.

COLOR. In males, the back is dull olive to brownish, the belly a rather yellow silver. Females are brighter than males, with a more metallic green color above and silver on the belly. Along the middle of each side in both sexes is a bright silver band which becomes dark in preserved specimens (photograph, page 98).

SIZE. The surf smelt reaches a length of about 25.4 cm in California (Roedel, 1953) but the maximum size of northern fish seems to be about 20 to 23 cm.

RANGE AND ABUNDANCE

The surf smelt is found along the coast of North America from Long Beach, California, in the south (Miller and Lea, 1972) to Chignik Lagoon in southwestern Alaska (Phinney and Dahlberg, 1968). A single specimen was taken in Herendeen Bay, on the northside of the Alaska Peninsula, in the summer of 1976. (I. Warner, Alaska Dept. Fish & Game, Kodiak, pers. comm.). On the western side of the Pacific, another subspecies ranges from southern Kamchatka to Korea.

The surf smelt is most abundant in the central part of its range, especially in Puget Sound and adjacent regions. Good runs occur in Alaska as far north as Prince William Sound. In the Columbia River to Puget Sound area, the surf smelt is fished not only for sport but also commercially. Landings of smelt contribute significant amounts to the fisheries of Oregon, Washington and British Columbia. However, abundance is far from uniform. In Puget Sound, for example, 57.3 km of beach are used by spawning smelt, but a particular 9.8 km produce more fish than the remaining 47.5.

HABITS

The surf smelt, as its name suggests, spawns along beaches in light to moderate surf. The spawning period for all populations stretches from March to May, according to locality and population (Yap-Chionggo, 1941). At spawning time, schools of smelt approach the beach, the females appearing a few days before the males. Spawning is most frequent when an afternoon or evening high tide is falling, and takes place from extreme low tide line to more than halfway up the beach (Thompson et al., 1936; Yap-Chionggo, 1941). Other observers have found surf smelt spawning most actively within one to one and one half hours before or after the flood (Loosanoff, 1937). At spawning, large numbers of males mill about near the edge of the surf. When a female is seen, numbers of males pursue her and try to get into spawning position. If she swims into deeper water, the males desert her. A ripe female, however, moves up the beach, accompanied by one to five males who swim parallel to and slightly behind her. The males press against the female, sometimes tilting their bodies to bring male and female vents close together. As they reach water 2.5 to 5 cm deep, the fish bend and vibrate, releasing eggs and sperm, then retreat to deeper water. Spawning may take place on both incoming and outgoing waves (Schaefer, 1936). The spawning act lasts only 5 to 10 seconds and may be repeated on several successive waves. A female usually requires several days to deposit all her ripe eggs, which number from about 1,500 to over 36,000 (Schaefer, 1936), depending on the race and size of the female. Females normally contain several size-groups of eggs at any given time and apparently spawn more than once in a single season. Although the female releases only a few eggs at a time, the males emit rather large quantities of milt, so that the water may become slightly milky on a heavily used beach. Preferred beaches are those not exposed to strong sun and composed of coarse sand and fine gravel .25 to .4 cm in diameter. Suitable-size substrate particles appear to be a most important factor in the selection of a spawning beach.

The eggs, about .1 to .12 cm in diameter after water-hardening, are pale yellow in color and are sticky and adhere to the particles of gravel. Shortly after fertilization, the outer membrane of each egg ruptures and turns inside out, adhering to the egg at the point where it sticks to the substrate and forming a short pedicle. Wave action buries the eggs, usually to a depth of 2.5 to 10 cm but sometimes to as deep as 30 cm.

Incubation requires 8 to 11 days at 12.2° to 15.5°C, but three or four times as long at 7.5° to 8.5°C. Once development is complete, hatching requires the stimulus of wetting, which is accomplished by the incoming tide. The young are .3 to .6 cm long at hatching and are transparent, with yellow eyes and a small yolk sac. The young are positively phototropic and swim actively toward the light. Thirteen days after hatching they are about .7 cm long.

Very little is known of the subsequent life history. Young smelt 3.5 cm long closely resemble the adults and may go up rivers, where they feed on Diptera and Ephemeroptera. Presumably those fish that do ascend rivers return to the sea very shortly, for only a few specimens have been taken in fresh water. One was recorded from the Sandy River, 16 km east of Portland, Oregon (McAllister, 1963).

The surf smelt matures at age 1+ or 2+, at a minimum length of 9 cm, with males maturing earlier than females. Within a single age group, larger fish mature and spawn earlier in the season than do smaller ones (Schaefer, 1936; Loosanoff, 1937). Maximum life is about two years for males, three for females.

Food in the sea consists of a wide variety of crustaceans, including copepods, amphipods, euphausiids, shrimp larvae, crabs, worms and jellyfish, as well as larval fishes (Hart and McHugh, 1944; Hart, 1973).

Nothing is known of the movments of the surf smelt. They disappear, presumably offshore, as young and reappear inshore as mature adults.

IMPORTANCE TO MAN

The surf smelt is one of the minor constituents of the total commercial fisheries of the west coast of North America. Total landings run to several hundred thousand kg per year and the surf smelt is considered *the* smelt in British Columbia. As food, it is considered a delicacy, being of fine flavor and texture. The size of the sport catch is unknown, but it is probably quite large.

EULACHON
ALSO KNOWN AS HOOLIGAN
Thaleichthys pacificus (Richardson)

DISTINCTIVE CHARACTERS

Large canine teeth on the vomer and 18 to 23 rays in the anal fin distinguish the eulachon (Figure 34).

DESCRIPTION

Body elongate, slender, slightly compressed in females; thicker in the back than in the belly (so that a cross-section is more or less pear-shaped) in adult males. Depth 15% to 20% of standard length. Head short, 20% to 26% of standard length, with rather prominent concentric striae present on gill covers. Tubercles present on heads of breeding males, but poorly developed or absent in females. Snout fairly long, 25% to 28% of head length. Eye round, small, its diameter 50% to 66% of snout length. Mouth oblique, large; maxilla reaches to or behind posterior margin of eye in adults. Small, pointed teeth present on both jaws, tongue and palatines; a pair of moderately large canine teeth present on vomer. All teeth tend to be lost at spawning. Gill rakers long, about 66% of eye diameter; 17 to 23 on first arch. Branchiostegals: 6 to 8. Lateral line complete, with 70 to 78 pored scales. Pyloric caeca quite long: 8 to 12. Vertebrae: 65 to 72; usually 68 to 70.

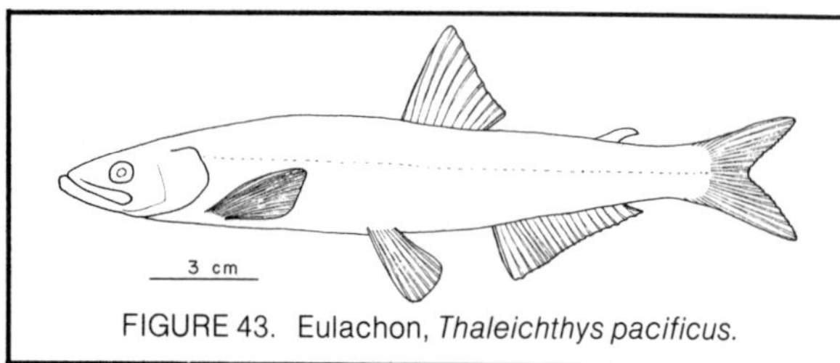

FIGURE 43. Eulachon, *Thaleichthys pacificus.*

FINS. Dorsal has 10 to 13 rays. Sickle-shaped adipose fin present. Anal has 18 to 23 rays; pectorals, 10 to 12; pelvics, 8. Caudal forked. Pectoral and pelvic fins longer in males than in females, pelvic fins of males sometimes reaching anus but always much shorter than that in females. All fins have well developed breeding tubercles in ripe males, but breeding tubercles are poorly developed or absent in females.

SCALES. Cycloid, rather small. Well developed breeding tubercles present on adult males, but tubercles only poorly developed on scales of females.

COLOR. Brown to dark bluish on the back, fading to silvery white or white on the belly. Fins transparent, although pectorals and caudal often dusky (photograph, page 98).

SIZE. Maximum length about 22.5 cm fork length (Taranetz, 1933), but generally not over 20 cm.

RANGE AND ABUNDANCE

The eulachon ranges from Bodega Head, California (Odemar, 1964) north along the coast of North America to Bristol Bay, Alaska, and westward in the Bering Sea to the Pribilof Islands. It is seasonally abundant in all its spawning streams.

HABITS

The eulachon is anadromous, spending most of its life in the sea but returning to freshwater streams to spawn. There is evidence, based on significant differences in meristic characters such as numbers of vertebrae, indicating that eulachon return to their natal streams (Hart and McHugh, 1944). The spawning run occurs in the spring, beginning in mid-March in the southern part of the range and extending well into May at the northern end. Males predominate in the early part of the run, but their numbers may be equalled or exceeded by females later. The fish apparently do not feed in fresh water (McHugh, 1939; Hart and McHugh, 1944).

Spawning takes place over coarse sand and pea-size gravel in water up to about 7.6 m deep. Water temperature at spawning time is usually between 4.4° and 7.8°C (McHugh, 1940; Smith and Saalfeld, 1955). The eggs are about .08 to .1 cm in diameter and a female produces from about 17,000 to as many as 60,000 eggs. Fecundity increases with the size and age of the individual. Shortly after the egg is extruded, its outer membrane splits, separates from the inner membrane and turns inside out, remaining attached to the inner membrane at one point and thus forming a short stalk. The free edges of the broken membrane are sticky and easily become attached to the bottom substrate. Hatching occurs after 30 to 40 days incubation at 4.4° to 7.2°C, but in less than 21 days at 9.4° to 12.8°C. The larvae are transparent, only .4 to .5 cm long. Weak swimmers, they stay near the bottom of the stream and are soon carried downstream to salt water. In the sea, the young fish are distributed in the scattering layer of coastal waters, where food is abundant. Food of the youngest fish seems to be mainly copepod larvae. Later young, 2.5 to 5 cm long, have a more varied diet, including phytoplankton, copepod eggs and adults, mysids, ostracods, barnacle larvae, cladocerans, worm larvae and the smaller larvae of the eulachon itself (Hart, 1973, citing unpublished studies by Barraclough). Juvenile eulachon feed heavily on euphausiids, which are abundant in these waters. By midwinter (December to February) the young fish average about 6.6 cm in length and by the time they are a full year old they are about 8 cm long. Subsequent growth is much slower. Two-year-old fish average not quite 9 cm; 3+, about 11.7 cm; 4+, about 15.4 cm in April. Adult eulachon in the sea feed on plankton, mostly euphausiids and cumaceans (Hart and McHugh, 1944; Smith and Saalfeld, 1955; McAllister, 1963; Barraclough, 1964).

Little else is known of the marine life of the eulachon. Occasional commercial catches of this smelt in near-shore waters suggest that the fish do not travel far offshore, probably moving about at no great distance from the natal river.

Sexual maturity may be attained at the end of the second year of life in some populations but not until the end of the third year in others. Most smelt die after spawning, but some survive and may spawn a second time. The spawning run from the sea begins when river temperatures rise to about 4.4°C, but the fish stop running if the temperature exceeds 7.8°C. Most of the runs occur in the larger rivers, such as the Columbia and Fraser, although smaller streams reaching the sea may also have eulachon populations. The spawning grounds may be in the major rivers themselves or in tributaries. Some of the spawning areas in the Columbia River are above Vancouver, Washington, more than 160 km from the ocean.

IMPORTANCE TO MAN

In Washington and Oregon, commercial fisheries exist which take more than 454,000 kg per year. A fishery of similar size once existed in British Columbia, but landings at present are much smaller. Eulachon are important in the subsistence fisheries, and have been for many years (Swan, 1881). Today, the native fishery in British Columbia probably takes more fish than does the province's commercial fishery (Scott and Crossman, 1973).

The flesh of the eulachon contains a high percentage of oil that can be rendered down to a fatty material of a color and consistency much like lard. This fat was highly prized by the Indians of the Pacific northwest. The fat content is so high that, when dried, the fish can be burned directly or with a wick threaded through it; hence the alternative name: candle fish.

Today the eulachon is utilized principally as food either for humans or for commercially reared fur-bearing animals. The flavor is good and the eulachon has a high place among gourmet food fishes. Indeed, it has been considered "unsurpassed by any fish whatsoever in delicacy of the flesh . . ." (Jordan and Evermann, 1908).

The eulachon is also important indirectly. When eulachon have congregated off river mouths preparatory to beginning their spawning runs, they are fed upon heavily by all sorts of predatory fishes including halibut, cod and salmon, as well as by such marine mammals as finback whales, porpoises, sea lions and seals. The eulachon thus forms an important link in the food chain between the small animals of the zooplankton and the large carnivores.

RAINBOW SMELT

Osmerus mordax (Mitchill)

DISTINCTIVE CHARACTERS

One or more large canine teeth on the vomer (often missing in spawning fish), 11 to 16 anal rays and a dorsal fin that originates above or ahead of the bases of the pelvic fins distinguish the rainbow smelt from other Alaskan osmerids (Figure 44).

DESCRIPTION

Body elongate, compressed, slender; depth about 12% to 19% of total length. Head moderate, length 16.5% to 23% of total length. Snout pointed, elongate, longer than eye diameter. Eye large, round, diameter 17.5% to 24% of head length. Mouth large, lower jaw longer than upper; maxilla reaches to middle of eye or farther back. Teeth well developed, caniniform, present on both jaws, tongue, vomer and palatines, the anterior teeth on tongue and vomer being enlarged. Gill rakers long, slender: 25 to 36 on first arch. Branchiostegals: usually 7 on each side, in rare cases 5, 6 or 8 on either or both sides. Lateral line is incomplete, has 14 to 28 pored scales. Pyloric caeca: 4 to 8. Vertebrae: 58 to 70, most often 60 to 66.

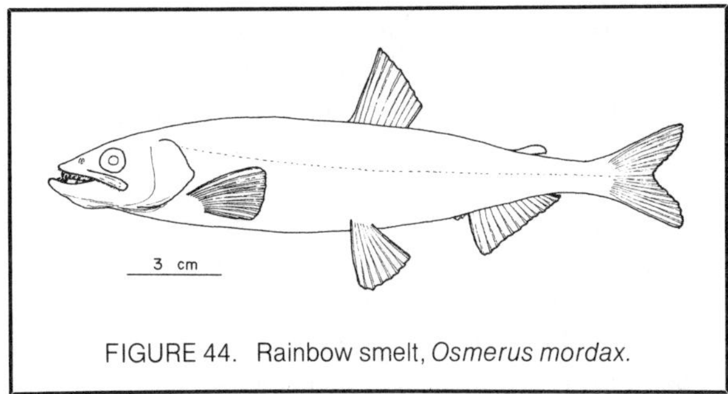

FIGURE 44. Rainbow smelt, *Osmerus mordax*.

FINS. Dorsal originates ahead of base of pelvic fins; 8 to 11 rays. Small adipose fin present. Anal has 12 to 16 rays; pectorals, which are shorter than head, 11 to 14 rays; pelvics, 8. Caudal forked.

SCALES. Cycloid, fairly large, thin and deciduous; 62 to 72 in a midlateral series. Prominent nuptial tubercles present on scales of spawning males, absent in females.

COLOR. Pale green to olive above, silvery below, with a bright, metallic silvery band along the sides. Sides often have purple, blue or pink iridescence. Fins colorless, sometimes with faint speckling (photograph, page 99).

SIZE. Reported up to 34 cm total length in the Anadyr River of Siberia (Berg, 1948), but North American smelt apparently only rarely exceed about 25 cm. The average rainbow smelt in commercial catches is about 15 cm long with a weight of about 30 grams.

RANGE AND ABUNDANCE

The range of the rainbow smelt along the Pacific Coast of North America is from Barkley Sound, Vancouver Island, north along the coast of British Columbia and Alaska (but not yet recorded between Lituya Bay and the tip of the Alaska Peninsula) through Bristol Bay, thence north to the arctic coast and east to Cape Bathurst. The species is also known from Saint Lawrence Island. On the Asian side, the rainbow smelt may be found from Korea and northern Japan to the Anadyr Peninsula and westward to the White Sea of Russia. Rainbow smelt are also native to the eastern coast of North America from northern New Jersey north to Hamilton Inlet on the northern coast of Labrador and westward in a number of lakes and streams in Quebec and Ontario (Dymond, 1937; Bigelow and Schroeder, 1963). References to rainbow smelt as far south as Virginia appear to be in error (Low, 1896; Backus, 1957; Bigelow and Schroeder, 1963).

Smelt were introduced into Michigan waters from Maine, beginning in 1906. Early plantings were unsuccessful, but a plant of 16.4 million eggs in Crystal Lake, Benzie County, made in 1912, took hold and appears to have produced the ancestors of most or all smelt in the western Great Lakes (Hankinson and Hubbs, 1922; Creaser, 1926; Savage, 1935). Introductions into New York waters were probably responsible for smelt in Lake Ontario, for they appeared there some years before they were taken in Lake Erie (Mason, 1933).

Wherever it is present, except perhaps in the most extreme ends of its range, the rainbow smelt is abundant although, because of its migratory habits, the abundance is local and seasonal.

HABITS

Little if anything is known from direct studies on the rainbow smelt of the Pacific coast. Most of the following account is derived from studies of east coast and Great Lakes populations. Presumably the life history of Pacific coast smelts is not much different.

Like other osmerids, the rainbow smelt is a springtime spawner. The adult fish begin to congregate near stream mouths early in the spring, often long before the ice goes out (Rupp, 1959). In most areas the majority of the fish are first-time spawners, usually 2+ fish. These constitute half to two-thirds of the run, with 3+ fish making up another 25% to 30% and the rest being older fish (McKenzie, 1964). Movement into the streams begins when water temperatures reach 2° to 4°C or higher. Warm days and cool nights seem to encourage the spawning migrations (Hoover, 1936). As a rule, the upstream run is short, at most a few km, and sometimes only a few hundred meters above the head of the tide; some rainbow smelt may even spawn in brackish water behind barrier beaches or in the tidal zone of estuaries (Bigelow and Schroeder, 1963; McKenzie, 1964). In the Yenisei River of Siberia, however, upstream migrations of more than 1,000 km have been observed (Berg, 1948), and of at least 320 km in the St. Lawrence River in Canada (Magnin and Beaulieu, 1965).

The movement from lake or river to the spawning grounds is usually made at night, although daytime spawning has been observed (Rupp, 1959). In most populations, there appears to be an influx of fish just after dusk, followed by a second group running around 2 a.m. (Creaser, 1926; Hoover, 1936; Baldwin, 1950). As a rule the males appear first, the females following an hour or so later. Spawning seems to be initiated, at least in part, by the presence of the proper sex ratio in the group, which has been indicated as being no more than four males to one female (Hoover, 1936; Rupp, 1965). In the spawning act, which takes place over sandy gravel, pebbles and rocks, the fish crowd together, all headed upstream. They move sideways in somewhat exaggerated swimming movements. Contact between males either brings about no reaction or a separation of the two fish, but when a male and female contact each other, eggs and milt are released. It has also been reported that the male pushes the female to the bottom or into shallow water after contact has been made (Hoover, 1936), but this action does not seem to be general. Apparently the prominent nuptial tubercles on the sides of the males provide a tactile stimulus for discriminating between the sexes. Females also may have nuptial tubercles on the top of the head and along the base of the dorsal fin, but the tubercles are poorly developed and located in positions where they could not function in the manner described (Hoover, 1936; Richardson, 1942; Rupp, 1965).

In the spawning act, a female deposits only about 50 eggs at a time (Hoover, 1936). Since the eggs are quite small (.08 to .1 cm) a single female produces a large number, from 1,700 to 69,600 (Langlois, 1935; Hoover, 1936; Berg, 1948; Bailey, 1964; McKenzie, 1964). Thus many spawning acts, spread over several hours each night for several nights, are required to deposit all the eggs.

Following each evening's activity, most of the fish drift, tailfirst, downstream to the larger body of water whence they came to the spawning grounds. Some, mostly males, may remain in the spawning stream during the day, but they avoid light as much as possible.

The larger members of an age group become

sexually ripe earlier in the season than do smaller ones, and older fish earlier than younger. Hence the spawning season may extend over several weeks, or even months, with newly ripe fish coming in as the spawned-out fish leave. Because of this correlation of spawning time with age and size, the average size of the fish tends to decrease as the run progresses.

Many of the spawned-out fish, especially males, die after spawning, but those that survive will spawn again the following year. Sexual maturity is achieved at the end of the second or third year of life. Since a few fish may live to six years, some obviously spawn several times during their lives (Creaser, 1926; Bailey, 1964).

Spawning is not always confined to streams, for rainbow smelt have been observed breeding in shallows along lake shores. Here the fish come inshore in small schools and swim about over rather restricted areas, apparently without any distinct pairing. The composition of the schools changes constantly, for individual fish apparently engage in spawning activities for only 15 to 30 minutes at a time, then leave the school (Lievense, 1954; Rupp, 1965).

Wherever spawning takes place, the eggs settle quickly to the bottom. Within 15 to 30 seconds of exposure to water, they become sticky and adhere to whatever they touch. As with the eggs of other smelt, the outer cover of rainbow smelt eggs ruptures and turns inside out, adhering to the egg at one point so that the egg is held above the substrate on a tiny pedestal. Hatching occurs in about 29 days at 6° to 7°C; 25 days at 7° to 8°C; 19 days at 9° to 10°C; 11 days at 12.2°C and 10 days at 15°C (Hoover, 1936; McKenzie, 1964). Density of eggs on the spawning grounds varies tremendously, depending on the number of adults using the area. Greatest production of larvae results when the density of eggs is on the order of 100,000 to 130,000 per square meter. Under these conditions, average survival to hatching is on the order of .5% to 2%. Major causes of mortality are mechanical crushing, abrading, dislodging by waves and currents, and fungus infections. However, year class abundance is not related to the number of larvae produced. Factors affecting the post-hatching survival of the young apparently are more important than the number of fish hatched (McKenzie, 1947, 1964; Rothschild, 1961; Rupp, 1965).

The young are about .5 to .6 cm long at hatching and are transparent. Being weak swimmers, they are soon carried downstream to the lake or estuary. They reach a length of 4 to 6 cm in three or four months (Anonymous, 1961; Gordon, 1961; Bigelow and Schroeder, 1963). Growth rates vary tremendously from one population to another. However, averages compiled from a number of sources yield the following approximate lengths at various ages: 1+, 11.1 cm; 2+, 16.7 cm; 3+, 19 cm; 4+, 21.8 cm; 5+, 22.8 cm; and 6+, 24.2 cm. Females grow faster, get bigger and live longer than males (Creaser, 1926; Beckman, 1942; Warfel et al., 1943; Baldwin, 1950; McKenzie, 1958; Bailey, 1964).

Except during spawning runs, the rainbow smelt apparently does not undertake definite migrations. Fish that go to sea stay within 8 to 10 km of shore and probably do not stray far along the coast from the estuary (Bigelow and Schroeder, 1963).

Although the rainbow smelt apparently returns to the river system in which it was hatched, the return to the spawning streams, both by first-time spawners and by older fish, is often not precise. The degree of homing seems to vary from one population to another and may be genetically controlled (McKenzie, 1964; Rupp and Redmond, 1966).

Food of young-of-the-year smelt is mostly copepods and cladocerans, as well as rotifers, eggs and algae. Adults in salt water feed on decapod and mysid shrimps, copepods, amphipods and small fishes, crabs, squid, worms and a variety of small shellfish. The diet in fresh water includes the same major groups: copepods, amphipods, cladocerans, mysids and small fishes as well as various insects, especially Ephemeroptera and Diptera nymphs and larvae. Feeding virtually ceases during spawning (Creaser, 1926, 1929; Kendall, 1927; Beckman, 1942; Baldwin, 1950; Gordon, 1961; Bigelow and Schroeder, 1963).

IMPORTANCE TO MAN

In areas where it is sufficiently abundant, such as New England and the Great Lakes region of the U.S. and Canada, the rainbow smelt is an important part of both the sport and commercial fisheries. Since 1960 the commercial catch by the U.S. and Canada in the Great Lakes and in the international lakes between Minnesota and Ontario has been between 4.5 and 9 million kg annually, averaging about 6.8 million, with a value of about $.07 per kg. These fish are taken mainly by trawls, traps and gill nets. In New England, landings of smelt reached 550,000 kg in 1889, but declined to a yearly average of only 215,250 kg from 1951 through 1954, and to an annual average of only 69,700 kg in 1969 through 1971. This decline probably resulted in part from lessened abundance caused by obstructions in, and pollution of, streams and in part from the high price commanded by New England smelts—a price about 10 times that of Great Lakes fish (Bigelow and Schroeder, 1963; Anonymous, 1972, 1973, 1974).

Great Lakes catches were formerly very large, but

an epidemic, attributed to either bacterial or viral infection, decimated the population in 1943 and 1944, causing an estimated loss to the commercial catch of nearly 23 million kg for the fishing seasons of 1943 through 1946 (Van Oosten, 1947). Other epidemic die-offs, particularly in New England, have been ascribed to the microspridian parasite *Glugea hertwigi* (Haley, 1952).

The rainbow smelt is also a popular sport fish. It is taken in dip nets or with hook and line, the latter being especially popular in winter through the ice. Sport catches in the U.S. are estimated to equal or exceed the commercial landings.

As food the rainbow smelt is highly esteemed and has been ever since white men came to North America. Its flesh is firm and tasty. It was not always considered an asset in lakes where it was introduced, as it was thought to be a serious predator on and competitor with various native fishes. In the early days it was considered a nuisance, as it fouled fishermen's nets set for other species. Later, however, it was fished for its own markets. However, there appears to be no evidence that smelt in the Great Lakes have had any adverse effect on other species (Gordon, 1961).

The rainbow smelt is too scarce in Alaska to be of any great importance, although it undoubtedly enters subsistence fisheries from time to time.

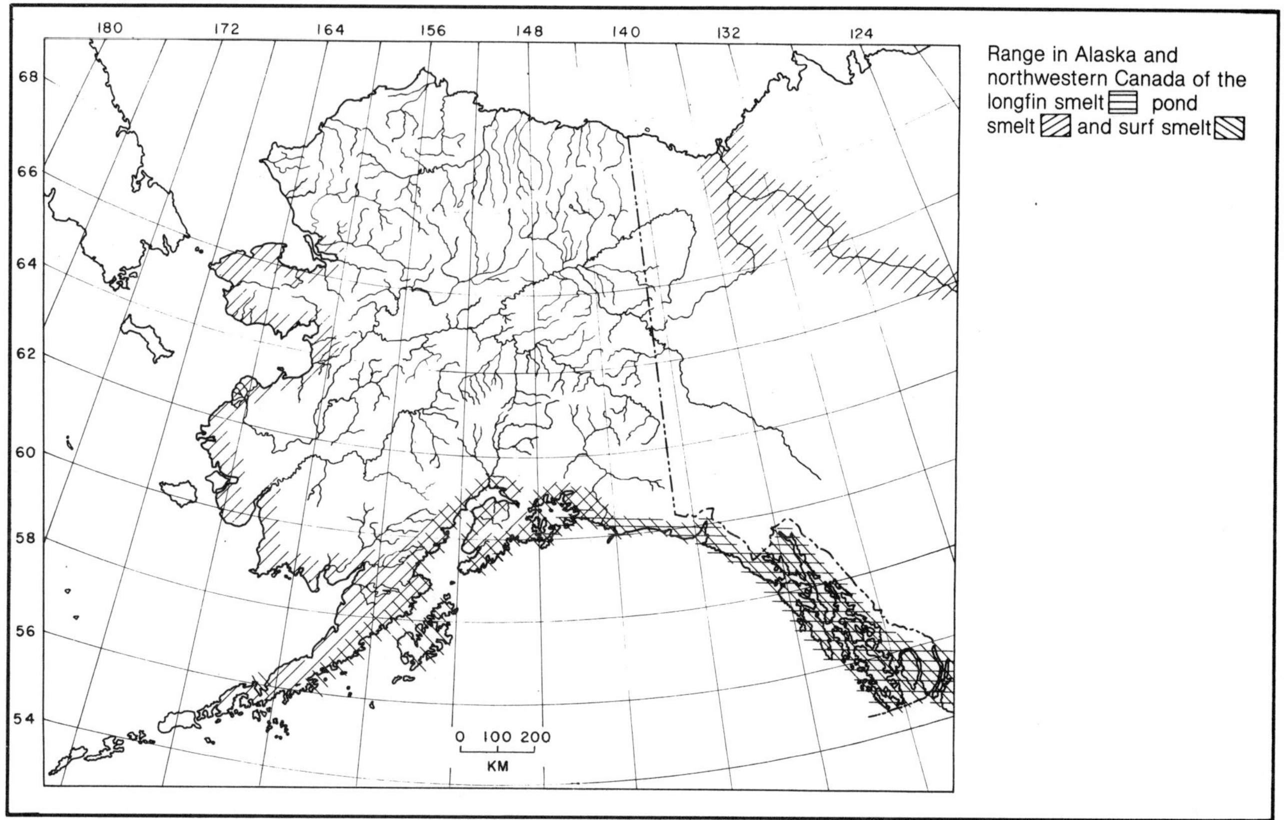

Range in Alaska and northwestern Canada of the longfin smelt ▤ pond smelt ▨ and surf smelt ▧

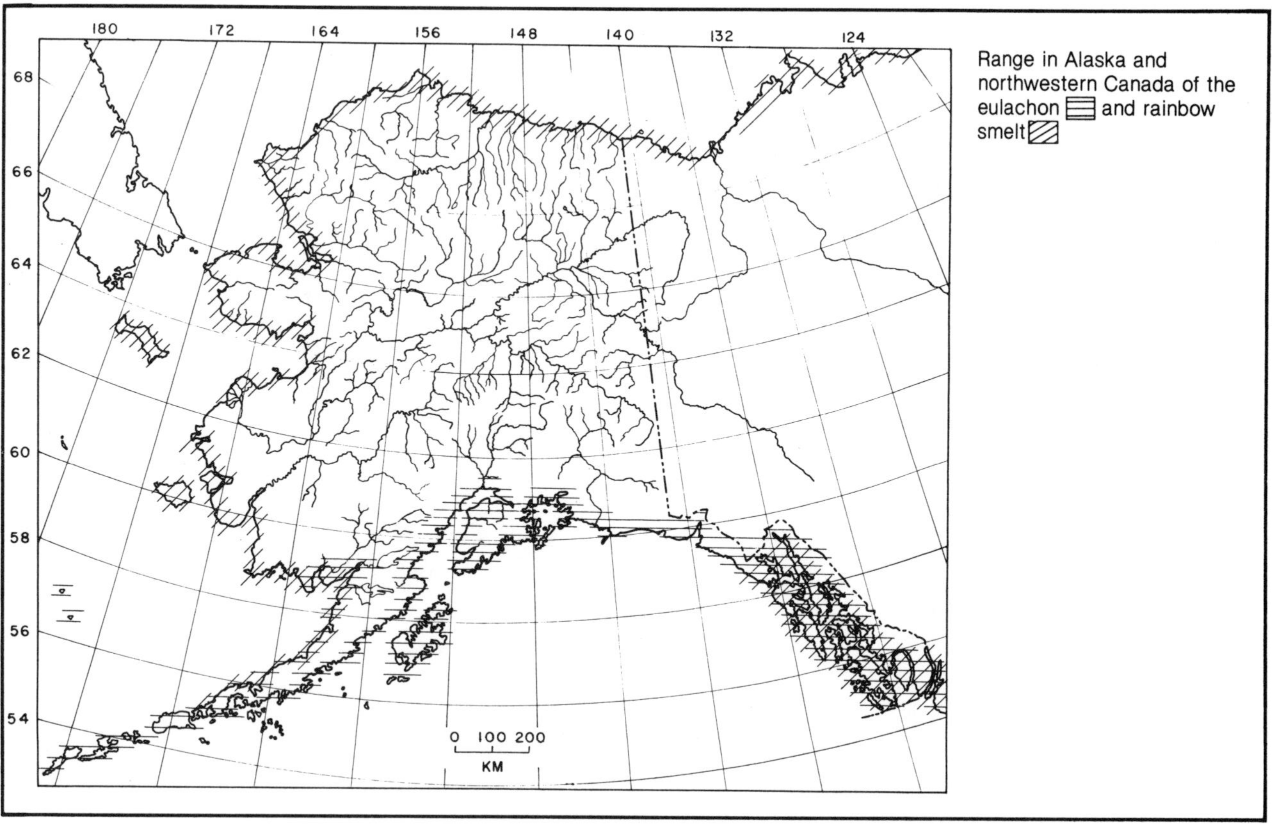

Range in Alaska and northwestern Canada of the eulachon ▤ and rainbow smelt ▨

Chapter Eight

MUDMINNOWS AND BLACKFISH

Family Umbridae

The five living species in this family, belonging to three genera, were previously classified in two or three separate families. Current ichthyological thinking lumps them all in one group. The family is strictly in the northern hemisphere in distribution. One species is found in eastern Europe, two more in eastern and central North America, another in northwestern Washington, and the fifth, *Dallia pectoralis,* in Alaska and western Siberia.

All members of the family are small, elongate fishes with rounded tails and rather broad, flattened heads. They live in small, muddy ponds and quiet streams with abundant vegetation. They are of no commercial value, but the Alaska blackfish may be used for food for both dogs and people.

ALASKA BLACKFISH

Dallia pectoralis Bean

DISTINCTIVE CHARACTERS

The Alaska blackfish is identified by its short, flattened snout, the rearward location of the dorsal and anal fins, the presence of about 33 rays in the pectoral fins, and the presence of a pelvic fin that has only three rays (Figure 45).

DESCRIPTION

Body elongate, cylindrical toward the head but compressed toward the tail. Depth of body about 16% of total length. Head short, blunt, somewhat flattened, about 20% of total length. Snout short, near 20% of head. Eye small, round, its diameter usually about 75% of snout length. Mouth large, broad, with lower jaw protruding; maxilla reaches behind middle of eye. Small, sharp teeth present on lower jaw, premaxilla, palatines and head of vomer. No teeth on maxilla or tongue. Gill rakers short: 9 to 12. Branchiostegals: 7 to 8. Lateral line has minute pores: 76 to 100 scales in midlateral series. No pyloric caeca. Vertebrae: 40 to 42.

FINS. Dorsal, which is located far back on body, has 10 to 14 rays. Anal, which is more or less under dorsal, 12 to 16 rays; pectorals, 32 to 36, with edge of fins round. Pelvics usually have 3 rays each, the fins very small and located just before anus. Caudal fin broad, rounded.

SCALES. Cycloid, small, more or less embedded in skin.

COLOR. Dark green or brown above and on upper sides, pale below with dark speckles; four to six irregular dark bars or blotches on sides. Fins have dark brownish speckling. Dorsal, anal and caudal fins have pale margins, which are pink to red in spawning males (photograph, page 99).

SIZE. In most of its normal habitat, the blackfish rarely exceeds 20 cm in length. However, in the Yukon-Kuskokwim Delta, fish up to about 25.5 cm are not uncommon. In the area around Anchorage, fish up to 30.4 cm and 366.0 g have been recorded (Trent and Kubik, 1974) and a single specimen of about 33 cm has been recorded by Alaska Department of Fish & Game, Anchorage.

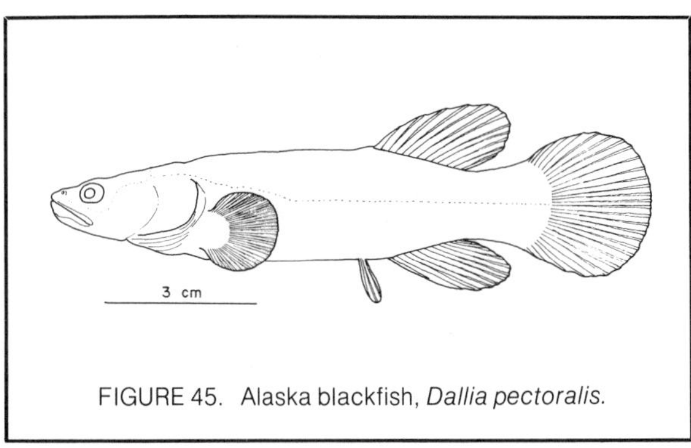

FIGURE 45. Alaska blackfish, *Dallia pectoralis.*

RANGE AND ABUNDANCE

The Alaska blackfish is found in lowland areas in eastern Siberia, Saint Matthew, Saint Lawrence and Nunivak islands in the Bering Sea, and in Alaska. On the mainland of Alaska its natural range is from the Colville River Delta on the arctic coast west and south to the central Alaska Peninsula near Chignik. It is present in the Yukon-Tanana drainage as far upstream as Big Eldorado Creek, near Fairbanks. Wherever it is present, it is usually quite abundant.

The Alaska blackfish was introduced successfully to Saint Paul Island in the Pribilofs and unsuccessfully to Ontario. It was accidentally introduced into Hood and Spenard lakes at the Anchorage airport in the early 1950s and has thrived there. Subsequently it spread via interconnecting waterways and illicit transplants to a number of other lakes in that area, where it now creates a serious problem in the management of the rainbow trout sport fishery.

HABITS

Little is known of the biology of the Alaska blackfish. Spawning occurs in spring and summer, beginning soon after breakup in May and continuing into July in the interior of Alaska, but apparently taking place only in late July in the Bristol Bay area (Blackett, 1962; Aspinwall, 1965). Upstream movement appears to coincide with a rise in water temperature to 10° to 15°C (Blackett, 1962). Spawning has not been observed, but the eggs, which are .15 to .23 cm in diameter, are probably deposited in vegetation at the bottom of shallow ponds and quiet streams (Nelson, 1887; personal observations). Females deposit from about 40 to 300 eggs, the number increasing with the size of the fish. Spawning of a particular female probably goes on over a period of several days, possibly longer, with only a few eggs being extruded at each spawning act. At any rate, partially spawned females have been found during most of the spawning season. Nearly ripe ovarian eggs are yellow and opaque, but are not capable of being fertilized. Fully ripe eggs are nearly transparent. The fertilized eggs are demersal and extremely sticky. Females normally contain two sets of eggs, the large, mature ones being about .2 cm in diameter, and a larger number of small recruitment eggs averaging less than .1 cm in diameter. This second group is presumably the eggs which will be spawned the following year.

Development to hatching requires about 10 days at 12° to 13°C under experimental conditions. The young are about .57 cm long at hatching and have a large yolk sac. By the 10th day after hatching, the young are about .9 cm long and the yolk sac has virtually disappeared. By the 22nd day, the little fish are about 1.2 cm long and are beginning to take on the characteristics of the adults. At 2 to 2.1 cm, reached in about 44 days, metamorphosis is virtually complete (Aspinwall, 1965). Subsequent growth in the first year of life is fairly rapid, but later slows. In interior Alaska and in the Anchorage area, the blackfish reach about 6.4 cm by 1+; 10.8 cm at 2+; 13.8 cm at 3+; and 17.8 cm at 4+. By contrast, fish

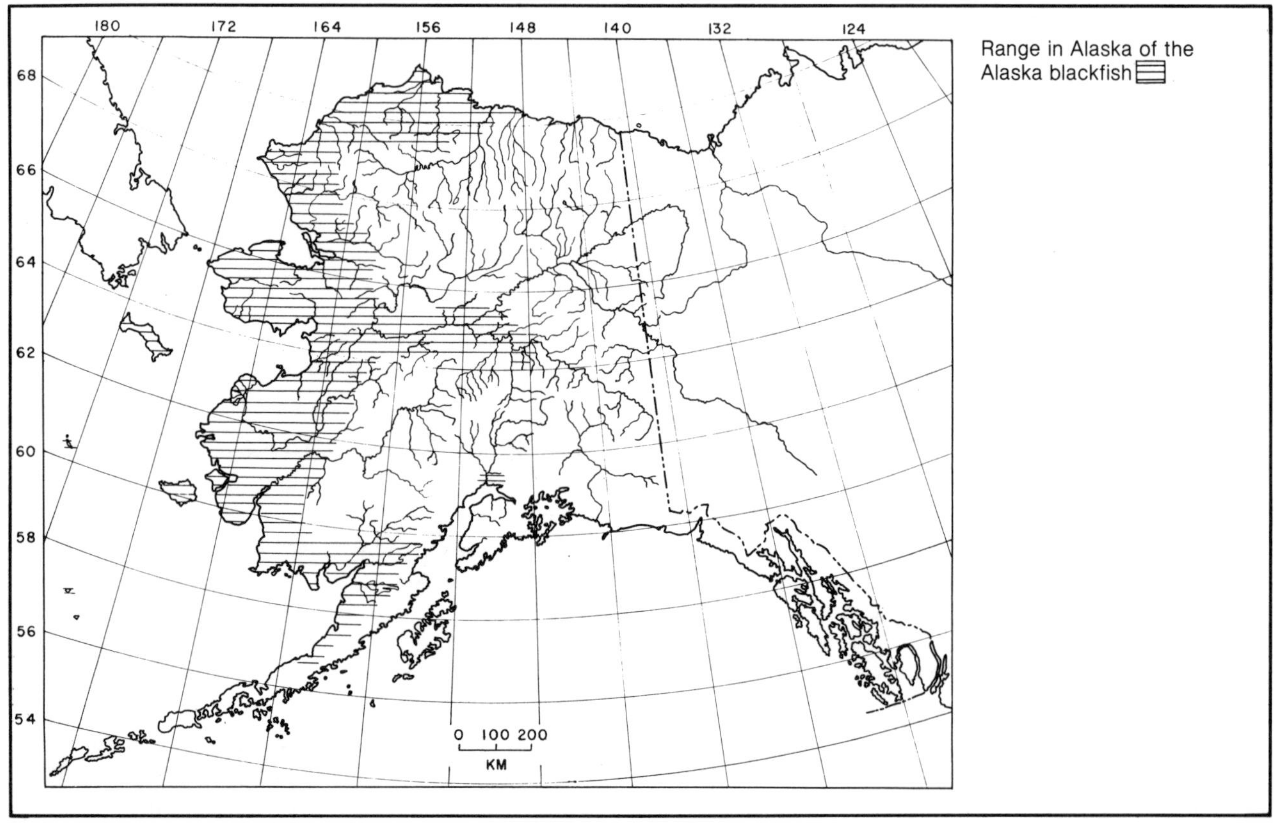

Range in Alaska of the Alaska blackfish

from Lake Aleknagik in the Bristol Bay area grow very slowly. A 2+ fish from that lake was only 3.6 cm long, a 3+ was 5 cm long, a 4+ fish was 6.3 cm long, and one of 8+ was only 13.5 cm long. Sexual maturity is reached at age 2+ or 3+, so some females probably spawn several times during their lives (Blackett, 1962; Aspinwall, 1965; Chlupach, 1975).

The blackfish does not undertake extensive movements, as far as is known. Its migrations appear to be limited to inshore or upstream movements to spawning grounds in the spring and (presumably) reverse migrations to deeper water in the fall.

Blackfish feed almost exclusively on small invertebrates. The smaller individuals subsist mostly on copepods and Cladocera, shifting as they grow larger to insects and small fishes. Hemiptera are especially important, but the diet also includes Diptera larvae, Trichoptera larvae, Ephemeroptera, Odonata, ostracods, mollusks, annelids and even algae (Ostdiek and Nardone, 1959; Chlupach, 1975). They also eat smaller members of their own kind. Because of their hardiness, their ability to tolerate crowding and low oxygen, and their diet, Alaska blackfish make tough competitors for rainbow trout wherever the two coexist.

Blackfish are renowned for their tolerance to cold and there is an old story of frozen blackfish being eaten by dogs, thawed by the heat of the dogs' stomachs and then vomited up alive (Turner, 1886). In spite of the story, blackfish cannot withstand complete freezing. Fish have, however, survived exposure to -20°C for up to 40 minutes, and can survive for a few days after complete freezing of parts of the body, even the head. Complete freezing, however, results in death (Borodin, 1934; Scholander et al., 1953). Blackfish can also withstand complete absence of oxygen for up to 24 hours if the temperature is 0° C (Bonnett, unpublished research).

IMPORTANCE TO MAN

The Alaska blackfish was formerly a most important source of food for Alaskan natives and their dogs. In the early 1880s, it was estimated that not less than 93,900 kg were taken annually in the Yukon-Kuskokwim Delta alone, with 62,600 kg taken from October through December. Total harvest all along the coast was estimated at not less than 140,600 kg and it was felt that double this amount might be a more realistic estimate (Nelson, 1884). Nowadays, however, such use has decreased greatly, although unknown quantities of blackfish are still used in some of the more remote villages.

The Alaska blackfish makes an interesting aquarium fish, but it should be noted that possession or export is prohibited by law unless a permit is secured.

Chapter Nine

PIKES

Family Esocidae

The pikes are elongate, somewhat compressed fishes, with elongate, flattened snouts and large, sharp teeth. Five species in one genus are distributed in the northern hemisphere. One species is confined to Siberia (except for introductions in Pennsylvania), three are native to eastern North America, and the fifth, the northern pike, *Esox lucius,* is of circumpolar distribution.

Pikes are carnivores, their diets consisting mainly of other fishes. They are classified as game fishes in North America, although the smaller members of the family might not be considered so by some people. They are quite edible when properly prepared, and commercial fisheries for northern pike are important in the larger lakes of Canada and the United States. The muskellunge reaches the largest size of any of the pikes, with an angling record of 31.8 kg. Next largest is the northern pike.

NORTHERN PIKE

Esox lucius Linnaeus

DISTINCTIVE CHARACTERS

The pike is easily recognized by its long, flat, "duck-bill" snout; its large mouth with many large, sharp teeth; and the rearward position of its dorsal and anal fins (Figure 46).

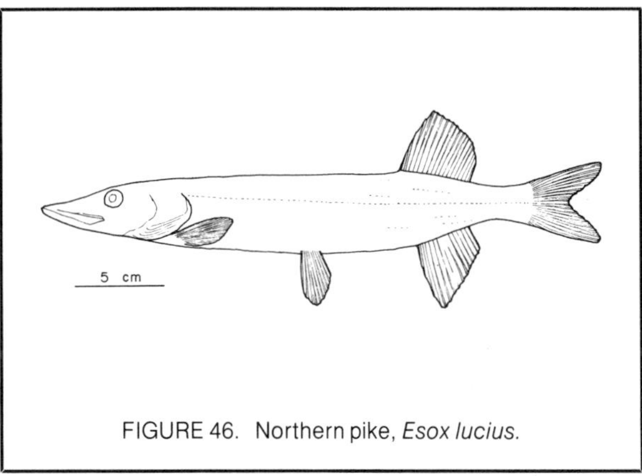

FIGURE 46. Northern pike, *Esox lucius.*

DESCRIPTION

Body elongate, slender, moderately compressed, its depth 10% to 17% of total length. Head long, 25% or more of total length. Snout elongate, flattened, 40% to 47% of head length. Eye round, large, near middle of head length and close to dorsal surface. Mouth large; maxilla reaches to eye; lower jaw often projects beyond upper. Usually five large sensory pores on each side of lower surface of lower jaw. Large sharp canine teeth on lower jaw, head of vomer and inner edge of palatines. Smaller sharp, curved teeth on premaxilla, tongue, vomer and palatines, as well as on basibranchials and pharyngobranchials behind tongue. Gill rakers present only as patches of sharp teeth on gill arches. Branchiostegals: 14 to 15. Lateral line has 55 to 65 pored scales, which are notched posteriorly. Number of scale rows along middle of sides: 105 to 148. No pyloric caeca. Vertebrae: 57 to 65.

FINS. Dorsal, which is located far to the rear, has 17 to 25 soft rays. Anal, located under and arising a little behind dorsal fin, has 14 to 22 rays. Pectorals low on the body, base under opercle; 14 to 17 rays. Pelvics are low on body, about at middle of total length; 10 or 11 rays. Paired fins rounded, paddle-shaped. Caudal fin slightly forked.

SCALES. Cycloid, moderately small, with numerous pitted scales scattered over body.

COLOR. In adults, back and sides dark grayish green to green or dark brownish, sides with numerous yellow spots arranged in irregular longitudinal rows. Scales usually have a tiny gold spot at edge. Belly and ventral surface of head creamy white. Dorsal, anal and caudal fins green to yellowish, sometimes more or less orange or red, marked with dark blotches. Pectoral and pelvic fins dusky. Head dark green above, pale below, with an inconspicuous dark line running below eye.

Color of young pike is similar to that of adults except that the sides are marked with irregular pale vertical bars instead of spots, and the eye bar is usually more conspicuous (photographs, page 100).

A color variant is known as the silver pike. Here the color is grayish green or deep blue on the back becoming silvery gray on the sides to creamy white below. There are no spots or bars on the sides, although pale marks may be present on the caudal peduncle. The fins are marked with small dark spots concentrated along the rays. This color variant is a genetic mutant that breeds true. It was first reported from the area near Sharbot Lake, Ontario (Prince, 1898), and subsequently has been found in north-central United States; in Ontario, Manitoba and MacKenzie in Canada; in Sweden; and in Alaska. It is said to be much hardier than the ordinary form (Eddy and Surber, 1947; Lawler, 1960, 1964; Bartholomew, et al., 1962).

SIZE. The northern pike in North America reaches at least 133 cm in length and 22.3 kg in weight. The angling record is a specimen of 21 kg and 133 cm from Sacandaga Reservoir, New York. A pike said to have weighed "about 45 pounds" (20.5 kg) was taken near Circle, Alaska, in the early

1960s. European pike apparently get bigger than those of North America. There are authentic records of pike up to 26 kg from Ireland and Scandinavia (Scott and Crossman, 1973) and an apparently authentic record of a fish of 34 kg from Lake Il'men' in Russia (Berg, 1948).

An ancient record, dating from 1765, of a large English pike, which appeared in a number of editions of *The Compleat Angler* (Walton, 1815), is as follows:

> On Tuesday last, at Lillieshall Lime Works, near Newport, a pool about 9 yards deep, that had not been fished for ages, was let off by means of a level brought up to drain the works, when an enormous pike was found; he was drawn out by means of a rope fastened round his head and gills, amidst hundreds of spectators, in which service a great many men were employed; he weighed upwards of 170 pounds, and is thought to be the largest ever seen. Some time ago the clerk of the parish was trolling in the above pool, when his bait was seized by this furious creature, which by a sudden jerk pulled him in, and doubtless would have devoured him also, had he not by wonderful agility and dexterous swimming escaped the dreadful jaws of this voracious animal.

This tale is, no doubt, somewhat exaggerated. Nevertheless, it is the sort of story which gives great encouragement to all honest anglers.

In most areas the average pike caught by sport fishermen will run between 1 and 3 kg in weight. A fish of over 7 kg is a very good one and one of more than 11 kg would be considered rather remarkable.

RANGE AND ABUNDANCE

The range of the northern pike is circumpolar in fresh water. It can be found in a wide range of locations in Europe; it is found as far south as Spain and northern Italy, and has an east-west distribution from the British Isles to the Pacific shores of Siberia. In North America, the pike ranges from western Alaska to eastern Canada (but is absent from the Keewatin Peninsula of the Northwest Territories) and from the arctic coast south to Nebraska, Missouri and southern New England. Except in the Ahrnklin River drainage in Alaska and the headwaters of the Alsek and Taku rivers in the Yukon Territory and British Columbia, pike do not occur naturally west of the continental divide. Pike have been introduced into a number of places in the United States, and the introductions are either a nuisance or a blessing, according to one's point of view. Illegal transplants in the 1970s by private individuals placed pike in the Susitna River drainage in Alaska.

HABITS

Pike spend the winter in relatively deep water in lakes and rivers. With the approach of spring, they begin to move inshore or upstream to the marsh areas where they spawn. This movement usually occurs soon after the ice goes out (Clark, 1950), but may start even before that in far northern areas (Cheney, 1972). Most of this movement to the spawning grounds takes place at night (Franklin and Smith, 1963). Spawning does not begin until water temperatures in the shallows reach about 6° to 9°C (Bennett, 1948; Clark, 1950; Cheney, 1971).

Pike tend to return to the same spawning area year after year. The spawning grounds are marshy areas with shallow water, emergent vegetation and mud bottoms covered with vegetation mats. Suitable vegetation and quiet water seem to be the most important factors in the choice of spawning areas. Actual spawning occurs in water less than 51 cm deep, with most activity in water of less than half that depth (Carbine and Applegate, 1946; Clark, 1950). A male (sometimes two or three males) courts a female by pushing with his snout against her head and pectoral region. If the female is not yet ripe or is spawned out, she repels the male by turning her head to one side and straightening with a jerk. She may also adopt the threat posture, with branchiostegals lowered, back arched, and paired fins spread downward. Although pike are not territorial or monogamous, when a male is attending a female, he may threaten other males with this same posture.

If the female is receptive, the male and female swim about side by side, apparently oriented eye to eye. At mating, both fish lower the branchiostegals and increase their swimming speed. The male flaps his caudal fin toward the female, then swings the caudal sharply away from her and brakes with his paired fins (photographs A and B, page 143). This thrusts his vent close to that of the female, and he ejects milt. At the same time, the female erects her pelvic fins, thrusts her caudal fin toward the male, and, by powerful contractions of her abdominal muscles, ejects some eggs (photograph C, page 143). The final return of the caudal fins to normal position mixes eggs and sperm, and scatters the eggs (photograph D, page 143). Only a few eggs, from 5 to 60, are released at a time. The spawning act is repeated every few minutes for up to several hours, after which the fish rest for some time before resuming. During this resting period, both male and female may take new mates, or they may continue together for several days until the female's eggs are all extruded. Spawning occurs only during daylight, and reduced light, as from cloud cover or ripples on the water, reduces spawning activity. Excessively cold nights have the same effect (Svärdson, 1949; Clark, 1950; Fabricius and Gustafson, 1958). The spawned-out adults may stay on the spawning grounds for as long as 14 weeks, but most leave within 6.

The eggs are .25 to .3 cm in diameter, tan to yellow in color. Egg number increases with the size of the fish, from as few as 2,000 in females of about 33 cm to nearly 600,000 in a fish weighing 14.5 kg. Ripe females contain both large ripe eggs and minute immature eggs that will ripen the following year. Thus, new eggs continue to develop during the life of the female. Some of the immature eggs are resorbed between spawning periods, as are all of the residual mature eggs (Carbine, 1944). Fertilization is usually highly efficient.

After fertilization, the eggs settle to rest on the weeds or the bottom. Development time to hatching varies inversely with temperature. At 6°C, 23 to 29 days are required, but at 18°C, only 4 or 5 days. Mortality rates of the eggs tend to increase with increasing temperatures (Swift, 1965). The newly hatched larvae are .65 to .93 cm long and have a yolk sac but no mouth. They cling to the weeds or substrate until the mouth develops when the fish reach a length of 1 to 1.2 cm, by which time the yolk sac is absorbed. Active feeding begins when the young fish are 1.1 to 1.3 cm long—about 10 days after hatching (Franklin and Smith, 1960). Early foods are various entomostracan zooplankters, especially copepods and cladocerans. As the young fish grow, they shift to eating insect larvae and nymphs, mainly Tendepedidae, then to fish and other small vertebrates. By the time they are about 5 cm long, the small pike are feeding almost exclusively on fish. They prefer soft-finned fishes and soon learn to avoid such prey as sticklebacks, which they cannot swallow because of the spines. Large pike, however, often feed heavily on sticklebacks, especially in summer when both pike and stickleback tend to be in the same areas (Hunt and Carbine, 1951; Frost, 1954; Mateeva, 1955; Franklin and Smith, 1960, 1963).

When the young have reached a length of about 2 cm they begin to move out of the marshes. Movement is in the daytime and is positively correlated with light intensity. Mortality from the fertilized egg to migrant fry is heavy, as much as 99.9%. Competition for food, predation and cannibalism are the most important factors here. Water quality also may be important, as the fry are rather sensitive to extremes of pH and to concentrations of carbonate and bicarbonate (Hunt and Carbine, 1951; McCarraher, 1962; Franklin and Smith, 1963).

Growth of the young is rapid, about .05 cm per day for the first 20 days, about .2 cm per day for the next 30 days, and about .1 cm per day for the next 40 days. The fastest growers are those that first make the shift to a fish diet. These young are especially likely to become cannibals. One fish of only 2.3 cm is known to have eaten another young pike of 1.6 cm (Hunt and Carbine, 1951). The fastest-growing fish may achieve a length of 44.6 cm and a weight of 460 g by mid-October. This represents a growth in length at the rate of .26 cm per day from hatching, and a growth in weight of .27 g per day (Carbine, 1945). Such fast-growing fish may mature as early as their second year of life (Mann, 1976), although most Alaskan pike do not mature until age 3+ or 4+ (Cheney, 1971).

Growth remains rapid in the first year, although it depends on temperature and the availability of food. Subsequently, as with most fishes, the growth rate slows (Rawson, 1932; Van Engel, 1940; Lagler, 1956; McCarraher, 1959; Cheney, 1972). Pike appear to require less food for maintenance than do most fishes and are therefore able to convert a relatively large portion of their food into growth. After maintenance requirements have been met, 1 g of food will produce .44 g of pike, a ratio of 2.29:1. Peak maintenance requirements occur in late spring, then decline and remain low through the winter, rising again in the spring (Johnson, 1966). This cycle appears to be related to the energy requirements of reproduction. Pike are well adapted to withstand long periods of starvation because they use lipid and glycogen reserves, thus conserving body proteins (Ince and Thorpe, 1976).

Growth rates tend to be faster in the warmer, southern parts of the range than in the far north, but northern fish live longer. However, even within a relatively small area, growth is highly variable from one body of water to another. The average size of fish of a given age may vary by a factor of two or even more, and the difference between the largest and smallest may represent almost a full order of magnitude. In the Minto Flats area of interior Alaska, pike reach average lengths of 14 cm by September of their first year; 18.6 cm at 1+, 28.7 cm at 2+, 55.5 cm at 5+, 80.1 cm at 10+, and 99 cm at 21+. These growth rates are somewhat faster than those found in Great Bear, Great Slave, Lesser Slave, and Athabasca lakes in northern Canada, or in a number of small lakes in the upper Tanana River drainage in Alaska (Miller and Kennedy, 1948b; Cheney, 1972).

Adult pike feed almost exclusively on fish, the kinds consumed depending largely on what is available. The variety of species eaten is tremendous and often includes smaller pike. Other organisms included in the diet include water fowl, frogs, small mammals such as mice and shrews, crayfish and insects. In Alaska, coregonids appear to be the major food item, followed by small pike, blackfish, burbot and suckers, as well as insects, especially Odonata naiads.

In feeding, the pike first aims itself toward its prey. If the distance between pike and prey is too great to be covered in one quick dash, the pike approaches slowly, often seeming scarcely to move. A short distance from the prey, the pike stops. Its body is slightly flexed and the caudal fin is bent almost at right angles to the body. The tail and body are straightened with one powerful stroke and the pike shoots forward. Its mouth is opened forcefully just as it reaches the prey, so the prey is sucked in as well as seized. By a series of movements of jaws and tongue, the pike turns the prey and then swallows it head first (Hoogland et al., 1957).

In general, pike seem to eat whatever they can catch and swallow (Lagler, 1956; Lawler, 1965b; Cheney, 1971). Digestion of fish is fairly rapid at usual summer temperatures, with digestion 50% complete in 20 hours. Birds, on the other hand, require a much longer time to digest, almost 130 hours for 50% digestion, due, no doubt, to the protection provided by the feathers (Solman, 1945; Seaburg and Moyle, 1964). Pike are believed to be serious predators of young waterfowl. This belief is no doubt valid in some places but not in others. In the deltas of the Saskatchewan and Athabasca rivers in Canada, pike were once estimated to eat nearly 10% of the young ducklings, but in the Seney National Wildlife Refuge in Michigan, only .2% of the pike stomachs examined contained waterfowl (Solman, 1945; Lagler, 1956).

Pike do not, as a rule, undertake long migrations, although occasional individuals may move considerable distances. In the Minto Flats, in interior Alaska, 36% of the fish tagged moved more than 16 km during the summers. The Minto Flats lakes become low in oxygen in winter and the pike must travel considerable distances to find suitable wintering areas. One fish moved 288 km downstream in 10 months (Cheney, 1971).

Different populations of pike often show statistically significant differences in such things as the numbers of fin rays, lateral line pores and vertebrae. These differences may indicate isolation in separate glacial refuges. However, since such differences have been found in lakes only 32 km apart and draining into the same river, any interpretation is open to question. There is certainly no strong evidence to indicate subspeciation (Morrow, 1964; McPhail and Lindsey, 1970; Cheney, 1972).

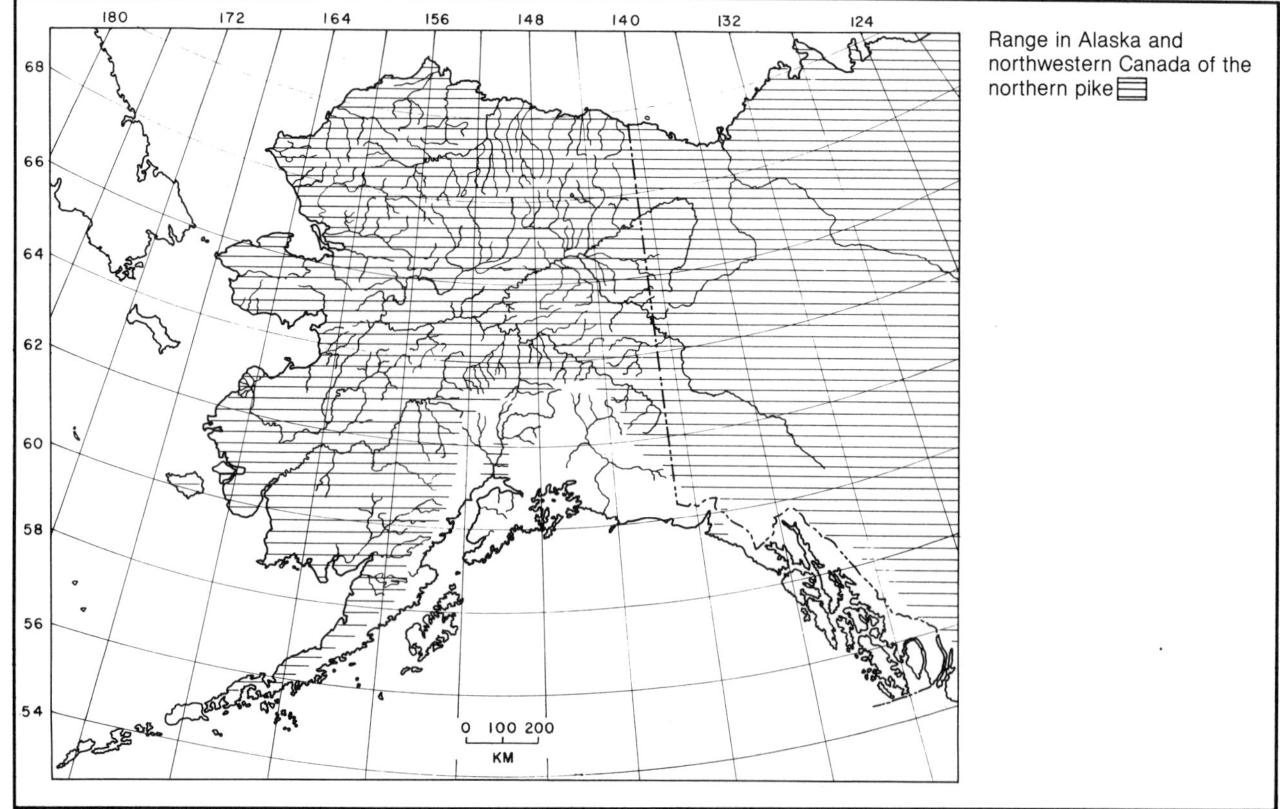

Range in Alaska and northwestern Canada of the northern pike

IMPORTANCE TO MAN

The pike enjoys a most varied reputation. In some areas it is considered a nuisance, scarcely worthy of being considered a fish, but in other regions it is highly regarded and attracts large numbers of anglers and dollars. Pike will take a large variety of lures and live baits. They put up a strong fight at first, but it is usually of fairly short duration. They seldom jump but will often rear out of the water, shaking their heads and all too frequently throwing the hook. Much of the reason behind the pike's poor reputation as a sport fish is the frequent use of gear that is too heavy. Taken on light tackle, pike give very good accounts of themselves. A short wire leader is a necessity, as the pike's sharp teeth are all too liable to cut a line. Pike quickly learn to avoid artificial lures such as spinners, but apparently cannot distinguish between live bait (a minnow) on a hook and free-swimming fishes (Beukema, 1970).

On the commercial side, the pike is unimportant in the United States. Landings from 1960 through 1970, almost entirely from the Great Lakes, averaged only a bit more than 79,500 kg per year. On the other hand, the Canadian catch runs on the order of 2.27 million kg per year, much of which is exported to the United States. Pike are usually sold fresh, generally in the round or gutted and beheaded.

For eating, pike are delicious. The meat is white, flaky and flavorful. The so-called muddy taste of which some people complain is confined to the skin. If the fish be thoroughly scaled, scrubbed and washed, the muddy taste is eliminated, but it is better and easier to skin the fish.

Another complaint against pike is its boniness. The dorsal ribs or Y-bones are only lightly fastened to the backbone and tend to come loose in the meat. However, with a very sharp knife and a little practice, it is easy to cut boneless filets of pike.

Pike are often used as farm-pond fish, particularly in combination with bluegills. They seem able to crop the forage fish at such a rate that the latter cannot overpopulate and become stunted.

Chapter Ten

MINNOWS

Family Cyprinidae

This is the largest of all families of fishes, including some 275 genera and more than 1500 species. The minnows are virtually worldwide in their distribution, being absent only from Australia, South America and Greenland. They are of variable shape, but generally are moderately elongate. They have no spines in the fins although in some forms, such as carp, the first one or two rays of the dorsal and/or anal fin may be stiffened and spinelike. Sexual dimorphism is often marked in the spawning season, when the males may develop breeding tubercles and/or bright colors. The larger species, such as carp, are used for human food in some parts of the world. However, most members of the family are small and their chief value is as forage for larger fishes.

LAKE CHUB

Couesius plumbeus (Agassiz)

DISTINCTIVE CHARACTERS

The spineless fins, normal jaws, and tiny barbel at the corner of the mouth distinguish the lake chub from other Alaskan fishes (Figure 47).

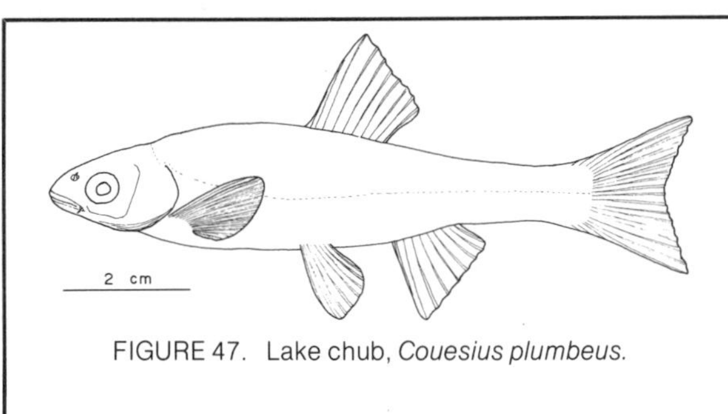

FIGURE 47. Lake chub, *Couesius plumbeus*.

DESCRIPTION

Body elongate, slender. Depth 14% to 21% of total length. Head short, about 19% to 22% of total length, being relatively longest in young fish. Snout moderate, rounded, a little shorter than eye diameter. Eye round, 20% to 33% of head. Mouth fairly small, slightly oblique, with upper jaw usually extending slightly beyond lower anteriorly and reaching rearward about to anterior edge of eye. A small but well-developed barbel near posterior end of maxilla. No teeth in jaws, but pharyngeal teeth well developed; number variable but usually 2 in left outer row, 4 in left inner row and in right inner row, 2 in right outer row. Gill rakers short, 4 to 9 on first arch. Branchiostegals: 3. Lateral line has 53 to 79 pores, usually 56 to 69. Vertebrae: 39 to 44, usually 40 or 41.

FINS. Dorsal has 8 rays; anal, 8 (in rare cases 7 or 9); pectorals, 13 to 18, most often 15 or 16; pelvics, 7 to 9, usually 8. Caudal moderately forked, with rounded lobes.

SCALES. Cycloid, small; those on back often smaller than those on sides. Breeding adults develop nuptial tubercles on the head and along the back to the dorsal fin as well as on the upper parts of the pectoral fins and on the breast. These tubercles are better developed in males than in females.

COLOR. Brown to greenish above, silvery below. A rather indistinct dark or lead-colored band is present along the sides, often extending forward onto the head in small specimens. Lower sides and belly often have fine dots of dark pigment. In some populations breeding males develop bright orange-red patches on sides of head and at bases of pectoral fins (Richardson, 1944), but the presence of this color varies from place to place. So far, orange patches have not been found in Alaskan lake chubs (photograph, page 100; Plate 25, page 136).

SIZE. Known to reach 22.7 cm total length in northern Quebec (Scott and Crossman, 1973), but most adults are 5 to 10 cm long.

RANGE AND ABUNDANCE

The lake chub is strictly North American. It ranges from interior Alaska east to Nova Scotia and from the arctic coast at the Mackenzie River Delta and Ungava Bay south to New England and the Great Lakes, except Lake Erie. Scattered, isolated populations are present in Iowa, Nebraska, Wyoming, Colorado, Montana and the Dakotas. In Alaska the lake chub seems to be confined to the Yukon-Koyukuk-Tanana-Porcupine drainage, from about Nulato on upstream. Wherever it is present at all, the lake chub is usually abundant.

HABITS

Despite the fact that the lake chub is widespread and common, very little is known about it. Spawning apparently occurs in the spring and summer, as early as April in the southern part of the range and as late as August in the far north (McPhail and Lindsey, 1970; Scott and Crossman, 1973). Spawning occurs in shallow water over rocky or gravelly bottoms in rivers and small streams (Allin, 1953; McPhail and Lindsey, 1970), the fish moving out of lakes or deeper parts of streams in large schools for this purpose. No nest or redd is built, nor do the adults guard the eggs (McPhail and Lindsey, 1970). In Lake Superior, the lake chub occasionally hybridizes with the longnose dace, *Rhinichthys cataractae* (Hubbs and Lagler, 1949). The eggs are yellowish in color. A female of 7 cm in length was estimated to contain about 500 eggs (Richardson, 1935). Nothing has been reported of spawning behavior or rate of development of eggs and young. In Pyramid Lake, Alberta, year-old chubs averaged about 2.8 cm in length; 2+ fish, 4.8 cm; 3+ fish, 7.1 cm; and 4+ fish, 11.4 cm (Rawson and Elsey, 1950). Lake chubs are thought to mature at age 3 or 4, seldom surviving beyond age 5, in central British Columbia. Females apparently grow faster and live longer than do males (McPhail and Lindsey, 1970).

Young lake chub feed primarily on zooplankton, chiefly cladocerans and copepods, while older fish eat mostly insect larvae and algae. Large chubs may also take small fishes (Simon, 1946; Rawson and Elsey, 1950; McPhail and Lindsey, 1970; Scott and Crossman, 1973).

The lake chub inhabits all sorts of waters—lakes, clear streams, heavily silted rivers. In general, it seems to be most common in fairly shallow water, but may move into deeper parts of lakes during hot weather. In some areas, as Great Bear Lake, Northwest Territories, it is found only in streams, in other places it inhabits streams almost exclusively, and in still other locations it seems to use stream habitats only for spawning (Hubbs and Lagler, 1949; Allin, 1953; Personius and Eddy, 1955; Johnson, 1975). My personal observations have been that in interior Alaska, in the Tanana and upper Yukon drainages, the lake chub is much more common in the heavily silted main rivers than in the clear tributaries.

The lake chub has been classified as a sight feeder, since it has large optic lobes and relatively few taste buds (Davis and Miller, 1967). However, since it is so common in heavily silted rivers, where visibility is virtually nil, other mechanisms for finding food must also be present.

IMPORTANCE TO MAN

The lake chub is of little direct importance to man. In some regions, anglers use it extensively for bait. It is said to be a nuisance in some trout fisheries, for it takes bait or a fly readily and "it is almost impossible to make a cast without catching one of these minnows" (Allin, 1953). Lake chub, in view of their diet, distribution and abundance, are probably an important forage species, but there are no data to confirm this.

In streams in Ontario, the lake chub is sometimes taken and eaten by smelt fishermen who do not recognize it (Scott and Crossman, 1973). It has been cold-smoked with satisfactory results (Lantz, 1962).

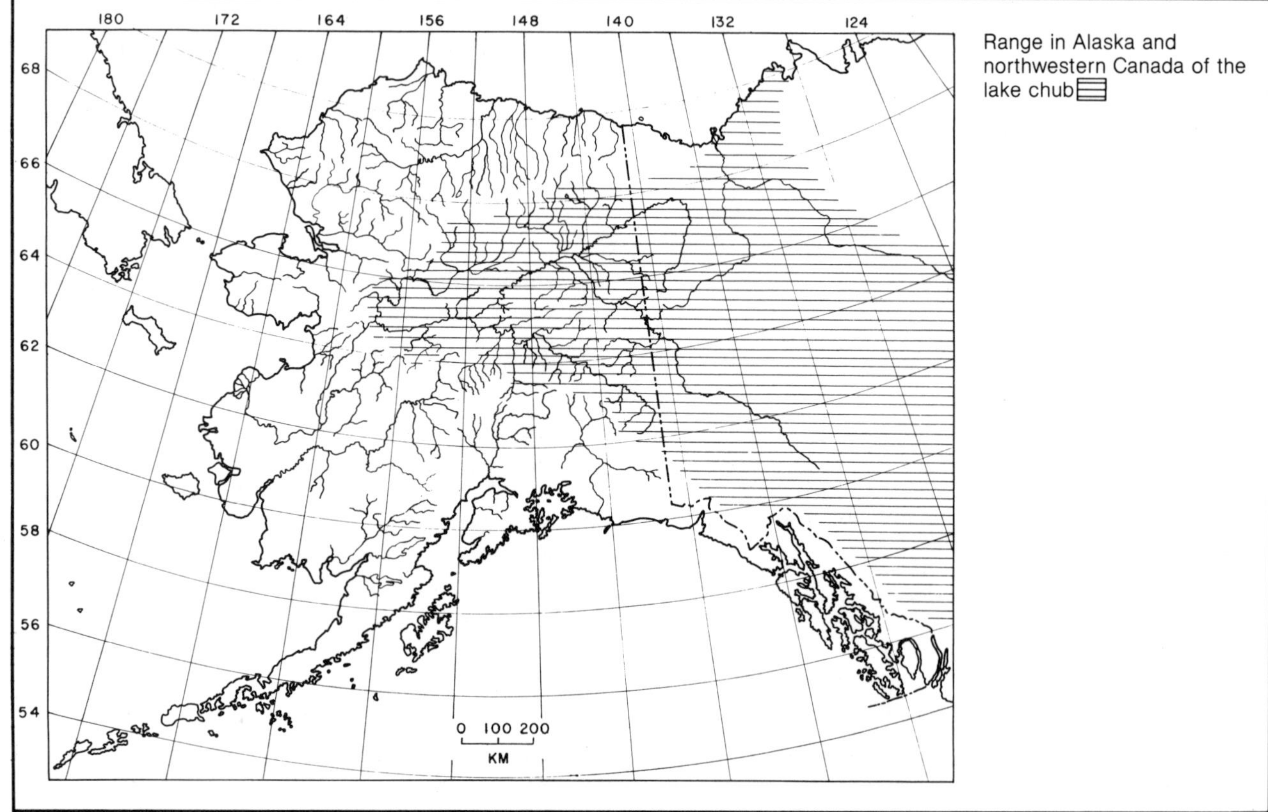

Range in Alaska and northwestern Canada of the lake chub

Chapter Eleven

SUCKERS

Family Catostomidae

These fishes are elongate and in most cases are nearly round in cross-section, with a protrusible mouth located on the underside of the head and no teeth in the jaws. Suckers feed by swimming slowly along the bottom, sucking up the bottom debris, which includes the small insect larvae and other invertebrates that live on or in the bottom. Some suckers may reach considerable size, weighing up to several kilos.

There are about 65 species of suckers, all but two of them found only in North America. One of the remaining species is endemic to southern China, while the other, the longnose sucker of North America, is also present in eastern Siberia.

Suckers are generally considered more of a nuisance than anything else, especially by trout fishermen. They are popularly believed to do great damage to the eggs of other fishes, but the supposed extent of this damage is probably greatly exaggerated. The larger species, especially the longnose sucker and white sucker, are taken commercially in the Great Lakes and the large Canadian lakes and are marketed as mullet. Suckers make excellent bait for large game fish such as pike and bass.

LONGNOSE SUCKER

Catostomus catostomus (Forster)

DISTINCTIVE CHARACTERS

The sucking mouth, which is located on the ventral side of the head and has thick, papillose lips, distinguishes the longnose sucker from all other Alaskan fishes (Figure 48).

DESCRIPTION

Body elongate, nearly cylindrical. Depth of body, which is greatest somewhat forward of dorsal fin, is 14% to 19% of total length. Head long, about 20% of total length; top of head rounded and scaleless. Snout long, 38% to 48% of head length, ending anteriorly in a rounded point. Eye round, small, its diameter about 22% to 31% of snout length. Mouth protrusible and ventrally located, behind tip of snout. Lips, especially upper, thick and covered with papillae. No teeth in jaws; numerous comblike pharyngeal teeth in single rows. Gill rakers short; 23 to 30 on first arch. Branchiostegals: 3. No proper, well-differentiated stomach; no pyloric caeca. Lateral line complete, inconspicuous, with 90 to 120 pored scales. Vertebrae: 45 to 47.

FINS. Dorsal has 9 to 11 rays; anal, 7 rays; pectorals, 16 to 18; pelvics, 10 or 11. Caudal moderately forked, the tips slightly rounded.

SCALES. Cycloid, small.

COLOR. Adults may be reddish brown, dark brassy green or gray to black above, paler on the lower sides, with the ventral parts white. Young fish are usually dark gray with mottling of paler color on the back. Young-of-the-year are gray with small black spots. Breeding males are usually dark above with a brilliant reddish stripe along each side, while females are greenish gold to copper, with a less brilliant red stripe. The breeding males show prominent tubercles on the rays of the anal and caudal fins and also on the head (photographs, page 101; Plate 26, page 137).

SIZE. The longnose sucker is reported to reach a length of 64.3 cm and a weight of 3.3 kg (Keleher, 1961), but the usual run of fish are much smaller.

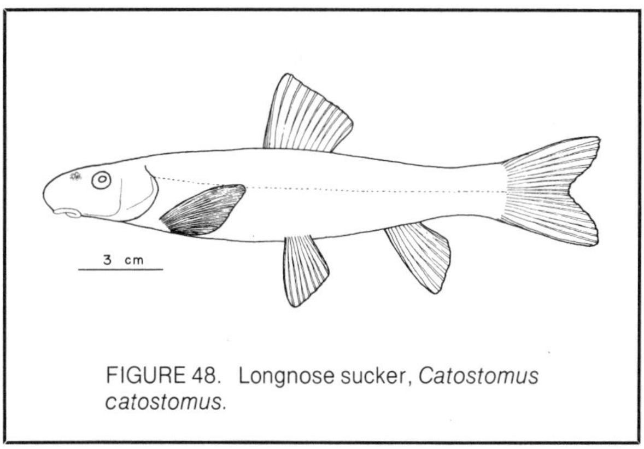

FIGURE 48. Longnose sucker, *Catostomus catostomus*.

RANGE AND ABUNDANCE

The longnose sucker ranges from New England to Labrador in the east, westward through the Great Lakes, the northern part of the Mississippi-Missouri river system and the Columbia to the west coast. It reaches the Arctic Ocean in northeastern Labrador but is absent from the arctic coast of Canada from Ungava to the Horton River. The longnose sucker is present throughout the rest of mainland Canada (except Nova Scotia and eastern Labrador) and Alaska, but absent from the islands along the Pacific and Bering coasts and from the arctic islands. It is found also in eastern Siberia from the Yana to the Anadyr rivers.

In North America, the longnose sucker is abundant throughout the northern part of its range, especially in the northwest.

HABITS

Breeding occurs in the spring, as early as May in the southern part of the range and as late as July in the far north. Spawning runs begin after water temperatures have reached 5°C, with greatest intensity occurring at temperatures above 10°C (Rawson and Elsey, 1950; Brown and Graham, 1954; Geen et al., 1966). The fish move from lakes into inlet streams or from slow, deep pools into shallow, gravel-bottomed portions of streams. Spawning occurs only during daylight hours, most commonly over gravel of .5 to 10 cm in diameter, in shallow water 10 to 60 cm deep with a current of 30 to 45 cm per second (Geen et al., 1966). At spawning time, the males lie close to the bottom in the current of the spawning area and show no aggressive behavior, while the females stay along the banks and in still water. In the breeding act a female swims out to the males, two to four of whom escort and crowd around her. With their dorsal fins erect, the males clasp the female with their pelvic fins and vibrate their anal fins against her. There is considerable thrashing about for a few seconds during which eggs and sperm are released. No nest is built. After a spawning, the female returns to the quiet water. She may spawn many times in an hour, with the same or different males. A single female may produce up to 60,300 eggs (Harris, 1962; Geen et al., 1966). Fish that have moved out of a lake to spawn generally return to the lake a few days after spawning is completed. However, river-resident fish may stay on or near the spawning area for much of the summer.

Post-spawning mortality of adults is on the order of 10% to 30%. Many fish spawn in two or even three consecutive years, while others may skip one or two years between spawnings (Geen et al., 1966).

The eggs are about .3 cm in diameter, yellow in color, adhesive and demersal, sinking to the bottom and lodging in crevices in the gravel. Development to hatching takes one to two weeks, according to temperature. The young are about .8 cm long at hatching and remain in the gravel for one to two weeks. In some areas a nocturnal downstream movement of fry begins as soon as the fish emerge from the gravel. However, in interior Alaska at least some of the young stay in the streams all summer.

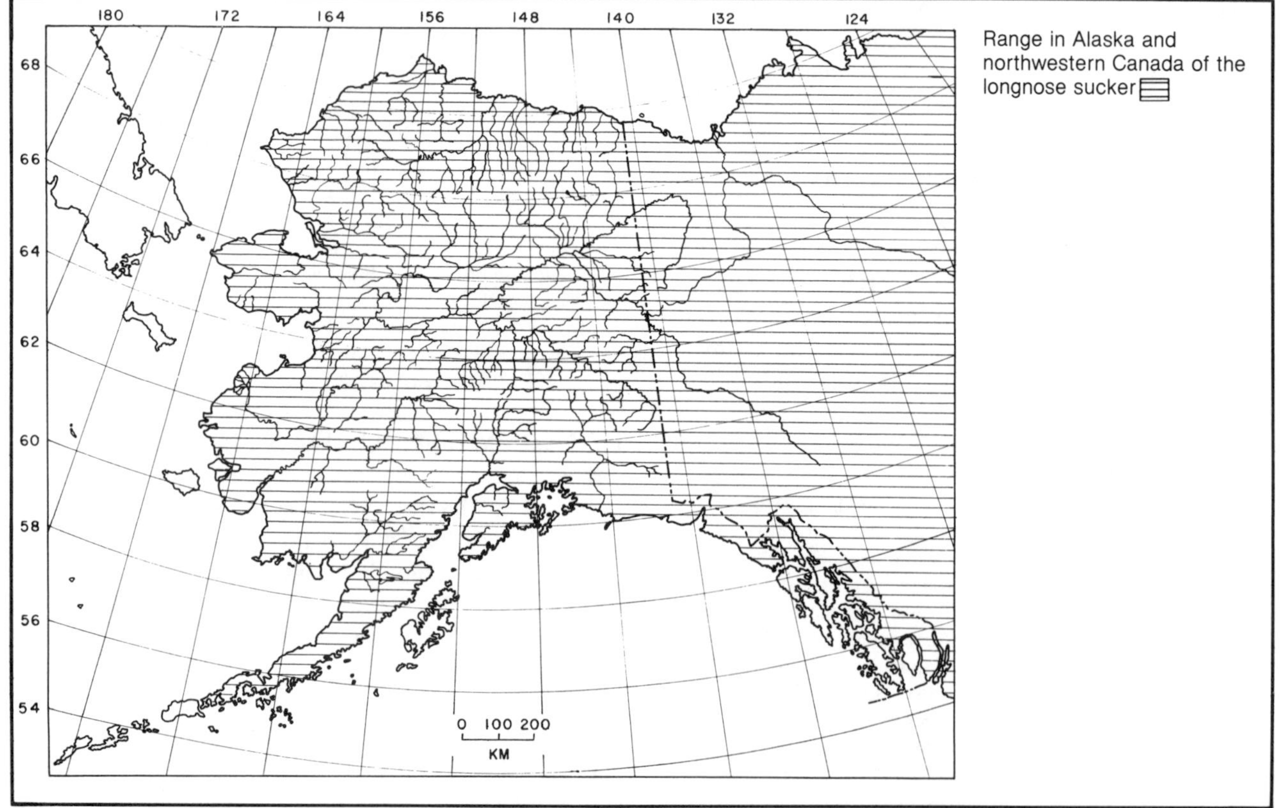

Range in Alaska and northwestern Canada of the longnose sucker

Growth rates vary tremendously from place to place, apparently correlated more with food supply than with temperature. In Great Slave Lake, young-of-the-year may reach 8 cm fork length by the end of August, but in Yellowstone Lake, Wyoming, they are less than half that length (Brown and Graham, 1954; Harris, 1962). Similar variations in growth rates are continued through later years of life. Even in a single population, the largest fish of a given age may be twice as long as the smallest. Age determinations by means of scales, which often underestimate the true age (Geen et al., 1966), have given the following age-length relationship for suckers from the south end of Great Slave Lake (Harris, 1962): 2+, 17.9 cm; 5+, 30.6 cm; 10+, 49.6 cm; 15+, 55.7 cm. This population is one that grows relatively fast.

Age at maturity increases with geographic latitude. Sexual maturity is reached at about age 2+ by males, 3+ by females in Colorado, 4+ or 5+ in Yellowstone Lake, but not until 9+ or 10+ in Great Slave Lake. The oldest fish on record is one of 19+ from the northern part of Great Slave Lake (Brown and Graham, 1954; Hayes, 1956; Harris, 1962).

Except for movement to and from the spawning areas, the longnose sucker apparently does not undertake any definite migrations. During the summer, fish in streams in interior Alaska appear to wander more or less at random, some going upstream, some down. The general trend of movement is downstream, however, so that by October no suckers remain in the upper reaches or in the spawning areas.

The longnose sucker feeds almost entirely on material found on the bottom. The fish swim slowly along, their protrusible lips touching the bottom in a way that suggests that the papillae have a sensory function. Food is sucked into the mouth and swallowed. In streams, major food items of the adults include algae and other plants, Diptera, Ephemeroptera, Trichoptera, Coleoptera, spiders and mollusks. Lake-dwelling adults feed mainly on various crustaceans, especially cladocerans and amphipods, as well as insect larvae and nymphs. Diptera and Ephemeroptera are the most important of these. Occasionally, large adult suckers will feed upside down on terrestrial insects floating on the surface of eddies. The very young fish seem to feed chiefly on Cladocera and insects.

The longnose sucker is reputed to destroy the spawn of other fishes, especially trout. Undoubtedly, fish eggs are eaten when available but, as far as trout eggs are concerned, these are undoubtedly floaters—eggs that were washed out of the redd or were dug up by subsequent spawners (Stenton, 1951).

IMPORTANCE TO MAN

Man's use of the longnose sucker ranges from no use at all to extensive use. In many areas the longnose sucker is a major source of dog food. In the Great Lakes and the Canadian lakes considerable amounts are landed and marketed, together with other suckers, as mullet. The flesh is said to be firm, white, flaky and sweet, although bony. This may be true of fish taken in the winter, but the flesh of spawning fish is soft and glutinous and has an unpleasant taste.

Because of the similarity in food habits, longnose suckers are important competitors with trout and other desirable sport fish. An intensive gill-netting program to remove longnose suckers from Pyramid Lake, Alberta, resulted only in improved growth of young suckers and did not improve angling success (Rawson and Elsey, 1950).

Chapter Twelve

TROUT-PERCHES

Family Percopsidae

This family, which includes only two species, gets its name because the fish have some of the characteristics of trouts and some of the characteristics of perches. They have, for example, an adipose fin and abdominally placed pelvic fins, like the trouts; but there are one or two spines in the dorsal, anal and pelvic fins and the scales are ctenoid, as in the perches.

The trout-perches are known only from North America. One species, the sand roller, is found in Washington, Oregon and Idaho; the other, the trout-perch, is widespread over much of the northern U.S. and Canada.

Trout-perches are important forage species for larger fishes.

TROUT-PERCH

Percopsis omiscomaycus (Walbaum)

DISTINCTIVE CHARACTERS

An adipose fin; small, weak spines in the dorsal and anal fins; rough, ctenoid scales; and pectoral fins reaching well behind the bases of the pelvic fins: this combination distinguishes the trout-perch from all other Alaskan freshwater fishes (Figure 49).

DESCRIPTION

Body elongate, terete, noticeably heavier toward the head. Greatest depth just behind head, about 18% of total length. Head large, more or less conical, its length 22% to 27% of total length. Snout long, rounded, 30% to 38% of head length. Eye round, large, 22% to 27% of head. Mouth small, subterminal, maxilla does not reach eye. Teeth small, bristlelike, in bands on lower jaw and premaxilla; no teeth elsewhere in mouth. Gill rakers short, stubby mounds with small teeth; 8 to 13 on first gill arch. Branchiostegals: 5 to 7, usually 6. Nearly straight lateral line has 41 to 60 pored scales. Pyloric caeca: 7 to 14. Vertebrae: 33 to 36.

FINS. Dorsal has 1 to 3 spines (usually 2), 9 to 11 rays. Adipose fin present. Anal has 1 spine, 5 to 8 rays; pectorals, 12 to 15 rays; pelvics, 8 or 9. Caudal forked.

SCALES. Rather large, ctenoid, noticeably rough to the touch when brushed from tail to head. No scales on head or nape.

COLOR. Pale yellowish to silvery, often almost transparent. A row of about 10 dark spots along midline of back, 10 or 11 spots along lateral line, and another row of spots high on sides above lateral line. Fins transparent (photograph, page 101; Plate 27, page 138).

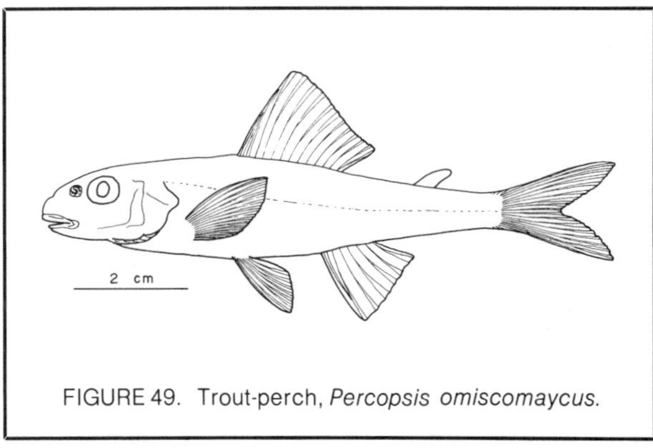

FIGURE 49. Trout-perch, *Percopsis omiscomaycus.*

SIZE. The maximum size attained in the southern part of the range is said to be about 20 cm. In most areas, however, the largest trout-perch are only about half this size. Alaskan specimens have run up to about 8 cm.

RANGE AND ABUNDANCE

Trout-perch are found in much of North America. They range from the peninsula formed by Delaware, Maryland and Virginia north to the shore of Hudson Bay; west through West Virginia, Tennessee and Missouri; northwesterly in the Mississippi drainage to the prairie provinces and northeastern British Columbia, northward in the Mackenzie drainage to the Arctic Coast and down the Porcupine and Yukon rivers almost to their mouths. In Alaska the trout-perch has been found at the mouths of the Tatonduk, Kandik and Charley rivers, at Circle and Nulato, and at the mouth of the Andreafsky River (UAFC #327; Morrow, 1965; McPhail and Lindsey, 1970).

The trout-perch appears to be rare in Alaska (Morrow, 1965), but in other areas it is an abundant species. In Heming Lake, Manitoba, the population of adult fish was estimated at 2,929 to 3,636 fish per hectare (Lawler and Fitz-Earle, 1968).

HABITS

Trout-perch spawning takes place in late spring and summer. In Red Lake, Minnesota, spawning fish were found from early June to mid-August

(Magnuson and Smith, 1963), while in Heming Lake, Manitoba, most spawning occurred in the latter half of May (Lawler, 1954). In Lake Erie, ripe individuals have been taken from early May to mid-August (Scott and Crossman, 1973). Ripe fish were once taken at Circle, Alaska, on June 28 (McPhail and Lindsey, 1970).

At spawning time, adults move inshore to shallow water or into shallow tributaries of lakes (Langlois, 1954; Magnuson and Smith, 1963). Males generally dominate the spawning population, sometimes by as much as 10:1. Some populations breed almost exclusively at night (Magnuson and Smith, 1963), but others show no variation from daytime spawning (Lawler, 1954). In the spawning act, two or more males cluster with a single female within 10 to 12.5 cm of the surface. They press close to the female, often breaking the surface of the water, and eggs and milt are released. The eggs are yellowish in color, about .15 cm in diameter before fertilization, demersal and sticky. They sink to the bottom and adhere to whatever they settle upon. Water-hardened eggs are about .19 cm in diameter. Females 6 to 7.8 cm in fork length produce 210 to 728 eggs, larger fish having more eggs (Lawler, 1954). Spawning has been observed in water with temperatures between 4.5° and 17°C (Lawler, 1954). Hatching occurs in about one week at 20° to 23°C (Lawler, 1954; Magnuson and Smith, 1963). Because Alaskan streams are so much colder than this, it is probable that trout-perch eggs in Alaska require at least twice as long to hatch.

The young are about .55 cm long at hatching. Each has a prominent yolk sac, an oval eye and a large head with a prominent pointed snout and a small, inferior mouth. The newly hatched young are unpigmented save for a number of large black stellate pigment cells on the yolk sac. By the time a young fish is .7 cm in length, the yolk sac has been absorbed and only a few large pigment cells are present on the right side of the stomach region. All fins except the pelvics are well-developed by the time the larvae are .95 cm long; the pelvics are just beginning to appear at this stage. The young trout-perch leave the shallows and move into deep water about three weeks after hatching (Magnuson and Smith, 1963). The young fish at 4 cm is completely transformed and is fully scaled (Fish, 1932). By the end of the first growing season, young trout-perch may achieve lengths of 5 to 8.4 cm, although Alaskan fish appear to grow much slower than this (Anonymous, 1961). Average length at one year of age is about 8.1 cm; at two years, 9.4 cm; at three, 10.2 cm; and at four, 11.5 cm. Females grow faster and live longer than males. Males apparently do not survive beyond the

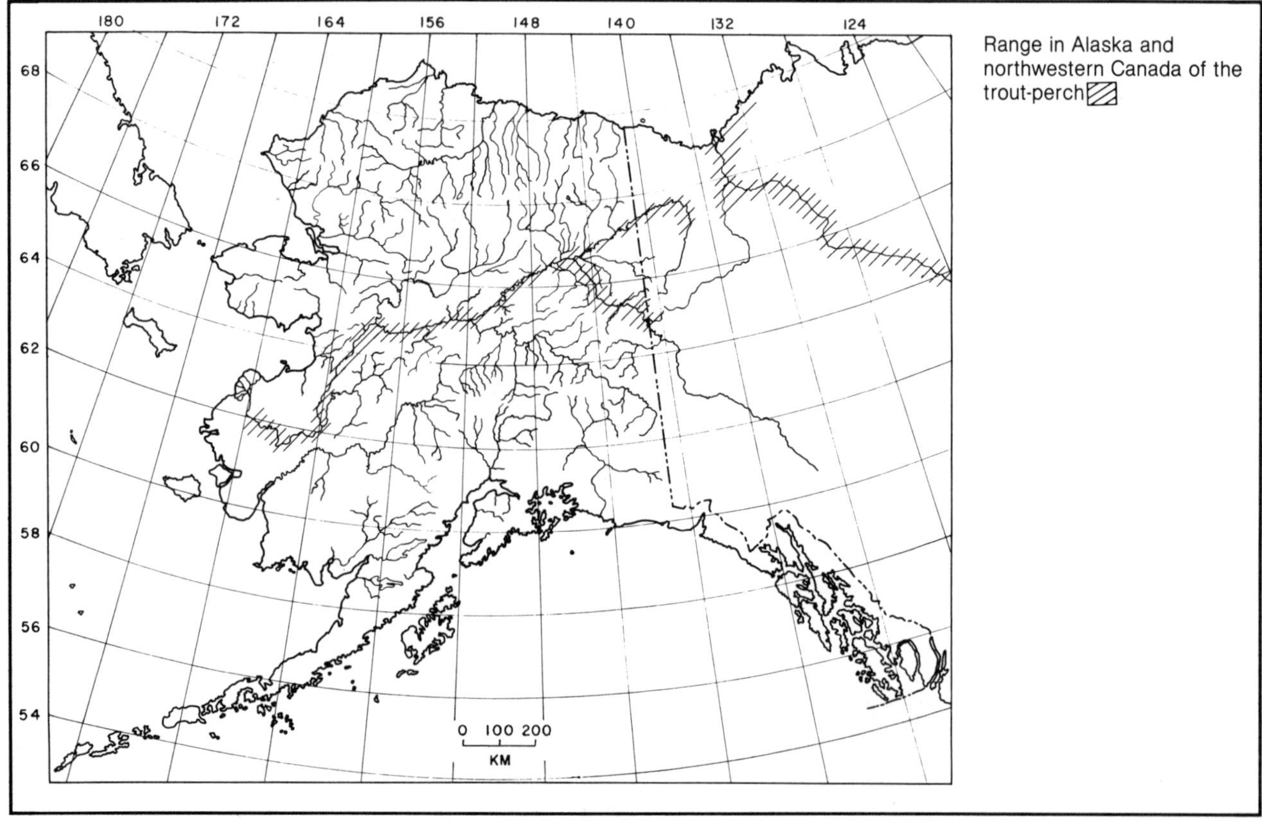

Range in Alaska and northwestern Canada of the trout-perch

third year (Trautman, 1957; Priegel, 1962; Magnuson and Smith 1963).

Males begin to mature in their second summer, but most females do not mature until a year later. This difference in age at first maturity apparently accounts, at least in part, for the predominance of males in the spawning populations. Spawning groups are 25% to 31% one-year-olds, 61% to 71% two-year-olds, 4% to 8% three-year-olds and up to 1% four-year-olds (Lawler, 1954; Magnuson and Smith, 1963). There is often, perhaps usually, heavy post-spawning mortality. Among two-year-olds, 96% of the males and 67% of the females die after spawning; among three-year-olds, 100% of the males and 96% of the females; and all of the four-year-old females (Magnuson and Smith, 1963).

Trout-perch are typically found in fairly deep water: in depths of 10 to 61 m in lakes, or in long, deep pools in streams. They move into shallow water for spawning. Daytime movements are rather noticeable, for the trout-perch spends the day either in deep water (in lakes) or under cut banks, roots, or debris (in streams), moving into the shallows to feed at night. Major foods are algae *(Microcystis),* Cladocera, amphipods and the larvae of chironomids and mayflies. Small fishes are sometimes eaten in the winter (Nurnberger, 1930; Langlois, 1954; Trautman, 1957).

IMPORTANCE TO MAN

The trout-perch is of no direct importance to man. However, it is an important forage fish for larger carnivores wherever it is abundant. It is known to be a major food for such fishes as pike, burbot, walleye, lake trout and others. Its habit of feeding in the shallows, then moving to deep water where it in turn is fed upon by larger fishes, may make it an important factor in nutrient transfer, especially in stratified lakes (Lawler, 1954, 1956; Langlois, 1954; McPhail and Lindsey, 1970).

Chapter Thirteen

CODFISHES

Family Gadidae

KEY TO THE ALASKAN SPECIES

SECTION	DESCRIPTION	THE FISH IS	PROCEED IN THIS KEY TO SECTION
1 a.	Three dorsal fins and 2 anal fins present.		**2**
b.	Two dorsal fins and a single anal fin present.	Burbot, *Lota lota* (Linnaeus), page 181.	
2 a.	Upper jaw longer than lower jaw. Less than 30 gill rakers.		**3**
b.	Lower jaw equal to or longer than upper jaw. More than 30 gill rakers.	Arctic cod, *Boreogadus saida* (Lepechin), page 184.	
3 a.	Length of chin barbel equal to at least three-fourths of eye diameter in young to longer than eye diameter in adults. Length of space between second and third dorsal fins less than eye diameter.	Pacific cod, *Gadus macrocephalus* Tilesius, page 185.	
b.	Barbel never longer than half of eye diameter, usually about equal to or shorter than diameter of pupil. Length of space between second and third dorsal fins equal to or greater than eye diameter.	Saffron cod, *Eleginus gracilis* (Tilesius), page 187.	

The codfishes are a large family, mostly made up of northern hemisphere marine fishes. The codfishes have large heads, wide gill openings, two or three dorsal fins, one or two anal fins, no spines in any fins and, usually, a small barbel at the tip of the chin.

Some of the codfishes enter fresh water. One species, the burbot, is found strictly in fresh water and has a circumpolar distribution in the northern hemisphere. A few species are known from the southern oceans.

The larger forms are very important food fishes and are the objects of widespread and intensive commercial fisheries.

BURBOT

Lota lota (Linnaeus)

DISTINCTIVE CHARACTERS

The long second dorsal fin, at least six times as long as the first, and a single barbel on the chin distinguish the burbot (Figure 50, page 182).

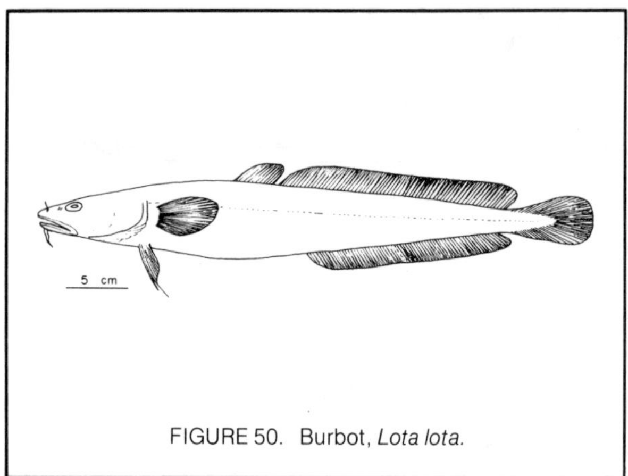

FIGURE 50. Burbot, *Lota lota.*

DESCRIPTION

Body elongate, robust and nearly round anteriorly, strongly compressed behind anus. Depth 13% to 15% of total length. Head flattened, broad, its length 19% to 20% of total length. Snout long, 27% to 33% of head length. Each nostril in a prominent tube. Eye small, its diameter about 30% of snout length. Mouth terminal, large, upper jaw reaching to below the eye. A single, prominent barbel present at tip of lower jaw. Teeth small and numerous, in bands on jaws and head of vomer. Gill rakers short, 7 to 12 on first arch. Branchiostegals: 6 to 8. Lateral line complete. Pyloric caeca: 31 to 168; 67 to 168 in Alaskan fish. Vertebrae: 50 to 67; 62 to 67 in Alaskan fish.

FINS. First dorsal short, with 8 to 16 rays; second dorsal long, at least 6 times length of first, with 60 to 80 rays and joined to caudal. Anal, 58 to 79 rays; joined to caudal. Pectorals are short and rounded, 17 to 21 rays. Pelvics, 5 to 8 rays; second ray is elongate and filamentous. Caudal rounded.

SCALES. Minute, cycloid, embedded in the skin.

COLOR. Yellowish through brown to dark olive green above and on sides; generally darker in northern regions but varying to some degree according to color of the local environment. Sides blotched and mottled with pale and dark shades; ventral parts usually pale yellow or white. Pelvic fins pale, others dark and mottled (photographs, page 102).

SIZE. Reported up to 34 kg in weight and 152.4 cm long in Alaska (Turner, 1886; Dall, 1898) but the angling record for the state is only 10.2 kg. The average fish caught by an angler probably weighs in the neighborhood of .5 to 1 kg.

RANGE AND ABUNDANCE

Distribution of the burbot is circumpolar in the northern hemisphere. It is present, in one or another of several subspecies, all across northern North America from about 40°N. to the Arctic Ocean, excluding only coastal Quebec and Labrador and the northeastern part of Keewatin in the Northwest Territories. In Europe and Asia it is to be found from the Pacific (though not on Kamchatka) to the Atlantic, but is missing from northern Scandinavia, Scotland and Ireland. Throughout its range it is moderately to extremely abundant. In some of the lakes of northcentral North America, burbot are so numerous as to be a nuisance to commercial gillnetters (Hewson, 1955).

HABITS

Burbot are winter spawners. The gonads begin to enlarge in August, but spawning does not begin until well into winter. Depending on geographical location, the actual spawning period may be from as early as mid-December to as late as early April, with most populations breeding in January or February (Cahn, 1936; Bjorn, 1940; Hewson, 1955; MacCrimmon, 1959; Lawler, 1963; Chen, 1969). In Alaska, as in most other areas, spawning apparently occurs in late January and February (Chen, 1969). In the spawning act—which is difficult to observe because it goes on at night under the ice and because the fish show strong negative phototrophism—the burbot congregate in moderately shallow water, .3 to more than 1.5 m deep but sometimes 18 to 20 m deep (Clemens, 1951b), over bottom composed of clean sand, gravel and stones. The males reach the spawning area first. At breeding, males and females form a great, globular mass of fish, individuals pushing toward the center and releasing eggs or sperm (Cahn, 1936), or at least milling around close together (MacCrimmon, 1959). There is no pairing, although Fabricius (1954) observed definite pairing of European burbot in an aquarium.

Burbot mature from age 2+ to 4+ in the southern part of the range, but not until they reach age 6+ or 7+ in interior Alaska (Chen, 1969). An average adult female will produce between 500,000 and 750,000 eggs, with numbers up to nearly 1.5 million having been recorded (Bjorn, 1940; Lawler, 1963; Chen, 1969). Egg size seems to be quite variable, from a diameter of .17 cm in Lake Erie to as little as .05 cm in Heming Lake, Manitoba. The eggs of fish in interior Alaska range between .07 and .09 cm (Fish, 1932; Lawler, 1963; Chen, 1969). The eggs are not sticky, but are demersal and contain an oil globule. After being spawned, they settle to the bottom and develop without any care from the parents. Development time varies with temperature, possibly also with the particular population. At 6.1°C, hatching occurs in about 30 days, but 71 days are needed at temperatures between about 0° and 3.6°C (Bjorn, 1940; MacCrimmon, 1959).

A newly hatched larva is only .3 to .4 cm long, colorless, transparent and without a yolk sac. Fin rays begin to appear in the dorsal, anal and caudal fins when the fish reaches 1 cm in length. By the time the young are about 1.9 cm long, fin rays are present in all fins, the chin barbel is present and the young fish is readily recognized as a burbot (Fish, 1932). Young burbot at this stage of development have been found in the Chena River of Alaska in June (Chen, 1969).

Growth rates are quite variable from place to place. As a generality, it may be said that fish in the northern part of the range tend to grow more slowly and to live longer than fish in more southern regions, although there are exceptions. Males tend to be shorter-lived than females and to grow more slowly after age 10. Typical lengths at various ages for burbot in interior Alaska are: 1+, 13.6 cm; 2+, 18.5 cm; 3+, 23.8 cm; 4+, 28.3 cm; 5+, 35.5 cm; 10+, 59.5 cm; 15+, 71.5 cm; 20+, 87.1 cm; 24+, 97.2 cm (Chen, 1969). Fish from lakes Erie, Simcoe (Ontario) and Winnipeg, for example, grew much faster than Alaskan fish, but those from Heming Lake, Manitoba, grew more slowly, at least after the first year (Clemens, 1951b; Hewson, 1955; MacCrimmon, 1959; Lawler, 1963). Chen's 24-year-old fish seems to be the oldest on record. In general, it appears that relatively few burbot live much beyond 15 years.

The burbot is usually a resident of fairly deep water, whether in lakes or in rivers. In lakes, burbot have been taken from as deep as 213 m and seem to be confined to the hypolimnion in the summertime. River fish tend to congregate in deep holes throughout the year, except at spawning. Optimum temperature for burbot is reported as 15.6° to 18.3°C (Scott and Crossman, 1973).

Migratory patterns of burbot are inadequately known. The fish are generally rather sedentary and do not move about much. However, there do appear to be definite movements toward spawning areas, although as a rule these are individual movements rather than migrations of a whole school together. Burbot also may move into shallow water to feed at night in the summer. They have been observed to make postspawning runs upriver, apparently for feeding (MacCrimmon, 1959).

In its food habits, the burbot is an omnivorous carnivore, although it displays strong preference for a fish diet. Young Alaskan burbot in their first and second years feed mostly on insect larvae, especially Plecoptera and Ephemeroptera, and on small sculpins, *Cottus cognatus*. Beginning in the third year, when the fish reach lengths of about 18 cm, there is a steady shift toward a diet of fishes of all sorts and away from invertebrates. From about age five on (at 35.5 cm total length), fishes of various sorts compose 67% to 90% of the food, with invertebrates making up less than 12% (Chen, 1969). In more southerly climates, the dependence on invertebrates seems to change at about the same age (five years) but at a much larger size (50 cm).

The list of food items is a long one, depending at least in part on what is available. In additon to those items already mentioned, it includes mollusks, asellids, *Mysis, Pontoporeia, Gammarus,* Trichoptera and crayfish as well as cisco eggs, mice, shrews and at least 20 species of fishes. Young burbot are an important food of large burbot (Nurnberger, 1930; Van Oosten and Deason, 1938; Clemens, 1951a; MacCrimmon and Devitt, 1954; Hewson, 1955; Beeton, 1956; Bonde and Maloney, 1960; Lawler, 1963; Chen, 1969). Two fish taken by the author in the Tanana River near Tetlin Junction, Alaska, in the early 1960s had adult bank swallows in their stomachs.

IMPORTANCE TO MAN

The burbot makes up a relatively small part of the freshwater fish catch of the United States. Maximum landings (over 277,000 kg per year) occurred in the late 1940s and early 1950s; landings declined slightly since then to an average of 173,600 kg per year for the years 1968 through 1973. Most of this catch comes from the Great Lakes and the international lakes, although since 1968 the upper Mississippi basin has supplied about 25% of the total. The price has fluctuated widely during this time, from less than $.02 to more than $.11 per pound. Fish from the Mississippi drainage generally commands a higher price than fish from the Great Lakes. Almost all burbot caught in the U.S. is used for food, either for people or for animals (Anonymous, 1971 to 1976). Attempts to popularize the burbot in Canada have thus far met with little success (Scott and Crossman, 1973). Burbot is an important commercial product in Siberia (Nikolskii, 1961).

As a food fish, burbot has enjoyed a mixed reputation. Early explorers in the Canadian Arctic ate it ". . . only in times of great scarcity" (Richardson, 1836), but the same author also noted that "When well bruised and mixed with a little flour, the roe can be baked into very good biscuits. . . ." The liver is also considered a delicacy, at least in Europe, and is used as a paté for canapés or is fried or smoked and eaten for itself. Burbot liver oil contains as much of vitamins A and D as does cod liver oil (Branion, 1930). Actually, burbot is an excellent food fish, for its flesh is white, flaky, of good flavor and almost boneless. The repulsive appearance of the fish apparently works against its popularity.

In Alaska small numbers of burbot are taken for subsistence. Sport fishermen probably take more than do the subsistence fisheries. Ice fishing for burbot in winter is reasonably popular and more and more anglers are learning that a burbot on light tackle is a worthy opponent at any time of year.

ARCTIC COD

Boreogadus saida (Lepechin)

DISTINCTIVE CHARACTERS

The distinctive characters of the arctic cod are the three dorsal and two anal fins; the lower jaw, which is as long as or slightly longer than the upper; the minute chin barbel; and the forked caudal fin (Figure 51).

DESCRIPTION

Body slender, elongate. Depth about 15% of fork length, greatest depth just behind head. Head moderate, 24% to 27% of fork length. Snout rather long, about 30% of head length. Eye round, large, its diameter 25% to 33% of head. Mouth fairly large, terminal. Teeth rather small, sharp, wide-set, in 2 rows in front of upper jaw, in one row on posterior part and in one row on lower jaw and vomer. A very small barbel usually present at anterior tip of lower jaw, sometimes scarcely visible. Gill rakers long and slender; 37 to 46. Lateral line discontinuous. Pyloric caeca: 20 to 37. Vertebrae: 53 to 57, in rare cases as few as 49.

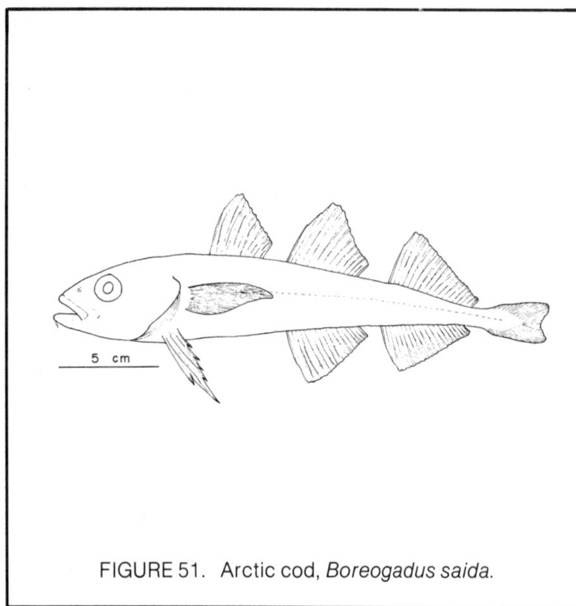

FIGURE 51. Arctic cod, *Boreogadus saida*.

FINS. First dorsal has 10 to 14 rays, rarely up to 16; second dorsal, 14 to 17 rays; third dorsal, 18 to 24. First anal, 15 to 20 rays; second anal, 18 to 24. Pectorals, about 19 rays; pelvics, 6, the second ray notably elongate. Caudal fin forked, the tips of the lobes slightly rounded.

SCALES. Cycloid, minute.

COLOR. Brownish or grayish brown above, sides above lateral line somewhat lighter, often with a yellow or purple tinge. Sides below lateral line, and ventral surface, silvery. Fine black dots scattered over body, most numerous on back. Fins dusky; dorsal and caudal with a narrow white edge; anal pale at base (photograph, page 102).

SIZE. One of the smallest of the cods. Most adults about 13 to 16 cm long, the largest specimen said to have been only 32.1 cm (Svetovidov, 1948). Weight to about 75 g.

RANGE AND ABUNDANCE

The arctic cod enjoys a circumpolar distribution in most of the Arctic Ocean, being absent only from the region just north of Scandinavia. On the Atlantic side of North America it has been found as far south as the Saint Lawrence River (Vladykov, 1945) and even to the estuary of the Miramichi River, New Brunswick (McKenzie, 1953). It ranges throughout the Arctic Ocean across the arctic coast of Canada and Alaska, south in the Bering Sea to Norton Sound on the east side, to the Gulf of Anadyr on the west; westward along the Siberian coast to about 37° to 38°E; and north probably to the North Pole (Andriyashev, 1954). Although primarily a marine species, the arctic cod seems to prefer the less saline waters, those with 15 to 30 parts per thousand salinity, and not infrequently runs far upstream in rivers. The arctic cod is one of the most abundant fishes present in arctic seas (Bean, 1887; Alverson and Wilimovsky, 1966). The density of juveniles in the eastern Chukchi Sea in September and October, 1970, was estimated at 28 fish per 1000 cubic meters of water, or about 700 kg of young fish per square kilometer (Quast, 1974).

HABITS

The arctic cod is a demersal species, the adults being associated with some kind of substrate, either the sea bottom or the underside of ice packs. The distribution of this fish is closely correlated with the presence of ice and/or lowered salinity. Sexual maturity is reached at three to four years of age, and the fish are reported to spawn only once in their lives (Nikolskii, 1961). The eggs are the largest of any gadid, .15 to .19 cm in diameter. The large eggs and the small size of the fish combine to produce low fecundity: 9,000 to 21,000 eggs per female. Spawning takes place from October to March, usually in January and February. At this time, the fish move close inshore, often in tremendous numbers. They may enter rivers, and spawning in fresh water has been recorded in Siberia (Svetovidov, 1948). The eggs are pelagic, floating in the surface waters.

Development to hatching requires several months.

The first larvae, about .5 cm long, appear from May to July. The larval stage lasts about two months. Small individuals .5 to .9 cm long have been taken in Siberian waters in May. Larger larvae, .9 to 1.8 cm long, are known from near the west coast of Greenland north of 68°N in late June. Transition to the juvenile stage occurs at the end of summer at lengths of 3 to 5 cm (Jensen, 1926; Andriyashev, 1954; Rass, 1968; Quast, 1974).

The young-of-the year appear to be negatively phototropic, avoiding light. They are much more numerous at depths below 20 m than above. This may be a mechanism whereby the fish reduce predation by sea birds (Quast, 1974).

Growth of arctic cod in the northern Bering Sea has been given as follows; 0+, 3.1 cm; 1+, 7.5 to 10 cm; 2+, 14.4 to 15.8 cm; 3+, 19 to 20 cm; 4+, 22 to 23 cm. This is rather faster growth than is found in more southerly regions along the east coast of Siberia (Andriyashev, 1954).

Arctic cod apparently undertake onshore-offshore migrations, which in part are associated with spawning and in part with movements of ice. The fish are common along the edge of pack ice, where they are said to swim rapidly between the blocks and to hide in cracks in the ice. The arctic cod shows strong preference for low temperatures. Eggs do well at 0° to 2°C, larvae at 2° to 5°C , and fry at 5° to 7°C (Rass, 1968). Older fish prefer lower temperatures. Adults seem to be most abundant in water with temperatures around -1° to -1.85°C (McKenzie, 1953; Backus, 1957; Leim and Scott, 1966).

Arctic cod feed mostly on plankton. Larvae and young fry eat copepod eggs and larval stages. Adults have a more varied diet, with euphausiids and calanoid copepods (especially *Calanus*) as the most important items but also including amphipods, shrimps, fish eggs and small fishes (Svetovidov, 1948; Andriyashev, 1954; Leim and Scott, 1966; Ponomarenko, 1967; Hognestad, 1968).

IMPORTANCE TO MAN

The arctic cod's chief importance to man is indirect. This fish is one of the major foods of many arctic marine animals including fishes, seals, belugas, narwhals and birds. At Cape Thompson, Alaska, Swartz (1966) estimated that the sea bird colony consumed about 13.1 million kg of fish per breeding season, of which the majority was arctic cod.

Direct importance to man is relatively low. The arctic cod is reported to be not very palatable. Hence, although it is fished commercially and in subsistence fisheries, especially by the Russians, most of the catch is used for animal food. The liver, however, contains up to 50% valuable oil.

PACIFIC COD

Gadus macrocephalus (Tilesius)

DISTINCTIVE CHARACTERS

Distinguishing characters of the Pacific cod are the presence of three dorsal and two anal fins, a long chin barbel (about three-fourths as long as the eye diameter in the young, longer than the eye diameter in adults) and a space between the second and third dorsal fins that is shorter than the eye diameter (Figure 52).

DESCRIPTION

Body elongate, nearly cylindrical toward the head, more or less compressed toward the tail. Depth about 20% of total length, deepest below first dorsal fin. Head large and broad, its length 26% to 29% of total length. Snout blunt, long, about 33% to 37% of head length. Eye round, its diameter 50% to 65% of snout length. Mouth large, subterminal, lower jaw shorter than upper; maxilla reaches to below eye. Small, sharp teeth present on both jaws and on head of vomer, the outer row of jaw teeth being larger than the others. Gill rakers: 18 to 23 on first arch. Lateral line has a prominent arch under first and second dorsal fins, is straight toward the tail, ending under third dorsal. Vertebrae: 49 to 55.

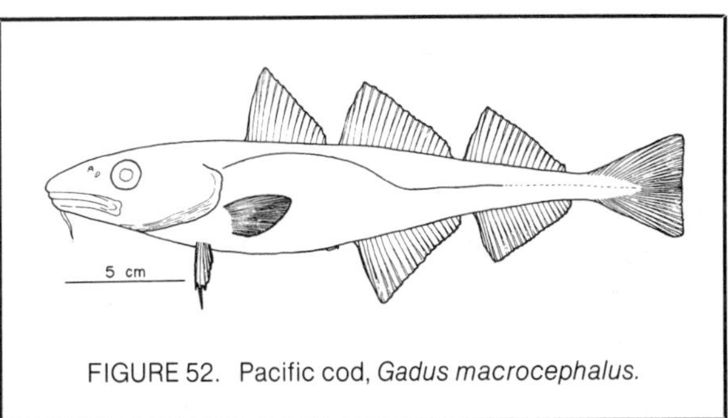

FIGURE 52. Pacific cod, *Gadus macrocephalus.*

FINS. First dorsal has 13 to 15 rays; second, 16 to 21; third, 15 to 21. First anal has 17 to 22 rays; second, 16 to 20. Pectorals, 19 to 22; pelvics, 6 or 7, with the second ray longest. Caudal fin truncate.

SCALES. Cycloid, small.

COLOR. Quite variable, usually brownish or olive gray above, paler below, with numerous brown or grayish spots on sides and back. Yellow color phases are known. Fins dusky; dorsal, anal and caudal fins have white edges that are wider on anal and caudal than on dorsal (photograph, page 103).

SIZE. Reaches a length of 1.2 m. Average size of trawl-caught fish is around 70 to 75 cm with a weight of about 4.5 kg.

RANGE AND ABUNDANCE

Pacific cod are found along the west coast from off Santa Monica, California, at 33° 59.5' S, north to Norton Sound and Saint Lawrence Island in the Bering Sea. On the Asian side the species is present from the southeastern tip of the Chukhotsk Peninsula through the Anadyr Gulf and southward to the Yellow Sea (Popov, 1933; Andriyashev, 1937, 1954; Svetovidov, 1948; Pinkas, 1967). It is rare south of Oregon, however, becoming most numerous, as well as larger, in the northern part of the range. From Puget Sound on northward and well into the Bering Sea, Pacific cod are abundant and support commercial fisheries of considerable size. Cod appear to prefer temperatures between 6° and 9°C (Ketchen, 1961).

HABITS

Like other codfishes, Pacific cod spawn in the winter, usually in January and February. Spawning grounds are in deep water, to as deep as 250 m. The eggs are small, average diameter being about .1 cm, and fecundity is high. Egg numbers tend to increase with the size of the fish. A female 40 cm long contains about 228,000 eggs while one of 80 cm may produce about 3.35 million. Egg counts as high as 5.7 million have been recorded. The eggs are demersal, with specific gravity of about 1.05, and are adhesive at first. They lose their adhesiveness about 30 hours after fertilization. Development to hatching requires about 8 to 9 days at 11°C but 29 days at 2°C. Experiments have shown that the maximum numbers of larvae are produced at salinities of about 19 parts per thousand and temperatures of about 5°C (Andriyashev, 1954; Thomson, 1962, 1963; Forrester, 1964, 1969b; Forrester and Alderdice, 1966).

The larvae are .35 to .48 cm long at hatching and have a fairly large yolk sac which is absorbed in 6 to 10 days, the time depending on temperature. Early growth is rapid and by the end of the first year of life the young fish are 23 to 26 cm long. Subsequent growth is, of course, much slower, and quite variable with different locations and populations. Typical lengths for various ages are: 2+, 50 cm; 3+, 61.4 cm; 4+, 67.3 cm; 5+, 72.6 cm; 6+, 76.2 cm. Use of otoliths for determining ages of Bering Sea cod results in much shorter lengths than these for corresponding ages. In contrast to most fishes, Pacific cod appear to grow just as fast in winter as they do in summer. However, cod on the Asian side of the Bering Sea do not grow as fast as the eastern Pacific fish. Sexual maturity is reached at age 2+ to 3+ in the southern parts of the range, but about two years later in the northern areas. Maximum age attained is about 13, but in most areas few live beyond about age 7 (Svetovidov, 1948; Mosher, 1953; Andriyashev, 1954; Forrester and Ketchen, 1955; Ketchen, 1961, 1964; Forrester, 1969b).

Pacific cod do not, as a rule, undertake extensive migrations. After spawning they move inshore to depths of 30 to 60 m; then, from late summer to midwinter, move out into the deeper water (100 to 250 m) of the spawning areas. In at least some North American stocks, there appears to be a good deal of movement from one bank to another. Most of these migrations are relatively short, but at least one tagged fish was recovered about 320 km from the point of release (Andriyashev, 1954; Forrester and Ketchen, 1955).

Young cod, like so many young fishes, probably feed largely on copepods and similar organisms. Adults feed heavily on shrimps, herring, sand lance and crabs, in that order, but also take almost any kind of small fish available, as well as worms, euphausiids, amphipods, isopods, echinoids, octopus and even ducks (Cobb, 1927; Hart, 1949; Andriyashev, 1954; Forrester and Ketchen 1955).

IMPORTANCE TO MAN

The Pacific cod is one of the more important secondary commercial fishes of the Pacific coast. Total landings in the U.S. and Canada run on the order of 5 to 10 million kg annually. The fishery began in 1863, when a Captain Turner, on the brig *Timandra,* brought a fare of salt cod to San Francisco from Sakhalin Island, U.S.S.R. A small fleet was organized and fished the Sakhalin region two years later. Fishing off the Shumagin Islands of Alaska began in 1867. Subsequently, nearly all the codfishing was done in Alaskan waters and the fishery prospered. Catches rose, more or less steadily, to a peak level of 2 to 4 million fish (probably about 10 to 20 million kg) in the 1920s. Nearly all the fish were landed at ports in Washington and California. Economic factors resulted in the decline of the Alaskan fisheries and the concommitant rise of the industry around British Columbia and Washington. By the late 1950s, the Alaska catch was no longer listed separately in the fisheries statistics and did not reappear until 1973 when landings of 72,000 kg were reported (Power, 1962; Anonymous, 1976).

The entire catch was salted in the early days, and the oil was extracted from the livers (38,000 l in 1866). With the advent of modern freezing techniques, more and more of the catch is frozen and used for fish sticks and similar products. The liver oil contains large quantities of vitamins A and D and in this respect is quite comparable to liver oil of Atlantic cod. Oil derived from the viscera is three to nine times as potent as oil from the liver, but the average yield is less than one-tenth that of the liver (Pugsley, 1938). The development of synthetic vitamins has adversely affected the market for these products.

SAFFRON COD

Eleginus gracilis (Tilesius)

DISTINCTIVE CHARACTERS

The saffron cod is set off by the presence of three dorsal and two anal fins, a lower jaw that is shorter than the upper, a chin barbel that is no longer than half the eye diameter, and a space between the second and third dorsal fins that is equal to or longer than the eye diameter (Figure 53).

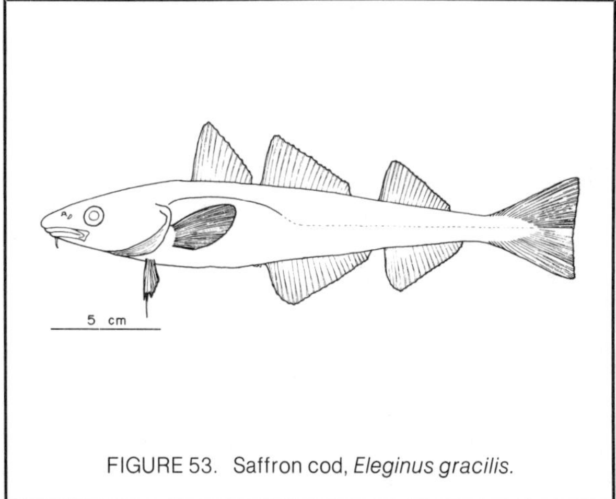

FIGURE 53. Saffron cod, *Eleginus gracilis*.

DESCRIPTION

Body elongate, nearly round in cross-section toward the head, slightly compressed toward the tail. Depth about 16% of total length. Head 21% to 25% of total length. Snout long, about 33% of head length. Eye round, moderate, its diameter about 18% of head length, or half of snout length. Mouth large, subterminal, with lower jaw distinctly shorter than upper; maxilla reaches to below eye. Teeth small, slender, curved backward; present in several rows in upper jaw, in 2 rows in anterior part of lower jaw and in a single row toward the rear. A patch of small teeth present on head of vomer. Gill rakers: 14 to 24, usually about 20, on first arch. Lateral line curved in the front, ending under second dorsal fin. Vertebrae: 57 to 64.

FINS. First dorsal has 11 to 15 rays; second, 15 to 23; third, 18 to 21. First anal has 20 to 24 rays; second, 19 to 23; pectorals, 20; pelvics, 6, the second ray produced. Caudal fin truncate or slightly emarginate.

SCALES. Cycloid, small; about 157 in a mid-lateral series.

COLOR. Grayish brown to olive above, upper part of sides paler, sometimes with a silvery-violet shading, often mottled with indistinct darker blotches. Lower sides and belly yellowish to silver white. Fins dusky, dorsals and caudal with white edges (photograph, page 103; Plate 28, page 139).

SIZE. Length usually around 25 to 35 cm but can reach about 50 cm and a weight of 1 kg.

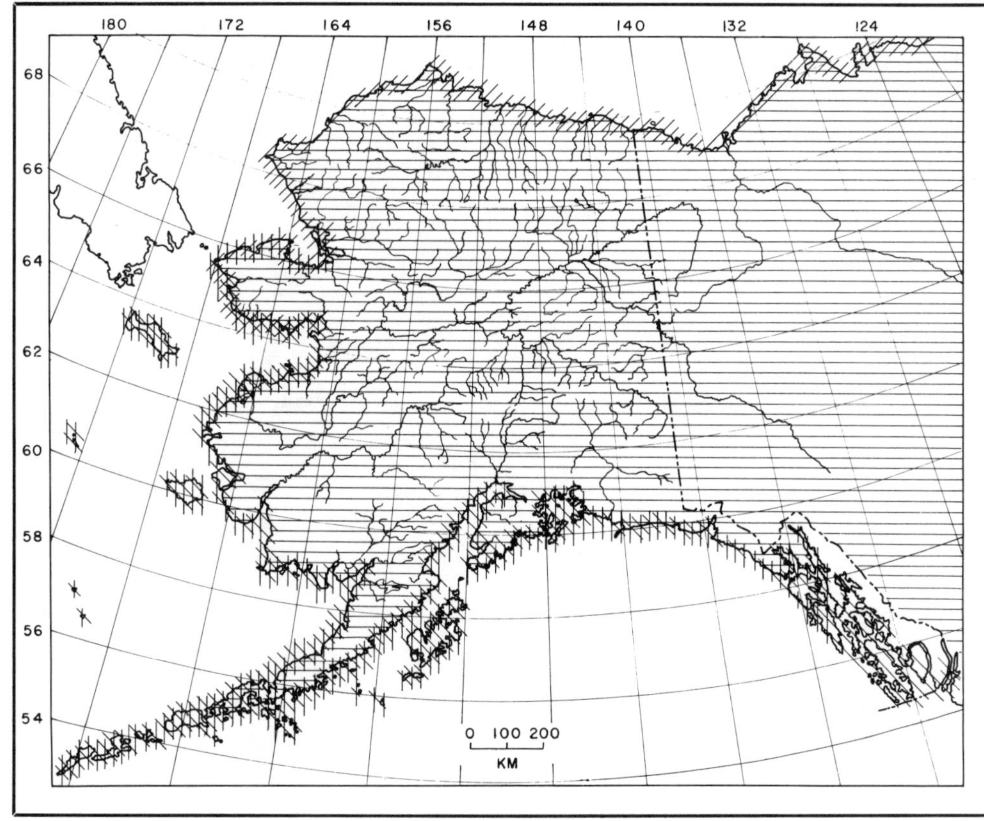

Range in Alaska and northwestern Canada of the burbot ▤ arctic cod ▨ Pacific cod ▧ and saffron cod ▥

RANGE AND ABUNDANCE

Confined to the north Pacific Ocean and the Bering and Chukchi seas; found from Sitka (Svetovidov, 1948) to at least as far north as Kotzebue on the Alaskan coast and from the Chukhotsk Peninsula south to Korea and the Yellow Sea on the Asian side. The saffron cod not infrequently enters rivers and may go considerable distances upstream. It has also been found in freshwater lakes on the Kamchatka Peninsula and on Bering Island, off Kamchatka (Jordan and Metz, 1913; Svetovidov, 1948; Andriyashev, 1954).

Throughout most of its range, the saffron cod is quite abundant, sufficiently so to be the object of commercial fisheries.

HABITS

Saffron cod spawn in the winter, from December to February. The fish move from water 30 to 60 m deep to shallower, inshore water for this purpose. In Norton Sound, saffron cod have been reported to spawn over pebbly bottoms (Turner, 1886). Water temperatures on the spawning grounds are -1.6° to -1.8°C. Fecundity is between 25,000 and 210,000 eggs per female. The eggs are said to be adhesive (Svetovidov, 1948). The young hatch in the spring, from April to June, and for the first few months of their lives are planktonic. They are frequently encountered under the bells of large jellyfish *(Cyania ferruginea)* (Andriyashev, 1954).

Growth is rather slow. Three-year-old fish average about 30 cm in length and weigh about 200 g; at 5+, 37.5 cm and 375 g; and at 7+, 46 cm and 800 to 900 g. Sexual maturity is reached at age 2+ or 3+, after which the fish spawn annually. (Svetovidov, 1948; Andriyashev, 1954).

Saffron cod do not migrate long distances. They move inshore in fall and winter for spawning and offshore in spring and summer to feed in deeper water. They often enter rivers and may go considerable distances upstream. However, they usually stay within regions of tidal influence. They apparently are restricted to the less frigid parts of the arctic seas, being replaced by the arctic cod in the colder regions (Popov, 1933; Svetovidov, 1948; Alverson and Wilimovsky, 1966).

Food of the saffron cod consists mainly of small crustaceans such as shrimps, amphipods and mysids, as well as polychaete worms and small fishes.

IMPORTANCE TO MAN

Along the coast of Alaska the saffron cod is used almost exclusively in subsistence fisheries. The coastal Eskimos catch considerable numbers with hand lines through holes in the ice. Along the Siberian coast, commercial fisheries of some magnitude are directed at this species. Current statistics are not available, but landings in the post-World War II years were on the order of 18 million kg annually. The flesh of the saffron cod is said to be very tasty in late fall and winter but not during the warmer months (Andriyashev, 1954).

Chapter Fourteen

STICKLEBACKS

Family Gasterosteidae

KEY TO THE ALASKAN SPECIES

SECTION	DESCRIPTION	THE FISH IS	PROCEED IN THIS KEY TO SECTION
a.	Two to 4 free spines, not connected by membranes, on midline of back in front of dorsal fin.	Threespine stickleback, *Gasterosteus aculeatus* Linnaeus, page 189.	
b.	Seven to 12 free spines on midline of back in front of dorsal fin.	Ninespine stickleback, *Pungitius pungitius* (Linnaeus), page 192.	

The members of this family are to be found in marine and fresh waters of Europe, Asia, North America and the western Mediterranean coast of Africa. Characteristically, they have three or more free spines in front of the dorsal fin and one before the anal fin. The pelvic fin is reduced to a single strong spine and 0 to 3 soft rays.

The sticklebacks are all small fishes and are often important in the food of larger fishes or birds. In some situations sticklebacks are strong competitors for food with young salmon. For an excellent detailed summation of the biology and behavior of sticklebacks, see Wootton (1976).

THREESPINE STICKLEBACK

Gasterosteus aculeatus Linnaeus

DISTINCTIVE CHARACTERS

The three (in rare cases two or four) sharp, free spines before the dorsal fin, the pelvic fin reduced to a sharp spine and a small ray, and the series of plates along the sides of the body identify the threespine stickleback (Figure 54).

DESCRIPTION

Body compressed, moderately robust, its depth about 25% of total length. (Deeper-bodied individuals are usually either gravid females or are infected with a cestode, *Schistocephalus,* which may fill the body cavity). Head almost 25% of total length.

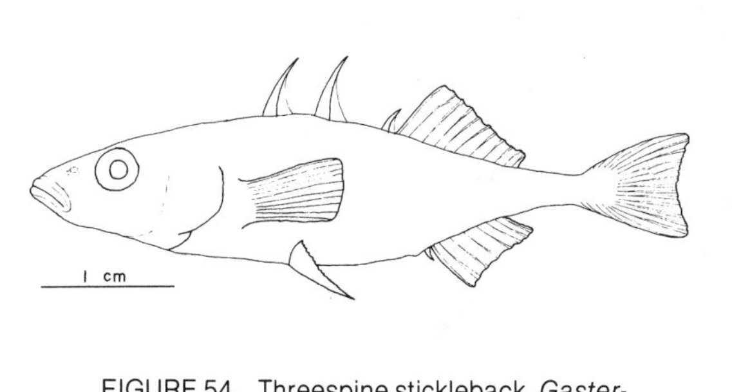

FIGURE 54. Threespine stickleback, *Gasterosteus aculeatus.*

Snout 27% to 31% of head length. Eye round, its diameter generally a little less than snout length. Mouth oblique, small; maxilla does not reach anterior margin of eye. Teeth small, fine, on both jaws. Gill rakers long and slender; 17 to 25 on first arch of strictly freshwater forms, 1 or 2 more in anadromous forms. Branchiostegals: 3 or 4. Lateral line more or less parallel to dorsal outline; pores microscopic. Pyloric caeca, short: 1 or 2. Vertebrae: 31 to 33, rarely as few as 29.

FINS. Dorsal has 2 to 4 (usually 3) spines and 10 to 14 rays; the spines are separate from each other and from the soft-rayed fin, each spine having a reduced membrane attached to its posterior side. Anal, 1 spine and 6 to 10 rays; spine is free from the rest of the fin. Pectorals, 9 to 11 rays; posterior margin of fins nearly truncate. Pelvics, 1 spine and 1 ray. Caudal truncate to slightly indented.

SCALES. No scales, but the sides have vertically enlarged bony plates. In freshwater populations, these plates usually number 5 to 9 on each side, with 7 the most common number. Marine and anadromous sticklebacks are completely armored with 22 to 37 plates. A few freshwater populations have 0 to 2 plates. The anadromous type has a keel along each side of the caudal peduncle.

COLOR. Freshwater forms usually mottled brown or greenish; anadromous fish silvery green to bluish black. A few isolated populations such as those in the Chehalis River system of Washington and in Mayer Lake, Queen Charlotte Islands, British Columbia, are black. Sides usually pale; belly yellow, white or silvery. Fins pale; pectoral rays often have dark dots (Greenbank and Nelson, 1959; McPhail, 1969; Moodie, 1972a, b).

Breeding males (except of the black forms) become brilliant bluish or green with blue or green eyes, and the forward part of the body, especially the breast region, turns bright red or orange (photograph, page 104; Plate 15, page 126).

SIZE. Maximum size reported to about 10 cm (Jordan and Evermann, 1896), but the size of adults in different populations is highly variable.

RANGE AND ABUNDANCE

The threespine stickleback is found along the Pacific coast of North America from Rio Rosario, Baja California, north to the Bristol Bay region of Alaska and Saint Lawrence Island. Recently recorded from Simpson Lagoon on the arctic coast of Alaska by Craig and Haldorson (1979). On the Asian coast of the Pacific it is found south to Korea. On the Atlantic side of North America, this stickleback is found from Chesapeake Bay north along the coast to the western shore of Hudson Bay, and to Baffin Island and Devon Island in the Canadian arctic. It is also present in southern Greenland, Iceland and most of western Europe. Wherever present, the threespine stickleback is usually abundant.

HABITS

Description of the habits of the threespine stickleback is not made any easier by the great variation shown among populations. It is quite probable that several subspecies or even full species are involved in this group, but adequate analysis has not yet been possible and authorities are divided in their opinions. Some suggest that the variations represent the response of a single plastic species to different environmental conditions. Others feel that various degrees of speciation have occurred; still others, that the differences are due to several lines of evolution (Hagen, 1967; McPhail, 1969; Miller and Hubbs, 1969; Hagen and McPhail, 1970; Moodie, 1972b; Ross, 1973; Bell, 1976). The discussion below is an attempt to provide a generalized summary based on many published accounts and personal observations.

Sticklebacks generally winter in deep water, moving inshore to the shallows early in spring. Breeding occurs in the spring and summer, usually June and July in Alaska, with a few fish in breeding condition as late as August. Just prior to the breeding season, males become strongly territorial and take on the breeding colors. They defend their territories by ritual displays, by a head-down position and by chasing and biting invading males. The resident male builds a barrel-shaped nest, using such things as grains of sand, bits of vegetation, etc., which he cements together with a glue secreted by a special portion of his kidney. After completing the nest, which has an entrance and an exit, the male courts females by doing a zigzag dance toward a female, then turning and swimming toward the nest. The intensity of the zigzag dance is extremely variable in different populations, ranging from short dashes each way to little more than head-wagging. Nonreceptive females ignore the dance and may be driven from the territory, but a receptive female will follow the male to the nest. There he points out the entrance by posing above it with his head down. The female enters the nest and deposits a clutch of eggs. At this time, males may butt the side of the nest, which apparently stimulates the female to lay her eggs. Fecundity ranges from 80 to nearly 1,300 eggs, but only 50 to 200 are deposited at one time. Females may lay eggs in several nests on several days or may be courted again by the same male. Between spawnings, which usually occur at intervals of three or four days, the female may eat her own weight of food. If an adequate food supply is not available, egg production goes on at the expense of body tissues, or spawning stops. A large, well-fed female may produce two or three times her own weight of eggs in a single season. Well-fed fish produce more eggs per spawning and spawn more times than do poorly-nourished females (Wootton, 1973a, b; Wootton and Evans, 1976).

When the female has laid her eggs, she leaves the nest by the exit. Attempts to back out of the nest are resisted by the male. Following egg deposition, which takes several minutes, the male may immediately enter the nest and fertilize the eggs, or, less frequently, he may court another female before entering the nest himself. In any case, the female is driven away after the eggs have been deposited. Several females generally are induced to deposit eggs in each nest, and it is not uncommon for a male to have several sets of eggs, at different stages of development, in a single nest.

Following courting and fertilizing, the male guards the nest. He also takes a characteristic position in front of the entrance or exit, maintaining his body at an angle of about 45° from horizontal with his head toward the nest, and fanning with his pectoral fins.

The eggs are sticky and adhere to each other. Diameter of newly laid eggs is .11 to .16 cm but they quickly swell to .15 to .19 cm. Hatching time may be as short as 6 days at 17 °C in California or as long as 14 days at 9 ° to 16 °C in Karluk Lake, Kodiak Island, Alaska. The young are about .42 to .45 cm long at hatching and each has a large spherical yolk sac. About 8 days after hatching, the young, now about .7 cm long and with the yolk sac absorbed, begin to emerge from the nest, and the male is kept busy catching them in his mouth and spitting them back into the nest. When the young are fully developed and free-swimming, they school around the male for a few days, then disperse. The male may now build a new nest and repeat the cycle.

Growth rates are extremely variable. In Karluk Lake, young threespine sticklebacks are about 2.8 cm in length by early August, but only about 1.2 cm long in the Dixon River, Glacier Bay National Monument. It is not known whether this reflects slower growth or later spawning in the latter area. Karluk Lake sticklebacks at age 1 are about 4.7 cm long; 6 cm at 2. In Cowichan Lake, British Columbia, threespine sticklebacks reach 6.4 cm in only 10 months. Normal life span in this population is 2.25 years; elsewhere it ranges from one to three years.

Sexual maturity is first attained at age 1, though most threespine sticklebacks do not mature until the second year. It is not known whether the early-maturing fish survive to spawn a second time. In at least some populations, the fish are hermaphroditic. Males have apparently nonfunctional ovaries while females may have functional testes and perhaps are capable of self-fertilizaton. At any rate, Karluk Lake females have been found with eyed eggs in the ovaries.

Freshwater threespine sticklebacks in summer generally inhabit shallow, well-oxygenated water in association with a modicum of aquatic vegetation. However, they have been found in large numbers at the surface over deep water in some Alaskan lakes and as deep as 24 m in Karluk Lake (Kuntz and Radcliffe, 1917; Tinbergen and Van Iersel, 1947; Vrat, 1949; Jones and Hynes, 1950; Carl, 1953; Greenbank and Nelson, 1959; Narver, 1969; Lewis et al., 1972).

The food of sticklebacks consists mostly of zooplankton and insects. Copepods, Cladocera and chironomids are the most imporant items, but the list is a long one, including rotifers, ostracods, oligochaetes, small mollusks, amphipods, beetle larvae, leeches, planarians, mites, and their own eggs and larvae (Markley, 1940; Hynes, 1950; Carl, 1953; Greenbank and Nelson, 1959; Manzer, 1976).

Although the number of lateral plates on freshwater threespine sticklebacks varies between zero and nine, the modal number in most populations is seven. This number of plates seems to be associated with behavioral traits which make those individuals less subject to predation by larger fishes such as trout and squawfish. The threespine stickleback relies mostly on camouflage and cryptic coloration for protection. Lying motionless in the water, as they often do, the fish resemble floating sticks or twigs. Individuals with more or less than seven lateral plates apparently are more active and thus more likely to attract the attention of predators than are seven-plated fish. Why this is so is unknown. When caught by a predator such as a pike, a stickleback erects all its spines and remains motionless. Since the spines can be locked into place because of the arrangement of the joints, this requires no expenditure of energy and the stickleback can maintain the erected spines indefinitely. This is quite an effective defense for, unless the predator is much larger than the stickleback, the erect spines prevent swallowing and the stickleback is spat out, usually uninjured. Pike, at least, soon learn to avoid sticklebacks and doubtless other predators do also (Hoogland et al., 1957; Greenbank and Nelson, 1959; Moodie, 1972a; Moodie et al., 1973; Hagen and Gilbertson, 1973).

The anadromous threespine stickleback differs from the freshwater form in a number of respects. Morphologically, this difference appears in the lateral plates and gill rakers. The anadromous form is fully plated, with up to 37 plates on the sides and a rather pronounced keel on each side of the caudal peduncle. In addition, the number of gill rakers on the first arch tends to be slightly higher in the anadromous form.

Life history also differs. Spawning behaviour is essentially like that of the freshwater form, but breeding may occur in either fresh or salt water in salinities at least as high as 28.5 parts per thousand (McPhail, 1969). Sexual maturity is more often reached at one year rather than two, and the spawning areas seem to be in thicker vegetation, such as eel-grass beds (Narver, 1969). The young leave the streams and estuaries where they were hatched and move out into salt water. At first they stay close to shore, sheltering in seaweeds and such, but they enter the open sea in the fall. Some remain near shore through the winter, but others apparently move out for considerable distances. Large numbers have been taken at the surface 800 km from shore in the Gulf of Alaska, and on Georges Bank in the Atlantic (Bigelow and Schroeder, 1953; Andriyashev, 1954; Clemens and Wilby, 1961; McPhail and Lindsey, 1970). Whether or not these little fish that go so far from shore ever find their way back is not known.

IMPORTANCE TO MAN

The threespine stickleback is of but little direct importance to man. It has occasionally been taken commercially in Scandinavia and rendered into meal and oil, the latter said to have a healing effect on wounds and burns (Bigelow and Welsh, 1925; Nikolskii, 1961). It is an important forage species for predaceous fish like Dolly Varden, lake trout and northern pike. Large populations in some lakes may have adverse effects on the growth of young sockeye salmon through competition for food, but its old reputation and the name salmon killer (Jordan and Evermann, 1896) seem to be completely unjustified. The threespine stickleback makes an interesting aquarium fish.

NINESPINE STICKLEBACK

Pungitius pungitius (Linnaeus)

DISTINCTIVE CHARACTERS

The ninespine stickleback is set off by the presence of 7 to 12 free spines in front of the dorsal fin and a long caudal keel that usually reaches to beneath the dorsal fin (Figure 55).

DESCRIPTION

Body elongate, slender, its greatest depth 19% to 22% of total length; caudal peduncle notably long and slender. Head short, 20% to 23% of total length. Snout about equal to eye diameter and about 25% of head. Mouth oblique, small, reaching back about to anterior margin of eye. Small, fine teeth present on both jaws. Gill rakers rather slender: 10 to 15 on first arch. Branchiostegals: 3. Lateral line nearly straight, the pores microscopic. No pyloric caeca. Vertebrae: 30 to 35, usually 32 to 34.

FINS. Dorsal has 6 to 12 spines, 9 to 13 rays; the spines are separate and each has a rudimentary membrane on its posterior side. Anal has 1 spine and 8 to 11 rays; the spine stout and curved. Pectorals, 10 to 11 rays; posterior edge of fin rounded. Pelvics, 1 ray, 1 spine, the ray pressed close to the spine. The pelvic girdle is occasionally reduced or absent (Nelson, 1971). Caudal fin usually truncate, varying from slightly indented to slightly rounded.

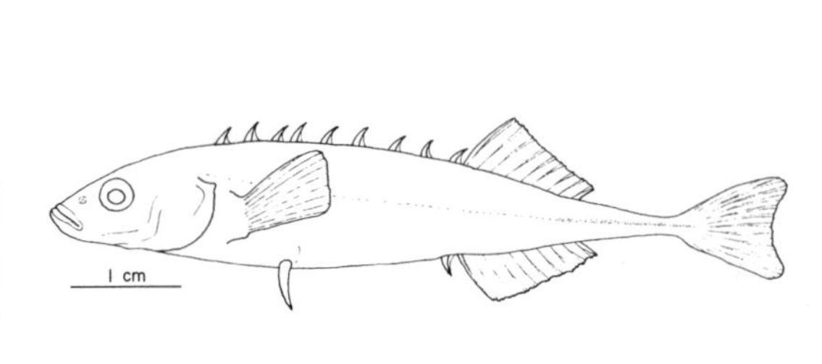

FIGURE 55. Ninespine stickleback, *Pungitius pungitius.*

SCALES. No scales; 0 to 15 small bony plates along anterior part of lateral line. Caudal peduncle has a noticeable keel that may reach forward to below front edge of dorsal fin.

COLOR. Dull olive to light brown above, sides mottled or blotched with darker patches of the same color. Belly yellowish to silvery white. Fins colorless. Breeding colors may be quite variable, depending on sex, population and stage of the breeding cycle. Colors of females are always less intense than those of males. Aggressive females become dark on the back and paler below, then sometimes become paler with more conspicuous saddle marks as actual breeding approaches (McKenzie and Keenleyside, 1970). Aggressive males become totally black except for the colorless fins and the membranes on the pelvic spines, which are white. At breeding, the males become paler on the back and more intensely black on the belly, especially under the chin (Morris, 1958; McKenzie and Keenleyside, 1970). Breeding males on the east coast of North America have been reported (Bigelow and Welsh, 1925) as reddish under the head and greenish on the belly (photograph, page 104; Plate 29, page 140).

SIZE. Up to 9 cm, but the average is about 6.5 cm or less.

RANGE AND ABUNDANCE

The ninespine stickleback is circumpolar in its total distribution. In Asia it ranges from the Yangtse River of China north to the Arctic Ocean, westward across northern Siberia to the Atlantic coast of Europe as far south as the Loire basin in France. It is present on the southern tip of Greenland. In North America, the species ranges from Cook Inlet, Alaska, north along the coast to the Arctic Ocean, east to the Atlantic. The arctic North American range of the ninespine stickleback includes Victoria and Baffin islands and most of the Arctic Archipelago in the Northwest Territories. From the mouth of the Mackenzie River, the ninespine stickleback ranges southeastward across Canada to the Great Lakes (except Lake Erie) and south along the coast to New Jersey. Isolated populations are present in the upper Mississippi drainage (Nelson, 1968a, b). There are two quite distinct forms in North America: a coastal, Bering form confined to Alaska and the coastal regions of Canada and eastern United States, and an inland, Mississippi form found in the rest of the range. The two groups are distinguished by the lower average number of gill rakers and dorsal spines and higher numbers of lateral plates in the Bering form (McPhail, 1963). Wherever it is present, the ninespine stickleback is abundant.

HABITS

The ninespine stickleback is strictly a freshwater form, one that can tolerate low oxygen concentrations. Although it can survive salinities up to 20 parts per thousand, it requires fresh water for spawning. The coastal form, however, may winter in the sea, at least in Hudson Bay, and has been taken in Norton Sound at Nome (Nelson, 1968c; McPhail and Lindsey, 1970; Lewis et al., 1972).

Ninespine sticklebacks spend the winter in deep water, moving into the shallows in spring. Spawning occurs in the spring and summer, generally from May to July, at water temperatures around 11° to 12°C, but ripe females have been found as early as April and as late as August (Nelson, 1968b; Griswold and Smith, 1973). The first indication of the onset of the breeding season is a breakdown of schooling and a beginning of aggressive behavior. Subsequently, both males and females set up territories which are defended against intruders of either sex. At this time males become black, females dark above and silvery below (see *Color* in section on description, preceding). Males construct nests of algae and bits of debris. The nests are generally located in aquatic vegetation 10 to 15 cm above the bottom, but may be on the bottom or even slightly sunk into it. In some areas, nests have been observed under or between rocks at depths as great as 2 m (McKenzie and Keenleyside, 1970). The nest is made of material stuck together with a glue secreted by the male's kidneys. Nests are more or less tubular or barrel-shaped, with an opening at each end. An exception is in the Apostle Islands region of Lake Superior, where ninespine sticklebacks breed in burrows in the mud bottom (Griswold and Smith, 1973).

As the nest is completed, the males become paler toward the back but more intensely black below, especially on the throat and forward part of the abdomen. They now begin to court the females, instead of attacking them. Courtship consists of a series of quick, head-down, dancing movements toward the female. This may be accompanied by bending the body in an *S* shape in front of the female. If the female is receptive, she lowers her tail, displaying her swollen belly to the male. He then dances back toward his nest, the female following with her snout between the male's pelvic spines. If the female is not responsive to courting, she may be attacked and driven from the male's territory. At the nest, the male takes up a position just above it, with his snout pointing to the opening, and fans with his pectoral fins. The female enters the nest, but, as she is longer than the nest, her head and tail protrude. The male then places his throat against the posterior part of one side of the female and quivers. This stimulates her to lay her eggs, after which she leaves the nest and the male enters the nest and fertilizes the eggs. In burrow nests, which have only one opening, the female enters, turns around, deposits her eggs and leaves; then the male enters the nest and fertilizes the eggs (Griswold and Smith, 1973). Total fecundity of a female is up to 960 eggs (Andriyashev, 1954), but only 50 to 80 are laid at a time. If the female is still near the nest when the male emerges, he attacks her and drives her out of his territory. The female soon begins feeding voraciously and in a day or so is ready to be courted again by the same or other males and to lay another clutch of eggs. The male usually collects several clutches of eggs from the females on adjoining territories.

Egg-laying and fertilization accomplished, the male again becomes black all over. He spends most of his time at one or the other entrances of the nest, in a nearly horizontal position, facing the nest and fanning with his pectoral fins. This keeps gentle currents of water moving over the eggs, bringing oxygen and removing metabolic wastes. The male also moves the eggs around in the nest and removes and eats any dead eggs. Sometimes the nest begins to fall apart before the eggs have hatched. The male may then build a new nest nearby and transfer the eggs to it (Morris, 1958).

The eggs, which are sticky and .1 to .15 cm in diameter, hatch in about a week at 18°C. At hatching, the male often enters the nest and removes the broken remains of the egg membranes. The newly hatched larvae move to the top of the nest and settle on it. At this time the male may construct a nursery, a loose mass of vegetation in the weeds a few centimeters above the nest. As the young develop and begin to move about, the male catches them in his mouth and spits them back into the nest or the nursery. As the young grow older and become still more active the male is less and less successful in getting the young back into the nest and finally loses interest in them except perhaps as food. The male may now build a new nest and start the reproductive cycle all over again, or the breeding season comes to an end (Morris, 1958).

Nothing is known of the growth rates of ninespine sticklebacks in northwestern North America. However, in the Apostle Islands regions of Lake Superior, the young sticklebacks are about .56 cm long at hatching. By the end of three weeks they have reached about 1.3 cm and reach about 4.5 cm by late fall, when they leave the shallow water. About half the annual growth occurs in the summer, before early August, with the remainder accomplished by December. The fish apparently do not grow during the winter. Females grow faster and live longer than do males. The fastest-growing fish of both sexes reach sexual maturity at one year of age, although a greater percentage of males than of females matures this early. Nearly all fish are mature at age 2; all are mature at 3. Males seldom live beyond age 3, due to heavy postspawning mortality, but females may live to age 5 or more. Two-year-old fish are about 6.1 cm long; 3 year males are about 6.6 cm long, and females a little longer; 5 year females are about 8 cm. By contrast, 3 year fish in certain English waters averaged only 3.7 cm in length and had a maximum life span of less than 3.5 years (Jones and Hynes, 1950; Griswold and Smith, 1973).

Of the migrations of the ninespine stickleback nothing definite is known. However, there would appear to be seasonal movements inshore to shallow water in the spring for spawning and, in the fall, offshore to deep water, or even to the less saline parts of the sea, by the young and such adults as survive spawning. Shortly after hatching the young are common in and just below the zone of rooted vegetation in lakes. Adults are common down to about 20 m and, in Lake Superior, at 90 to 110 m. They appear to be most numerous in water of temperatures between 6° and 12°C (Dryer, 1966; Nelson, 1968b).

Food of ninespine sticklebacks consists mostly of copepods and chironomids, but they also eat Cladocera and other small crustaceans, ostracods and oligochaete worms and, on occasion, their own eggs and larvae (Hynes, 1950; Morris, 1958). They in turn are fed upon by various predaceous fishes such as arctic charr, Dolly Varden, lake trout, walleye, grayling and fish-eating birds (Rawson, 1957; Dryer et al., 1965; McPhail and Lindsey, 1970).

IMPORTANCE TO MAN

The ninespine stickleback is too small and of too uncertain occurrence to be of direct value to man. However, the fish may be so abundant at certain times of year that the natives of Siberia, of the Yukon-Kuskokwim Delta and of other similar regions catch them for food both for dogs and for people. Ninespine sticklebacks have also been used as a source of oil in some areas (Bigelow and Welsh, 1925; Nikolskii, 1961; McPhail and Lindsey, 1970).

Indirect importance is probably greater than the direct, for ninespine sticklebacks may form a significant part of the food of larger fishes.

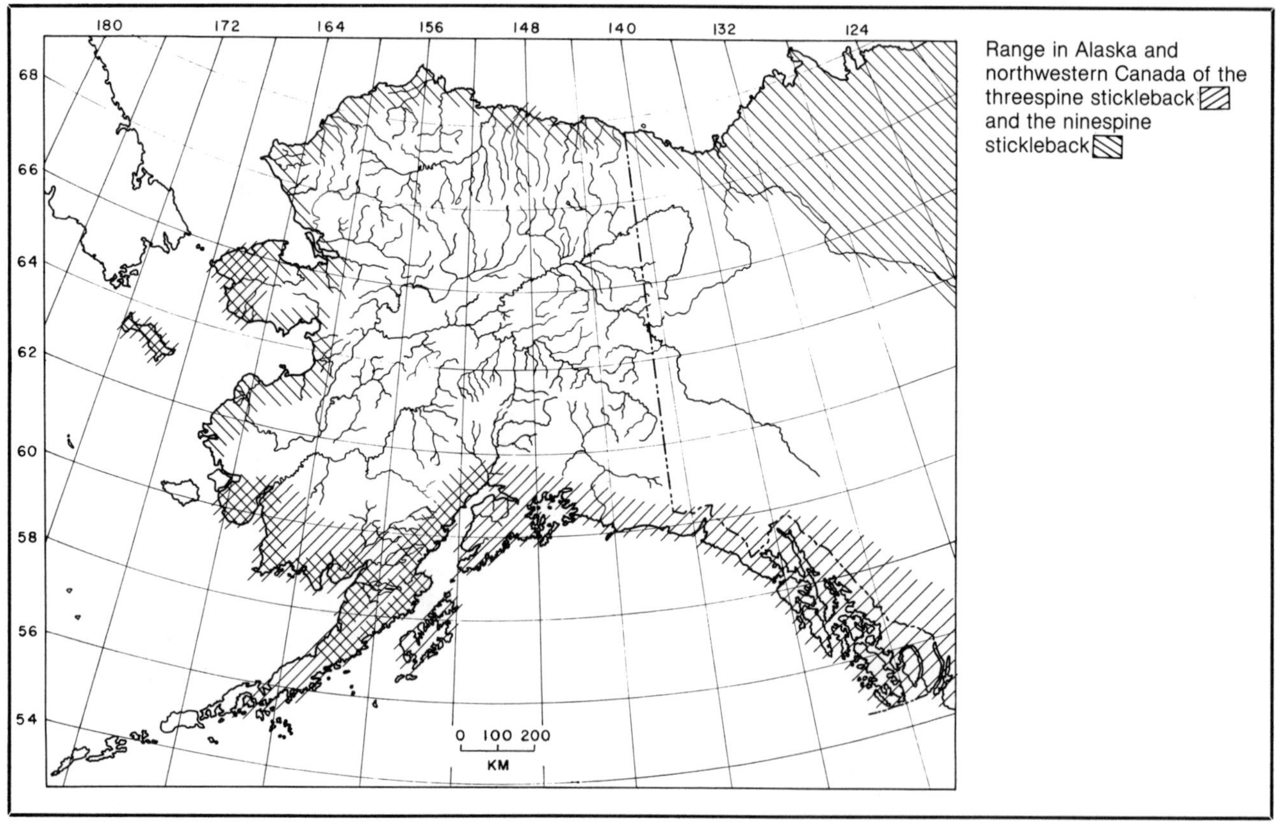

Range in Alaska and northwestern Canada of the threespine stickleback and the ninespine stickleback

Chapter Fifteen

SURFPERCHES

Family Embiotocidae

The members of this family, numbering about 20 North American species, are almost all marine. One species lives in fresh water in California and another, the shiner perch, is mainly marine but often enters rivers.

The surfperches are live-bearers, bringing forth living young rather than laying eggs. In appearance they are typically perchlike, with a dorsal fin having both spines and rays, and a three-spined anal fin. However, the scales are cycloid rather than ctenoid. A remarkable feature of this group is the fact that, in at least some species, the males are sexually mature at birth.

Surfperches are small fishes, rarely exceeding 15 cm in length. They are utilized to some extent for human food or as bait for larger fishes.

SHINER PERCH

Cymatogaster aggregata Gibbons

DISTINCTIVE CHARACTERS

The rather deep, compressed body, the large scales, and the three spines in the anal fin distinguish the shiner perch from other freshwater fishes of Alaska (Figure 56).

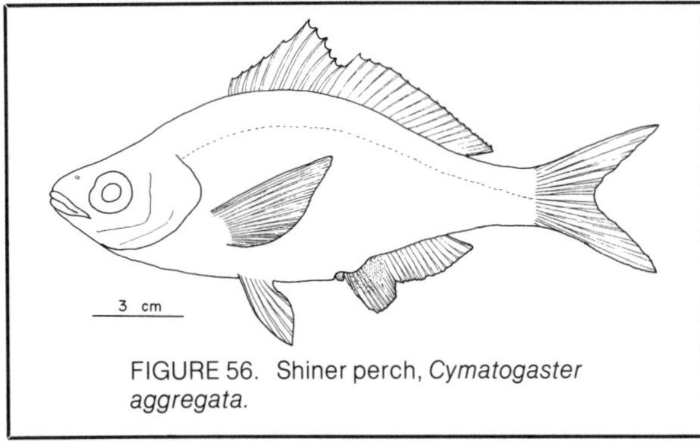

FIGURE 56. Shiner perch, *Cymatogaster aggregata.*

DESCRIPTION

Body compressed, deep, its depth 33% to 38% of fork length. Head compressed, moderate, its length 27% to 34% of fork length. Snout length, 26% to 33% of head, usually slightly greater than eye diameter. Eye moderate, round or nearly so, diameter 24% to 30% of head. Nostrils double on each side. Mouth terminal, rather small, directed slightly upward, upper jaw reaching backward to below anterior margin of eye. Small conical teeth present on both jaws, but absent on vomer and palatines. Gill rakers short, slender; 28 to 33 on first arch. Branchiostegals: 5 or 6. Lateral line slightly arched, complete; 36 to 43 pored scales. Vertebrae: 33 to 37.

FINS. Dorsal has 8 to 11 spines, usually 9, and 19 to 22 rays, usually 20; the spiny portion of the fin is higher than the soft-rayed part. Anal has 3 spines, 22 to 25 rays, usually 24. Pectorals, 19 or 20 rays; pelvics, 1 spine, 5 rays. Caudal forked.

SCALES. Large, cycloid. Scale sheath present along posterior three-fourths of base of dorsal fin, separated from body scales by a furrow.

COLOR. Generally silvery, with back dusky to greenish. On middle of sides toward head are scales with groups of fine black dots on them, forming about eight longitudinal stripes. The stripes are often interrupted, especially in females, by three pale yellow, vertical bands. Paired fins colorless. Dorsal and caudal fins plain or dusky. Anal usually colorless, sometimes with a yellow blotch toward the front (photograph, page 105). Breeding males may be almost solid black (Eigenmann and Ulrey, 1894).

SIZE. Reported up to 20.3 cm (Evermann and Goldsborough, 1907), but the vast majority are between about 10 and 12.7 cm. Males are generally smaller than females.

RANGE AND ABUNDANCE

The shiner perch is found along the west coast of North America from San Quintin Bay, Baja California (Miller and Lea, 1972), north to Wrangell, Alaska (Bean, 1884). It appears to be rather scarce at the extreme ends of the range but is abundant from about San Diego to Ketchikan. Occasionally found in brackish or fresh water (Bailey et al., 1970).

HABITS

The shiner perch is viviparous, bearing fully developed young, which develop in the ovarian cavity of the female. Mating is preceded by courtship. The male moves slowly toward the female, who retreats. Her flight stimulates pursuit by up to 10 males. During the pursuit, males attempt to bring their anal regions in contact with that of the female. One male heads off the female, urging her away from the group of males and also driving them away. The female is conducted to the shelter of a rock or other object, where the courtship dance begins. In this dance the male, with dorsal fin fully erect, swims by means of his pectoral fins in a figure eight pattern over the female, undulating in both the horizontal and vertical planes. The male then stops, faces the female head to head, quivers, moves his jaws and undulates his dorsal fin. He then moves beside the female, facing in the same direction, and repeats the movements. Finally, the male tilts on his side, the female tilts slightly away from him, and the anal regions are brought in contact with each other. Copulation lasts less than a second (Hubbs, 1917; Wiebe, 1968b).

Males are mature and ripe at birth. Juvenile females are mated soon after being born. Shortly before breeding, the males develop fleshy lobes on both sides of the anal fin. One lobe ends in a tubular intromittant organ—a nonmammalian penis—that points more or less forward and downward. Mating takes place in June and early July in most areas, less commonly in May or August. Sperm is stored in the female's ovary until about December, when fertilization occurs. Gestation of the young requires five to six months and they are born in June or July, about a year after the parents have mated (Eigenmann, 1894; Turner, 1938).

The eggs are extremely small, only about .03 cm in diameter, and they shrink still further during early development to about .02 cm (Eigenmann, 1894). Fertilization occurs while the eggs are still in the follicles, but development does not begin until after their release. Eggs that are not ripe at the time of fertilization degenerate and may contribute to the nourishment of the developing embryos. During gestation the epithelial cells of the ovary become filled with fluid and slough off. The embryos are nourished by these cells as well as by the ovarian fluid itself; both cells and fluid enter the embryonic alimentary canal through the gill opening, later through the mouth as well. Later, the embryo's respiration comes about through the development of highly vascularized tissues along the margins of the dorsal and anal fins. These tissues are in close contact with vascularized portions of the ovary and most probably function in the exchange of oxygen and carbon dioxide. In about half the embryos, one gill opening is invaded by a fold of tissue from the ovary wall, apparently another respiratory device (Tarp, 1952; Turner, 1952). Brood size ranges from 3 to 36 young. Older and larger females produce more and larger young and generally give birth earlier in the season than do smaller, younger fish. The development of sex products and secondary sex characters of the male is enhanced by warm temperatures and increasing day lengths. Development of egg cells of the female, by contrast, is encouraged by cool

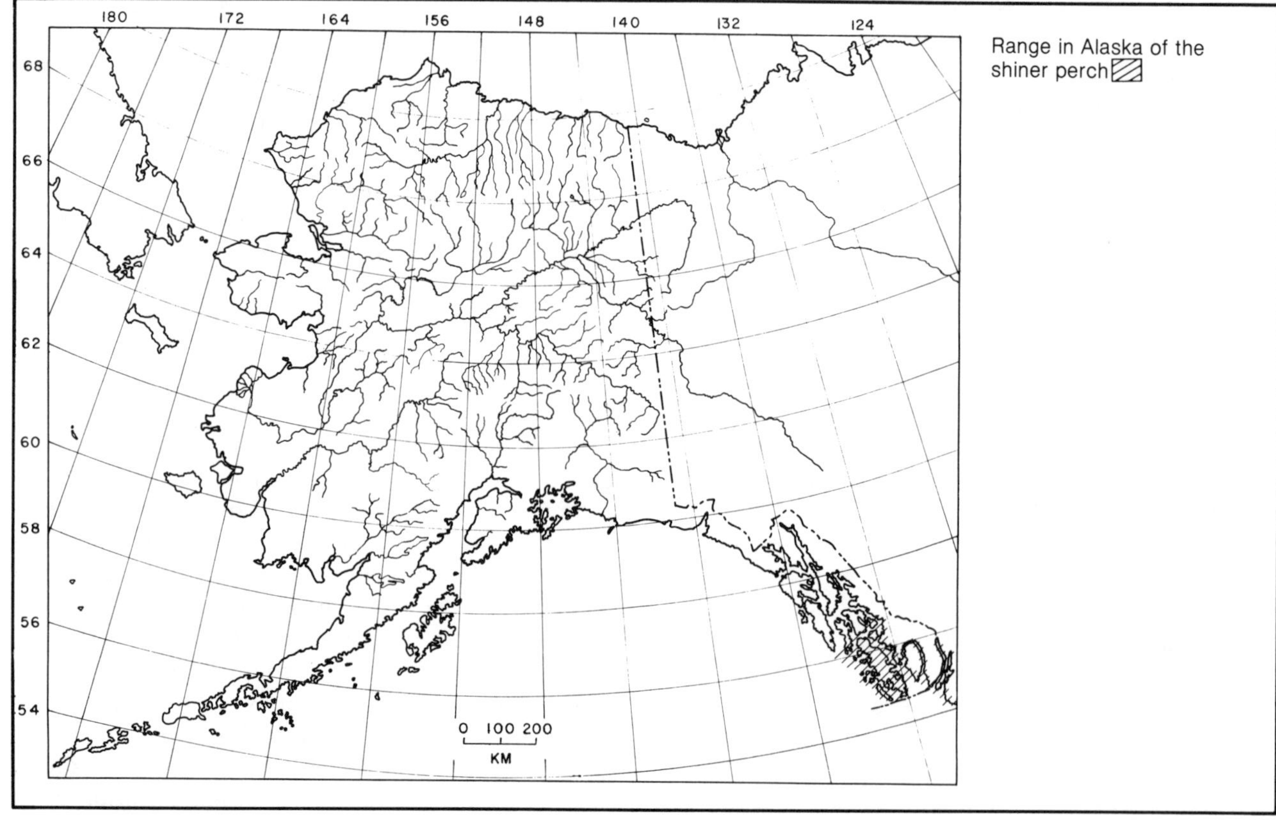

Range in Alaska of the shiner perch

temperatures and decreasing light, although development of the embryos is promoted by warmth (Eigenmann, 1894; Evermann and Goldsborough, 1907; Wiebe, 1968a, b; Wilson and Millemann, 1969). Breeding apparently occurs annually during the life of the individual.

The young fish are 3.4 to 4.4 cm long at birth and are ready to mate at this time. Males are smaller than females, a relation which continues throughout life. At age 1+, females average about 9.3 cm long in Yaquina Bay, Oregon. At 2+, they are about 11.1 cm; at 3+, 11.8 cm; at 4+, 13 cm; at 5+, 13.3 cm; and at 6+, about 13.7 cm (Eigenmann, 1894; Wilson and Millemann, 1969).

Except for seasonal onshore-offshore movements, the shiner perch apparently does not migrate. However, the fish does appear in shallow water inshore in the summer and has been taken in trawls as deep as 128 m in winter (Clemens and Wilby, 1946; Hart, 1973).

Food of the shiner perch varies with the size of the individual and the time of year. The young feed mainly on copepods, while the adults eat various small crustaceans, mollusks and algae. Adults often eat the appendages of barnacles on piers and rocks (Clemens and Wilby, 1946; Gordon, 1965).

IMPORTANCE TO MAN

The shiner perch is of little importance to man. Some are marketed in British Columbia, chiefly for the oriental trade in Vancouver (Clemens and Wilby, 1946) and also in California, especially in San Francisco and Los Angeles. However, the shiner perch is only a minor constituent of the so-called "perch" landings in California (Roedel, 1948). The shiner perch is used to a slight extent as bait for larger fishes and provides considerable sport in the summer, when numbers are found close inshore, for juvenile anglers. It has been said to be "a very fair pan fish" (Evermann and Goldsborough, 1907).

Chapter Sixteen

SCULPINS

Family Cottidae

KEY TO THE ALASKAN SPECIES

SECTION	DESCRIPTION	THE FISH IS	PROCEED IN THIS KEY TO SECTION
1 a.	Dorsal fins touch each other or are only very slightly separated.		**2**
b.	Dorsal fins are separated by a distinct space.		**5**
2 a.	Upper preopercular spine moderately long, branched and antlerlike, with 3 or 4 spinules.	Pacific staghorn sculpin, *Leptocottus armatus* Girard, page 205.	
b.	Upper preopercular spine short, simple and not branched.		**3**
3 a.	Lateral line ends under middle of second dorsal, although there may be isolated pores farther behind. Two pores on tip of chin at midline (Figure 57A, page 200).	Slimy sculpin, *Cottus cognatus* Richardson, page 200.	
b.	Lateral line extends to behind anal fin. One pore on tip of chin at midline (Figure 58A, page 202).		**4**
4 a.	Well-developed palatine teeth present.	Prickly sculpin, *Cottus asper* Richardson, page 202.	
b.	Palatine teeth absent or only poorly developed.	Coastrange sculpin, *Cottus aleuticus* Gilbert, page 204.	
5 a.	Two spines on preoperculum. No teeth on palatines.	Fourhorn sculpin, *Myoxocephalus quadricornis* (Linnaeus), page 207	
b.	One spine on preoperculum. Teeth present on palatines.	Sharpnose sculpin, *Clinocottus acuticeps* (Gilbert), page 209	

Sculpins are bottom-dwelling fishes, mostly marine but sometimes freshwater, with a few of the marine forms entering rivers and on occasion moving considerable distances upstream. There are at least 300 species in the family. A sculpin has a large head with gill covers which are usually armed with sharp spines; a robust body tapering to a narrow caudal peduncle; both a spiny and a soft dorsal fin; a single spine in each pelvic fin but none in the anal; and ctenoid-type scales, but with scalation usually much reduced and the scales often highly modified.

The sculpins are primarily fishes of the northern

temperate and arctic seas. One genus, *Cottus,* is circumpolar in fresh water in the northern hemisphere. Most are fairly small fishes, especially the freshwater forms, but a few of the marine species may reach lengths of 60 cm or more. Freshwater sculpins occasionally prey upon the young of various salmonids, but only rarely does this reach significant levels. In turn, the sculpins are eaten by larger fishes such as lake trout and burbot.

A number of old records of freshwater sculpins in Alaska were based on misidentifications. Kevin M. Howe, Department of Fisheries and Wildlife, Oregon State University, in the mid-1970s re-examined the specimens that formed the basis for Evermann and Goldsborough's (1907) record of the riffle sculpin, *Cottus gulosus,* from the settlement of Loring and from the Boca de Quadra. Howe finds these specimens to be a mixture of coastrange sculpins, *Cottus aleuticus,* and prickly sculpins, *Cottus asper.*

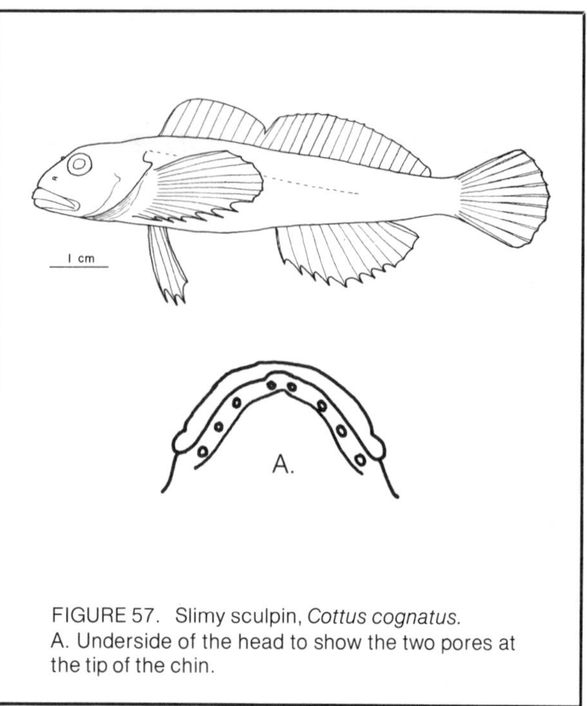

FIGURE 57. Slimy sculpin, *Cottus cognatus.* A. Underside of the head to show the two pores at the tip of the chin.

SLIMY SCULPIN

Cottus cognatus Richardson

DISTINCTIVE CHARACTERS

The two pores on the chin and the short lateral line ending under the second dorsal fin distinguish the slimy sculpin (Figure 57; Plate 30C, page 141).

DESCRIPTION

Body tadpole-shaped, nearly round in cross-section near the head, strongly compressed toward the tail. Depth 17% to 21% of total length. Head broad, somewhat flattened, expanded posteriorly, its length 22% to 28% of total length. Snout rounded and broad as seen from above, its length 27% to 28% of head length. Nostrils in short tubes; one above middle of upper jaw on each side, another near antero-dorsal margin of each eye. Eyes more or less on top of head, their diameters a little less than snout length. Mouth broad, terminal, with upper jaw projecting and maxilla reaching anterior margin of eye or farther back. Fine teeth on jaws and vomer, none on palatines (teeth rarely present on palatines, according to McAllister, 1964). Gill rakers short and stubby, about 6 on first gill arch. Branchiostegals: 6. Lateral line incomplete, ending under middle of soft dorsal fin and usually having a few isolated pores behind this point; main portion of lateral line has 12 to 26 pores. Pyloric caeca: 2 to 5. Vertebrae: 31 to 35.

FINS. First dorsal has 7 to 10 spines; second dorsal, 14 to 19 rays; anal, 10 to 14 rays. In the pectorals, which are large and fan-shaped, tips of lower rays are projecting; 12 to 16 rays. Pelvics, 1 spine and 3, sometimes 4 rays, but the fourth ray is much reduced. Caudal rounded.

SCALES. No scales, but small prickles sometimes present behind pectoral fins.

COLOR. Rather dark brown or green to dark gray on back and sides, whitish below, with vague, dark mottlings or bars below soft dorsal. Belly sometimes with orange tints. Soft dorsal, pectoral and caudal fins usually barred, pelvics and anal usually immaculate but sometimes barred. Spiny dorsal dark at the base, with a clear margin that may turn orange in breeding males. Breeding males usually dark, sometimes black, all over (photograph, page 106).

SIZE. Known to reach 12.1 cm total length (Van Vliet, 1964), but most do not exceed about 7.5 cm.

RANGE AND ABUNDANCE

The slimy sculpin is distributed all across northern North America from eastern New Brunswick to western Alaska, including Nunivak and Saint Lawrence islands. On the east coast of the U.S. it is found as far south as Virginia and north to Ungava Bay, Quebec, though it has not been recorded from the northernmost parts of Newfoundland and northwestern Labrador, nor the most northerly parts of Keewatin, in the Northwest Territories. It is present in all the Great Lakes, the upper Mississippi drainage and northwesterly from there across most of Saskatchewan to northern Alberta (but is absent from most of southern Alberta). Present in the upper Columbia drainage and the Fraser River, north through British Columbia east of the continental divide, reaching the west coast in southeastern Alaska. Present throughout the Northwest Territories (except northeastern Keewatin), Yukon Territory and mainland Alaska. Also known from the eastern part of the Chukhotsk Peninsula in Siberia.

Throughout its range the slimy sculpin is an abundant species. It inhabits lakes to considerable depths, being most common in Lake Superior at depths between 90 and 110 m. In Lake Michigan it has been found all the way from near shore to depths of 128 m (Deason, 1939). It is common in streams, particularly those with fairly fast current and rocky bottoms, where it stays on the bottom, darting from place to place when disturbed. Its quiescent, bottom-dwelling habits and cryptic coloration make it difficult to observe until it moves.

HABITS

Spawning takes place in the spring, shortly after breakup, at water temperatures between 4.5° and 10°C. This may occur as early as late March in the southern part of the range to late May or even later in the far north. Before spawning, males select nest sites, usually under such things as rocks, logs or boards, in shallow water from about 2 cm to more than 30 cm deep. The floor of the nest is often sandy and may be excavated to some extent by strong swimming or fanning movements on the part of the male. He may also remove gravel from the nest by picking up small particles in his mouth and moving them outside. The nest is usually 2 to 4 cm high, both height and width depending on the size of the fish. At this time, the male assumes a dark brown to black color and the orange margin of the first dorsal fin is bright (Koster, 1936; Van Vliet, 1964).

Nesting males are strongly territorial and aggressive toward other males. They defend the nest by "barking"—quickly opening and closing the mouth—at intruders, which may be followed by a quick dart with gill covers spread and head flattened, and by fighting. In contrast to most fishes, in which antagonistic behavior is usually ritual, the loser of a fight between two male sculpins is often killed (Koster, 1936; Van Vliet, 1964).

Courtship begins when a ripe female approaches the nest. The male barks, undulates and twitches his body and fins, then rushes to the side of the female and drives her into the nest. Within the nest, there is more barking, as well as butting or biting the female's side near the vent. Both fish turn upside-down and the female deposits her eggs on the roof of the nest. The male presses her against the roof, which may help in extruding the eggs, and he releases milt (Koster, 1936). After spawning, the female leaves the nest and shows no further interest in the eggs.

Spawning apparently goes on at any time of the day or night. The female deposits all her eggs in a single mass. Fecundity ranges from about 42 to 1,420 eggs, the number tending to increase with the size of the female. The average size of a clutch is 150 to over 600 eggs. Males usually mate with two or three females in the same nest, but nests have been found with as many as 10 egg masses (Koster, 1936; Van Vliet, 1964; Craig and Wells, 1976).

The eggs are quite large for so small a fish, .25 to .3 cm in diameter, and are yellow to pink in color. Development to hatching requires about 30 days. During this time the male remains in or near the nest, guarding it against intruders, fanning the eggs with his pectoral fins and removing debris and dead eggs. The young are about .72 cm long at hatching, with a large spherical yolk sac. They seek the bottom of the nest and remain there for about a week. By that time the yolk has been absorbed, the young are nearly 1.1 cm long and they leave the nest to take up the solitary life characteristic of this species.

Growth rates vary from locality to locality, with 1+ fish as small as 3.6 cm total length in the Cree River, Saskatchewan, or as long as 9.3 cm at Otter Rapids on the Churchill River (Van Vliet, 1964). In general, however, growth seems to be rather slow. Most fish mature in their second year, although in the Chandalar River of Alaska, the usual age at maturity was 4. Maximum age recorded is 7, in the Chandalar River fish (Craig and Wells, 1976).

Except for probable movement into shallow water for spawning, slimy sculpins apparently do not migrate. It is not known whether the sculpins found at considerable depths in the Great Lakes breed at those depths or whether they go in to shore in the spring. The slimy sculpin is quite sedentary, rarely moving more than a few meters, even when violently disturbed. However, slimy sculpins have been seen to travel considerable distances through the semi-consolidated, jellylike sediments on the bottoms of some deep lakes on the Canadian shield (Emery, 1973). In some areas they are common in brackish water (Dunbar and Hildebrand, 1952). Presumably, these individuals must migrate to and from fresh water, at least for spawning.

The slimy sculpin is almost exclusively insectivorous in its food habits. In most areas, the major items are the larvae of Diptera, Ephemeroptera and Trichoptera, with Odonata and Amphipoda sometimes important for larger individuals. The smaller fish feed most heavily on Diptera, especially chironomids and simuliids, while larger fish tend to make more use of the larger items (Kendall and Goldsborough, 1908; Rimsky-Korsakoff, 1930; Sibley and Rimsky-Korsakoff, 1931; Pate, 1933; Koster, 1936, 1937; Van Vliet, 1964; Petrosky and Waters, 1975; Craig and Wells, 1976). Although the slimy sculpin has often been accused of devouring the eggs and young of trout and other salmonids, it seems that this happens but seldom. Fish are rarely eaten, and young sculpins, as well as sculpin eggs, are consumed far more frequently than are other fishes. Sculpins do, on occasion, eat larval trout; however, salmonid eggs are too well protected by the redd to be vulnerable to sculpins large enough to eat them and the salmonid eggs are too large to be eaten by sculpins small enough to burrow into a redd (Koster, 1936, 1937; Kogl, 1965; Clary, 1972; Petrosky and Waters, 1975; Craig and Wells, 1976).

IMPORTANCE TO MAN

The slimy sculpin is of no direct importance to man. In some places it may be used as bait for larger fishes, but even this seems to be rare. Indirectly, however, it may be more significant. This sculpin is almost exclusively a bottom feeder and the salmonid fishes with which it frequently coexists are mostly middepth and surface feeders, but the two groups feed on much the same groups of organisms at different developmental stages. In a Minnesota stream, it has been found that slimy sculpins made up about a third of the total annual fish production, with three trouts *(Salvelinus fontinalis, Salmo gairdneri* and *Salmo trutta)* contributing the remaining two-thirds. In the Chatanika River, Alaska, sculpins and grayling share many of the same food items. It is conceivable that a large population of sculpins could compete strongly with the salmonids and limit the production of the latter, although this possibility has not been proven (Schallock, 1966; Vascotto, 1970; Petrosky and Waters, 1975; Craig and Wells, 1976).

PRICKLY SCULPIN

Cottus asper Richardson

DISTINCTIVE CHARACTERS

The complete lateral line, a single pore at the tip of the chin, the presence of 15 to 19 anal rays, and well-developed palatine teeth distinguish the prickly sculpin (Figure 58; Plate 30d, page 141).

DESCRIPTION

Body elongate, broad and nearly cylindrical near the head, compressed toward the tail. Depth 16% to 18% of total length. Head large, 25% to 32% of total length. Snout 21% to 27% of head length. Eye round, its size variable, 18% to 33% of head length. Two nostrils on each side, each in a short tube; anterior nostril near edge of upper jaw, posterior nostril close to anterior margin of eye. Mouth large; maxilla reaches middle of eye or farther back in adults. Teeth small but well developed, present on both jaws, palatines and vomer. Gill rakers short: 5 or 6. Branchiostegals: 5 to 7, usually 6. Lateral line complete; 32 to 43 pores. Pyloric caeca short; 4 to 6. Vertebrae: 34 to 36.

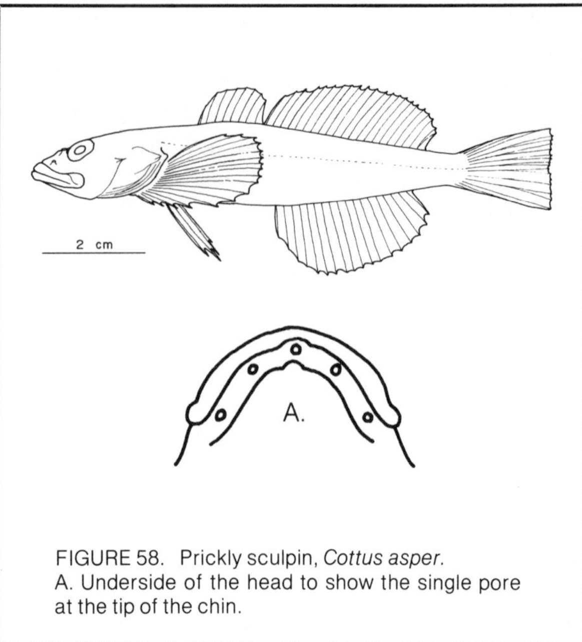

FIGURE 58. Prickly sculpin, *Cottus asper.*
A. Underside of the head to show the single pore at the tip of the chin.

FINS. Dorsal has 7 to 10 spines, 18 to 23 rays. Anal, 15 to 19 rays; pectorals, which are large and fan-shaped, 15 to 18 rays. Pelvics, 1 spine, 4 rays (in rare cases 3 or 5). Caudal truncate or slightly rounded.

SCALES. No true scales. Prickles on body, their distribution ranging from most of the skin (except on abdomen) to a small patch behind base of pectoral fins.

COLOR. Dark brown, olive or gray above and on sides, whitish yellow to white below. Usually three dark irregular blotches or bars below soft dorsal fin. Vague irregular dark marks on sides. Fins (except anal) have dark bars; first dorsal has a dark spot toward the rear. Both sexes show an orange band on the edge of the first dorsal fin at spawning time (photograph, page 106).

SIZE. This is the largest species of the genus *Cottus,* said to reach about 30 cm (Jordon and Evermann, 1896), but the majority are generally not over 15 cm. However, the original specimen, on which the description was based, was 24.1 cm in length (Richardson, 1836) and Jordan and Gilbert (1882) listed 24.5 cm as the maximum length.

RANGE AND ABUNDANCE

Known from the Ventura River, California, in the south, northward in coastal streams of the Pacific coast to Seward, Alaska. Ranges well inland in the San Joaquin and Sacramento rivers of California, the northern part of the Columbia River drainage (but not the Snake River) as well as in the Fraser and other major Pacific coastal rivers of British Columbia (Krejsa, 1967a). Isolated populations are present in the Peace River drainage in British Columbia as far downstream as McLeod Lake (Lindsey, 1956). An abundant form wherever present.

HABITS

The prickly sculpin exhibits at least two genetically distinct forms. The inland form is generally more densely prickled over a larger portion of the body and does not migrate to estuaries to spawn, while the coastal form shows a reduced number of prickles and spawns in brackish water (Krejsa, 1976b). Except for the difference in spawning localities, the life histories of the two are quite similar, as far as is known.

Spawning may occur as early as February in the south and as late as July in the north. Prior to breeding, the males move downstream and select nest sites under such places as cobbles or large flat rocks. The females aggregate some distance upstream, then move down singly to the spawning area. They display to the male, who courts a female and brings her to his nest. Further courtship goes on in the nest. The orange eggs, somewhat less than .1 cm in diameter, are sticky and adhere to the roof of the nest. Fecundity ranges between 280 and 7,410 eggs per female (Patten, 1971). Since males may mate with as many as 10 females, there may be 25,000 to 30,000 eggs in a single nest (Krejsa, 1967b; Ringstad, 1974). After spawning, the female goes back upstream to feed, while the male remains at the nest, fanning and guarding the eggs. He does not feed until the eggs have hatched. Spawning takes place in water temperatures of 8° to 13° C. Development to hatching requires 15 to 16 days at 12°C, but about 21 days at 8°C (Krejsa, 1967b).

Within a few hours of hatching, the larvae, about .5 cm long, swim up to the surface, where they remain in a planktonic existence for the next 30 to 35 days. They are positively responsive to currents and swim actively, in short bursts, against currents greater than 1 cm per second. They are probably swept up and down the estuary by tidal currents, but any carried out to sea doubtless perish, as none have been taken in the ocean. However, in late spring and early summer, the larvae are numerous around and below the spawning grounds (Krejsa, 1967b; Pearcy and Myers, 1974; Mason and Machidori, 1976). Larvae hatched upstream in fresh water may be carried into a lake or estuary during this phase of existence (McLarney, 1968).

During the planktonic stage of life, the larvae of the freshwater, nonanadromous form in lakes show distinct diurnal vertical migrations. They are most abundant at the surface during the darkest hours of the night, between 9 p.m. and 4 a.m. During the day and on bright moonlight nights, they apparently stay deep in the water (Sinclair, 1968).

Metamorphosis has been completed by the end of the planktonic period and the young fish take up a demersal mode of life. The adults move back upstream during the late summer, followed by the young in the early fall, although the young may remain in the estuary for a full year. Upstream movement is usually no more than a few kilometers and may be blocked by relatively small obstructions such as falls of 30 cm in height (Krejsa, 1967b; Ringstad, 1974; Mason and Machidori, 1976).

Yearling fish (and possibly older ones also) have been observed to form schools in shallow water in lakes (Northcote and Hartman, 1959). Whether this is related to feeding or represents a remnant of their pelagic life or has some other explanation is not known.

The prickly sculpin grows rather slowly and shows wide variations in growth rates within and between year classes, as well as from place to place. Some approximate lengths at different ages for fish from Oregon and Vancouver Island are: 1+, 4.5 to 4.6 cm; 2+, 5.2 to 6.5 cm; 3+, 7.1 to 8.9 cm; 4+, 8.5 to 9.8 cm. The establishment of typical lengths at different ages is difficult because of the fact that this sculpin appears to make about 50% of an entire year's growth in only two months, July and August. Hence, the time of collection makes a great difference in the observed average lengths (Bond, 1963; Ringstad, 1974; Mason and Machidori, 1976).

The oldest specimen reported was a 7-year-old fish from Oregon (Bond, 1963). If the very large specimens (24 to 30 cm) reported in the literature grew at the rates shown here, they must have been at least 13 to 17 years old.

Food of the prickly sculpin consists mainly of invertebrate animals of various sorts; as would be expected, these are mostly bottom-dwelling organisms and the developmental stages of insects. The list is a long one and includes cladocerans, copepods, ostracods, amphipods, mollusks, mites, at least seven orders of insects, and small fishes. Among the insects, the Trichoptera, Ephemeroptera and Diptera seem to be the most important. However, the relative ranking of food items varies with season and locality and depends largely on availability. In some areas the eggs and fry of sockeye, pink and chum salmon, and even year-old sockeye, are eaten in considerable numbers. Up to 111 sockeye fry have been found in the stomach of a single prickly sculpin. This sculpin also eats other fishes, including its own kind. One was found that had swallowed another sculpin more than half as long as itself (Pritchard, 1936b; Ricker, 1941; Robertson, 1949; Northcote, 1954; Hunter, 1959).

IMPORTANCE TO MAN

The prickly sculpin is of no direct importance to man. It is too small to be used as food and too difficult to capture in large numbers to be used for anything else. Indirectly, however, this species may be of considerable importance as a predator on the young of more valuable species and as food for the adults. It is an important item in the food of several fish-eating birds such as mergansers.

COASTRANGE SCULPIN

Cottus aleuticus Gilbert

DISTINCTIVE CHARACTERS

The coastrange sculpin is distinguished by having only a single pore on the tip of the chin, no palatine teeth, and no pronounced gap between the first and second dorsal fins (Figure 59; Figure 57A, page 200; Plate 30D, page 141).

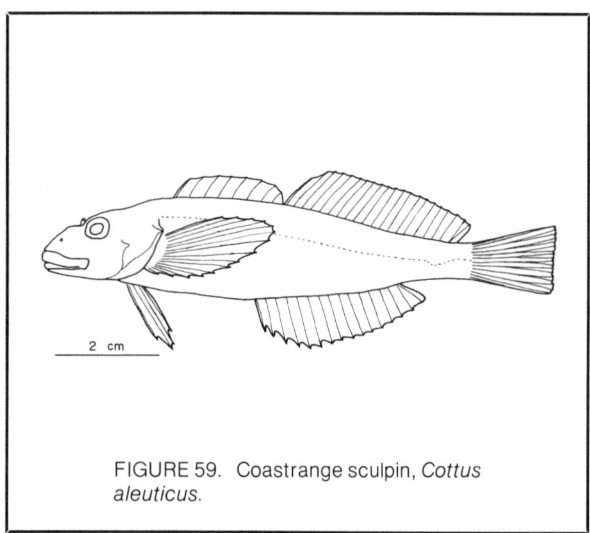

FIGURE 59. Coastrange sculpin, *Cottus aleuticus.*

DESCRIPTION

Body elongate, rather round near the head, compressed toward the tail; depth about 18% of total length. Head moderate, 20% to 23% of total length. Snout 27% to 33% of head. Eye small, round, its diameter less than snout length. Nostrils 2 on each side, well separated, each in a short tube; posterior nostril at forward medial margin of eye. Mouth moderate, broad; maxilla reaches almost to below anterior edge of eye. Teeth small but well developed in both jaws and on vomer; absent from palatines. Gill rakers short: 5 to 7 on first arch. Branchiostegals: 6. Lateral line complete, with 34 to 44 pores, generally with a marked flexion on caudal peduncle. Pyloric caeca: 3 to 6. Vertebrae: 34 to 38.

FINS. Dorsal has 8 to 10 spines, 17 to 20 rays; Anal, 12 to 15 rays; pectorals, 13 to 16, usually 14; pelvics, 1 spine, 4 rays. Caudal truncate.

SCALES. No scales. Skin smooth except for a small patch of prickles behind each pectoral fin.

COLOR. Dark brown to greenish or grayish on back and sides, with darker blotches. Sides lighter, ventral areas white. Usually two or three dark saddlelike blotches below soft part of dorsal fin. Dark bars on dorsal, anal, pectoral and caudal fins. Orange edge on spiny dorsal fin of spawning males (photograph, page 107).

SIZE. Up to 17.2 cm in southern California according to Hubbs (1921), but generally not over about 11.5 cm, with most ranging between 5 and 10 cm.

RANGE AND ABUNDANCE

From Piedras Blancas Point, California, north in coastal streams to Bristol Bay, Alaska, and westward in the Aleutians to Kiska Island. An isolated population is found in the Kobuk River of Alaska, some 800 km north of the nearest Bristol Bay fish. Apparently isolated populations also are present in Lake Washington, Washington, and Cultus Lake, British Columbia, and perhaps also in other lakes of that general area (Ricker, 1960; Ikesumiju, 1975; Larson and Brown, 1975). The coastrange sculpin is one of the more abundant small fishes throughout its range.

HABITS

Spawning generally takes place in the lower reaches of the streams and in the estuaries, but may occur well upstream as well. The eggs are deposited in clumps and clusters in crevices between rocks or, more often, on the underside of logs, cutbanks, or rocks (Ringstad, 1974; personal observation). The eggs are yellow to orange, sticky, about .12 to .19 cm in diameter, and are usually present in at least two distinct groups of different stages of development. Spawning behavior has not been observed, so it is not known whether the clumps represent several spawnings by a single female or single spawnings by several females, but judging from the fact that over 7,000 eggs have been found in a single nest, it is almost certainly the latter. Fecundity ranges from 100 to 1,764 eggs per female (McPhail and Lindsey, 1970; Patten, 1971). The male guards the nest until all eggs have hatched.

Spawning occurs in the spring, as early as mid-February to as late as August, but mostly in May and June, in water temperatures around 6° to 8°C (Ikesumiju, 1975). Time required for development to hatching is 19 to 20 days at 10° to 12°C under laboratory conditions (Mason and Machidori, 1976). Larvae are about .5 cm long at hatching and swim to the surface within a few hours. The young are planktonic, floating near the surface, and are carried downstream to the intertidal portions of estuaries or out into the open waters of large lakes. Feeding begins 6 to 10 days after hatching, by which time the yolk is noticeably depleted and most of the larvae have drifted down to the lake or estuary (Mason and Machidori, 1976). Young coastrange sculpins may be

2 to 3 cm long in the intertidal zone by mid-August (Heard, 1965; McLarney, 1968). In Carnation Creek, British Columbia, they average 4.15 cm long at age 1 (in August), 5.7 cm at age 2, 7 cm at age 3 and 7.95 cm at age 4. Sexual maturity is achieved in the third year (Ricker, 1960; Patten, 1971). Maximum age recorded is 8 years, although in Oregon the fish apparently do not survive beyond 4 years (Bond, 1963; Mason and Machidori, 1976).

The coastrange sculpin undertakes regular seasonal migrations. The adults move downstream to estuaries or at least the lower reaches of rivers in the spring, moving mostly at night. This migration is associated with spawning, although in some streams spawning takes place in the normal winter habitat upstream (McLarney, 1968; Mason and Machidori, 1976). A reverse, upstream migration of yearlings and adults occurs in late summer to early winter, from August to December. The young fish apparently spend nearly a full year in the downstream habitat. The winter is spent in the upper parts of the streams (McLarney, 1968; Ringstad, 1974). Where coastrange sculpins co-exist with prickly sculpins, in the lower portions of streams, the latter occupy sheltered areas of low current velocities, while the former are found more often on the heads and tails of riffles in swifter water. In the absence of the prickly sculpin, especially upstream, the coastrange sculpin occupies both swift and quiet water (Ringstad, 1974). The coastrange sculpin is generally solitary, but large aggregations have been seen. It is not uncommon to find two or three individuals in the general vicinity of a nest (Greenbank, 1957; personal observations).

Food of the coastrange sculpin consists mainly of benthic insect larvae and nymphs. However, depending on the season of the year and the time of day, feeding habits vary. Feeding is most intense at night. During daylight hours in summer, Trichoptera larvae dominate as food. In late evening and early morning, Plecoptera and Ephemeroptera nymphs and chironomid larvae are important. In some streams this sculpin preys heavily on pink salmon fry. Other foods include ostracods, mysids, cladocerans, amphipods and isopods. Coastrange sculpin can survive without food for 94 days or more, but they lose about 33% of their weight in such circumstances (Hunter, 1959; Sheridan and Meehan, 1962; Ringstad, 1974; Ikesumiju, 1975).

IMPORTANCE TO MAN

The coastrange sculpin is of no direct importance to man. However, in some situations it may be a significant predator on salmon fry of several species, and has been shown to compete for food, sometimes severely, with coho salmon fry (Ringstad, 1974). In turn the planktonic larvae of this sculpin are eaten by juvenile sockeye salmon, and the adults may be important food items for larger predatory fishes such as Dolly Varden.

PACIFIC STAGHORN SCULPIN

Leptocottus armatus Girard

DISTINCTIVE CHARACTERS

The Pacific staghorn sculpin is set off by the large upper preopercular spine ending in three or four sharp, upturned, curved spinules and by the large, dark spot on the posterior part of the spiny dorsal fin (Figure 60).

DESCRIPTION

Body elongate, more or less cylindrical toward the head, somewhat compressed toward the tail. Depth about 17% to 20% of total length. Head rather flat and broad, its length about 33% of total length. Snout about 25% of head length. Eye oval, the horizontal diameter greater than the vertical; length 13% to 18% of head. Mouth moderate, terminal, lower jaw slightly shorter than upper, with upper jaw reaching back to below eye. Small sharp teeth present in bands on both jaws, vomer and palatines. Gill rakers reduced to flat, bony plates, each bearing a cluster of small teeth; 8 or 9 on lower portion of first arch, none on upper portion. Branchiostegals: 6. Lateral line nearly straight, with 37 to 42 pores, each associated with a small subdermal cartilaginous plate. Pyloric caeca long and fingerlike: 8 to 10. Vertebrae: 37 to 39.

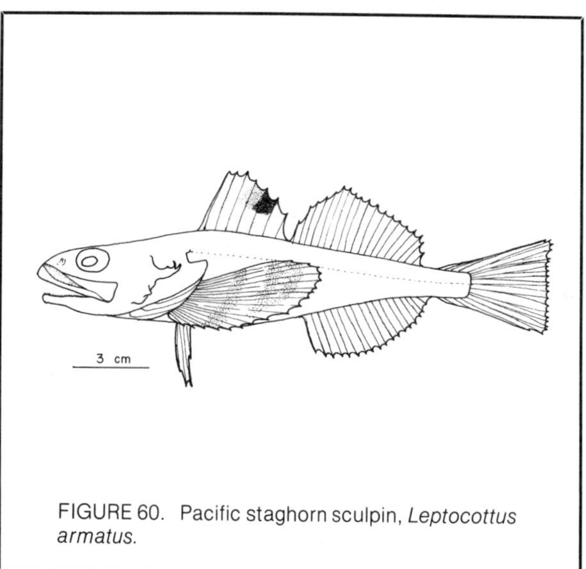

FIGURE 60. Pacific staghorn sculpin, *Leptocottus armatus.*

FINS. First dorsal has 6 to 8 spines; second dorsal, 15 to 20 rays, the spinous and soft parts separated by a short gap. Anal has 15 to 20 rays;

pectorals, 19; pelvics, 1 spine and 4 rays. Caudal slightly rounded.

SCALES. No scales. Skin smooth and naked except for the lateral line plates.

COLOR. Grayish olive to rather green, occasionally with some yellow, dorsally. Orange-yellow to white or silvery below lateral line. Spiny dorsal fin dusky, with a black spot near tips of last 3 spines, a white band below it. Soft dorsal dusky, with several oblique white to yellowish bands. Pectorals yellow with 5 or 6 dark greenish bars. Caudal dusky with one or two pale bands. Anal and pelvic fins pale (photograph, page 108; Plate 16, page 127).

SIZE. Reaches about 46 cm total length.

RANGE AND ABUNDANCE

Found along the Pacific coast of North America from San Quintin Bay, Baja California (Roedel, 1948) to Izembek Lagoon in the southeastern Bering Sea (Tack, 1970; Paulson and Smith, 1974). Throughout most of its range the Pacific staghorn sculpin is a common fish of the subtidal zone and tide pools. Even in the Bering Sea, at the northern limit of its range, it is not at all uncommon in favorable locations. Although a marine fish, the Pacific staghorn sculpin can tolerate fresh water and not infrequently penetrates rivers and even fairly fast small streams. It has been found in fresh water on Admiralty Island, Alaska, among other places (Gunter, 1942).

HABITS

The Pacific staghorn sculpin spawns from October to March, but the majority of reproductive activity takes place in January and February. Spawning areas are probably most common in bays and estuaries with relatively stable salinities, but must also exist in the ocean, for very young staghorn sculpins have been found in areas far from freshwater inputs. Eggs develop normally in salinities between 10.2 and 34.3 parts per thousand, with greatest survival in the range of 17.6 to 26.4 parts per thousand. The higher of these two figures is probably close to the optimum salinity (Jones, 1962).

Development to hatching under laboratory conditions requires 9 to 14 days at 15 °C, with most of the eggs hatching in between 10 and 12 days. The newly hatched larvae are .39 to .48 cm long, each having a large, globular yolk sac (Jones, 1962). Growth and longevity appear to vary tremendously in different localities. Fish from Walker Creek, Tomales Bay (north of Point Reyes, California) were reported to grow exceedingly fast, reaching an average total length of 12.7 cm at age 1+, 15.6 cm at 2+ and 19.7 cm at 3+. The maximum age observed in this population was 3+ (Jones, 1962). By contrast, fish from Puget Sound, near Friday Harbor, reached age 10+, with average calculated total lengths at I, 3.4 cm; II, 5.5 cm; III, 8 cm; IV, 10.1 cm; VII, 17.4 cm; X, 22.8 cm (Weiss, 1969). Females appear to reach greater size and age than do males.

Recently metamorphosed young move from the spawning areas in the estuarine regions into completely fresh water, where they remain for up to six weeks. Because of the extended spawning period, the fish farthest upstream are usually somewhat older and larger than those in the lower estuary. However, this migration into fresh water is not an essential part of the life history, for staghorn sculpins may spend their entire lives in highly saline water (MacGinitie, 1935). Adults apparently tend to remain in shallow water in the lower estuary, or farther offshore. The adult staghorn sculpin is often one of the dominant species of the sand flats and in some regions, at least, is common to as deep as 90 m (Jones, 1962; Tack, 1970; Isakson et al., 1971; Paulson and Smith, 1974; Pearcy and Myers, 1974). This broad distribution reflects the considerable degree to which this sculpin can tolerate different salinities. This tolerance range goes from essentially zero (fresh water) to a maximum of about 51 to 53 parts per thousand, considerably higher than ordinary sea water (Hubbs, 1947; Erkkila et al., 1950; Carpelan, 1961).

The Pacific staghorn sculpin is essentially a sedentary fish, resting on or moving about slowly just over the bottom. However, it is capable of rapid movement over short distances when occasion demands. When violently disturbed, it "rushes rapidly to a new place and buries itself, leaving only the eyes exposed" (MacGinitie, 1935). This mode of life is reflected in the food habits. Juveniles in the Walker Creek estuary subsisted almost entirely on amphipods of the genus *Corophium,* but also consumed nereid worms, gammarid amphipods, insect larvae and nymphs, and 18 other items of minor importance. Adults in San Francisco Bay had fed chiefly on four species of bottom-dwelling shrimps, smelt and crabs, with other fishes and invertebrates occurring in small amounts in the stomach contents (Jones, 1962).

IMPORTANCE TO MAN

The Pacific staghorn sculpin is of little direct importance to man. Although it is edible, the large head and slender body result in a small yield of meat per fish. To anglers it is sometimes a nuisance, greedily taking baited hooks intended for more desirable fishes. It probably competes strongly for food with other fishes, especially in confined regions such as bays and estuaries. It is an important food for herons, loons, ducks and cormorants (MacGinitie, 1935; Clemens and Wilby, 1961).

FOURHORN SCULPIN

Myoxocephalus quadricornis (Linnaeus)

DISTINCTIVE CHARACTERS

The fourhorn sculpin is identified by the four bony protuberances on the top of the head (the protuberances are smaller in females and young and absent in the freshwater form), the chainlike lateral line, the sharp, straight spines on the preoperculum, and the absence of palatine teeth (Figure 61).

DESCRIPTION

Body tadpole-shaped, tapering toward the tail. Depth about 25% of total length. Head moderately large, 27% to 30% of total length, broad and flattened, its width notably greater than its depth. Four bony or warty protuberances on top of head, 2 between the eyes and 2 on occiput. Four preopercular spines on each side; upper spine long, straight and sharp, longer in males than in females; the second spine shorter than the upper; the 2 lower spines short and pointing downward. Snout broad, long, 26% to 30% of head length. Eye small, 60% to 80% of snout length. Mouth large, terminal, lower jaw included; maxilla reaches to below middle of eye or farther back. Jaws and vomer have bands of small teeth. Gill rakers reduced to rounded, spiny protuberances: 7 to 8 on first arch. Branchiostegals: 6. Lateral line chainlike, with about 45 pores, each with a small embedded plate. Pyloric caeca: 5 to 9. Vertebrae: 37 to 42.

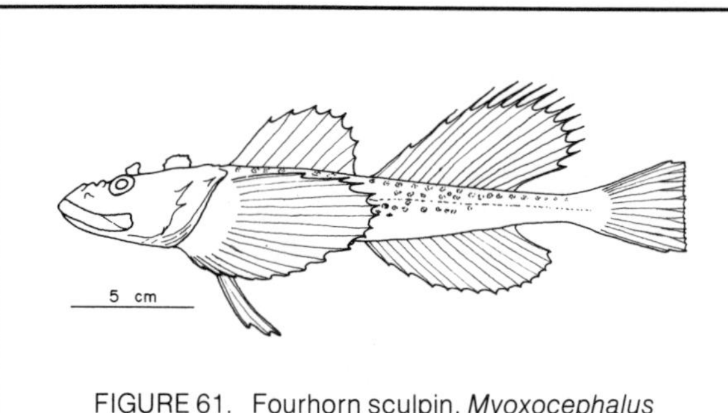

FIGURE 61. Fourhorn sculpin, *Myoxocephalus quadricornis.*

FINS: Dorsal has 7 to 9 spines, 13 to 16 rays; the spiny and soft parts are separated by a space about equal to eye diameter. Soft dorsal often much enlarged in adult males. Anal, 13 to 17 rays; pectorals, 15 to 18; pelvics, 1 spine, 3 or 4 rays. Caudal truncate to slightly rounded.

SCALES. No true scales. Lateral line has embedded bony plates. Sides above and below lateral line have several irregular rows of round bony, prickly plates which are best developed and most numerous in adult males, are poorly developed or absent in females and young.

COLOR. Young are gray above, with three or four dark saddles below dorsal fins and a dark spot on dorsal side of caudal peduncle. Adults are darker. Spiny dorsal fin dusted with black; soft dorsal, anal, pectorals and caudal have dark bars. Pelvics pale (photograph, page 109).

SIZE. Reported to reach a length of 36.5 cm (Andriyashev, 1954) but most adults do not exceed about 28 cm and a weight of about 260 g.

There are two distinct forms of *M. quadricornis:* the marine, brackish-water and riverine form described here and the dwarf, strictly lacustrine (lake-dwelling) form, which is often considered a separate subspecies, *M. quadricornis thomsoni.* In Canada, this lacustrine form is known as the deepwater sculpin. It differs from the marine type chiefly in its small size and in its lack of bony protuberances on the head and spiny plates on the sides. The deepwater sculpin has not yet been found in Alaska but may be present in some of the deep, unexplored lakes of the arctic.

RANGE AND ABUNDANCE

The range of the fourhorn sculpin is circumpolar in cold brackish and moderately saline water. In Europe this fish is found from the Baltic eastward along the Siberian coast to the Chukchi and Bering seas and south in the Bering Sea to the Anadyr River. It ranges from northwestern Greenland westward along the arctic coast of Canada and the Canadian arctic archipelago, to the north coast of Alaska and south in the eastern Bering Sea to Norton Sound and Saint Lawrence Island. This sculpin ascends rivers for considerable distances. It has been found in the Meade River, Alaska, as much as 144 km upstream, and 192 km up the Mackenzie River in Canada. It is an abundant species as far as is known.

HABITS

Most of the knowledge of the biology of the fourhorn sculpin comes from studies made in the Baltic Sea. Presumably the life history of the fish in Alaska is not very different.

Spawning takes place from mid-December through January at depths of 15 to 20 m and in water temperatures of 1.5° to 2°C. With the approach of the spawning season, males become territorial and aggressive toward other males. When an intruding male appears on his territory, the resident male advances toward the intruder in quick, short darts, stopping 3 to 5 cm from the intruder with his dorsal and pectoral fins spread. At the same time, the resident produces a low-pitched humming sound, with a frequency of 125 cycles per second. The intruder usually lowers his dorsal fin and turns away. If he does not, the resident male bites him.

Two or three days before spawning, the females become restless, swimming about between short periods of rest. When a female swims over a male, he undulates his body from side to side and raises his spiny dorsal fin. If the female comes to rest near the male, he moves close to her in a series of short darts.

Both sexes fan rhythmically with their pectoral fins, sometime for hours, thus making a hole 20 to 25 cm in diameter and 10 to 15 cm deep in the soft bottom. Finally the male and female lie side by side, with the male's caudal fin twisted under that of the female. The male makes rhythmic motions toward the female with his tail, and the motions apparently stimulate her to release her eggs (Westin, 1969, 1970b).

The eggs are adhesive and are extruded in a single clump. They are quite large, .24 to .29 cm in diameter. The color varies from greenish or bluish to yellow. At one time the different egg colors were thought to indicate genetic differences (Svärdson, 1958; 1961) but subsequent investigation has shown that the colors of the eggs are controlled by diet (Nyman and Westin, 1968, 1969; Westin, 1968a, c). As would be expected with such large eggs, fecundity is low, 792 to 6,150, but in some populations reaches to almost 18,000 eggs per female (Andriyashev, 1954; Westin, 1968a).

After spawning, the female leaves and shows no further interest in the eggs. The male, however, remains with the egg mass, guarding it and attacking any fish that comes within about 30 cm. He generally lies close to the eggs, fanning them with his pectoral fins and occasionally picking them up in his mouth and spitting away the dead ones. This cleaning is essential to successful hatching, for without it the eggs soon become infested with fungi and die. The male guards and cares for the eggs until they hatch (photographs, page 144), and does not feed during this period. Hatching requires 97 days at 1.5°C, 74 days at 2°C or 55 days at 4.7°C. At 10.5°C, all eggs die before hatching (Westin, 1969).

Fry hatch in the spring and reach a length of 2 to 2.4 cm by August. Little is known of subsequent growth except that it is slow. One-year-old fish are 4 to 5.5 cm long; 2+ fish are about 9.7 cm long; 5+ or 6+ are 21 to 24 cm, 7- or 8-year-olds are 24 to 27 cm, and at 10+ the average length is about 30 to 31 cm. Fish from lagoons along the coast of the Beaufort Sea of Alaska tend to be slightly smaller. Females, especially in the older age groups, are generally larger than males. Sexual maturity is first reached at age 3 to 5, most fish being mature at 6 (Andriyashev, 1954; Lukyanichov and Tugarina, 1965, Griffiths et al., 1975, 1977).

The fourhorn sculpin is most active in the daytime during the winter (November to April) but is largely nocturnal the rest of the year (Westin, 1971). It is quite strictly a cold-water fish, although under proper conditions of acclimation it can stand temperatures up to 25.5°C. In its adaptation to very cold temperatures, around 0°C, it develops an organic "antifreeze" in the blood. At low temperatures, about 4°C, it adapts more readily to slight rises of temperature than to equal drops in temperature (Westin, 1968b; Oikari and Kristoffersson, 1973).

The fourhorn sculpin lives permanently near the coast. Barring short onshore-offshore seasonal movements and mass movements of fry into shallow water in summer (Andriyashev, 1954; Westin, 1970a), there are no migrations of large numbers of fish. Movements into fresh water and long distances up rivers are apparently undertaken by relatively few individuals at a time, except that juveniles are often common in the lower reaches of streams along the Beaufort Sea. Food of the fourhorn sculpin consists primarily of invertebrates of various sorts. The list includes priapulids, mysids, isopods, amphipods, mollusks, small fishes and fish eggs, the eggs most commonly being the eggs of its own species. In the Baltic, the most important individual food items are the isopod *Mesidotea entomon* and the amphipod *Pontoporeia affinis.* It is the latter that gives the characteristic greenish or bluish color to the eggs. Fish living on diets that do not include *Pontoporeia* have yellow eggs (Andriyashev, 1954; Westin, 1968c, 1970a). In other areas mysids may compose as much as 90% of the food (Lukyanichov and Tugarina, 1965). In Kaktovik Lagoon, Alaska, amphipods and isopods composed about 78% of the food of adults. Young-of-the-year fed mostly on Notostraca in early summer, shifting later to Mysidacea and then to amphipods (Griffiths et al., 1977).

Almost nothing is known of the biology of the deep-water lake-dwelling fourhorn sculpin. It lives at such great depths that its presence is often known only from the examination of stomach contents of deep-feeding carnivores like burbot and lake trout. It is present in the Great Lakes and in a number of deep lakes in Canada. It is most abundant at depths below about 75 m in the Great Lakes and at 25 to 37 m in Great Slave Lake. Its diet includes mysids, copepods, amphipods and chironomid larvae and pupae. This is a dwarf form. The three largest on record are a specimen 19.9 cm long from Lake Ontario and two of 10.3 and 10.9 cm from Lake Michigan. Similar and perhaps identical sculpins are known from a number of lakes in Europe. The forms living in lakes most recently cut off from the sea, such as the lakes on Victoria Island, Northwest Territories, and Lake Ladoga in Russia, are morphologically intermediate between those in older lakes and those in the sea (Deason, 1939; Rawson, 1951; Martin and Chapman, 1965; Dryer, 1966; Delisle and Van Vliet, 1968; Mc Phail and Lindsey, 1970; McAllister and Ward, 1972; Dyatlov, 1974).

IMPORTANCE TO MAN

The fourhorn sculpin is of no direct importance to man. Although it is edible and is used for food in some regions of the arctic coast, its distribution far from centers of population and the small yield of meat per fish work against its being used much. The deep-water lacustrine form is, where available, one of the first fish foods eaten by young lake trout and is a minor constituent of the diets of adult lake trout and burbot (Andriyashev, 1954; Rawson, 1961).

SHARPNOSE SCULPIN

Clinocottus acuticeps (Gilbert)

DISTINCTIVE CHARACTERS

The flattened, tripartite anal papilla and the cirri on the eyeballs, head, lateral line and at the tip of each dorsal spine distinguish the sharpnose sculpin from its freshwater relatives (Figure 62).

DESCRIPTION

Body elongate, slender, slightly compressed. Depth 15% to 19% of total length. Head rather small, about 23% of total length. Snout sharp, short, its length about 25% of head length. Eye nearly round, its diameter about equal to or a little less than snout length; a slender cirrus present on upper part of eyeball. Mouth terminal, with upper jaw reaching to a point below anterior edge of pupil. Small teeth in bands on both jaws. Gill rakers reduced to low smooth mounds; about 6 on lower limb of first arch, none on upper limb. Branchiostegals: 6. Lateral line high toward the head, curving downward to middle of sides, straight toward the tail; 33 to 36 pores on body, often 1 or 2 more on tail, each of the anterior 15 or so pores having a slender cirrus. Vertebrae: 32 or 33 (from a sample of 4 specimens). Anus located well forward, about one-third the distance from pelvic base to anal origin, with a broad, flattened, tripartite anal papilla.

FINS. Dorsal has 7 to 9 spines, 14 to 16 rays. Anal, 10 to 13 rays, the next to last ray longer than the rays before and behind it. Pectorals, which reach to or just beyond front of anal, have 13 rays. Pelvics are short; 1 spine, 3 rays. Caudal rounded.

SCALES. No scales. On each side, an unbranched cirrus is present at inner side of base of nasal spine, one on upper part of eyeball. There is 1 cirrus above the eye and 2 or 3 behind it on the head; 1 or 2 at the angle of the gill opening, 1 above each of the anterior pores of the lateral line, and 1 at tip of each dorsal spine.

COLOR. Varies with the environment. Sometimes nearly uniform bright green but more often green to light brown above with dark wedge-shaped saddles, broader below, on upper part of sides, with lighter color between. Sometimes, along or below lateral line, a dark longitudinal stripe that is in some cases interrupted with light spots. Ventral region creamy to white. Three dark lines radiating from the eye, the first to the snout, another downward to behind the mouth, the third rearward to base of preopercular spine. Spiny dorsal fin with a dark blotch between first and third spines. Pelvic fins plain, others usually dusky, mottled or indistinctly barred (photograph, page 109).

SIZE. A very small fish, maximum size about 6.3 cm.

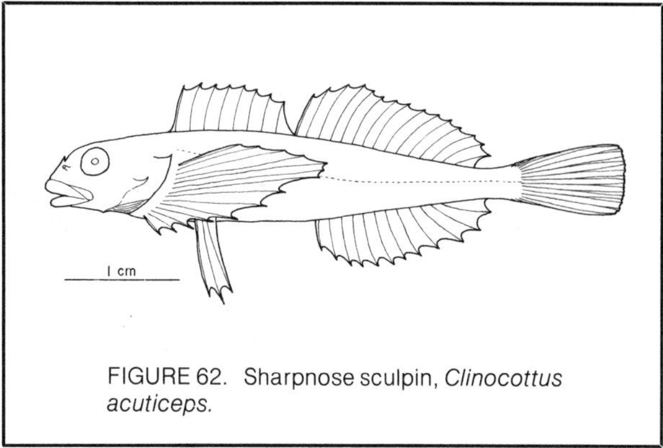

FIGURE 62. Sharpnose sculpin, *Clinocottus acuticeps.*

RANGE AND ABUNDANCE

The sharpnose sculpin is known from the Big Sur River, California, north along the coast to Alaska and westward along the Aleutian Chain to Attu Island. It has been recorded from the Bering Sea side of Unimak and Unalaska islands in the Aleutians (Wilimovsky, 1964; Miller and Lea, 1972). Within this range it is a common member of the inshore rock/algae community, especially in sheltered tide-pools in the upper intertidal zone (Green, 1971). At Amchitka Island in the Aleutians it is most abundant from late spring to early fall (Isakson et al., 1971). It occasionally ventures into fresh water.

HABITS

Virtually nothing is known of the biology of the sharpnose sculpin. It spawns in the spring and summer, for breeding has been observed at the San Juan Islands of Washington on July 4 and a ripe female was taken on April 28. The eggs are brown, about .1 cm in diameter (Hart, 1973).

At Amchitka Island the sharpnose sculpin is most abundant near shore in warm weather (Isakson et al., 1971). Presumably it moves into deeper, more sheltered areas to escape the rigors of winter.

Judging by its size and habitat, the sharpnose sculpin probably feeds on the small invertebrates common among the seaweeds and tide pools. However, nothing is known on this subject.

IMPORTANCE TO MAN

The sharpnose sculpin is a small, zoological curiosity, but as far as is known it is otherwise of no importance to man.

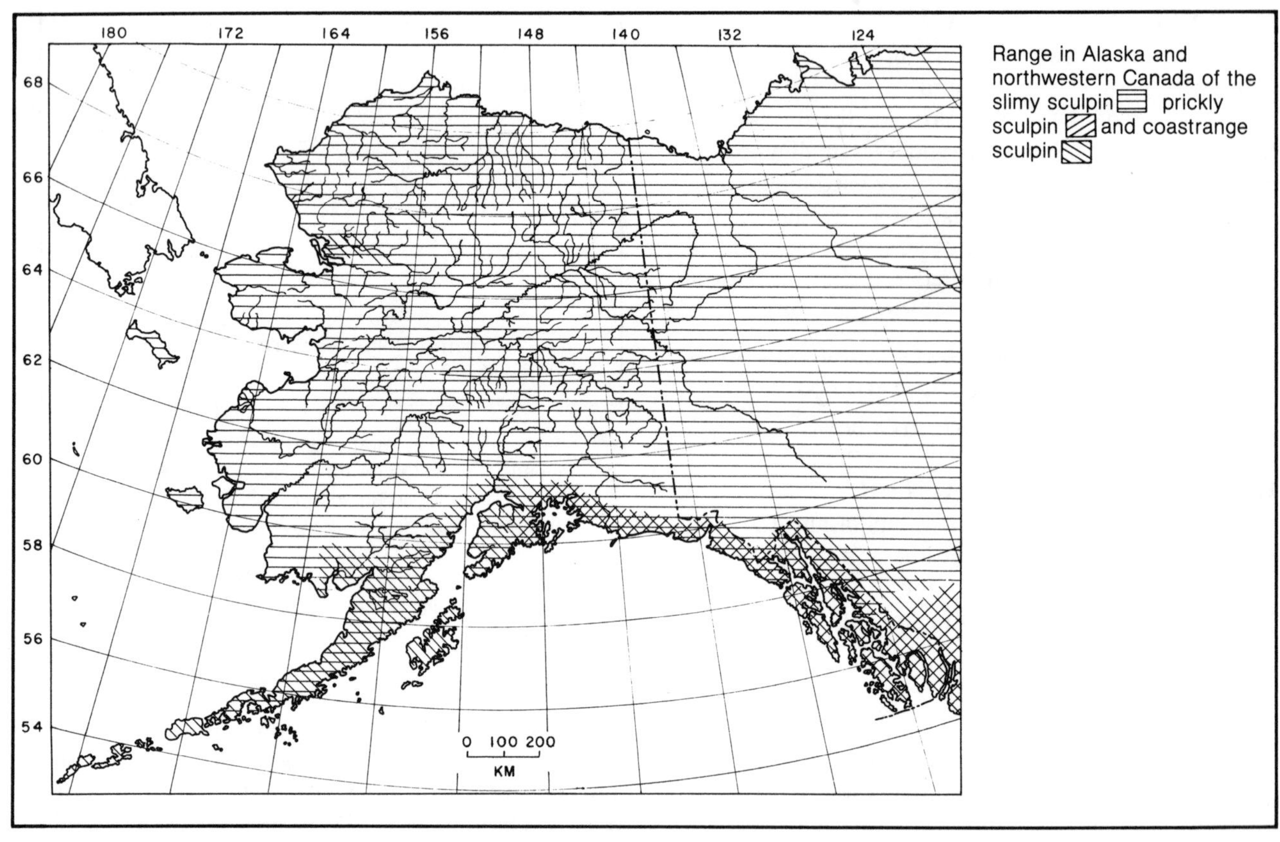

Range in Alaska and northwestern Canada of the slimy sculpin ▤ prickly sculpin ▨ and coastrange sculpin ▧

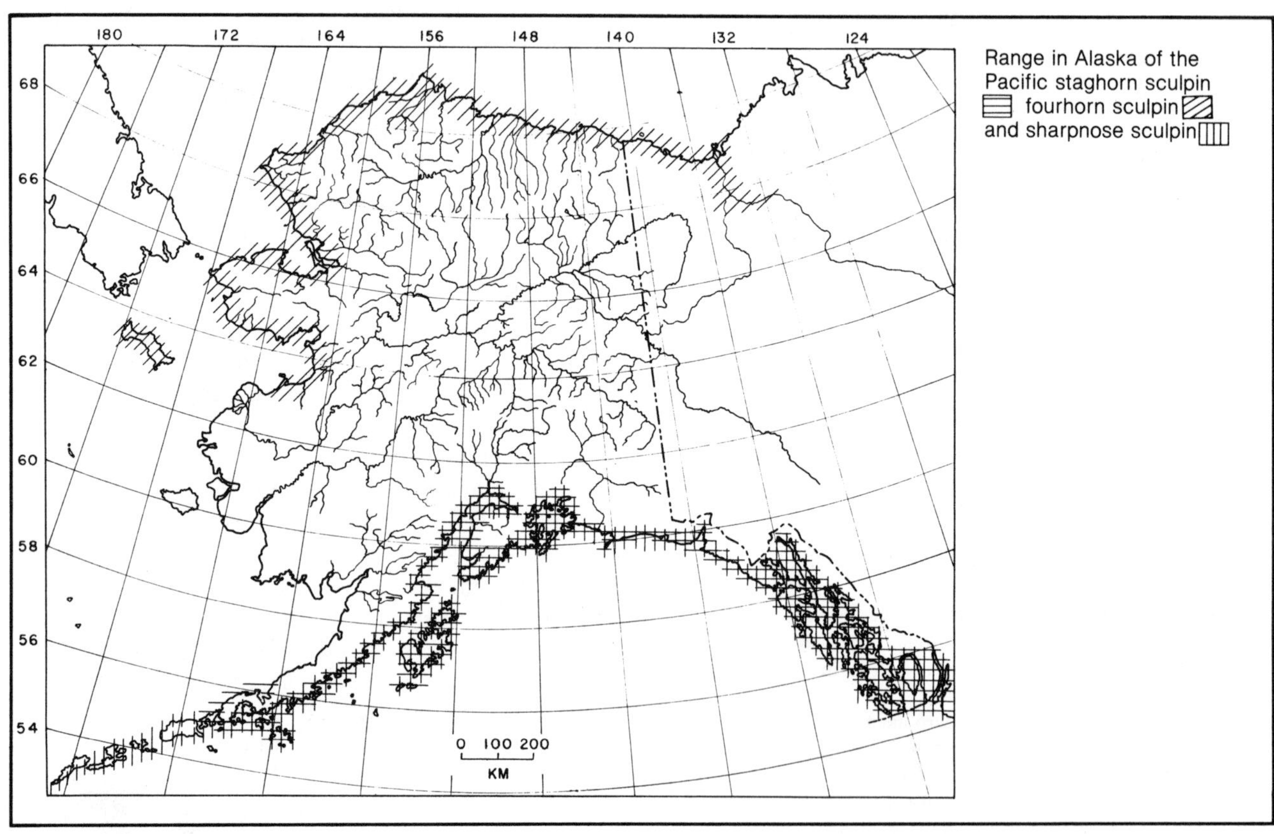

Range in Alaska of the Pacific staghorn sculpin ▤ fourhorn sculpin ▨ and sharpnose sculpin ▥

Chapter Seventeen

FLOUNDERS

Family Pleuronectidae

KEY TO THE ALASKAN SPECIES

SECTION	DESCRIPTION	THE FISH IS	PROCEED IN THIS KEY TO SECTION
a.	Fins uniformly colored. Eyed side of fish covered with typical scales, has no bony tubercles.	Arctic flounder, *Liopsetta glacialis* (Pallas), page 211.	
b.	Dorsal and anal fins have alternating light and dark vertical bars. Eyed side of fish has numerous star-shaped tubercles, including a row along base of dorsal fin and of anal fin.	Starry flounder, *Platichthys stellatus* (Pallas), page 212.	

The flounders are a remarkable group of fishes that have both eyes on the same side of the head. The young are symmetrical at hatching and swim in an upright position. During larval development, one eye, usually the left, moves over the top of the head and comes to rest beside the other eye. The fish settles to the bottom, blind side down, and takes up a demersal mode of life. The eyed side is colored, usually brownish or greenish brown, and the blind side is white. The dorsal and anal fins are long, extending almost the entire length of the body, and have no spines.

Flounders are all marine, but a few species enter fresh water. Several species are highly important food fishes and are the objects of commercial fisheries. The group is of worldwide distribution in the ocean, but the greatest numbers of species and individuals are to be found in the northern hemisphere.

ARCTIC FLOUNDER

Liopsetta glacialis (Pallas)

DISTINCTIVE CHARACTERS

The presence of both eyes on the same side of the head, normal scales (as opposed to the tubercled scales of the starry flounder) and generally plain coloration distinguish the arctic flounder (Figure 63).

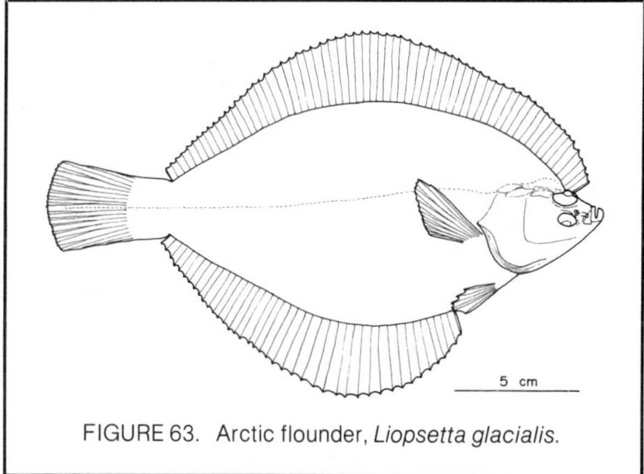

FIGURE 63. Arctic flounder, *Liopsetta glacialis.*

DESCRIPTION

Body strongly compressed, broad, its depth 38% to 46% of total length. Head short, 22% to 26% of total length. Snout short, its length 14% to 18% of head. Eye a little longer than wide, its diameter about equal to snout length; right (lower) eye a little in front of left. Nostrils in short tubes. Mouth small, oblique, asymmetric; jaws of blind side a little longer than on eyed side; maxilla reaches about to anterior edge of lower eye. Teeth incisorlike, small; upper jaw has 3 to 6 teeth on eyed side, 12 to 21 on blind side; lower jaw has 4 to 16 and 15 to 22. Gill rakers: 9 to 15 on first arch. Branchiostegals: 5 to 6. Lateral line has a very low curve above pectoral fin, is straight behind and has a short accessory branch on head; 73 to 76 pores in main portion. In males the lateral line is complete but in females as large as about 20 cm it is an open groove on the posterior part of the body (Walters, 1955). Pyloric caeca: 3 (from a sample of 7 specimens). Vertebrae: 37 or 38 (7 specimens).

FINS. Dorsal has 50 to 62 rays, the most anterior ray being above the eye. Anal, 35 to 44 rays, with an embedded forward-pointing spine before first ray. Pectorals, 9 to 11 rays (in rare cases 12); pelvics, 6. Caudal rounded.

SCALES. Weakly ctenoid on both sides of the body in males, with cycloid scales on the abdominal region of the blind side. Females usually have cycloid scales over most of the body and narrow bands of ctenoid scales along the bases of the dorsal and anal fins. In some populations the females are scaled like the males (Norman, 1934; Andriyashev, 1954; Walters, 1955).

COLOR. Eyed side dark olive green to brown, sometimes with scattered black dots or indefinite dark blotches. Blind side white, rarely with brown lapping over from the eyed side. Fins pale brownish, sometimes with a somewhat yellow tinge or traces of dark spots (photograph, page 110).

SIZE. This is one of the smaller flounders, only rarely reaching 35 cm. Most are much smaller than 25 cm.

RANGE AND ABUNDANCE

The arctic flounder is almost circumpolar in its distribution. It is found in the Arctic Ocean from Queen Maude Gulf in arctic Canada westward along the coasts of North America and Siberia to the White Sea and the Barents Sea. On the American side of the Pacific it is present in the Chukchi and Bering seas southward to Bristol Bay, and on the Siberian side to the northern part of the Sea of Okhotsk. The arctic flounder is a fish of the coastal waters, not found far offshore. In some places it is very abundant, at least inshore in summer. It often enters rivers (Jordan, 1884; Bean, 1887c; Andriyashev, 1954; Walters, 1955; Nikolskii, 1961; Alverson and Wilmovsky, 1966).

HABITS

As with so many arctic fishes, little is known about the arctic flounder. Spawning usually takes place in coastal areas from January to March, but may be as late as May in some regions. Spawning goes on in shallow water at depths of 5 to 10 m in regions that have pronounced tidal currents, temperatures below -1°C and salinities of about 27 to 28 parts per thousand. Fecundity, compared to that of other flounders, is relatively low: 31,000 to 230,000 eggs per female. The fish usually reach maturity at age 4+ to 5+, although maturity as early as 2+ has been reported. Spawning is said to occur only every second year. Females grow more rapidly than males, but growth is slow in both sexes. In the Barents Sea 5+ males average only 17.7 cm in length; females, 19.9 cm, with 9+ females being about 24.9 cm. Arctic flounders appear to move offshore in the fall and onshore in spring. They move close inshore in the evenings, especially on a rising tide. Their food is mainly small mollusks, crustaceans and fishes (Turner, 1886; Bean, 1887c; Probatov, 1940; Esipov, 1949; Andriyashev, 1954; Nikolskii, 1961).

IMPORTANCE TO MAN

The arctic flounder is of little importance to man. Small quantities are taken commercially in the eastern parts of the Barents and White seas. In Alaska, this species was formerly (and perhaps still is) used in coastal subsistence fisheries, especially eaten raw. Opinions of early writers vary as to its utility. Jordan (1884) wrote that ". . . its great abundance and fine flavor make it an important article of food." By contrast, Turner (1886) found it "not palatable" and noted that in summer the fish often developed repulsive tumors along the fins.

STARRY FLOUNDER

Platichthys stellatus (Pallas)

DISTINCTIVE CHARACTERS

The starry flounder is distinguished by the presence of both eyes on the same side of the head, dorsal and anal fins that are marked with dark and light (white to orange) bars and, especially, by the stellate, bony tubercles scattered over its body (Figure 64).

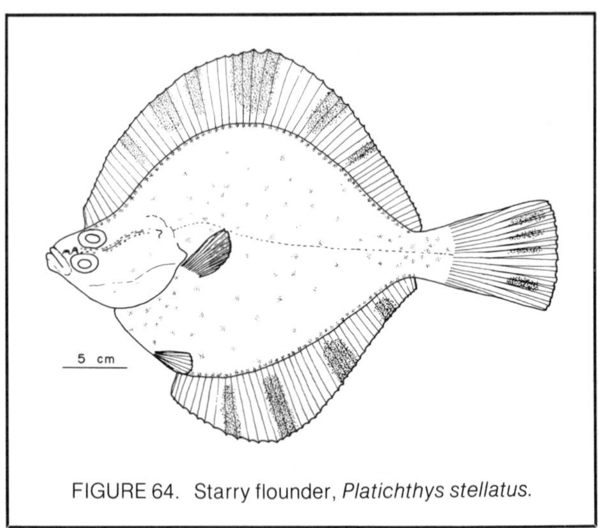

FIGURE 64. Starry flounder, *Platichthys stellatus.*

DESCRIPTION

Body strongly compressed, asymmetrical, colored on one side only. Depth 40% to 48% of total length. Head moderate, 23% to 26% of total length. Snout rather pointed, 15% to 18% of head length. Nostrils in short tubes, 1 at anterior dorsal margin of lower eye, the other just anterior to the first. Eye small, diameter about equal to snout length or a little longer. Both eyes on same side of head; may be on either right or left side. Mouth terminal, oblique, with lower jaw protruding. Teeth incisorlike; about 10 on eyed side of upper jaw, 15 on blind side, 12 and 16 on lower jaw. Gill rakers: 6 to 11 on first arch. Branchiostegals: 4. Lateral line has a slight arch over pectoral fin; 63 to 78 pores. Pyloric caeca:

usually 2 in North American specimens, but sometimes 3 or 4; usually 4 in Asian fish. Vertebrae: 34 to 37.

FINS. Dorsal, which originates over middle of upper eye, has 52 to 66 rays. Anal, 38 to 47, with a sharp, forward-pointing spine (often buried in skin) before first ray. Pectorals, which are bluntly pointed, about 11 rays; pelvics, 6. Caudal slightly rounded.

SCALES. Stellate tubercles with well-developed spines are scattered over head and body and in a row along bases of dorsal and anal fins. Tubercles more numerous on eyed side than on blind side, and increase in number with size and age. Embedded cycloid scales present between the stellate tubercles, but distribution of the embedded scales seems to be quite variable (Norman, 1934; Orcutt, 1950; Batts, 1964).

COLOR. Eyed side dark brown to nearly black, sometimes with indefinite blotchings. Alaskan specimens occasionally have a greenish tinge. Blind side white to creamy. Dorsal fin has 4 to 7 dark bars with white to orange spaces between; anal fin has 4 to 6 such bars. Caudal fin has 3 or 4 dark longitudinal bars on its posterior part (photograph, page 110; Plate 17, page 128). In rare cases the blind side may be partly or completely colored like the eyed side, or white may be present on the eyed side, creating a piebald effect (Gudger, 1941; Follett, 1954).

SIZE. One of the largest, if not the largest, of the true flounders. Reported to reach nearly 1 m in length and 9.1 kg in weight.

RANGE AND ABUNDANCE

The starry flounder ranges along the coast of North America from around Santa Barbara, California, north to the Arctic Ocean, then east along the arctic coast of Canada to Bathurst Inlet, possibly even as far east as Queen Maude Gulf (Walters, 1955). To the west, starry flounders are found along the Chukchi and Bering coasts of Siberia (but not the Arctic Ocean coast) and southward to Japan and Korea. In the central parts of its range the starry flounder is abundant, and from northern California to the Bering Sea it is perhaps the most abundant of the flounders in near-shore areas. It is common in brackish water and may ascend rivers for some distance, even into fresh water (Gunter, 1942; Hubbs, 1947). Alverson and Wilimovsky (1966) observed that the starry flounder apparently does not venture far from shore or into water of high salinity; this was also my personal observation in the Chukchi and Bering seas in August, 1974.

HABITS

Spawning occurs in the winter and spring, from November to February off California, February to April in Puget Sound and British Columbia, and still later farther north, with the height of the spawning season apparently corresponding with water temperatures near 11 °C (Orcutt, 1950; Andriyashev, 1954; Hart, 1973). The eggs are quite small, .089 to .094 cm in diameter, colorless to pale orange, with a thin vermiculated membrane. They are slightly less dense than sea water, so tend to rise and float near the surface. A medium-size female of 56.5 cm standard length (about 69 cm total length) contained an estimated 11 million eggs. Hatching occurs about 68 hours after fertilization when the eggs are kept at 12.5 °C, but in 110 hours at 10.5 °C. The newly hatched larvae are about .2 cm long, with large yolk sacs. For the first few hours, they are largely quiescent and tend to float with the yolk sac uppermost. After 24 hours, however, the larvae, now about .3 cm long, have become quite active. The yolk is completely absorbed in about 10 days. The time of metamorphosis is unknown, but this phenomenon takes place when the young reach a length between .34 and 1.05 cm, probably closer to the latter (Orcutt, 1950).

Minute cycloid scales are present when the young reach 2.5 cm, and these scales soon begin to develop into the typical stellate plates. Specimens of 10 cm show these plates on the eyed side of the head and along the dorsal and anal fin bases on both sides of the body. At 20 cm there are broad bands of rough scales above and below the lateral line on the eyed side, on the head and in double lines above and below the lateral line on the blind side. As the fish continue to grow, the tubercles become more numerous and cover more and more of the entire body (Orcutt, 1950).

During the first 18 months of life there is a noticeable seasonal difference in growth rate; growth is rapid through spring and early summer, then slows through the fall to accelerate again in midwinter through the following spring. The same growth pattern exists in older fish but is less obvious. Typical lengths (converted from standard to total length by multiplying by 1.22) for fish from southern California are 1+, 12.9 cm (male) and 13.3 cm (female); 2+, 28.7 (male) and 29.4 (female); 3+, 36.4 (male) and 38.4 (female); 5+, 47.7 (male) and 51.9 (female); 7+, 62 cm (female). A fish of this last length will weigh about 3.25 kg (Orcutt, 1950). Large individuals in more northern waters grow about 2.5 cm per year (Manzer, 1952).

Sexual maturity is reached at age 2+ for males, 3+ for females. Females grow faster, reach a larger size and live longer than do males.

The starry flounder makes inshore-offshore migrations with the seasons. During the summer the fish are inshore, often in very shallow water and in estuaries; they tend to move into deeper water, up to

300 m deep, in the winter. However, they may occur in the deep water at all times of year, for commercial fishermen fishing for other species have taken them at these depths in May (Turner, 1886; Bean, 1887c; Orcutt, 1950; Andriyashev, 1954). Except for these seasonal movements, starry flounders do not migrate much. The young, however, do move up rivers, and the adults may also, for as much as 120 km. But few adults have been taken far up rivers. A few fish tagged at the mouth of the Columbia River and in British Columbia waters had moved 96 to 200 km, but most were recovered within 5 km of the tagging area (Manzer, 1952; Westrheim, 1955).

The pelagic young feed on minute plankton. Demersal copepods and amphipods are important food items for the starry flounder after metamorphosis and adoption of a bottom-dwelling life style. As the fish grow, larger and larger items are included in the diet. From the time the fish reach a length of about 10 cm, food includes clams, snails, starfish, amphipods, polychaete worms, crabs, mysids and nemerteans. Fish are eaten only by the larger flounders, mostly those over 45 cm long. Small starry flounders graze on the siphon tips of clams, which lie buried in the bottom with only the ends of the siphons exposed. In Puget Sound, the starry flounder feeds heavily from July to October, stops feeding in January and apparently does not eat again until June. It is not known whether this feeding cycle occurs in other areas (Orcutt, 1950; Andriyashev, 1954; Miller, 1967).

When the fish is at rest, the dorsal and anal fins are curled towards the blind side, holding the body slightly off the bottom. Movement is most often a sort of crawling, with the fish using the rays of the dorsal and anal fin in the manner of the legs of a caterpillar. In quick, short movements, the pectoral fins are used as paddles. When disturbed, the starry flounder flutters its dorsal, anal and caudal fins so as to wave a covering of sand or mud over its body. It may bury itself so deeply that even the eyes are covered, and may be so confident of its concealment that force must be used to move it.

Adaptive coloration is pronounced. Starry flounders can alter their colors and color patterns to simulate the bottoms on which they lie. Fish on mud bottoms are dark, those on sand tend to be brownish, while fish on extremely light-colored bottoms are gray (Orcutt, 1950).

A major point of interest concerning the starry flounder lies in the fact that, although it belongs to a group that normally has color and the eyes on the right side, the starry flounder may have eyes and color either on the right side (dextral) or the left side

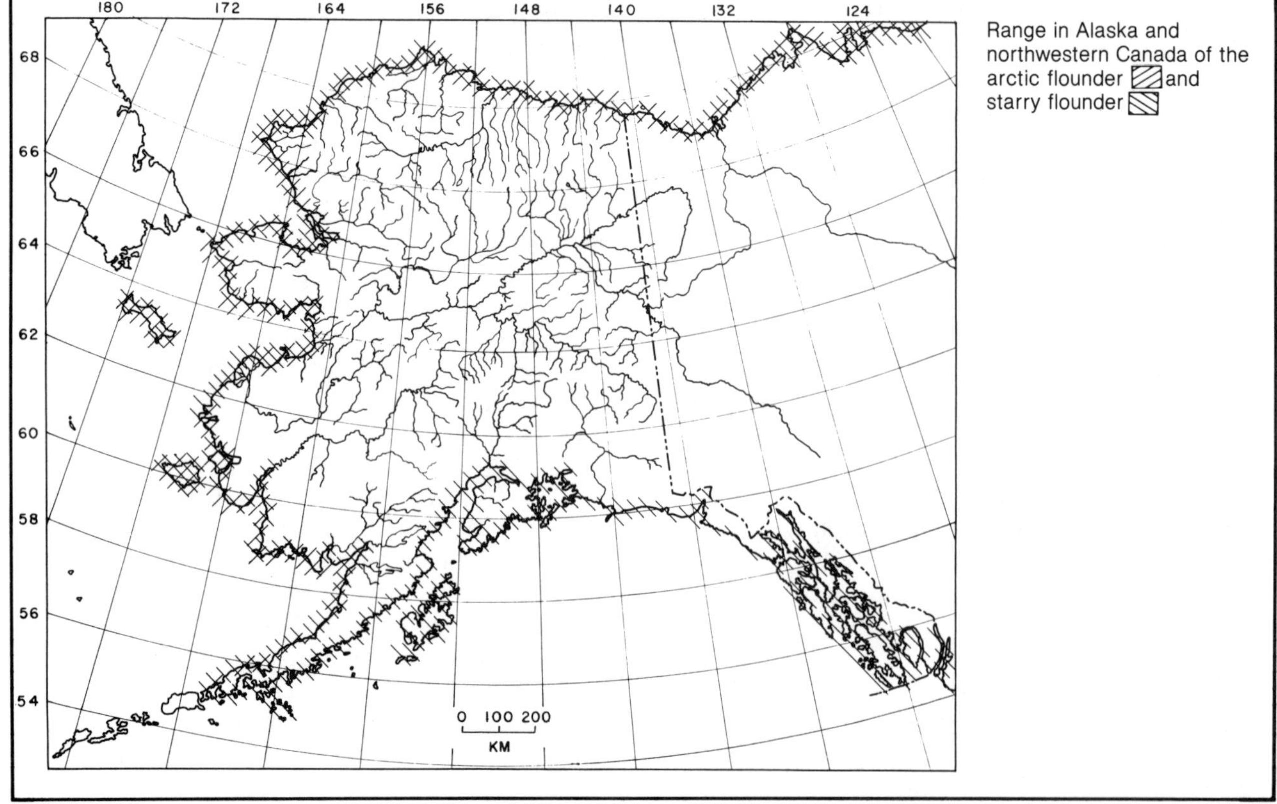

Range in Alaska and northwestern Canada of the arctic flounder [hatched] and starry flounder [cross-hatched]

(sinistral). There is some evidence, although inconclusive, suggesting that sinistral individuals are less viable than dextral, at least in some areas (Hubbs and Hubbs, 1944). Against this is the fact that over most of the range, sinistral starry flounders outnumber dextral ones. There appears to be a general trend, with irregularities, for sinistrality to increase to the north and west. Off California, sinistral individuals make up 55.2% to 59.5% of the population; off the outer coast of Oregon, 49.2%; at the mouth of the Columbia River, 60.4%; off Washington, 66.4%; southeast Alaska, 58.2%; Kodiak Island and the Alaska Peninsula, 68%; Japan, nearly 100%. Sinistrality and dextrality are not correlated with sex, both males and females showing the same degree of reversal in a given population (Townsend, 1937; Hubbs and Kuronuma 1942; Orcutt, 1950; Andriyashev, 1954; Forrester, 1969).

The starry flounder hybridizes with at least two other species, the Japanese *Kareius bicoloratus* and the North American *Parophrys vetulus*. Both hybrids were given scientific names before their hybrid status was realized. The North American hybrid, *Inopsetta ischyra,* is not uncommon and has been studied to some degree. The hybrids have been found from Drake's Bay, California, north to the Bering Sea. Reproductive level of the hybrid is low due to abnormal development of eggs and sperm (Schultz and Smith, 1936; Herald, 1941; Hubbs and Kuronuma, 1942; Aron, 1958; Reed, 1964).

IMPORTANCE TO MAN

Although the starry flounder is abundant and widespread, it is of relatively small importance. It is taken commercially, but mostly as an incidental catch during fishing for other species. Starry flounder is marketed, along with several other flatfishes, as sole, so it is difficult to determine how much is taken. In California, landings have been fairly steady for many years at between 136,000 and 227,000 kg per year. Total landings of unclassified flounders on the west coast in 1971 amounted to about 909,000 kg. Probably about 75% of this was starry flounder. Smaller fish are considered superior to large ones for eating purposes, as the flesh of the latter is said to be somewhat coarse. Opinions vary as to the quality of the flavor. In Kamchatka it was once canned as a luxury item for export (Andriyashev, 1935, Ripley, 1949; Orcutt, 1950; Anonymous, 1974).

The starry flounder is reasonably popular as a sport fish, for it bites readily most of the time and can often make the difference between a "dry" day and a successful one.

BIBLIOGRAPHY

Allen, G. H. 1965. Ocean migration and distribution of fin-marked coho salmon. J. Fish. Res. Bd. Canada 23(7): 1043-1061.

Allin, A. E. 1953. Records of the creek northern chub from Ontario. Canadian Field-Nat. 67(3):128-130.

Alt, K. T. 1965. Food habits of inconnu in Alaska. Trans. Amer. Fish. Soc. 94(3):272-274.

Alt, K. T. 1968. Sheefish and pike investigations of the upper Yukon and Kuskokwim drainages with emphasis on Minto Flats drainages. Alaska Dept. Fish Game. Fed. Aid Fish Restor., Ann. Rept. Progress 1967-1968, Project F-5-R-9, Job 17-B. 9:307-321.

Alt, K. T. 1969. Taxonomy and ecology of the inconnu, *Stenodus leucichthys nelma,* in Alaska. Biol. Pap. Univ. Alaska. 12:1-61.

Alt, K. T. 1971a. Distribution, movements, age and growth, and taxonomic status of whitefish *(Coregonus* sp.) in the Tanana-Yukon drainage and North Slope. Alaska Dept. Fish Game. Fed. Aid Fish Restor., Ann. Rept. Progress, Project F-9-3, Job R-II-F. 12:19-31.

Alt. K. T. 1971b. The sheefish in Alaska. Alaska Dept. Fish Game, Wildl. Notebook Ser., Fishes: No. 6. 2 pp.

Alt, K. T. 1971c. Occurrence of hybrids between inconnu, *Stenodus leucichthys nelma* (Pallas) and humpback whitefish, *Coregonus pidschian* (Linnaeus) in Chatanika River, Alaska. Trans. Amer. Fish. Soc. 100(2):362-365.

Alt, K. T. 1973a. Age and growth of the inconnu *(Stenodus leucichthys)* in Alaska. J. Fish. Res. Bd. Canada 30(3):457-459.

Alt, K. T. 1973b. Distribution, movements, age and growth, and taxonomic status of whitefish in the Arctic-Yukon-Kuskokwim area. Alaska Dept. Fish Game. Fed. Aid Fish Restor., Ann. Progress Rept., Project F-9-5, Job R-II-C. 14:23-31.

Alt, K. T. 1973c. Contributions to the biology of the Bering cisco *(Coregonus laurettae)* in Alaska. J. Fish. Res. Bd. Canada 30(12-1):1885-1888.

Alt, K. T. 1977. Inconnu, *Stenodus leucichthys,* migration studies in Alaska 1961-74. J. Fish. Res. Bd. Canada 34(1):129-133.

Alt, K. T., and D. R. Kogl. 1973. Notes on the whitefish of the Colville River, Alaska. J. Fish. Res. Bd. Canada 30(4): 554-556.

Alverson, D. L., and N. J. Wilimovsky. 1966. Fishery investigations of the southeastern Chukchi Sea. p. 843-860. *In:* Wilimovsky, N. J., and J. N. Wolfe (eds.). Environment of the Cape Thompson region, Alaska. U.S. Atomic Energy Commission, Washington, D.C.

Anas, R. E. 1959. Three-year-old pink salmon. J. Fish. Res. Bd. Canada 16 (1):91-92.

Anderson, A. W., and C. E. Peterson. 1953. Fishery statistics of the United States 1950. U.S. Fish Wildl. Serv., Stat. Digest 27.

Anderson, A. W., and E. A. Power. 1946. Fishery statistics of the United States 1942. U.S. Fish Wildl. Serv., Stat. Digest 11.

Anderson, A. W., and E. A. Power. 1957. Historical fishery statistics. Pacific herring fishery, 1882-1955. p. 407-411. *In:* Fishery statistics of the United States 1955. U.S. Fish Wildl. Serv., Stat. Digest 41.

Andrews, C. W., and E. Lear. 1956. The biology of the Arctic char *(Salvelinus alpinus* L.) in northern Labrador. J. Fish. Res. Bd. Canada 13(6):843-860.

Andriyashev, A. P. 1935. Geographical distribution of the marine food fishes of the Bering Sea and problems connected there-with. Explor. Mers URSS. 22:135-145. (Not seen. Cited by Orcutt, 1950).

Andriyashev, A. P. 1937. A contribution to the knowledge of the fishes from the Bering and Chukchi seas. Explor. Mers URSS. 25:292-355. Transl. U.S. Fish Wildl. Serv. Spec. Sci. Rept. Fisheries 145.

Andriyashev, A. P. 1954. Fishes of the northern seas of the U.S.S.R. Keys to the fauna of the U.S.S.R. No. 53, 617 pp. Israel Program for Scientific Translations 1964.

Anonymous. 1953a. Preparation for stocking in suitable waters—southeastern Alaska. U.S. Fish Wildl. Serv. and Alaska Game Comm. Fed. Aid Fish Restor., Quarterly Progress Rept. 1953, Project F-1-R-2. 2(4):8-9.

Anonymous. 1953b. The largest lake trout ever caught. Hunting and Fishing in Canada. 19(8):20.

Anonymous. 1954. An unusual catch of green sturgeon. Fish. Res. Bd. Canada, Pac. Prog. Rep. 100:19.

Anonymous. 1961. Great Lakes fishery investigations. Comm. Fish. Rev. 23(6):23-24.

Anonymous. 1971. Fishery statistics of the United States 1968. U.S. Nat. Mar. Fish. Serv., Stat. Digest 62.

Anonymous. 1972. Fishery statistics of the United States 1969. U.S. Nat. Mar. Fish. Serv., Stat. Digest 63.

Anonymous. 1973. Fishery statistics of the United States 1970. U.S. Nat. Mar. Fish. Serv., Stat. Digest 64.

Anonymous. 1974. Fishery statistics of the United States 1971. U.S. Nat. Mar. Fish. Serv., Stat. Digest 65.

Anonymous. 1975. Fishery statistics of the United States. 1972 U.S. Nat. Mar. Fish. Serv., Stat. Digest 66.

Anonymous. 1976. Fishery statistics of the United States. 1973 U.S. Nat. Mar. Fish. Serv., Stat. Digest 67.

Armstrong, R. H. 1965a. Some migratory habits of the anadromous Dolly Varden in southeastern Alaska. Alaska Dept. Fish Game Res. Rept. 3:1-36.

Armstrong, R. H. 1965b. Some feeding habits of the anadromous Dolly Varden *Salvelinus malma* (Walbaum) in southeastern Alaska. Alaska Dept. Fish Game Info. Leaflet 51:1-26.

Armstrong, R. H. 1967. Investigations of anadromous Dolly Varden in the Hood Bay drainages, southeastern Alaska. Alaska Dept. Fish Game. Fed. Aid Fish Restor., Ann. Rept. Progress, Project F-5-R-8. 8:33-56.

Armstrong, R. H. 1971a. Age, food, and migration of sea-run cutthroat trout, *Salmo clarki,* at Eva Lake, southeastern Alaska. Trans. Amer. Fish. Soc. 100(2):302-306.

Armstrong, R. H. 1971b. Life history of Dolly Varden. Alaska Dept. Fish Game. Fed. Aid Fish Restor., Ann. Progress Rept., Project F-9-3, Rept. R-IV-A. 12:1-11.

Armstrong, R. H., and J. E. Morrow, 1980. The dolly varden charr, p. 99-140. *In:* Balon, E. K. (ed.). Charrs: Salmonid fishes of the genus *Salvelinus.* Dr. W. Junk b.v., Publishers. The Hague, Netherlands.

Aro, K. V., and M. P. Shepard. 1967. Salmon of the north Pacific Ocean—Part IV. Spawning populations of north Pacific salmon. 5. Pacific salmon in Canada. Bull. Int. N. Pac. Fish. Comm. 23:225-327.

Aron, W. 1958. Cytological and histological studies on the hybrid of *Platichthys stellatus* x *Parophrys vetulus,* with notes on its backcross to *P. vetulus.* Copeia 1958(2):105-111.

Aspinwall, N. 1965. Spawning characteristics and early life history of the Alaskan blackfish, *Dallia pectoralis* Bean. M.S. Thesis, Univ. Washington, Seattle. 78 pp.

Atkinson, C. E., J. H. Rose and T. O. Duncan. 1967. Salmon of the north Pacific Ocean—Part IV. Spawning populations of north Pacific salmon. 4. Pacific salmon in the United States. Bull. Int. N. Pac. Fish. Comm. 23:43-223.

Baade, R. T. 1957. Environmental studies of the cutthroat trout, S.E. Alaska. U.S. Fish Wildl. Serv. and Alaska Game Comm. Fed. Aid Fish Restor., Quart. Prog. Rept., Project F-1-R-6. 6:62-67.

Baade, R. T. 1962. Inventory and cataloging of the sport fish and sport fish waters in lower southeast Alaska. Alaska Dept. Fish Game. Fed. Aid Fish Restor., Ann. Rept. Progress 1961-1962, Project F-5-R-3, Job 1-A. 3:1-13.

Backus, R. H. 1957. The fishes of Labrador. Bull. Amer. Mus. Nat. Hist. 113(4):277-337.

Bailey, J. E., and D. R. Evans. 1971. The low-temperature threshold for pink salmon eggs in relation to a proposed hydroelectric installation. Fish. Bull. 69(3):587-593.

Bailey, J. E., B. L. Wing and C. R. Mattson. 1975. Zooplankton abundance and feeding habits of fry of pink salmon, *Oncorhynchus gorbuscha,* and chum salmon, *Oncorhynchus keta,* in Traitors Cove, Alaska, with speculations on carrying capacity of the area. Fish. Bull. 73(4):846-861.

Bailey, M. M. 1963. Age, growth, and maturity of round whitefish of the Apostle Islands and Isle Royale regions, Lake Superior. Fish Bull. U.S. Fish Wildl. Serv. 63(1):63-75.

Bailey, M. M. 1964. Age, growth, maturity, and sex composition of the American smelt, *Osmerus mordax* (Mitchill), of western Lake Superior. Trans. Amer. Fish. Soc. 93(4):382-395.

Bailey, R. M., J. E. Fitch, E. S. Herald, E. A. Lachner, C. C. Lindsey, C. A. Robins and W. B. Scott. 1970. A list of common and scientific names of fishes from the United States and Canada. Amer. Fish. Soc. Spec. Publ. No. 6. 149 pp.

Bajkov, A. D. 1951. Migration of white sturgeon *(Acipenser transmontanus)* in the Columbia River. Oregon Fish Comm. Res. Briefs 3(2):8-21.

Bajkov, A. D. 1955. White sturgeon with seven rows of scutes. Calif. Fish Game 41:347-348.

Baldwin, N. S. 1950. The American smelt, *Osmerus mordax* (Mitchill), of South Bay, Manitoulin Island, Lake Huron. Trans. Amer. Fish. Soc. 78:176-180.

Baldwin, N. S. 1957. Food consumption and growth of brook trout at different temperatures. Trans. Amer. Fish. Soc. 86:323-328.

Barraclough, W. E. 1964. Contribution to the marine life history of the eulachon *Thaleichthys pacificus.* J. Fish. Res. Bd. Canada 21(5):1333-1337.

Barraclough, W. E. 1967. Occurrence of larval herring *(Clupea pallasii)* in the Strait of Georgia during July 1966. J. Fish. Res. Bd. Canada 24(11):2455-2460.

Barraclough, W. E., and D. Robinson. 1972. The fertilization of Great Central Lake. III. Effect on juvenile sockeye salmon. Fish. Bull. 70(1):37-48.

Bartholomew, M. A., J. DiVall and J. E. Morrow. 1962. Silver pike, an atypical *Esox lucius,* in Alaska, a first record. Copeia 1962(2):449-450.

Batts, B. S. 1964. Lepidology of the adult pleuronectiform fishes of Puget Sound, Washington. Copeia 1964(4):666-673.

Bean, T. H. 1884. Notes on a collection of fishes made in 1882 and 1883 by Capt. Henry E. Nichols, U.S.N., in Alaska and British Columbia, with a description of a new genus and species, Prionistius macellus. Proc. U.S. Nat. Mus. 6:353-361.

Bean, T. H. 1887. Notes on Alaskan fishes. p. 201-322. *In:* Nelson, E. W. Report upon the natural history collections made in Alaska between the years 1877 and 1881. Arctic. Ser. Publ. Signal Serv. U.S. Army, No. III. Gov't Printing Office, Washington, D.C.

Bean, T. H. 1903. Catalogue of the fishes of New York. Bull. N.Y. St. Mus. 60:1-784.

Beckman, W. C. 1942. Length-weight relationship, age, sex-ratio and food habits of smelt *(Osmorus mordax)* from Crystal Lake, Benzie County, Michigan. Copeia 1942(2):120-124.

Beeton, A. M. 1956. Food habits of the burbot *(Lota lota lacustris)* in the White River, a Michigan trout stream. Copeia 1956(1):58-60.

Bell, M. A. 1976. Evolution of phenotypic diversity in *Gasterosteus aculeatus* superspecies on the Pacific coast of North America. Syst. Zool. 25(3):211-227.

Bennett, L. H. 1948. Pike culture at the New London, Minnesota, station. Prog. Fish-Cult. 10(2):95-97.

Berg, L. S. 1948. Freshwater fishes of the U.S.S.R. and adjacent countries. Guide to the fauna of the U.S.S.R. No. 27. Vol. 1, 4th ed. Akad. Nauk SSSR Zool. Inst., Moscow. Translated from Russian by Israel Program for Scientific Translations, 1962. Office of Technical Services, U.S. Dept. Commerce, Washington, D.C. 504 pp.

Beukema, J. J. 1970. Acquired hook-avoidance in the pike, *Esox lucius* L. fished with artificial and natural baits. J. Fish Biol. 2(2):155-160.

Bigelow, H. B. 1963. Genus *Salvelinus* Richardson 1836. Fishes of the western North Atlantic. Sears Found. Mar. Res., Mem. 1(3):503-542.

Bigelow, H. B., and W. C. Schroeder. 1953. Fishes of the Gulf of Maine. Fish Bull. U.S. Fish Wildl. Serv. 53(74):1-577.

Bigelow, H.B., and W.C. Schroeder. 1963. Family Osmeridae. Fishes of the Western North Atlantic. Sears Found. Mar. Res., Mem. 1(3):553-597.

Bigelow, H. B., and W. W. Welsh. 1925. Fishes of the Gulf of Maine. Bull. U.S. Bur. Fish. 40:1-567.

Birman, I. B. 1950. Parastism of salmon of the genus *Oncorhynchus* by The Pacific lamprey. Izvestia Tinro 32:158-160. Fish. Res. Bd. Canada Trans. 290.

Birman, I. B. 1953. Dinamika chislennosti i sovre mennoe sostoyanie zapasov kety i gorbushi basseina Amura. Trudy Soveshch. Ikhtiol. Kom. Acad. Nauk SSSR 4:22-37.

Bishop, F. G. 1971. Observations on spawning habits and fecundity of the Arctic grayling. Prog. Fish-Cult. 33(1):12-19.

Bjorn, E. E. 1940. Preliminary observations and experimental study of the ling, *Lota maculosa* (LeSueur), in Wyoming. Trans. Amer. Fish. Soc. 69:192-196.

Black, E. C. 1953. Upper lethal temperature of some British Columbia freshwater fishes. J. Fish. Res. Bd. Canada 10(4):196-210.

Black, E. C., A. R. Connor, K.-C. Lam and W.-G. Chiu. 1962. Changes in glycogen, pyruvate and lactate in rainbow trout *(Salmo gairdneri)* during and following muscular activity. J. Fish. Res. Bd. Canada 19(3):409-436.

Blackett, R. F. 1962. Some phases of the life history of the Alaskan blackfish, *Dallia pectoralis.* Copeia 1962(1):124-130.

Blackett, R. F. 1968. Spawning behavior and early life history of anadromous Dolly Varden, *Salvelinus malma* (Walbaum), in southeastern Alaska. Alaska Dept. Fish Game Res. Rept. 6:1-85.

Bond, C. E. 1963. Distribution and ecology of freshwater sculpins, genus *Cottus,* in Oregon. Ph.D. Thesis, Univ. Michigan, Ann Arbor. 186 pp. (Not seen. Cited by McPhail and Lindsey, 1970).

Bonde, T., and J. E. Maloney. 1960. Food habits of burbot. Trans. Amer. Fish. Soc. 89(4):374-376.

Borodin, N. A. 1934. The anabiosis or phenomenon of resuscitation of fishes after being frozen. Zool. Jahrb., Abt. Allg. Zool. Physiol. Tiere 53(3):313-342.

Boulva, J., and A. Simard. 1968. Présence du *Salvelinus namaycush* (Pisces: Salmonidae) dans les eaux marine de l'Arctique occidental Canadien. J. Fish. Res. Bd. Canada 25(7):1501-1504.

Bower, W. T. 1919. Alaska fisheries and fur industries in 1918. Rept. U.S. Comm. Fish. 1918 (1919), App. VII: 1-128.

Bower, W. T., and H. C. Fassett. 1914. Fishery industries. *In:* Alaska fisheries and fur industries in 1913. Rept. U.S. Comm. Fish. 1913 (1914), App. II: 1-172.

Branion, H. 1930. The marketing of ling (burbot). Trans. Amer. Fish. Soc. 60:199-203.

Brett, J. R. 1952. Temperature tolerance in young Pacific salmon, genus *Oncorhynchus.* J. Fish. Res. Bd. Canada 9(6):265-323.

Brett, J. R., and D. MacKinnon. 1952. Some observations on olfactory perception in migrating adult coho and spring salmon. Fish. Res. Bd. Canada, Pac. Prog. Rept. 90:21-23.

Brett, J. R., and D. MacKinnon. 1954. Some aspects of olfactory perception in migrating adult coho and spring salmon. J. Fish. Res. Bd. Canada 11(3):310-318.

Briggs, J. C. 1953. The behavior and reproduction of salmonid fishes in a small coastal stream. Calif. Fish Bull. 94. 62 pp.

Brown, C.J.D. 1938a. The feeding habits of the Montana grayling *(Thymallus montanus).* J. Wildl. Mgt. 2(3):135-145.

Brown, C.J.D. 1938b. Observations on the life-history and breeding habits of the Montana grayling. Copeia 1938(3):132-136.

Brown, C.J.D. 1952. Spawning habits and early development of the mountain whitefish, *Prosopium williamsoni,* in Montana. Copeia 1952(2):109-113.

Brown, C.J.D., and C. Buck, Jr. 1939. When do trout and grayling fry begin to take food? J. Wildl. Mgt. 3(2):134-140.

Brown, C.J.D., and R. J. Graham. 1954. Observations on the longnose sucker in Yellowstone Lake. Trans. Amer. Fish. Soc. 83: 38-46.

Browning, R. J. 1974. Fisheries of the North Pacific. Alaska Northwest Publ. Co., Anchorage. 408 pp.

Brunson, R. B., and D. G. Block. 1957. The first report on the white sturgeon of Flathead Lake, Montana. Proc. Montana Acad. Sci. 17:61-62.

Budd, J. 1957. Movements of tagged whitefish in northern Lake Huron and Georgian Bay. Trans. Amer. Fish. Soc. 86:128-134.

Burdick, G. E., E. J. Harris, H. J. Dean, T. M. Walker, J. Skea and D. Colby. 1964. The accumulation of DDT in lake trout and the effect on reproduction. Trans. Amer. Fish. Soc. 93(2):127-136.

Burns, J. W., and A. Calhoun. 1966. Trout stream management. p. 178-181. *In:* A. Calhoun (ed.). Inland fisheries management. Calif. Dept. Fish Game, Sacramento.

Burrows, R. E., and N. L. Karrick. 1947. A biological assay of the nutritional value of certain salmon cannery waste products. p. 71-89. *In:* Utilization of Alaskan salmon cannery waste. U.S. Dept. Commerce, Office Tech. Serv., Indust. Res. Devel. Div. Rept. 1.

Buss, K. 1960. Data on known age hatchery trout. Pers. Comm. quoted by Carlander, 1969.

Buss, K., and J. E. Wright Jr. 1956. Results of species hybridization within the family Salmonidae. Prog. Fish-Cult. 18(4):149-158.

Buss, K., and J. E. Wright. 1958. Appearance and fertility of trout hybrids. Trans. Amer. Fish. Soc. 87:172-181.

Butler, C., and D. Miyauchi. 1947. The preparation of vitamin oils from salmon cannery offal by the alkali digestion process. p. 52-70. *In:* Utilization of Alaskan salmon cannery waste. U.S. Dept. Commerce, Office Tech. Serv., Indust. Res. Devel. Div. Rept. 1.

Cahn, A. R. 1936. Observations on the breeding of the lawyer, *Lota maculosa.* Copeia 1936(3):163-165.

Calhoun, A. J. 1944. Black-spotted trout in Blue Lake, California. Calf. Fish Game 30(1):22-42.

Canadian Department of Fisheries. 1961. Trade News. Sept. 1961:10. (Not seen. Cited by McAfee, 1966).

Carbine, W. F. 1944. Egg production of the northern pike, *Esox lucius* L., and the percentage survival of eggs and young on the spawning grounds. Pap. Mich. Acad. Sci. Arts Lett. 29:123-137.

Carbine, W. F. 1945. Growth potential of the northern pike *(Esox lucius).* Pap. Mich. Acad. Sci. Arts Lett. 30:205-220.

Carbine, W. F., and V. C. Applegate. 1946. The movement and growth of marked northern pike *(Esox lucius* L.) in Houghton Lake and the Muskegon River. Pap. Mich. Acad. Sci. Arts Lett. 32:215-238.

Carl, G. C. 1953. Limnobiology of Cowichan Lake, British Columbia. J. Fish. Res. Bd. Canada 9(9):417-449.

Carlander, K. D. 1969. Handbook of freshwater fishery biology, Vol. 1. Iowa State Univ. Press, Ames. 752 pp.

Carlson, H. R. 1974. Foods of juvenile sockeye salmon, *Oncorhynchus nerka,* in the inshore coastal waters of Bristol Bay, Alaska, 1966-67. Fish. Bull. 74(2):458-462.

Carpelan, L. H. 1961. Salinity tolerances of some fishes of a southern California coastal lagoon. Copeia 1961(1):32-39.

Cating, J. P. 1953. Determining age of Atlantic shad from their scales. Fish. Bull. U.S. Fish Wildl. Serv. 54(85):187-199.

Chadwick, H. K. 1959. California sturgeon tagging studies. Calif. Fish Game 45:297-301.

Chamberlain, F. M. 1907. Some observations on salmon and trout in Alaska. Rept. U.S. Comm. Fish. 1906 (1907), Spec. Pap. Bur. Fish. Doc. 627. 112 pp.

Chatwin, B. M. 1953. Age and size of chum salmon from the Johnstone Strait area. Fish. Res. Bd. Canada, Prog. Rept. Pac. Coast Sta. 97:9-10.

Cheek, R. P. 1968. The American shad. U.S. Fish Wildl. Serv. Fishery Leaflet 614. 13 pp.

Chen, L. C. 1969. The biology and taxonomy of the burbot, *Lota lota leptura,* in interior Alaska. Biol. Pap. Univ. Alaska 11:1-51.

Cheney, W. L. 1971. Life history investigations of northern pike in the Tanana River drainage. Alaska Dept. Fish Game. Fed. Aid Fish Restor., Ann. Prog. Rept., Project F-9-3, Study R-III. 12:1-24.

Cheney, W. L. 1972. Life history investigations of northern pike in the Tanana River drainage. Alaska Dept. Fish Game. Fed. Aid Fish Restor., Ann. Prog. Rept., Project F-9-4, Study R-III. 13:1-30.

Chlupach, R. S. 1975. Studies of introduced blackfish in waters of southcentral Alaska. Alaska Dept. Fish Game. Fed. Aid Fish Restor., Ann. Performance Rept., Project F-9-7, Study G-II. 16:62-78.

Christie, W. J. 1963. Effects of artificial propagation and the weather on recruitment in the Lake Ontario whitefish fishery. J. Fish. Res. Bd. Canada 20(3):597-646.

Clark, C. F. 1950. Observations on the spawning habits of the northern pike, *Esox lucius,* in northwestern Ohio. Copeia 1950(4):285-288.

Clary, J. R. 1972. Predation on the brown trout by the slimy sculpin. Prog. Fish-Cult. 34(2):91-95.

Claussen, L. G. 1959. A southern range extension of the American shad to Todos Santos Bay, Baja California, Mexico. Calif. Fish Game 45(3):217-218.

Clemens, H. P. 1951a. The food of the burbot *Lota lota maculosa* (LeSueur) in Lake Erie. Trans. Amer. Fish. Soc. 80:56-66.

Clemens, H. P. 1951b. The growth of the burbot *Lota lota maculosa* (LeSueur) in Lake Erie. Trans. Amer. Fish. Soc. 80:163-173.

Clemens, W. A. 1928. The food of trout from the streams of Oneida County, New York State. Trans. Amer. Fish. Soc. 58:183-197.

Clemens, W. A., and G. V. Wilby. 1946. Fishes of the Pacific coast of Canada. Bull. Fish. Res. Bd. Canada 68. 368 pp.

Clemens, W. A., and G. V. Wilby. 1961. Fishes of the Pacific coast of Canada. Bull. Fish. Res. Bd. Canada. 68 (2 ed.). 443 pp.

Cobb, J. N. 1927. Pacific cod fisheries. Rept. U.S. Comm. Fish. (1926), App. 7:385-499.

Coble, D. W. 1961. Influence of water exchange and dissolved oxygen in redds on survival of steelhead trout embryos. Trans. Amer. Fish. Soc. 90(4):469-474.

Cohen, D. M. 1954. Age and growth studies on two species of whitefishes from Point Barrow, Alaska. Stanford Ichthyol. Bull. 4:168-187.

Cooper, A. C. 1965. The effect of transported stream sediments on the survival of sockeye and pink salmon eggs and alevins. Bull. Int. Pac. Salmon Fish. Comm. 18:1-71.

Cooper, E. L. 1951. Validation of the use of scales of brook trout, *Salvelinus fontinalis,* for age determination. Copeia 1951(2):141-148.

Cooper, E. L. 1970. Growth of cutthroat trout *(Salmo clarki)* in Chef Creek, Vancouver Island, British Columbia. J. Fish. Res. Bd. Canada 27(11):2063-2070.

Corson, B. W. 1955. Four years progress in the use of artificially controlled light to induce early spawning in brook trout. Prog. Fish-Cult. 17(3):99-102.

Craig, J. A., and R. L. Hacker. 1940. The history and development of the fisheries of the Columbia River. Bull. U.S. Bur. Fish. 49(32):133-216.

Craig, P. C. 1977. Ecological studies of anadromous and resident populations of arctic charr in the Canning River drainage and adjacent coastal waters of the Beaufort Sea, Alaska. Arctic Gas Biol. Rept. Series 41(1):1-116.

Craig, P. C., and L. Haldorson. 1979. Ecology of fishes in Simpson Lagoon, Beaufort Sea, Alaska. Ann. Rept. Beaufort Sea Barrier Island-Lagoon Ecological Process Studies. OCSEAP, NOAA, Boulder, Colorado. 100 p. Processed.

Craig, P. C., and J. Wells. 1976. Life history notes for a population of slimy sculpin *(Cottus cognatus)* in an Alaskan arctic stream. J. Fish. Res. Bd. Canada 33(7):1639-1642.

Creaser, C. W. 1926. The establishment of the Atlantic smelt in the upper waters of the Great Lakes. Pap. Mich. Acad. Sci. Arts Lett. 5:405-423.

Creaser, C. W. 1929. The food of yearling smelt from Michigan. Pap. Mich. Acad. Sci. Arts Lett. 10:427-431.

Crossman, E. J., and K. Buss. 1966. Artificial hybrid between kokanee *(Oncorhynchus nerka)* and brook trout *(Salvelinus fontinalis).* Copeia 1966(2):357-359.

Dall, W. H. 1898. The Yukon Territory. Downey and Co., London. 438 pp.

Davidson, F. A., and S. J. Hutchinson. 1938. The geographical distribution and environmental limits of the Pacific salmon (genus *Oncorhynchus).* Bull. U.S. Bur. Fish. 48(26):667-692.

Davis, B. J., and R. J. Miller. 1967. Brain patterns in minnows of the genus *Hybopsis* in relation to feeding habits and habitat. Copeia 1967(1):1-39.

Davis, W. S. 1957. Ova production of American shad in Atlantic coast rivers. U.S. Fish Wildl. Serv. Res. Rept. 49:1-5.

Deason, H. J. 1939. The distribution of cottid fishes in Lake Michigan. Pap. Mich. Acad. Sci. Arts, Lett. 24(2):105-115.

Dees, L. T. 1961. Sturgeons. U.S. Fish Wildl. Serv. Fishery Leaflet 526. 8 pp.

DeGraaf, D. 1974. Life history of the pond smelt, *Hypomesus olidus* Pallas (Osmeridae), in a small unnamed lake in the northern Yukon Territory. Canad. Arctic Gas Study Ltd./Alaskan Arctic Gas Study Co., Biol. Rept. Series 18(2):1-89.

DeLacy, A. C., and W. M. Morton. 1943. Taxonomy and habits of the charrs, *Salvelinus malma* and *Salvelinus alpinus,* of the Karluk drainage system. Trans Amer. Fish. Soc. 72:79-82.

Delisle, C., and W. VanVliet. 1968. First records of the sculpins *Myoxocephalus thompsonii* and *Cottus ricei* from the Ottawa valley, southwestern Quebec. J. Fish. Res. Bd. Canada 25(12):2733-2737.

DeRoche, S. E., and L. H. Bond. 1957. The lake trout of Cold Stream Pond, Enfield, Maine. Trans. Amer. Fish. Soc. 85:257-270.

DeWitt, J. W., Jr. 1954. A survey of the coast cutthroat trout, *Salmo clarki clarki* Richardson, in California. Calif. Fish Game 40(3):329-335.

Dizon, A. E., R. M. Horrall and A. D. Hasler. 1973a. Long term olfactory "memory" in coho salmon, *Oncorhynchus kisutch.* Fish. Bull. 71(1):315-317.

Dizon, A. E., R. M. Horrall and A. D. Hasler. 1973b. Olfactory encephalographic responses of homing coho salmon, *Oncorhynchus kisutch,* to water conditioned by conspecifics. Fish. Bull. 71(3):893-896.

Dodge, D. P., and H. R. MacCrimmon. 1970. Vital statistics of a population of Great Lakes rainbow trout *(Salmo gairdneri)* characterized by an extended spawning season. J. Fish. Res. Bd. Canada 27(3):613-618.

Donaldson, L. R., and G. H. Allen. 1958. Return of silver salmon, *Oncorhynchus kisutch* (Walbaum), to point of release. Trans. Amer. Fish. Soc. 87:13-22.

Drucker, B. 1972. Some life history characteristics of coho salmon of the Karluk River system, Kodiak Island, Alaska. Fish. Bull. 70(1):79-94.

Dryer, W. R. 1963. Age and growth of the whitefish in Lake Superior. Fish Bull. U.S. Fish Wildl. Serv. 63(1):77-95.

Dryer, W. R. 1964. Movements, growth, and rate of recapture of whitefish tagged in the Apostle Islands area of Lake Superior. Fish. Bull. U.S. Fish Wildl. Serv. 63(3):611-618.

Dryer, W. R. 1966. Bathymetric distribution of fish in the Apostle Islands region, Lake Superior. Trans. Amer. Fish. Soc. 95(3):248-259.

Dryer, W. R., L. F. Erkkila and C. L. Tetzloff. 1965. Food of lake trout in Lake Superior. Trans. Amer. Fish. Soc. 94(2):169-176.

Dryfoos, R. L. 1961. Four range extensions of fishes from the northeastern Pacific. Copeia 1961(4):476-477.

Dunbar, M. J., and H. H. Hildebrand. 1952. Contribution to the study of the fishes of Ungava Bay. J. Fish. Res. Bd. Canada 9(2):83-128.

Dyatlov, M. A. 1974. Nekotorye dannye o biologii ladozhskoi rogatki *Myoxocephalus quadricornis lonnbergi* Berg. Vopr. Ikhtiol. 14(1):171-173.

Dymond. J. R. 1937. New records of Ontario fishes. Copeia 1937(1):59.

Dymond, J. R. 1943. The coregonine fishes of northwestern Canada. Contrib. Roy. Ontario Mus. Zool. 24:171-232. Reprinted from Trans. Roy. Canadian Inst. 24(2):171-231.

Eddy, S., and T. Surber. 1947. Northern fishes with special reference to the upper Mississippi valley. Univ. Minnesota Press, Minneapolis. 276 pp.

Eigenmann, C. H. 1894. *Cymatogaster aggregatus* Gibbons; a contribution to the ontogeny of viviparous fishes. p. 401-478. *In:* Eigenmann, C. L. On the viviparous fishes of the Pacific coast of North America. Bull. U.S. Bur. Fish. 12:381-478.

Eigenmann, C. L., and A. B. Ulrey. 1894. A review of the Embiotocidae. p. 382-400. *In:* Eigenmann, C. L. On the viviparous fishes of the Pacific coast of North America. Bull. U.S. Bur. Fish. 12:381-478.

Embody, G. C. 1934. Relation of temperature to the incubation periods of eggs of four species of trout. Trans. Amer. Fish. Soc. 64:281-292.

Emery, A. R. 1973. Sediments of deep Canadian shield lakes: Observations of gross structure and biological significance. Science 181(4100):655-657.

Erkkila, L. F., J. W. Moffett, O. B. Cope, B. R. Smith and R. S. Nielson. 1950. Sacramento—San Joaquin fishery resources: Effects of Tracy pumping plant and delta cross channel. U.S. Fish Wildl. Serv. Spec. Sci. Rept. Fisheries 56. 109 pp.

Eschmeyer, P. H. 1955. The reproduction of lake trout in southern Lake Superior. Trans. Amer. Fish. Soc. 84:47-74.

Eschmeyer, P. H., and R. M. Bailey. 1955. The pygmy whitefish, *Coregonus coulteri,* in Lake Superior. Trans. Amer. Fish. Soc. 84:161-199.

Eschmeyer, P. H., R. Daly and L. F. Erkkila. 1953. The movement of tagged lake trout in Lake Superior, 1950-52. Trans. Amer. Fish. Soc. 82:68-77.

Esipov, V. K. 1949. Promyslovye ryby SSSR. (Commercial fish of the USSR). (Not seen. Cited by Andriyashev, 1954).

Everhart, W. H. 1958. Fishes of Maine. 2 ed. Maine Dept. Inl. Fish Game. 94 pp.

Evermann, B. W., and E. L. Goldsborough. 1907. The fishes of Alaska. Bull. U.S. Bur. Fish. 26:219-360.

Faber, D. J. 1970. Ecological observations on newly hatched lake whitefish in South Bay, Lake Huron. p. 481-500. *In:* Lindsey, C. C., and C. S. Woods (eds.). Biology of coregonid fishes. Univ. Manitoba Press, Winnipeg.

Fabricius, E. 1953. Aquarium observations on the spawning behaviour of the char, *Salmo alpinus.* Rept. Inst. Freshwater Res. Drottningholm 34:14-48.

Fabricius, E. 1954. Aquarium observations on the spawning behaviour of the burbot, *Lota vulgaris* L. Rept. Inst. Freshwater Res. Drottningholm 35:51-57.

Fabricius, E., and K.-J. Gustafson. 1954. Further aquarium observations on the spawning behaviour of the char, *Salmo alpinus* L. Rept. Inst. Freshwater Res. Drottningholm 35:58-104.

Fabricius, E., and K.-J. Gustafson. 1958. Some new observations on the spawning behavior of the pike, *Esox lucius* L. Rept. Inst. Freshwater Res. Drottningholm 39:23-54.

Fiedler, R. H. 1943. Fishery statistics of the United States 1940. U.S. Fish Wildl. Serv., Stat. Digest 4.

Finger, G., and R. H. Armstrong. 1965. Fishery and biological characteristics of salmon caught by sport gear in southeastern Alaska. Alaska Dept. Fish Game Info. Leaflet 57:1-58.

Fish, M. P. 1932. Contributions to the early life histories of sixty-two species of fishes from Lake Erie and its tributary waters. Bull. U.S. Bur. Fish 47, Bull. 10:293-398.

Foerster, R. E., and W. E. Ricker, 1941. The effect of reduction of predacious fishes on survival of young sockeye salmon at Cultus Lake. J. Fish. Res. Bd. Canada 5(4):315-336.

Follett, W. I. 1954. The case of the piebald flounder. Pac. Discovery 7(5):24-25.

Forrester, C. R. 1964. Laboratory observations on embryonic development and larvae of the Pacific cod *(Gadus macrocephalus* Tilesius). J. Fish. Res. Bd. Canada 21(1):9-16.

Forrester, C. R. 1969a. Sinistrality in *Platichthys stellatus* of British Columbia. J. Fish. Res. Bd. Canada 26(1):191-196.

Forrester, C. R. 1969b. Life history information on some groundfish species. Fish. Res. Bd. Canada, Tech. Rept. 105:1-17.

Forrester, C. R., and D. R. Alderdice. 1966. Effects of salinity and temperature on embryonic development of the Pacific cod *(Gadus macrocephalus).* J. Fish. Res. Bd. Canada 23(3):319-340.

Forrester, C. R., and K. S. Ketchen. 1955. Preliminary results of gray cod tagging in Georgia strait in the winter of 1954-1955. Fish. Res. Bd. Canada, Prog. Rept. Pac. Sta. 103:8-10.

Foskett, D. R. 1951. Young salmon in the Nanaimo area. Fish. Res. Bd. Canada, Prog. Rept. Pac. Coast Sta. 86:18-19.

Franklin, D. R., and L. L. Smith, Jr. 1960. Note on the early growth and allometry of the northern pike, *Esox lucius* L. Copeia 1960(2):143-144.

Franklin, D. R., and L. L. Smith, Jr. 1963. Early life history of the northern pike, *Esox lucius* L., with special reference to the factors influencing the numerical strength of year classes. Trans. Amer. Fish. Soc. 92(2):91-110.

French, R. R., and R. G. Bakkala. 1974. A new model of ocean migration of Bristol Bay sockeye salmon. Fish. Bull. 72(2):589-614.

French, R. R., and R. J. Wahle. 1959. Biology of chinook and blueback salmon and steelhead in the Wenatchee River system. U.S. Fish Wildl. Serv. Spec. Sci. Rept. Fisheries 304. 17 pp.

Frost, W. E. 1954. The food of the pike, *Esox lucius* L., in Windermere. J. Anim. Ecol. 23:339-360.

Fujita, T., and S. Kokubo. 1927. Studies on herring. Bull. Sch. Fish. Hokkaido Univ. 1(1):1-141. (Not seen. Cited by Shmidt 1950).

Fuller, W. A. 1955. The inconnu *(Stenodus leucichthys mackenziei)* in Great Slave Lake and adjoining waters. J. Fish. Res. Bd. Canada 12(5):768-780.

Furniss, R. A. 1974. Inventory and cataloging of Arctic area waters. Alaska Dept. Fish Game. Fed. Aid Fish Restor., Ann. Performance Rept., Project F-9-6, Job G-I-I. 15:1-45.

Garside, E. T., and J. S. Tait. 1958. Preferred temperature of rainbow trout *(Salmo gairdneri* Richardson) and its unusual relationship to acclimation temperature. Canadian J. Zool. 36(3):563-567.

Gazeteer of Canada. 1971. Northwest Territories. Surveys and Mapping Branch; Dept. Energy, Mines, Resources. 74 pp.

Geen, G. H., T. H. Northcote, G. F. Hartman and C. C. Lindsey. 1966. Life histories of two species of catostomid fishes in Sixteenmile Lake, British Columbia, with particular reference to inlet stream spawning. J. Fish. Res. Bd. Canada 23(11):1761-1788.

Gilbert, C. H. 1895. The ichthyological collections of the steamer *Albatross* during the years 1890 and 1891. Rept. U.S. Comm. Fish. 19:393-476.

Gilbert, C. H. 1924. The salmon of the Yukon River. Bull. U.S. Bur. Fish 38:317-332.

Godfrey, H. 1959. Variations in annual average weight of British Columbia pink salmon, 1944-1958. J. Fish. Res. Bd. Canada 16(3):329-337.

Gordon, C. D. 1965. Aspects of the age and growth of *Cymatogaster aggregata.* M.S. Thesis, Univ. British Columbia, Vancouver. 90 pp. (Not seen. Cited by Hart, 1973).

Gordon, W. G. 1961. Food of the American smelt in Saginaw Bay, Lake Huron. Trans. Amer. Fish. Soc. 90(4):439-443.

Gould, H. 1938. They came in millions. Alaska Sportsman 4(5):12, 24.

Grainger, E. H. 1953. On the age, growth, migration, reproductive potential and feeding habits of the Arctic char (Salvelinus alpinus) of Frobisher Bay, Baffin Island. J. Fish. Res. Bd. Canada 10(6):326-370.

Greeley, J. R. 1932. The spawning habits of brook, brown and rainbow trout, and the problem of egg predators. Trans. Amer. Fish. Soc. 62:239-248.

Green, J. M. 1971. Local distribution of *Oligocottus maculosus* Girard and other tide pool cottids of the west coast of Vancouver Island, British Columbia. Canad. J. Zool. 49(8):1111-1128.

Greenbank, J. 1957. Aggregational behavior in a freshwater sculpin. Copeia 1957(2):157.

Greenbank, J., and P. R. Nelson. 1959. Life history of the threespine stickleback *Gasterosteus aculeatus* Linnaeus in Karluk Lake and Bare Lake, Kodiak Island, Alaska. Fish. Bull. U.S. Fish Wildl. Serv. 59(153):537-559.

Griffiths, W. B., J. K. den Beste and P. C. Craig. 1977. Fisheries investigations in a coastal region of the Beaufort Sea (Kaktovik Lagoon, Alaska). Arctic Gas Biol. Rept. Serv. 40(2):1-190.

Griffiths, W., P. C. Craig, G. Walder and G. Mann. 1975. Fisheries investigations in a coastal region of the Beaufort Sea (Nunaluk Lagoon, Yukon Territory). Arctic Gas Biol. Rept. Serv. 34(2):1-219.

Griswold, B. L., and L. L. Smith, Jr. 1973. The life history and trophic relationship of the ninespine stickleback, *Pungitius pungitius,* in the Apostle Islands area of Lake Superior. Fish. Bull. 71(4):1039-1060.

Groot, C. 1965. On the orientation of young sockeye salmon *(Oncorhynchus nerka)* during their seaward migration out of lakes. Behaviour, Supp. 14:1-198.

Gudger, E. W. 1941. A totally ambicolorate flounder, *Platichthys stellatus,* from Alaskan waters. Copeia 1941(1):28-30.

Gudger, E. W. 1942. Giant fishes of North America. Nat. Hist. 49:115-121.

Günther, A.C.L.G. 1877. An account of the fishes collected by Capt. Fielden between 78° and 83° N. lat. during the Arctic Expedition of 1875-76. Proc. Zool. Soc. London 1877:293-295.

Gunter, G. 1942. A list of fishes of the mainland of North and Middle America recorded from both freshwater and sea water. Amer. Midl. Nat. 28(2):305-326.

Hacker, V. A. 1957 Biology and management of lake trout in Green Lake, Wisconsin. Trans. Amer. Fish. Soc. 86:71-83.

Hagen, D. W. 1967. Isolating mechanisms in threespine sticklebacks *(Gasterosteus).* J. Fish. Res. Bd. Canada 24(8):1637-1692.

Hagen, D. W., and L. G. Gilbertson. 1973. Selective predation and the intensity of selection acting upon the lateral plates of threespine sticklebacks. Heredity 30:373-387.

Hagen, D. W., and J. D. McPhail. 1970. The species problem within *Gasterosteus aculeatus* on the Pacific coast of North America. J. Fish. Res. Bd. Canada 27(1):147-155.

Haley, A. J. 1952. Preliminary observations on a severe epidemic of microsporidiosis in the smelt, *Osmerus mordax* (Mitchill). J. Parasit. 38(2):183.

Hanamura, N. 1966. Salmon of the north Pacific Ocean—Part III. A review of the life history of North Pacific salmon. 1. Sockeye salmon in the far east. Bull. Int. N. Pac. Fish. Comm. 18:1-28.

Hanavan, M. G. 1954. Survival of pink-salmon spawn in the intertidal area with special reference to influence of crowding. Fish. Bull. U.S. Fish Wildl. Serv. 56(95):167-176.

Hanavan, M. G., and G. K. Tanonaka. 1959. Experimental fishing to determine distribution of salmon in the North Pacific Ocean and Bering Sea, 1956. U.S. Fish Wildl. Serv. Spec. Sci. Rept. Fisheries 302. 22 pp.

Hankinson, T. L., and C. L. Hubbs. 1922. The establishment of the smelt in Great Lakes waters. Copeia 109:57-59.

Harper, F. 1948. Fishes of the Nueltin Lake expedition, Keewatin, 1947. Part 2—Historical and field notes. Proc. Acad. Nat. Sci. Phila. 50:153-184.

Harris, R.H.D. 1962. Growth and reproduction of the longnose sucker, *Catostomus catostomus* (Forster), in Great Slave Lake. J. Fish. Res. Bd. Canada 19(1):113-126.

Hart, J. L. 1930. The spawning and early life history of the whitefish, *Coregonus clupeaformis,* in the Bay of Quinte, Ontario. Contr. Canadian Biol. Fish. 6(7):167-214.

Hart, J. L. 1949. Food of fish of the cod family. Fish. Res. Bd. Canada, Prog. Rept. Pac. Stations 79:35-36.

Hart, J. L. 1973. Pacific fishes of Canada. Bull. Fish. Res. Bd. Canada 180. 740 pp.

Hart, J. L., and J. L. McHugh. 1944. The smelts (Osmeridae) of British Columbia. Bull. Fish. Res. Bd. Canada 64. 27 pp.

Hartman, G. F. 1965. The role of behavior in the ecology and interaction of underyearling coho salmon *(Oncorhynchus kisutch)* and steelhead trout *(Salmo gairdneri)*. J. Fish. Res. Bd. Canada 22(4):1035-1081.

Hartman, G. F., and C. A. Gill. 1968. Distribution of juvenile steelhead and cutthroat trout *(Salmo gairdneri* and *S. clarki clarki)* within streams in southwestern British Columbia. J. Fish. Res. Bd. Canada 25(1):33-48.

Hartman, G. F., T. G. Northcote and C. C. Lindsey. 1962. Comparison of inlet and outlet spawning runs of rainbow trout in Loon Lake, British Columbia, J. Fish. Res. Bd. Canada 19(2):173-200.

Hartman, W. L. 1959. Biology and vital statistics of rainbow trout in the Finger Lakes region, New York. N.Y. Fish Game Jour. 6(2):121-178.

Hartman, W. L., C. W. Strickland and D. T. Hoopes. 1962. Survival and behavior of sockeye salmon fry migrating into Brooks Lake, Alaska. Trans. Amer. Fish. Soc. 91(2):133-139.

Hasler, A. D. 1966. Underwater guideposts: homing of salmon. Univ. Wisconsin Press, Madison. 155 pp.

Hayes, M. L. 1956. Life history studies of two species of suckers in Shadow Mountain Reservoir, Grand County, Colorado. M.S. Thesis, Colorado A and M College, Fort Collins. 126 pp. (Not seen. Cited by Carlander, 1969).

Hazzard, A. S. 1932. Some phases of the life history of the eastern brook trout, *Salvelinus fontinalis* Mitchill. Trans. Amer. Fish. Soc. 62:344-350.

Heard, W. R. 1965. Limnetic cottid larvae and their utilization as food by juvenile sockeye salmon. Trans. Amer. Fish. Soc. 94(2):191-193.

Heard, W. R. 1966. Observations on lampreys in the Naknek River system of southwest Alaska. Copeia 1966(2):332-339.

Heard, W. R., and W. L. Hartman. 1966. Pygmy whitefish *Prosopium coulteri* in the Naknek River system of southwest Alaska. Fish. Bull. U.S. Fish Wildl. Serv. 65(3):555-579.

Heiser, D. W. 1966. Age and growth of anadromous Dolly Varden char *Salvelinus malma* (Walbaum) in Eva Creek, Baranof Island, southeastern Alaska. Alaska Dept. Fish Game Res. Rept. 5:1-29.

Henderson, N. E. 1963. Influence of light and temperature on the reproductive cycle of the eastern brook trout, *Salvelinus fontinalis* (Mitchill). J. Fish. Res. Bd. Canada 20(4):859-897.

Herald, E. S. 1941. First record of the hybrid flounder, *Inopsetta ischyra,* from California. Calif. Fish Game 27(2):44-46.

Hewson, L. C. 1955. Age, maturity, spawning and food of burbot, *Lota lota,* in Lake Winnipeg. J. Fish. Res. Bd. Canada 12(6):930-940.

Higley, D. L., and C. E. Bond. 1973. Ecology and production of juvenile spring chinook salmon, *Oncorhynchus tshawytscha,* in a eutrophic reservoir. Fish. Bull. 71(3):877-891.

Hildebrand, S. F. 1963. Family Clupeidae. Fishes of the western North Atlantic. Mem. Sears Foundation Mar. Res. 1(3): 257-454.

Hildebrand, S. F., and I. L. Towers. 1927. Food of trout in Fish Lake, Utah. Ecology 8(4):389-397.

Hoag, S. H. 1972. The relationship between the summer food of juvenile sockeye salmon, *Oncorhynchus nerka,* and the standing stock of zooplankton in Iliamna Lake, Alaska. Fish. Bull. 70(2): 355-362.

Hoar, W. S. 1956. The behavior of migrating pink and chum salmon fry. J. Fish. Res. Bd. Canada 13(3):309-325.

Hochachka, P. W., and A. C. Sinclair. 1962. Glycogen stores in trout tissues before and after stream planting. J. Fish. Res. Bd. Canada 19(1):127-136.

Hognestad, P. T. 1968. Observations on the polar cod in the Barents Sea. Rapp. Proc. Verb. Cons. Perm. Internat. Explor. Mer 158:126-130.

Hollis, E. H. 1948. The homing tendency of shad. Science 108:332-333.

Hoogland, R., D. Morris and N. Tinbergen. 1957. The spines of sticklebacks *(Gasterosteus* and *Pygosteus)* as means of defense against predators *(Perca* and *Esox)*. Behaviour 10:205-236.

Hoopes, D. T. 1962. Ecological distribution of spawning sockeye salmon in three lateral streams, Brooks Lake, Alaska. Ph.D. Thesis, Iowa St. Univ., Ames. 235 pp.

Hoopes, D. T. 1972. Selection of spawning sites by sockeye salmon in small streams. Fish. Bull. 70(2):447-458.

Hoover, E. E. 1936. The spawning activities of fresh water smelt with special reference to the sex ratio. Copeia 1936(2):85-91.

Hourston, A. S. 1958. Population studies on juvenile herring in Barkley Sound, British Columbia. J. Fish. Res. Bd. Canada 15(5):909-960.

Hourston, A. S. 1959. Effects of some aspects of environment on the distribution of juvenile herring in Barkley Sound. J. Fish. Res. Bd. Canada 16(3):283-308.

Houston, A. H. 1961. Influence of size upon the adaptation of steelhead trout *(Salmo gairdneri)* and chum salmon *(Oncorhynchus keta)* to sea water. J. Fish. Res. Bd. Canada 18(3):401-415.

Hubbs, C. 1947. Mixture of marine and fresh-water fishes in the lower Salinas River, California. Copeia 1947(2):147-149.

Hubbs, C. L. 1917. The breeding habits of the viviparous perch. Cymatogaster. Copeia 47:72-74.

Hubbs, C. L. 1921. Notes on Cottus asper and Cottus aleuticus. Copeia 90:7-8.

Hubbs, C. L. 1925. A revision of the osmerid fishes of the North Pacific. Proc. Biol. Soc. Wash. 38:49-56.

Hubbs, C. L. 1946. Wandering of pink salmon and other salmonid fishes into southern California. Calif. Fish Game 32(2):81-86.

Hubbs, C. L., and L. C. Hubbs. 1944. Bilateral symmetry and bilateral variation in fishes. Pap. Mich. Acad. Sci. Arts Lett. 30:229-310.

Hubbs, C. L., and K. Kuronuma. 1942. Hybridization in nature between two genera of flounders in Japan. Pap. Mich. Acad. Sci. Arts Lett. 27:267-306.

Hubbs, C. L., and K. F. Lagler. 1949. Fishes of Isle Royale, Lake Superior, Michigan. Pap. Michigan Acad. Sci. Arts Lett. 33:73-133.

Hume, L. C. 1955. Rainbow trout spawn twice a year. Calif. Fish Game 41(1):117.

Hunt, B. P., and W. F. Carbine. 1951. Food of young pike, *Esox lucius* L., and associated fishes in Peterson's Ditches, Houghton Lake, Michigan. Trans. Amer. Fish. Soc. 80:67-83.

Hunter, J. G. 1959. Survival and production of pink and chum salmon in a coastal stream. J. Fish. Res. Bd. Canada 16(6): 835-886.

Hynes, H.B.N. 1950. The food of fresh-water sticklebacks *(Gasterosteus aculeatus* and *Pygosteus pungitius),* with a review of methods used in studies of the food of fishes. J. Anim. Ecol. 19:36-58.

Ikesumiju, K. 1975. Aspects of the ecology and life history of the sculpin, *Cottus aleuticus* (Gilbert), in Lake Washington. J. Fish. Biol. 7(2): 235-246.

Ince, B. W., and A. Thorpe. 1976. The effects of starvation and force-feeding on the metabolism of the northern pike, *Esox lucius* L. J. Fish Biol. 8(1):79-88.

Isakson, J. S., C. A. Simenstad and R. L. Burgner. 1971. Fish communities and food chains in the Amchitka area. Bioscience 21(12):666-670.

Ivanova, E. I. 1952. On finding smallmouth smelt in northern Europe. (In Russian). Tr. Vses. Gidrobiol. Obshchest. 4:252-259. (Not seen. Cited by McAllister, 1963).

Jensen, A. S. 1926. Investigations of the "Dana" in West Greenland waters, 1925. Rapp. Proc. Verb. Cons. Perm. Internat. Explor. Mer 39:85-102.

Johnson, L. 1966. Experimental determination of food consumption of pike, *Esox lucius,* for growth and maintenance. J. Fish. Res. Bd. Canada 23(10):1495-1505.

Johnson, L. 1975. Distribution of fish species in Great Bear Lake, Northwest Territories, with reference to zooplankton, benthic invertebrates, and environmental conditions. J. Fish. Res. Bd. Canada 32(11):1989-2004.

Jonas, R.E.E., H. S. Shedev and N. Tomlinson. 1962. Blood pH and mortality in rainbow trout *(Salmo gairdneri)* and sockeye salmon *(Oncorhynchus nerka).* J. Fish. Res. Bd. Canada 19(4):619-624.

Jones, A. C. 1962. The biology of the euryhaline fish Leptocottus armatus Girard (Cottidae). Univ. California Publ. Zool. 67:321-367.

Jones, D. E. 1973. Steelhead and sea-run cutthroat life history in southeast Alaska. Alaska Dept. Fish Game. Ann. Prog. Rept., Anad. Fish Stud., AFS-42-1. 14:1-18.

Jones, D. E. 1975. Steelhead and sea-run cutthroat trout life history study in southeast Alaska. Alaska Dept. Fish Game. Ann. Perform. Rept., Anad. Fish Stud., AFS-42-3. 16:1-42.

Jones, J. W., and H.B.N. Hynes. 1950. The age and growth of *Gasterosteus aculeatus, Pygosteus pungitius* and *Spinachia vulgaris,* as shown by their otoliths. J. Anim. Ecol. 19:59-73.

Jordan, D. S. 1884. The flat fishes and soles of the Pacific coast. p. 184-189. *In:* Goode, G. B. The fisheries and fishery industries of the United States. Section I. Natural history of useful aquatic animals. Part III. Fishes. Gov't. Printing Office, Washington, D.C.

Jordan, D. S., and B. W. Evermann. 1896. The fishes of North and Middle America. Bull. U.S. Nat. Mus. 47(1):1-954.

Jordan, D. S., and B. W. Evermann. 1908. American food and game fishes. Doubleday, Page and Co., N.Y. 572 pp.

Jordan, D. S., B. W. Evermann and H. W. Clark. 1930. Check-list of the fishes and fishlike vertebrates of North and Middle American north of the northern boundary of Venezuela and Columbia. Rep. U.S. Comm. Fish. 1928(1930), App. X. 670 pp.

Jordan, D. S., and C. H. Gilbert. 1882. Synopsis of the fishes of North America. Bull. U.S. Nat. Mus. 16. 1018 pp.

Jordan, D. S., and C. W. Metz. 1913. A catalogue of the fishes known from the waters of Korea. Mem. Carnegie Mus. 6:1-65.

Karzanovskii, M. Y. 1962. Food of migrating fry of *Oncorhynchus gorbuscha* and *Salvelinus malma* in the rivers of Sakhalin. Rybnoe Khoz. 38(6):24-25. (Biol. Abst. 41(5): Abst. No. 20992).

Karzinkin, G. S. 1951. K normativam kormleniia molodi osetrovykh u belorybitsy. Trudy Vses. Nauchno-issled. Inst. Morsk. Ryb. Khoz. Okeanogr. 19:25-38.

Katz, M. 1948. The fecundity of herring from various parts of the north Pacific. Trans. Amer. Fish. Soc. 75:72-76.

Keleher, J. J. 1961. Comparison of largest Great Slave Lake fish with North American records. J. Fish. Res. Bd. Canada 18(3):417-421.

Kendall, W. C. 1921. Further observations on Coulter's whitefish. Copeia 1921(90):1-4.

Kendall, W. C. 1927. The smelts. Bull. U.S. Bur. Fish. 42:217-375.

Kendall, W. C., and E. L. Goldsborough. 1908. The fishes of the Connecticut Lakes and adjacent waters, with notes on the plankton environment. 77 p. *In:* Rept. U.S. Comm. Fish. 1907. Bur. Fish Doc. 633.

Kennedy, W. A. 1953. Growth, maturity, fecundity and mortality in the relatively unexploited whitefish, Coregonus clupeaformis, of Great Slave Lake. J. Fish. Res. Bd. Canada 10(7): 413-441.

Kennedy, W. A. 1954. Growth, maturity and mortality in the relatively unexploited lake trout, *Cristivomer namaycush,* of Great Slave Lake. J. Fish. Res. Bd. Canada 11(6):827-852.

Kepler, P. P. 1973. Population studies of northern pike and whitefish in the Minto Flats complex with emphasis on the Chatanika River. Alaska Dept. Fish Game. Fed. Aid Fish Restor., Ann. Progress Rept., Project F-9-5, Job G-II-J. 14:59-81.

Ketchen, K. S. 1961. Observations on the ecology of the Pacific cod *(Gadus macrocephalus)* in Canadian waters. J. Fish. Res. Bd. Canada 18(4):513-558.

Ketchen, K. S. 1964. Preliminary results of studies on growth and mortality of Pacific cod *(Gadus macrocephalus)* in Hecate Strait, British Columbia. J. Fish. Res. Bd. Canada 21(5):1051-1067.

Kimsey, J. B. 1951. Notes on kokanee spawning in Donner Lake, California, 1949. Calif. Fish Game 37(3):273-279.

Kimsey, J. B. 1960. Note on spring food habits of the lake trout, *Salvelinus namaycush.* Calif. Fish Game 46(2):229-230.

Kliewer, E. V. 1970. Gillraker variation and diet in lake whitefish *Coregonus clupeaformis* in northern Manitoba. p. 147-165. *In:* Lindsey, C. C., and C. S. Woods (eds.). Biology of coregonid fishes. Univ. Manitoba Press, Winnipeg.

Knight, A. E. 1963. The embryonic and larval development of the rainbow trout. Trans. Amer. Fish Soc. 92(4):344-355.

Koelz, W. 1929. Coregonid fishes of the Great Lakes. Bull. U.S. Bur. Fish. 43, Pt. 2:297-643.

Kogl, D. R. 1965. Springs and ground-water as factors affecting survival of chum salmon spawn in a sub-arctic stream. M.S. Thesis, Univ. Alaska, College. 59 pp.

Kogl, D. R. 1971. Monitoring and evaluation of Arctic waters with emphasis on the North Slope drainages: Colville River study. Alaska Dept. Fish Game. Fed. Aid Fish Restor., Ann. Progress Rept., Project F-9-3, Job G-III-A. 12:23-61.

Koster, W. J. 1936. The life history and ecology of the sculpins (Cottidae) of central New York. Ph.D. Thesis, Cornell Univ., Ithaca. 87 pp. and Appendix.

Koster, W. J. 1937. The food of sculpins (Cottidae) in central New York. Trans. Amer. Fish. Soc. 66:374-382.

Kramer, R. H., and L. L. Smith, Jr. 1965. Effects of suspended wood fiber on brown and rainbow trout eggs and alevins. Trans. Amer. Fish. Soc. 94(3):252-258.

Kratt, L. F., and R.J.F. Smith. 1978. Breeding tubercles occur on male and female arctic grayling *(Thymallus arcticus).* Copeia 1978 (1):185-188.

Krejsa, R. J. 1967a. The systematics of the prickly sculpin, *Cottus asper* Richardson, a polytypic species. Part I. Synonymy, nomenclatural history, and distribution. Pac. Sci. 21(2): 241-251.

Krejsa, R. J. 1967b. The systematics of the prickly sculpin, *Cottus asper* Richardson, a polytypic species. Part II. Studies of the life history, with especial reference to migration. Pac. Sci. 21(4):414-422.

Kruse, T. E. 1959. Grayling of Grebe Lake, Yellowstone National Park, Wyoming. Fish. Bull. U.S. Fish Wildl. Serv. 59(149): 307-351.

Kuntz, A., and L. Radcliffe. 1917. Notes on the embryology and larval development of twelve teleost fishes. Bull. U.S. Bur. Fish. 35:87-134.

Kuznetsov, N. F. 1932. O pomesyakh nel'my s sigovymi. pp. 47-66. *In:* Materialy k ikhtiofaune r. Leny. Tr. Kom. Izuch. Yakutsk SSSR 3. (English summary pp. 65-66).

Lagler, K. F. 1956. The pike, *Esox lucius* Linnaeus, in relation to waterfowl on the Seney National Wildlfe Refuge, Michigan. J. Wildl. Mgt. 20(2):114-124.

Lagler, K. F., and A. T. Wright. 1962. Predation of the Dolly Varden, *Salvelinus malma,* on young salmons, *Oncorhynchus* spp., in an estuary of southeastern Alaska. Trans. Amer. Fish. Soc. 91(1):90-93.

Laird, J. A. 1928. Grayling in the east. Trans. Amer. Fish. Soc. 58:167-169.

Langlois, T. H. 1935. Notes on the spawning habits of the Atlantic smelt. Copeia 1935(3):141-142.

Langlois, T. H. 1954. The western end of Lake Erie and its ecology. J. W. Edwards, Ann Arbor, Mich. 479 pp.

Lantz, A. W. 1962. Specialty fish products. Circ. (Gen Ser.) Biol. Sta. London, Ontario. 4:10-28. (Not seen. Cited by Scott and Crossman, 1973).

LaPerriere, J. D. 1973. Laboratory rearing experiments on artificially propagated inconnu *(Stenodus leucichthys).* Univ. Alaska, Inst. Water Resources, Rept. IWR-40. 25 pp. Processed.

LaPointe, D. F. 1958. Age and growth of the American shad, from three Atlantic rivers. Trans. Amer. Fish. Soc. 87:139-150.

Larson, K. W., and G. W. Brown, Jr. 1975. Systematic status of a midwater population of freshwater sculpin *(Cottus)* from Lake Washington, Seattle, Washington. J. Fish. Res. Bd. Canada 32(1):21-28.

Lawler, G. H. 1954. Observations on the trout perch *Percopsis omiscomaycus* (Walbaum), at Heming Lake, Manitoba. J. Fish. Res. Bd. Canada 11(1):1-4.

Lawler, G. H. 1960. A mutant pike, *Esox lucius.* J. Fish. Res. Bd. Canada 17(5):647-654.

Lawler, G. H. 1963. The biology and taxonomy of the burbot, *Lota lota,* in Heming Lake, Manitoba. J. Fish. Res. Bd. Canada 20(2):417-433.

Lawler, G. H. 1965a. Fluctuations in the success of year-classes of whitefish populations with special reference to Lake Erie. J. Fish. Res. Bd. Canada 22(5):1197-1227.

Lawler, G. H. 1965b. The food of the pike, *Esox lucius,* in Heming Lake, Manitoba. J. Fish. Res. Bd. Canada 22(6): 1357-1377.

Lawler, G. H., and M. Fitz-Earle. 1968. Marking small fish with stains for estimating populations at Heming Lake, Manitoba. J. Fish. Res. Bd. Canada 25(2):255-266.

LeBrasseur, R. J. 1965. Stomach contents of salmon and steelhead trout in the northeastern Pacific Ocean. J. Fish. Res. Bd. Canada 23(1):85-100.

LeBrasseur, R. J. 1966a. Stomach contents of salmon and steelhead trout in the northeastern Pacific Ocean. J. Fish. Res. Bd. Canada 23(1):85-100.

LeBrasseur, R. J. 1966b. Growth of juvenile chum salmon *(Oncorhynchus keta)* under different feeding regimes. J. Fish. Res. Bd. Canada 26(6):1631-1645.

LeBrasseur, R. J., and O. D. Kennedy. 1972. The fertilization of Great Central Lake. II. Zooplankton standing stock. Fish. Bull. 70(1):25-36.

LeBrasseur. R. J., and R. R. Parker. 1964. Growth rate of central British Columbia pink salmon *(Oncorhynchus gorbuscha).* J. Fish. Res. Bd. Canada 21(5):1101-1128.

Lehman, B. A. 1953. Fecundity of Hudson River shad. U.S. Fish Wildl. Serv. Res. Rept. 33: 1-8.

Leim, A. H. 1924. The life history of the shad *(Alosa sapidissima* (Wilson)) with special reference to the factors limiting its abundance. Contrib. Canadian Biol. NS 2(11):161-284.

Leim, A. H., and W. B. Scott. 1966. Fishes of the Atlantic coast of Canada. Bull. Fish. Res. Bd. Canada 155. 485 pp.

Levanidov, V. Y., and I. M. Levanidova. 1957. Food of downstream migrant young summer chum salmon and pink salmon in Amur tributaries. Isvest. Tikhookean. Nauchno-issled. Inst. Ryb. Khoz. Okeanogr. 45:3-16. (Not seen. Cited by Scott and Crossman, 1973).

Lewis, D. B., M. Walkey and H.J.G. Dartnall. 1972. Some effects of low oxygen tension on the distribution of the three-spined stickleback *Gasterosteus aculeatus* L. and the nine-spined stickleback *Pungitius pungitius* L. J. Fish Biol. 4(1):103-108.

Lievense, S. J. 1954. Spawning of American smelt, *Osmerus mordax,* in Crystal Lake, Benzie County, Michigan. Copeia 1954(3):232-233.

Lindsey, C. C. 1956. Distribution and taxonomy of fishes in the Mackenzie drainage of British Columbia. J. Fish. Res. Bd. Canada 13(6):759-789.

Lindsey, C. C. 1963a. Status of the whitefish species *Coregonus nelsonii* Bean, and designation of a new type. Copeia 1963(1): 173-174.

Lindsey, C. C. 1963b. Sympatric occurrence of two species of humpback whitefish in Squanga Lake, Yukon Territory. J. Fish. Res. Bd. Canada 20(3):749-767.

Lindsey, C. C. 1964. Problems in zoogeography of the lake trout, *Salvelinus namaycush.* J. Fish. Res. Bd. Canada 21(5): 977-994.

Lindsey, C. C., J. W. Clayton and W. G. Franzin. 1970. Zoogeographic problems and protein variation in the *Coregonus clupeaformis* whitefish species complex. p. 127-146. *In:* Lindsey, C. C., and C. S. Woods (eds.). Biology of coregonid fishes. Univ. Manitoba Press, Winnipeg.

Lindsey, C. C., T. G. Northcote and G. F. Hartman. 1959. Homing of rainbow trout to inlet and outlet spawning streams at Loon Lake, British Columbia. J. Fish. Res. Bd. Canada 16(5):695-719.

Loftus, K. H. 1958. Studies on river-spawning populations of lake trout in eastern Lake Superior. Trans. Amer. Fish. Soc. 87:259-277.

Loosanoff, V. L. 1937. The spawning run of the Pacific surf smelt, *Hypomesus pretiosus* [Girard]. Int. Rev. ges. Hydrobiol. 36:170-183.

Lord, R. F. 1932. Notes on Montana grayling at the Pittsford, Vt., experimental trout hatchery. Trans. Amer. Fish. Soc. 62:171-178.

Lorz, H. W., and T. G. Northcote. 1965. Factors affecting stream location, and timing and intensity of entry by spawning kokanee *(Oncorhynchus nerka)* into an inlet of Nicolai Lake, British Columbia. J. Fish. Res. Bd. Canada 22(3):665-687.

Lovetskaya, E. A. 1948. Materialy po biologii amurskoi kety. Izv. Tikhookean. Nauchno-issled. Inst. Ryb. Khoz. Okeanogr. 27:115-137.

Low, A. P. 1896. Report on explorations in the Labrador Peninsula along the East Main, Koksoak, Hamilton, Manicuagan and portions of other rivers in 1892-93-94-95. App. III. List of the principal food fishes of the Labrador Peninsula with short notes on their distribution. Ann. Rept. Geol. Surv. Canada NS8, Rept. L. 387 pp.

Lowry, G. R. 1965. Movement of cutthroat trout, *Salmo clarki clarki* (Richardson) in three Oregon coastal streams. Trans. Amer. Fish. Soc. 94(4):334-338.

Lowry, G. R. 1966. Production and food of cutthroat trout in three Oregon coastal streams. J. Wildl. Mgt. 30(4):754-767.

Lukyanichov, F. V., and P. Y. Tugarina. 1965. Ledovitomorskaya rogatka *Myoxocephalus quadricornis labradoricus* (Girard) Khatangskoi guby. Izv. biologo-geogr. nauchno-issled. Inst., Irkutsk 18(1/2):181-186. (Biol. Abst. 49: Abst. No. 43881.)

Lyles, C. H. 1969. Fishery Statistics of the United States 1967. U.S. Fish Wildl. Serv., Stat. Digest 61.

Magnin, E. 1959. Répartition actuelle des acipenserides. Rev. Trav. Inst. Pêches Marit. 23(3):277-285.

Magnin, E., and G. Beaulieu. 1965. Quelques données sur la biologie de l'éperlan *Osmerus eperlanus mordax* (Mitchill) du Saint-Laurent. Nat. Canad. 92:81-105.

Magnuson, J. J., and L. L. Smith, Jr. 1963. Some phases of the life history of the trout-perch. Ecology 44(1):83-95.

Mahon, E. F., and W. S. Hoar. 1956. The early development of the chum salmon, *Oncorhynchus keta* (Walbaum). J. Morph. 98(1):1-48.

Mann, R.H.R. 1976. Observations on the age, reproduction and food of the pike *Esox lucius* (L.) in two rivers in southern England. J. Fish Biol. 8(2):179-197.

Manning, T. H. 1942. Notes on some fishes of the Canadian eastern arctic. Canadian Field-Nat. 56(8, 9):128129.

Manzer, J. I. 1952. Notes on dispersion and growth of some British Columbia bottom fishes. J. Fish. Res. Bd. Canada 8(5): 374-377.

Manzer, J. I. 1964. Preliminary observations on the vertical distribution of Pacific salmon (Genus *Oncorhynchus)* in the Gulf of Alaska. J. Fish. Res. Bd. Canada 21(5):891-903.

Manzer, J. I. 1969. Stomach contents of juvenile Pacific salmon in Chatham Sound and adjacent waters. J. Fish. Res. Bd. Canada 26(8):2219-2223.

Manzer, J. I. 1976. Distribution, food, and feeding of threespine stickleback, *Gasterosteus aculeatus,* in Great Central Lake, Vancouver Island, with comments on competition for food with juvenile sockeye salmon, *Oncorhynchus nerka.* Fish. Bull. 74(3):647-668.

Manzer, J. I., T. Ishida, A. E. Peterson and M. G. Hanavan. 1965. Salmon of the north Pacific Ocean. Part V. Offshore distribution of salmon. Bull. Int. N. Pac. Fish. Comm. 15:1-452.

Margolis, L., F. C. Cleaver, Y. Fukuda and H. Godfrey. 1966. Salmon of the north Pacific Ocean. Part IV. Sockeye salmon in offshore waters. Bull. Int. N. Pac. Fish. Comm. 20:1-70.

Markley, M. H. 1940. Notes on the food habits and parasites of the stickleback, *Gasterosteus aculeatus* (Linnaeus), in the Sacramento River, California. Copeia 1940(4):223-225.

Martin, N. V. 1952. A study of the lake trout, *Salvelinus namaycush,* in two Algonquin Park, Ontario, lakes. Trans. Amer. Fish. Soc. 81:111-137.

Martin, N. V. 1954. Catch and winter food of lake trout in certain Algonquin Park lakes. J. Fish. Res. Bd. Canada 11(1):5-10.

Martin, N. V. 1957. Reproduction of lake trout in Algonquin Park, Ontario. Trans. Amer. Fish. Soc. 86:231-244.

Martin, N. V. 1960. Homing behaviour in spawning lake trout. Canad. Fish Cult. 26:3-6.

Martin, N. V. 1966. The significance of food habits in the biology, exploitation and management of Algonquin Park, Ontario, lake trout. Trans. Amer. Fish. Soc. 95(4):415-422.

Martin, N. V. 1970. Long-term effects of diet on the biology of lake trout and the fishery in Lake Opeongo, Ontario. J. Fish. Res. Bd. Canada 27(1):125-146.

Martin, N. V., and N. S. Baldwin. 1960. Observations on the life history of the hybrid between eastern brook trout and lake trout in Algonquin Park, Ontario. J. Fish. Res. Bd. Canada 17(4):541-551.

Martin, N. V., and L. J. Chapman. 1965. Distribution of certain crustaceans and fishes in the region of Algonquin Park, Ontario. J. Fish. Res. Bd. Canada 22(4):969-976.

Martin, N. V. and F. K. Sandercock. 1967. Pyloric caeca and gill raker development in lake trout, *Salvelinus namaycush,* in Algonquin Park, Ontario. J. Fish. Res. Bd. Canada 24(5): 965-974.

Marvich, E. S. 1952. Sport fish. Ann. Rept. Alaska Fish. Bd. and Alaska Dept. Fish. 3:55-61.

Marvich, E. S., and A. H. McRea. 1953. Sport fish. Ann. Rept. 1952 Alaska Fish Bd. and Alaska Dept. Fish. 4:45-54.

Marvich, E. S., A. H. McRea, R. J. Simon and W. J. Cahill. 1954. Sport fish. Ann. Rept. 1953 Alaska Fish Bd. and Alaska Dept. Fish. 5:55-66.

Mason, E.J.R. 1933. Smelts in Lake Ontario. Copeia 1933(1):34.

Mason, J. C. 1974a. Aspects of the ecology of juvenile coho salmon *(Oncorhynchus kisutch)* in Great Central Lake, B.C. Fish. Res. Bd. Canada Tech. Rept. 438:1-37.

Mason, J. C. 1974b. A first appraisal of the response of juvenile coho salmon *(O. kisutch)* to supplemental feeding in an experimental stream. Canada Dept. Environ. Fish. Mar. Serv. Res. Div. Tech. Rept. 469:1-21.

Mason, J. C. 1974c. A further appraisal of the response to supplemental feeding of juvenile coho *(O. kisutch)* in an experimental stream. Canada Dept. Environ. Fish. Mar. Serv. Res. Div. Tech. Rept. 470:1-26.

Mason, J. C. 1976. Some features of coho salmon, *Oncorhynchus kisutch,* fry emerging from simulated redds and concurrent changes in photobehavior. Fish. Bull. 74(1):167-175.

Mason, J. C., and S. Machidori. 1976. Populations of sympatric sculpins, *Cottus aleuticus* and *Cottus asper,* in four adjacent salmon-producing coastal streams on Vancouver Island, B.C. Fish. Bull. 74(1):131-141.

Mason, J. E. 1965. Salmon of the north Pacific Ocean. Part IX. Coho, chinook and masu salmon in offshore waters. 2. Chinook salmon in offshore waters. Bull. Int. N. Pac. Fish. Comm. 16:41-73.

Mateeva, R. P. 1955. The nutrition of the young pike in the spawning-cultivation establishment in 1953. Vop. Ikhtiol. 1955(5):61-70. (Biol. Abst. 32(7):Abst. 22146.)

Meehan, W. R., and D. B. Siniff. 1962. A study of the downstream migrations of anadromous fishes in the Taku River, Alaska. Trans. Amer. Fish. Soc. 91(4):399-407.

Merrell, T. R. 1961. Unusual white sturgeon diet. Oregon Fish. Comm. Res. Briefs 8(1):77.

Merriman, D. 1935. Squam Lake trout. Bull. Boston Soc. Nat. Hist. 75:3-10.

Mighell, J. L., and J. R. Dangel. 1975. Hatching survival of hybrids of *Oncorhynchus masou* with *Salmo gairdneri* and with North American species of *Oncorhynchus.* Fish. Bull. 73(2):447-449.

Miller, B. S. 1967. Stomach contents of adult starry flounder and sand sole in East Sound, Orcas Island, Washington. J. Fish. Res. Bd. Canada 24(12):2515-2526.

Miller, D. J., and R. N. Lea. 1972. Guide to the coastal marine fishes of California. Calif. Fish Bull. 157. 225 pp.

Miller, D. J., and J. Schmidtke. 1956. Report on the distribution and abundance of the Pacific herring *(Clupea pallasi)* along the coast of central and southern California. Calif. Fish Game 42(3):163-187.

Miller, R. B. 1946. Notes on the Arctic grayling, *Thymallus signifer* Richardson, from Great Bear Lake. Copeia 1946(4): 227-236.

Miller, R. B., and W. A. Kennedy. 1948a. Observations on the lake trout of Great Bear Lake. J. Fish. Res. Bd. Canada 7(4): 176-189.

Miller, R. B., and W. A. Kennedy. 1948b. Pike *(Esox lucius)* from four northern Canadian lakes. J. Fish. Res. Bd. Canada 7(4): 190-199.

Miller, R. B., and F. Miller. 1962. Diet, glycogen and resistance to fatigue in hatchery rainbow trout. Part II. J. Fish. Res. Bd. Canada 19(3):365-375.

Miller, R. R., and C. L. Hubbs. 1969. Systematics of *Gasterosteus aculeatus,* with particular reference to intergradation and introgression along the Pacific coast of North America: A commentary on a recent contribution. Copeia 1969(1):52-69.

Milne, D. J., and E.A.R. Ball. 1958. The tagging of spring and coho salmon in the Strait of Georgia in 1956. Fish. Res. Bd. Canada, Prog. Rept. Pac. Coast Sta. 111:14-18.

Mitchill, S. L. 1818. Description of three species of fish. J. Acad. Nat. Sci. Phila. 1(2):407-412.

Moodie, G.E.E. 1972a. Predation, natural selection and adaptation in an unusual threespine stickleback. Heredity 28(2): 155-167.

Moodie, G.E.E. 1972b. Morphology, life history, and ecology of an unusual stickleback *(Gasterosteus aculeatus)* in the Queen Charlotte Islands, Canada. Canad. J. Zool. 50(6):721-732.

Moodie, G.E.E., J. D. McPhail and D. W. Hagen. 1973. Experimental demonstration of selective predation on *Gasterosteus aculeatus.* Behaviour 47(1'2):95-105.

Moore, J. W. 1975. Reproductive biology of anadromous arctic char, *Salvelinus alpinus* (L.), in the Cumberland Sound area of Baffin Island. J. Fish Biol. 7(2):143-151.

Moore, J. W., and I. A. Moore. 1974. Food and growth of arctic char, *Salvelinus alpinus* (L.), in the Cumberland Sound area of Baffin Island. J. Fish Biol. 6(1):79-92.

Morris, D. 1958. The reproductive behaviour of the ten-spined stickleback *(Pygosteus pungitius* L.). Behaviour Supp. 6. 154 pp.

Morrow, J. E. 1964. Populations of pike, *Esox lucius,* in Alaska and northeastern North America. Copeia 1964(1):235-236.

Morrow, J. E. 1965. First record of the trout-perch, *Percopsis omiscomaycus,* from Alaska. Copeia 1965(2):232.

Morrow, J. E. 1974. Illustrated keys to the fresh-water fishes of Alaska. Alaska Northwest Publ. Co., Anchorage. 78 pp.

Morrow, J. E. 1980. Analysis of the dolly varden charr, *Salvelinus malma,* of northwestern North America and northeastern Siberia. p. 323-338. *In:* Balon, E. K. (ed.). Charrs: Salmonid fishes of the genus *Salvelinus.* Dr. W. Junk b.v., Publishers. The Hague, Netherlands.

Morrow, J. E., E. W. Schallock and G. E. Bergtold. 1977. Feeding by Alaska whitefish, *Coregonus nelsoni,* during the spawning run. Fish. Bull. 75(1):234-235.

Mosher, K. H. 1953. Use of otoliths for determining the age of several fishes from the Bering Sea. J. Cons. Perm. Internat. Explor. Mer 19(3):337-344.

Mraz, D. 1964a. Age and growth of round whitefish in Lake Michigan. Trans. Amer. Fish. Soc. 93(1):46-52.

Mraz, D. 1964b. Age, growth, sex ratio, and maturity of the whitefish in central Green Bay and adjacent waters of Lake Michigan. Fish. Bull. U.S. Fish Wildl. Serv. 63(3):619-634.

Murai, T., and J. W. Andrews. 1972. Growth and food conversion of rainbow trout reared in brackish and fresh water. Fish. Bull. 70(4):1293-1295.

McAfee, W. R. 1966. Eastern brook trout. p. 242-260. *In:* Calhoun, A. (ed.). Inland fisheries management. Calif. Dept. Fish Game, Sacramento.

McAllister, D. E. 1963. A revision of the smelt family, Osmeridae. Bull. Nat. Mus. Canada 191. 53 pp.

McAllister, D. E. 1964. Distinguishing characters for the sculpins Cottus bairdii and C. cognatus. J. Fish. Res. Bd. Canada 21(5):1339-1342.

McAllister, D. E. and J. C. Ward. 1972. The deepwater sculpin, *Myoxocephalus quadricornis thompsoni,* new to Alberta, Canada. J. Fish Res. Bd. Canada 29(3):344-345.

McCarraher, D. B. 1959. The northern pike-bluegill combination in north-central Nebraska farm ponds. Prog. Fish-Cult. 21(4):188-189.

McCarraher, D B. 1962. Northern pike, *Esox lucius,* in alkaline lakes of Nebraska. Trans. Amer. Fish. Soc. 91(3):326-329.

McCart, P. 1965. Growth and morphometry of four British Columbia populations of pygmy whitefish *(Prosopium coulteri).* J. Fish. Res. Bd. Canada 22(5):1229-1259.

McCart, P. 1967. Behavior and ecology of sockeye salmon fry in the Babine River. J. Fish. Res. Bd. Canada 24(2):375-428.

McCart, P. 1970. Evidence for the existence of sibling species of pygmy whitefish *(Prosopium coulteri)* in three Alaskan lakes. p. 81-98. *In:* C. C. Lindsey and C. S. Woods, (eds.). Biology of coregonid fishes. Univ. Manitoba Press, Winnipeg.

McCart, P., P. Craig and H. Bain. 1972. Report on fisheries investigations in the Sagavanirktok River and neighboring drainages. Alyeska Pipeline Service Co. 165 pp. (Processed).

MacCrimmon, H. R. 1959. Observations on spawning of burbot in Lake Simcoe, Ontario. J. Wildl. Mgt. 23(4):447-449.

MacCrimmon, H. R. 1971. World distribution of rainbow trout *(Salmo gairdneri).* J. Fish. Res. Bd. Canada 28(5):663-704.

MacCrimmon, H. R., and J. S. Campbell. 1969. World distribution of brook trout, *Salvelinus fontinalis.* J. Fish. Res. Bd. Canada 26(7):1699-1725.

MacCrimmon, H. R., and O. E. Devitt. 1954. Winter studies on the burbot, *Lota lota lacustris,* of Lake Simcoe, Ontario. Canad. Fish. Cult. 16:34-41.

McDonald, M. 1891. Introduction and acclimation of new species. p. LI-LII. *In:* Report of the commissioner. Rept. U.S. Comm. Fish. 15(1887).

MacGinitie, G. E. 1935. Ecological aspects of a California marine estuary. Amer. Midl. Nat. 16(5):629-765.

McGuire, H. D. 1896. Third and fourth annual reports of the state fish and game protector of the state of Oregon 1895-1896. W. H. Leeds, Salem. 115 pp. and appendix.

McHenry, E. T. 1973. Silver salmon studies in Resurrection Bay. Alaska Dept. Fish Game. Fed. Aid Fish Restor., Ann. Prog. Rept., Study G-II. 14:1-22.

McHugh, J. L. 1939. The eulachon. Fish. Res. Bd. Canada, Pac. Prog. Rept. 40:17-22.

McHugh, J. L. 1940. Where does the eulachon spawn. Fish. Res. Bd. Canada, Pac. Prog. Rept. 44:18-19.

McInerney, J. E. 1964. Salinity preference: an orientation mechanism in salmon migration. J. Fish. Res. Bd. Canada 21(5):995-1018.

McKenzie, J. A., and M.H.A. Keenleyside. 1970. Reproductive behavior of ninespine sticklebacks *(Pungitius pungitius(L.))* in South Bay, Manitoulin Island, Ontario. Canad. J. Zool. 48(1):55-61.

McKenzie, R. A. 1947. The effect of crowding of smelt eggs on the production of larvae. Fish. Res. Bd. Canada, Prog. Rept. Atlantic Coast Sta. 39:11-13.

McKenzie, R. A. 1953. Arctic or polar cod, *Boreogadus saida,* in Miramichi Bay, New Brunswick. Copeia 1953(4):238-239.

McKenzie, R. A. 1958. Age and growth of smelt, *Osmerus mordax* (Mitchill), of the Miramichi River, New Brunswick. J. Fish. Res. Bd. Canada 15(6):1313-1327.

McKenzie, R. A. 1964. Smelt life history and fishery in the Miramichi River, New Brunswick. Bull. Fish. Res. Bd. Canada 144. 77 pp.

McLarney, W. O. 1968. Spawning habits and morphological variation in the coastrange sculpin, *Cottus aleuticus,* and the prickly sculpin, *Cottus asper.* Trans. Amer. Fish. Soc. 97(1):46-48.

McPhail, J. D. 1961. A systematic study of the *Salvelinus alpinus* complex in North America. J. Fish. Res. Bd. Canada 18(5): 793-814.

McPhail, J. D. 1963. Geographic variation in North American ninespine sticklebacks, *Pungitius pungitius.* J. Fish. Res. Bd. Canada 20(1):27-44.

McPhail, J. D. 1966. The *Coregonus autumnalis* complex in Alaska and northwestern Canada. J. Fish. Res. Bd. Canada 23(1):141-148.

McPhail, J. D. 1969. Predation and the evolution of a stickleback *(Gasterosteus).* J. Fish. Res. Bd. Canada 26(12):3183-3208.

McPhail, J. D., and C. C. Lindsey. 1970. Freshwater fishes of northwestern Canada and Alaska. Bull. Fish. Res. Bd. Canada 173. 381 pp.

Nagasaki, F. 1958. The fecundity of Pacific herring *(Clupea pallasi)* in British Columbia coastal waters. J. Fish. Res. Bd. Canada 15(3):313-330.

Nagata, T. H. 1967. Artificial spawning of anadromous Dolly Varden. Prog. Fish-Cult. 29(1):26.

Narver, D. W. 1966. Pelagial ecology and carrying capacity of sockeye salmon in Chignik Lakes, Alaska. Ph.D. Thesis, Univ. Washington, Seattle. 348 pp.

Narver, D. W. 1969. Phenotypic variation in threespine sticklebacks *(Gasterosteus aculeatus)* of the Chignik River system, Alaska. J. Fish. Res. Bd. Canada 26(2):405-412.

Narver, D. W., and M. L. Dahlberg. 1965. Estuarine food of Dolly Varden at Chignik, Alaska. Trans. Amer. Fish. Soc. 94(4): 405-408.

Neave, F. 1953. Principles affecting the size of pink and chum salmon populations in British Columbia. J. Fish. Res. Bd. Canada 9(9):450-491.

Neave, F. 1955. Notes on the seaward migration of pink and chum salmon fry. J. Fish. Res. Bd. Canada 12(3):369-374.

Needham, P. R. 1938. Trout streams. Comstock Publ. Co., Ithaca, N.Y. 233 pp.

Needham, P. R. 1961. Observations on the natural spawning of eastern brook trout. Calif. Fish Game 47(1):27-40.

Needham, P. R., and T. M. Vaughan. 1952. Spawning of the Dolly Varden, *Salvelinus malma,* in Twin Creek, Idaho. Copeia 1952(3):197-199.

Nelson, E. W. 1884. The blackfish of Alaska-Dallia pectoralis Bean. p. 466-467. *In:* Goode, G. B. The fisheries and fishery industries of the United States. Section I. Natural history of useful aquatic animals. Gov't Printing Office, Washington, D.C.

Nelson, E. W. 1887. Report upon the natural history collections made in Alaska between the years 1877 and 1881. Arctic Ser. Publ. Signal Serv. U.S. Army, No. III. 337 pp. Gov't. Printing Office, Washington, D.C.

Nelson, J. S. 1968a. Distribution and nomenclature of North American kokanee, *Oncorhynchus nerka.* J. Fish. Res. Bd. Canada 25(2):409-414.

Nelson, J. S. 1968b. Deep-water ninespine sticklebacks, *Pungitius pungitius,* in the Mississippi drainage, Crooked Lake, Indiana. Copeia 1968(2):326-334.

Nelson, J. S. 1968c. Salinity tolerance of brook sticklebacks, *Culaea inconstans,* freshwater ninespine sticklebacks, *Pungitius pungitius,* and freshwater fourspine sticklebacks, *Apeltes quadracus.* Canad. J. Zool. 46(4):663-667.

Nelson, J. S. 1971. Absence of the pelvic complex in ninespine sticklebacks, *Pungitius pungitius,* collected in Ireland and Wood Buffalo National Park region, Canada, with notes on meristic variation. Copeia 1971(4):707-717.

Nelson, M. L. 1964. Abundance, size and age of red salmon smolts from the Wood River system, 1963. Alaska Dept. Fish Game Info. Leaflet 37:1-22.

Nelson, P. H. 1954. Life history and management of the American grayling *(Thymallus signifer tricolor)* in Montana. J. Wildl. Mgt. 18(3):324-342.

Nikolskii, G. V. 1952. O tipe dinamiki stada i kharaktere neresta gorbushi *O. g.* (Walb.) i kety *O. k.* (Walb.) v Amure. Doklady Akad. Nauk SSSR. 86(4). (Not seen. Cited by Nikolskii, 1961).

Nikolskii, G. V. 1956. Fishes of the Amur Basin. Results of the 1945-1949 Amur ichthyological expedition. (In Russian). Izdatelstvo Akad. Nauk SSSR. 551 pp.

Nikolskii, G. V. 1961. Special ichthyology. 2 ed. Israel Program for Scientific Translations. 538 pp.

Norden, G. R. 1959. Comparative morphology of certain salmonid fishes with particular reference to the grayling *(Thymallus arcticus)*, and its phylogeny. PhD Thesis, Univ. Michigan, Ann Arbor. 214 pp.

Norman, J. R. 1934. A systematic monograph of the flatfishes (Heterosomata). British Museum, London. 459 pp.

Normandeau, D. A. 1969. Life history and ecology of the round whitefish, *Prosopium cylindraceum* (Pallas), of Newfound Lake, Bristol, New Hampshire. Trans. Amer. Fish. Soc. 98(1): 7-13.

Norris, K. S. 1957. Second record of the green sturgeon in southern California. Calif. Fish Game 43:317.

Northcote, T. G. 1954. Observations on the comparative ecology of two species of fish, *Cottus asper* and *Cottus rhotheus*, in British Columbia. Copeia 1954(1):25-28.

Northcote, T. G. 1962. Migratory behaviour of juvenile rainbow trout, *Salmo gairdneri*, in inlet and outlet streams of Loon Lake, British Columbia. J. Fish. Res. Bd. Canada 19(2): 201-270.

Northcote, T. G., and G. F. Hartman. 1959. A case of "schooling" behavior in the prickly sculpin, *Cottus asper* Richardson. Copeia 1959(2):156-158.

Northcote, T. G., and H. W. Lorz. 1966. Seasonal and diel changes in food of adult kokanee *(Oncorhynchus nerka)*. J. Fish. Res. Bd. Canada 23(8):1259-1263.

Novotny, A. J., and C.V.W. Mahnken. 1971. Predation on juvenile Pacific salmon by a marine isopod *Rocinela belliceps pugettensis* (Crustacea, Isopoda). Fish. Bull. 69(3):699-701.

Nurnberger, P. K. 1930. The plant and animal food of the fishes of Big Sandy Lake. Trans. Amer. Fish. Soc. 60:253-259.

Nyman, L., and L. Westin. 1968. On the problem of sibling species and possible intraspecific variation in fourhorn sculpin, Myoxocephalus quadricornis (L.). Rept. Inst. Freshwater Res. Drottningholm 48:57-66.

Nyman, L., and L. Westin. 1969. Blood protein systematics of *Cottidae* in the Baltic drainage area. Rept. Inst. Freshwater Res. Drottningholm 49:164-174.

Odemar, M. W. 1964. Southern range extension of the eulachon, *Thaleichthys pacificus*. Calif. Fish Game 50(4):305-307.

Ohmer, E. N. 1929a. Ohmer discusses trout and salmon. Pac. Fisherman 27(6):25.

Ohmer, E. N. 1929b. Ohmer again convicts the trout. Pac. Fisherman 27(11):29.

Oikari, A., and R. Kristoffersson. 1973. Plasma ionic levels in *Myoxocephalus quadricornis* (L.) in brackish water during temperature acclimation, particularly to cold. Ann. Zool. Fenn. 10(4):495-499.

Orcutt, H. G. 1950. The life history of the starry flounder *Platichthys stellatus* (Pallas). Calif. Fish Bull. 78. 64 pp.

Orth, D. J. 1967. Dictionary of Alaska place names. U.S. Geol. Surv. Prof. Pap. 567. 1084 pp.

Ostdiek, J. L., and R. M. Nardone. 1959. Studies on the Alaskan blackfish *Dallia pectoralis*. 1. Habitat, size and stomach analyses. Amer. Midl. Nat. 61(1):218-229.

Parker, R. B. 1966. Marine mortality schedule of pink salmon of the Bella Coola River, central British Columbia. J. Fish. Res. Bd. Canada 25(4):757-794.

Parker, R. R. 1960. Critical size and maximum yield for chinook salmon *(Oncorhynchus tshawytscha)*. J. Fish. Res. Bd. Canada 17(2):199-210.

Parker, R. R., and W. Kirkness. 1951. Biological investigations. Ann. Rept. Alaska Dept. Fish. 2:25-41.

Pate, V.S.L. 1933. Studies on fish food in selected areas. pp. 130-156. *In:* A biological survey of the upper Hudson watershed. Supp. 22nd Ann. Rept. N.Y. State Conservation Dept.

Patten, B. J. 1971. Spawning and fecundity of seven species of northwest American Cottus. Amer. Midl. Nat. 85(2):493-506.

Paulson, A. C., and R. L. Smith. 1974. Occurrence of Pacific staghorn sculpin *(Leptocottus armatus)* in the southern Bering Sea. J. Fish. Res. Bd. Canada 31(7):1262.

Pearcy, W. G., and S. S. Myers. 1974. Larval fishes of Yaquina Bay, Oregon: A nursery ground for marine fishes? Fish. Bull. 72(1):201-213.

Personius, R. G., and S. Eddy. 1955. Fishes of the Little Missouri River. Copeia 1955(1):41-43.

Petrosky, C. E., and T. F. Waters. 1975. Annual production by the slimy sculpin population in a small Minnesota trout stream. Trans. Amer. Fish. Soc. 104(2):237-244.

Phinney, D. E., and M. L. Dahlberg. 1968. Western range extension of the surf smelt, *Hypomesus pretiosus pretiosus*. J. Fish. Res. Bd. Canada 25(1):203-204.

Pinkas, L. 1967. First record of a Pacific cod in southern California waters. Calif. Fish Game 53(2):127-128.

Pletcher, F. T. 1963. The life history and distribution of lampreys in the Salmon and certain other rivers in British Columbia. M.S. Thesis, Univ. British Columbia, Vancouver. 195 pp.

Ponomarenko, V. P. 1967. Pitanie lichinok i mal kov saiki *(Boreogadus saida* Lepechin) v Barents-evom i Karskom moryakh. Mater. Rybokhoz Issled. Sev. Basseina 10:20-27. (Not seen. Cited by Quast, 1974).

Popov, A. M. 1933. Fishes of Avatcha Bay on the southern coast of Kamchatka. Copeia 1933(2):59-67.

Power, E. A. 1962. Fishery statistics of the United States 1960. U.S. Fish Wildl. Serv., Stat. Digest 53.

Prakash, A. 1962. Seasonal changes in feeding of coho and chinook (spring) salmon in southern British Columbia waters. J. Fish. Res. Bd. Canada 19(5):851-866.

Prakash, A., and D. J. Milne. 1958. Food as a factor affecting the growth of coho salmon off the east and west coast of Vancouver Island, B.C. Fish. Res. Bd. Canada, Prog. Rept. Pac. Coast Sta. 112:7-9.

Price, J. W. 1940. Time temperature relations in the incubation of the whitefish *Coregonus clupeaformis* (Mitchill). J. Gen. Physiol. 23:449-468.

Priegel, G. 1962. Plentiful but unknown (the trout-perch, Percopsis omiscomaycus, in Lake Winnebago). Wisc. Conserv. 27(3):13.

Prince, E. E. 1898. On the Esocidae (or Luciidae) of Canada. Rept. 67th Meeting British Assoc. Advance. Sci. 1897. p. 688. (Not seen. Cited by Scott and Crossman, 1973).

Pritchard, A. L. 1936a. Factors influencing the upstream spawning migration of the pink salmon, *Oncorhynchus gorbuscha* (Walbaum). J. Fish. Res. Bd. Canada 2(4):383-389.

Pritchard, A. L. 1936b. Stomach content analyses of fishes preying upon the young of Pacific salmon during fry migration at McClinton Creek, Masset Inlet, British Columbia. Canadian Field-Nat. 50(6):104-105.

Pritchard, A. L., and A. L. Tester. 1939. The food of spring salmon in British Columbia waters during 1939. Fish. Res. Bd. Canada, Prog. Rept. Pac. Sta. 42:3-7.

Pritchard, A. L., and A. L. Tester. 1940. The food of spring salmon in British Columbia waters in 1940. Fish. Res. Bd. Canada, Prog. Rept. Pac. Sta. 47:14-18.

Pritchard, A. L., and A. L. Tester. 1942. The food of spring salmon in British Columbia waters in 1941. Fish. Res. Bd. Canada, Prog. Rept. Pac. Sta. 53:3-6.

Pritchard, A. L., and A. L. Tester. 1943. Notes on the food of coho salmon in British Columbia. Fish. Res. Bd. Canada, Prog. Rept. Pac. Coast Sta. 55:10-11.

Probatov, A. N. 1940. Polyarna kambala Karskoi guby *(Liopsetta glacialis* Pall.). (The arctic flounder *(Liopsetta glacialis* Pall.) in the Kara Bay.) Trudy Novorossiisk. Biol. Sta. 2(3):3-20. (Not seen. Cited by Andriyashev, 1954).

Pugsley, L. I. 1938. The vitamin A potency of gray cod, ling cod, and red cod liver and visceral oils. Fish. Res. Bd. Canada, Prog. Rept. Pac. Stations 36:22-24.

Pycha, R. L. 1956. Progress report on white sturgeon studies. Calif. Fish Game 42:23-35.

Quast, J. C. 1974. Density distribution of juvenile arctic cod, *Boreogadus saida,* in the eastern Chukchi Sea in the fall of 1970. Fish. Bull. 72(4):1094-1105.

Radtke, L. D. 1966. Distribution of smelt, juvenile sturgeon, and starry flounder in the Sacramento-San Joaquin delta with observations on food of sturgeon. Calif. Fish. Bull. 136: 115-129.

Randle, A. C., and F. R. Cramer. 1941. The Squaw Creek test stream. Calif. Fish Game 27(3):172-184.

Rass, T. S. 1968. Spawning and development of polar cod. Rapp. Proc. Verb. Cons. Perm. Internat. Explor. Mer 158:135-137.

Rawson, D. S. 1932. The pike of Waskesiu Lake, Saskatchewan. Trans. Amer. Fish. Soc. 62:323-330.

Rawson, D. S. 1951. Studies of the fish of Great Slave Lake. J. Fish. Res. Bd. Canada 8(4):207-240.

Rawson, D. S. 1957. The life history and ecology of the yellow walleye, *Stizostedion vitreum,* in Lac la Ronge, Saskatchewan. Trans. Amer. Fish. Soc. 86:15-37.

Rawson, D. S. 1961. The lake trout of Lac la Ronge, Saskatchewan. J. Fish. Res. Bd. Canada 18(3):423-462.

Rawson, D. S., and C. A. Elsey. 1950. Reduction in the longnose sucker population of Pyramid Lake, Alberta, in an attempt to improve angling. Trans. Amer. Fish. Soc. 78:13-31.

Rearden, J. 1975a. Alaska's herring. Part I. *ALASKA* ® magazine 41(10):30-32.

Rearden, J. 1975b. Alaska's herring. Part II. *ALASKA* ® magazine 41(11):20-22.

Reckahn, J. A. 1970. Ecology of young lake whitefish *(Coregonus clupeaformis)* in South Bay, Manitoulin Island, Lake Huron. p. 437-460. *In:* Lindsey, C. C., and C. S. Woods (eds.). Biology of coregonid fishes. Univ. Manitoba Press, Winnipeg.

Reed, P. H. 1964. Recent occurrences of intergeneric hybrid flounders, *Inopsetta ischyra* (Jordan and Gilbert), from California and Oregon. Calif. Fish Game 50(2):118-121.

Reed, R. J. 1964. Life history and migration patterns of Arctic grayling, *Thymallus arcticus* (Pallas), in the Tanana River drainage of Alaska. Alaska Dept. Fish Game Res. Rept. 2:1-30.

Reed, R. J. 1967a. Observations of fishes associated with spawning salmon. Trans. Amer. Fish. Soc. 96(1):62-67.

Reed, R. J. 1967b. Age and growth of Prince of Wales, Alaska, Dolly Varden, *Salvelinus malma* (Walbaum), and rainbow trout, *Salmo gairdneri* Richardson. Trans. Amer. Fish. Soc. 96(2):223-224.

Reimers, N., J. A. Maciolek and E. P. Pister. 1955. Limnological study of the lakes in Convict Creek basin, Mono County, California. Fish. Bull. U.S. Fish Wildl. Serv. 56(103):437-503.

Revet, L. 1962. A preliminary study of the migration and growth of the Dolly Varden char in Kitoi Bay, Alaska. Alaska Dept. Fish Game Info. Leaflet 17:1-6.

Rice, H. J. 1884. Experiments upon retarding the development of eggs of the shad, made in 1879, at the United States shad-hatching station at Havre de Grace, Md. Rep. U.S. Comm. Fish. 1881(1884):787-794.

Rice, S. D., and R. M. Stokes. 1975. Acute toxicity of ammonia to several developmental stages of rainbow trout, *Salmo gairdneri*. Fish. Bull. 73(1):207-211.

Richardson, J. 1823. Notice of the fishes. pp. 705-728. *In:* Appendix to narrative of a journey to the shores of the polar sea in the years 1819, 1820, 1821 and 1822 by John Franklin. Appendix 6. John Murray, London.

Richardson, J. 1836. Fauna boreali-americana or the zoology of the northern parts of British America. Part third. The fish. Richard Bentley, London. 327 pp.

Richardson, L. L. 1942. The occurrence of nuptial tubercles on the female of *Osmerus mordax* (Mitchill). Copeia 1942(1): 27-29.

Richardson, L. R. 1935. The freshwater fishes of eastern Quebec. Ph.D. Thesis, McGill Univ., Montreal. 196 pp. (Not seen. Cited by Scott and Crossman, 1973).

Richardson, L. R. 1944. Brief records of fishes from central northern Quebec. Copeia 1944(4):205-208.

Ricker, W. E. 1930. Feeding habits of speckled trout in Ontario waters. Trans. Amer. Fish. Soc. 60:64-72.

Ricker, W. E. 1932. Studies of speckled trout *(Salvelinus fontinalis)* in Ontario. Univ. Toronto Stud. Biol. Ser. 36, Publ. Ontario Fish. Res. Lab. 44:67-110.

Ricker, W. E. 1940. On the origin of kokanee, a freshwater type of sockeye salmon. Trans. Roy. Soc. Canada (3)34, Sec. 5:121-135.

Ricker, W. E. 1941. The consumption of young sockeye salmon by predaceous fishes. J. Fish. Res. Bd. Canada 5(3):293-313.

Ricker, W. E. 1960. A population of dwarf coastrange sculpins *(Cottus aleuticus)*. J. Fish. Res. Bd. Canada 17(6):929-932.

Ricker, W. E. 1962. Comparison of ocean growth and maturity of sockeye salmon during their last two years. J. Fish. Res. Bd. Canada 19(4):531-560.

Ricker, W. E. 1964. Ocean growth and mortality of pink and chum salmon. J. Fish. Res. Bd. Canada 21(5):905-931.

Ricker, W. E. 1966. Salmon of the north Pacific Ocean—Part III. A review of the life history of North Pacific salmon. 4. Sockeye salmon in British Columbia. Bull. Int. N. Pac. Fish. Comm. 18:59-69.

Rimsky-Korsakoff, V. N. 1930. The food of certain fishes of the Lake Champlain watershed. p. 88-104. *In:* A biological survey of the Champlain watershed. Supp. 19th Ann. Rept. N.Y. State Conservation Dept.

Ringstad, N. R. 1974. Food competition between freshwater sculpins (Genus *Cottus)* and juvenile coho salmon *(Oncorhynchus kisutch)*: an experimental and ecological study in a British Columbia coastal stream. Environment Canada Fish. Mar. Serv. Tech. Rept. 457. 88 pp.

Ripley, W. E. 1949. Bottom fish. pp. 63-75. *In:* The commercial fish catch of California for the year 1949 with an historical review 1916-1947. Calif. Fish. Bull. 74. 267 pp.

Robertson, J. G. 1949. Sockeye fry production in a small British Columbia watershed. Fish. Res. Bd. Canada, Prog. Rept. Pac. Sta. 80:55-57.

Robertson, O. H. 1949. Production of the silvery smolt stage in rainbow trout by intramuscular injection of mammalian thyroid extract and thyrotropic hormone. J. Exp. Zool. 110:337-355.

Roedel, P. M. 1941. A sturgeon in southern California waters. Calif. Fish Game 27(3):191.

Roedel, P. M. 1948. Common marine fishes of California. Calif. Fish. Bull. 68. 153 pp.

Roedel, P. M. 1953. Common ocean fishes of the California coast. Calif. Fish. Bull. 91. 184 pp.

Roelofs, E. W. 1958. Age and growth of whitefish, *Coregonus clupeaformis* (Mitchill), in Big Bay deNoc and northern Lake Michigan. Trans. Amer. Fish. Soc. 87:190-199.

Rogers, D. E. 1968. A comparison of the food of sockeye salmon fry and threespine sticklebacks in the Wood River Lakes. pp. 1-43. *In:* Burgner, R. L. (ed.). Further studies of Alaska sockeye salmon. Univ. Washington Publ. Fish. New Series, Vol. 3.

Rogers, D. E. 1972. Wood River sockeye salmon studies. pp. 17-18. *In:* 1971 research in fisheries. Univ. Washington Coll. Fish. Contrib. 355.

Rogers, D. E. 1973. Abundance and size of juvenile sockeye salmon, *Oncorhynchus nerka,* and associated species in Lake Aleknagik, Alaska, in relation to their environment. Fish. Bull. 71(4):1061-1075.

Roguski, E. A., and E. Komarek, Jr. 1971. Monitoring and evaluation of Arctic waters with emphasis on North Slope drainages: Arctic Wildlife Range study. Alaska Dept. Fish Game. Fed. Aid Fish Restor., Ann. Progress Rept., Project F-9-3, Job G-III-A. 12:1-22.

Roguski, E. A., and C. E. Spetz. 1968. Inventory and cataloging of sport fish and sport fish waters in the interior of Alaska. Alaska Dept. Fish Game. Fed. Aid Fish Restor., Ann. Rept. Progress, Project F-5-R-9. 9:265-285.

Roos, J. F. 1959. Feeding habits of the Dolly Varden, Salvelinus malma (Walbaum), at Chignik, Alaska. Trans. Amer. Fish. Soc. 88(4):253-260.

Roos, J. F. 1960. Predation of young coho salmon on young sockeye salmon fry at Chignik, Alaska. Trans. Amer. Fish. Soc. 89(4):377-379.

Ross, S. T. 1973. The systematics of *Gasterosteus aculeatus* (Pisces: Gasterosteidae) in central and southern California. Los Angeles Co. Nat. Hist. Mus. Contrib. Sci. 243:1-20.

Rothschild, B. J. 1961. Production and survival of eggs of the American smelt, *Osmerus mordax* (Mitchill), in Maine. Trans. Amer. Fish. Soc. 90(1):42-48.

Rounsefell, G. A. 1930. Contribution to the biology of the Pacific herring, *Clupea pallasii,* and the condition of the fishery in Alaska. Bull. U. S. Bur. Fish. 45:227-320.

Rounsefell, G. A. 1957. Fecundity of North American Salmonidae. Fish. Bull. U.S. Fish Wildl. Serv. 57(122):451-468.

Rounsefell, G. A. 1958. Factors causing decline in sockeye salmon of the Karluk River, Alaska. Fish. Bull. U.S. Fish Wildl. Serv. 58(130):83-169.

Royce, W. F. 1951. Breeding habits of lake trout in New York. Fish. Bull. U.S. Fish. Wildl. Serv. 52(59):59-76.

Royce, W. F., L. S. Smith and A. C. Hartt. 1968. Modes of oceanic migration of Pacific salmon and comments on guidance mechanisms. Fish. Bull. U.S. Fish Wildl. Serv. 66(3):441-462.

Rupp, R. S. 1959. Variation in the life history of the American smelt in inland waters in Maine. Trans. Amer. Fish. Soc. 88(4):241-252.

Rupp, R. S. 1965. Shore-spawning and survival of eggs of the American smelt. Trans. Amer. Fish. Soc. 94(2):160-168.

Rupp, R. S., and M. A. Redmond. 1966. Transfer studies of ecologic and genetic variations in the American smelt. Ecology 47(2):253-259.

Rutter, C. 1908. The fishes of the Sacramento-San Juan basin, with a study of their distribution. Bull. U.S. Bur. Fish. 27:105-115.

Ryder, J. A. 1884a. The protozoa and protophytes considered as the primary or indirect source of the food of fishes. Rep. U.S. Comm. Fish. 1881(1884):755-770.

Ryder, J. A. 1884b. On the retardation of the development of the ova of shad (Alosa sapidissima) with observations on the egg fungus and bacteria. Rep. U.S. Comm. Fish. 1881(1884): 795-811.

Sato, R. 1952. Biological observation on the pond smelt, *Hypomesus olidus* (Pallas), in Lake Kogawara, Aomori Prefecture, Japan. II. Early life history of the fish. Tohoku J. Agr. Res. 3(1):175-184.

Savage, J. 1935. Smelts in the Canadian waters of Lake Huron. Copeia 1935(4):194.

Savvaitova, K. A. 1978. Ecology and systematics of freshwater charrs of the genus *Salvelinus* (Nilsson) from some bodies of water in Kamchatka. J. Ichthiol. 13(1):56-68.

Scattergood, L. W., C. J. Sindermann and B. E. Skud. 1959. Spawning of North American herring. Trans. Amer. Fish. Soc. 88(3):164-168.

Schaefer, M. B. 1936. Contribution to the life history of the surf smelt *(Hypomesus pretiosus)* in Puget Sound. Washington Dept. Fish., Biol. Rept. 35 B. 45 pp.

Schaefer, M. B. 1937. Notes on the spawning of the Pacific herring, *Clupea pallasii.* Copeia 1937(1):57.

Schallock, E. W. 1966. Grayling life history related to a hydroelectric development on the Chatanika River, Alaska. M.S. Thesis, Univ. Alaska, College. 113 pp.

Scholander, P. F., W. Flagg, R. J. Hock and L. Irving. 1953. Studies on the physiology of frozen plants and animals in the Arctic. J. Cell. Comp. Physiol. 42, Supp. 1:1-56.

Schreiber, M. R. 1961. Observations on the food habits of juvenile white sturgeon. Calif. Fish. Game 48:79-80.

Schultz, L. P. 1938. The breeding habits of salmon and trout. Ann. Rept. Smithson. Inst. 1937(1938):365-376.

Schultz, L. P., and R. T. Smith. 1936. Is *Inopsetta ischyra* (Jordan and Gilbert) from Puget Sound, Washington, a hybrid flat-fish? Copeia 1936(4):199-203.

Schultz, L. P., and Students. 1935. The breeding activities of the little redfish, a landlocked form of the sockeye salmon, Oncorhynchus nerka. Mid-Pac. Mag., Pan-Pac. Res. Inst., Section 10(1):67-77.

Scott, D. P. 1962. Effect of food quantity on fecundity of rainbow trout, *Salmo gairdneri.* J. Fish. Res. Bd. Canada 19(4): 715-731.

Scott, W. B., and E. J. Crossman. 1973. Freshwater fishes of Canada. Bull. Fish. Res. Bd. Canada 184. 966 pp.

Seaburg, K. G., and J. B. Moyle. 1964. Feeding habits, digestive rates, and growth of some Minnesota warm water fishes. Trans. Amer. Fish. Soc. 93(3):269-285.

Seeley, G. M., and G. W. McCammon. 1966. Kokanee. p. 274-294. *In:* A. Calhoun (ed.). Inland Fisheries Management. Calif. Dept. Fish Game, Sacramento.

Seidelman, D. L., P. B. Cunningham and R. B. Russell. 1973. Life history studies of rainbow trout in the Kvichak drainage of Bristol Bay. Alaska Dept. Fish Game. Fed. Aid Fish Restor., Ann. Prog. Rept., Project F-9-5, Study G-II. 14:1-50.

Semakula, S. N., and P. A. Larkin. 1968. Age, growth, food, and yield of the white sturgeon *(Acipenser transmontanus)* of the Fraser River, British Columbia. J. Fish. Res. Bd. Canada 25(12):2589-2602.

Shapovalov, L., and A. C. Taft. 1954. The life histories of the steelhead rainbow trout *(Salmo gairdneri gairdneri)* and silver salmon *(Oncorhynchus kisutch)* with special reference to Waddell Creek, California, and recommendations regarding their management. Calif. Fish Bull. 98. 375 pp.

Shebley, W. H. 1931. Trout lives 19 years. Calif. Fish Game 17(4):441.

Shmidt, P. Y. 1950. Fishes of the Sea of Okhotsk. Acad. Sci. U.S.S.R., Trans. Pacific Committee 6: Israel Program Sci. Trans. 1965.

Sibley, C. K., and V. Rimsky-Korsakoff. 1931. Food of certain fishes in the watershed. p. 109-120. *In:* A biological survey of the St. Lawrence watershed. Supp. 20th Ann. Rept. N.Y. State Conservation Dept.

Simon, J. R. 1946. Wyoming fishes. Bull. Wyoming Game Fish Dept. 4:1-129. (Not seen. Cited by Scott and Crossman, 1973).

Simon, R. C., and R. E. Noble. 1968. Hybridization in *Oncorhynchus* (Salmonidae). I. Variability and inheritance in artificial crosses of chum and pink salmon. Trans. Amer. Fish. Soc. 97(2):109-118.

Sinclair, D. C. 1968. Diel limnetic occurrence of young *Cottus asper* in two British Columbia lakes. J. Fish. Res. Bd. Canada 25(9):1997-2000.

Sinclair, S., S. Trachtenberg and M. L. Beckford. 1967. Physical and economic organization of the fisheries of the District of Mackenzie, Northwest Territories. Bull. Fish. Res. Bd. Canada 158. 70 pp.

Skud, B. E. 1955. Length-weight relationship in migrating fry of pink salmon *(Oncorhynchus gorbuscha)* in Sashin Creek, Little Port Walter, Alaska. Copeia 1955(3):204-207.

Smith, H. D., A. H. Seymour and L. H. Donaldson. 1966. The salmon resource. p. 861-876. *In:* Wilimovsky, N. J., and J. N. Wolfe (eds.). Environment of the Cape Thompson region, Alaska. U.S. Atomic Energy Comm., Washington, D. C.

Smith, H. M. 1896. A review of the history and results of the attempts to acclimatize fish and other water animals in the Pacific states. Bull. U.S. Fish Comm. 15:379-472.

Smith, M. W., and J. W. Saunders. 1958. Movements of brook trout, *Salvelinus fontinalis* (Mitchill), between and within fresh and salt water. J. Fish. Res. Bd. Canada 15(6):1403-1449.

Smith, M. W., and J. W. Saunders. 1967. Movements of brook trout in relation to an artificial pond on a small stream. J. Fish. Res. Bd. Canada 24(8):1743-1761.

Smith, O. R. 1941. The spawning habits of cutthroat and eastern brook trouts. J. Wildl. Mgt. 5(4):461-471.

Smith, O. R. 1947. Returns from natural spawning of cutthroat trout and eastern brook trout. Trans. Amer. Fish. Soc. 74:281-296.

Smith, S. B. 1960. A note on two stocks of steelhead trout *(Salmo gairdneri)* in Capilano River, British Columbia. J. Fish. Res. Bd. Canada 17(5):739-741.

Smith, W. E., and R. W. Saalfeld. 1955. Studies on Columbia River smelt *Thaleichthys pacificus* (Richardson). Washington Dept. Fish., Res. Pap. 1(3):3-26.

Solman, V.E.F. 1945. The ecological relations of pike, *Esox lucius* L., and waterfowl. Ecology 26(2):157-170.

Sparrow, R.A.H. 1968. A first report of chum salmon fry feeding in fresh water of British Columbia. J. Fish. Res. Bd. Canada 25(3):599-602.

Sprules, W. M. 1952. The arctic char of the west coast of Hudson Bay. J. Fish. Res. Bd. Canada 9(1):1-15.

Starks, E. C. 1918. The herrings and herring-like fishes of California. Calif. Fish Game 4(2):58-65.

Stenton, J. E. 1951. Eastern brook trout eggs taken by longnose suckers in Banff National Park, Canada. Copeia 1951(2): 171-172.

Stevenson, J. C. 1962. Distribution and survival of herring larvae *(Clupea pallasii* Valenciennes) in British Columbia waters. J. Fish. Res. Bd. Canada 19(5):735-810.

Straty, R. R. 1974. Ecology and behavior of juvenile sockeye salmon *(Oncorhynchus nerka)* in Bristol Bay and eastern Bering Sea. pp. 285-320. *In:* Hood, D. W., and E. J. Kelley (eds.). Oceanography of the Bering Sea with emphasis on renewable resources. Inst. Mar. Sci. Univ. Alaska, Occ. Publ. No. 2.

Sumner, F. H. 1948. Age and growth of steelhead trout, *Salmo gairdnerii* Richardson, caught by sport and commercial fishermen in Tillamook County, Oregon. Trans. Amer. Fish. Soc. 75:77-83.

Sumner, F. H. 1953. Migrations of salmonids in Sand Creek, Oregon. Trans. Amer. Fish. Soc. 82:139-150.

Sumner, F. H. 1962. Migration and growth of the coastal cutthroat trout in Tillamook County, Oregon. Trans. Amer. Fish. Soc. 91(1):77-83.

Sutherland, D. F. 1973. Distribution, seasonal abundance, and some biological features of steelhead trout, *Salmo gairdneri,* in the North Pacific Ocean. Fish. Bull. 71(3):787-807.

Svärdson, G. 1949. Note on the spawning habits of Leuciscus eryophthalmus (L.), Abramis brama (L.) and Esox lucius L. Rept. Inst. Freshwater Res. Drottningholm 29:102-107.

Svärdson, G. 1958. Tvillingarter bland brackvattensfiskarna. Fauna Flora, Upps. 53:150-174.

Svärdson, G. 1961. Young sibling fish species in western Europe. pp. 498-513. *In:* Blair, W. F. (ed.). Vertebrate speciation. Univ. Texas Press, Austin.

Svetovidov, A. N. 1948. Fishes. Gadiformes. Fauna of the U.S.S.R. Vol. 9, No. 4. Idat. Akad. Nauk. Israel Program Sci. Trans. 1962. 304 pp.

Swan, J. G. 1881. The eulachon or candle-fish of the northwest coast. Proc. U.S. Nat. Mus. 3:257-264.

Swartz, L. G. 1966. Sea cliff birds. p. 611-678. *In:* Wilimovsky, N. J., and J. N. Wolfe (eds.). Environment of the Cape Thompson region, Alaska. U.S. Atomic Energy Commission, Washington, D.C.

Swift, D. R. 1965. Effect of temperature on mortality and rate of development of the eggs of the pike *(Esox lucius* L.) and the perch *(Perca fluviatilis* L.). Nature (London) 206(4983):528.

Tack, S. L. 1970. The summer distribution and standing stock of the fishes of Ixembek Lagoon, Alaska. M.S. Thesis, Univ. Alaska, College. 111 pp.

Taft, A. C., and L. Shapovalov. 1938. Homing instinct and straying among steelhead trout *(Salmo gairdneri)* and silver salmon *(Oncorhynchus kisutch).* Calif. Fish Game 24(2):118-125.

Talbot, G. B., and J. E. Sykes. 1958. Atlantic coast migrations of American shad. Fish. Bull. U.S. Fish Wildl. Serv. 58 (142):473-490.

Taranetz, A. Y. 1933. New data on the ichthyofauna of the Bering Sea. Vestn. Dal'nevost. Filial Akad. Nauk SSSR (Vladivostok) (1/3):67-68.

Tarp, F. H. 1952. A revision of the family Embiotocidae (The surf-perches). Calif. Fish. Bull. 88. 99 pp.

Thompson, R. B. 1959. Fecundity of the arctic char, *Salvelinus alpinus,* of the Wood River Lakes, Bristol Bay, Alaska. Copeia 1959(4):345-346.

Thompson, R. B., and D. F. Tufts. 1967. Predation by Dolly Varden and northern squawfish on hatchery-reared sockeye salmon in Lake Wenatchee, Washington. Trans. Amer. Fish. Soc. 96(4):424-427.

Thompson, W. F., F. H. Bell, H. A. Dunlop, L. P. Schultz and R. Van Cleve. 1936. The spawning of the silver smelt, *Hypomesus pretiosus.* Ecology 17:158-168.

Thomson, J. A. 1962. On the fecundity of Pacific cod *(Gadus macrocephalus* Tilesius) from Hecate Strait, British Columbia. J. Fish. Res. Bd. Canada 19(3):497-500.

Thomson, J. A. 1963. On the demersal quality of the fertilized eggs of Pacific cod, *Gadus macrocephalus* Tilesius. J. Fish. Res. Bd. Canada 20(4):1087-1088.

Thorsteinson, F. V. 1962. Herring predation on pink salmon fry in a southeastern Alaska estuary. Trans. Amer. Fish. Soc. 91(3):321-323.

Thorsteinson, F. V., and T. R. Merrell, Jr. 1964. Salmon tagging experiments along the south shore of Unimak Island and the southwestern shore of the Alaskan Peninsula. U.S. Fish Wildl. Serv. Spec. Sci. Rept. Fisheries. 486. 15 pp.

Tinbergen, N., and J.J.A. VanIersel. 1947. "Displacement reactions" in the three-spined stickleback. Behaviour 1(1):56-63.

Townsend, A. H., and P. P. Kepler. 1974. Population studies of northern pike and whitefish in the Minto Flats complex with emphasis on the Chatanika River. Alaska Dept. Fish Game. Fed. Aid Fish Restor., Ann. Rept. Performance, Project F-9-6, Job G-II-J. 15:59-79.

Townsend, L. D. 1937. Geographical variation and correlation in Pacific flounders. Copeia 1937(2):92-103.

Townsend, L. D. 1942. The occurrence of flounder post-larvae in fish stomachs. Copeia 1942(2):126-127.

Trautman, M. B. 1957. The fishes of Ohio. Ohio State Univ. Press, Columbus. 683 pp.

Trent, T. T., and S. W. Kubik. 1974. Studies of introduced blackfish in waters of southcentral Alaska. Alaska Dept. Fish Game. Fed. Aid Fish Restor., Ann. Rept. Performance, Study G-II. 15:81-85.

Turner, C. E., and H. T. Bilton. 1968. Another pink salmon *(Oncorhynchus gorbuscha)* in its third year. J. Fish. Res. Bd. Canada 25(9):1993-1996.

Turner, C. L. 1938. Histological and cytological changes in the ovary of *Cymatogaster aggregatus* during gestation. J. Morph. 62(2):351-368.

Turner, C. L. 1952. An accessory respiratory device in embryos of the embiotocid fish, *Cymatogaster aggregata,* during gestation. Copeia 1952(3):146-147.

Turner, L. M. 1886. Contributions to the natural history of Alaska. Arctic Ser. Publ. Signal Serv. U.S. Army, No. II. 226 p. Gov't. Printing Office, Washington, D.C.

Ueno, T., and K. Abe. 1966. On rare or newly found fishes from the waters of Hokkaido (I) and (II). Jap. J. Ichthyol. 13:220-236.

Van Engel, W. A. 1940. The rate of growth of the northern pike, *Esox lucius* Linnaeus, in Wisconsin waters. Copeia 1940(3): 177-188.

Van Oosten, J. 1946. Maximum size and age of whitefish. The Fisherman 14(8):17-18. (Not seen. Cited by Scott and Crossman, 1973).

Van Oosten, J. 1947. Mortality of smelt, *Osmerus mordax* (Mitchill), in Lakes Huron and Michigan during the fall and winter of 1943-1944. Trans. Amer. Fish. Soc. 74:310-337.

Van Oosten, J., and H. Deason. 1938. The food of the lake trout *(Cristivomer namaycush namaycush)* and of the lawyer *(Lota maculosa)* of Lake Michigan. Trans. Amer. Fish. Soc. 67:155-177.

Van Vliet, W. H. 1964. An ecological study of *Cottus cognatus* Richardson in northern Saskatchewan. M.S. Thesis, Univ. Saskatchewan, Saskatoon. 155 pp.

Van Wyhe, G. L., and J. W. Peck. 1969. A limnological survey of Paxson and Summit lakes in interior Alaska. Alaska Dept. Fish Game Info. Leaflet 124:1-40.

Vascotto, G. L. 1970. Summer ecology and behavior of the grayling of McManus Creek, Alaska. M.S. Thesis, Univ. Alaska, College. 132 pp.

Vascotto, G. L., and J. E. Morrow. 1973. Behavior of the arctic grayling, Thymallus arcticus, in McManus Creek, Alaska. Biol. Pap. Univ. Alaska. 13:29-38.

Vladykov, V. D. 1945. Trois poissons nouveaux pour la Province de Quebec. Nat. Canad. 72(1'2):27-39.

Vladykov, V. D. 1954. Taxonomic characters of the eastern North American chars *(Salvelinus* and *Cristivomer).* J. Fish. Res. Bd. Canada 11:904-932.

Vladykov, V. D. 1955. *Lampetra zanandreai,* a new species of lamprey from northern Italy. Copeia 1955(3):215-223.

Vladykov, V. D. 1956. Fecundity of wild speckled trout *(Salvelinus fontinalis)* in Quebec lakes. J. Fish. Res. Bd. Canada 13(6):799-841.

Vladykov, V. D., and W. I. Follett. 1958. Redescription of *Lampetra ayresii* (Günther) of western North America, a species of lamprey (Petromyzonidae) distinct from *Lampetra fluviatilis* (Linnaeus) of Europe. J. Fish. Res. Bd. Canada 15(1):47-77.

Vladykov, V. D., and W. I. Follett. 1965. *Lampetra richardsoni,* a new nonparasitic species of lamprey (Petromyzonidae) from western North America. J. Fish. Res. Bd. Canada 22(1): 139-158.

Vladykov, V. D., and E. Kott. 1978. A new nonparasitic species of the holarctic lamprey genus *Lethenteron* Creaser and Hubbs 1922 (Petromyzonidae) from northwestern North America with notes on other species of the same genus. Biol. Pap. Univ. Alaska 19:1-74.

von Westernhagen, H., and H. Rosenthal. 1976. Predator-prey relationship between Pacific herring, *Clupea harengus pallasi,* larvae and a predatory hyperiid amphipod, *Hyperoche medusarum.* Fish. Bull. 74(3):669-674.

Vork, F. I. 1948. Nel'ma *(Stenodus leucichthys nelma* Pallas) reki Ob. Trudy Sib. Otd. VNIORX. Krasnoyarsk 3(2):1-79.

Vrat, V. 1949. Reproductive behavior and development of eggs of the three-spined stickleback *(Gasterosteus aculeatus)* of California. Copeia 1949(4):252-260.

Vreeland, R.R., R. J. Wahle and A. H. Arp. 1975. Homing behavior and contribution to Columbia River fisheries of marked coho salmon released at two locations. Fish. Bull. 73(4):717-725.

Wadman, R. 1962. Inventory and cataloging of sport fish and cataloging of sport fish and sport fishing waters in upper southeast Alaska. Alaska Dept. Fish Game. Fed. Aid Fish Restor., Ann. Rept. Progress 1961-1962, Project F-5-R-3, Job 3-A. 3:21-29.

Wales, J. H. 1941. Development of steelhead trout eggs. Calif. Fish Game 27(4):250-260.

Wales, J. H. 1962. Introduction of pond smelt from Japan into California. Calif. Fish Game 48(2):141-142.

Walters, V. 1955. Fishes of western arctic America and eastern arctic Siberia. Bull. Amer. Mus. Nat. Hist. 106(5):255-368.

Walton, I. 1815. The compleat angler, or contemplative man's recreation: being a discourse on rivers, fish ponds, fish and fishing. 8th ed. S. Bagster, London. 514 pp.

Ward, J. C. 1951. The breeding biology of the Arctic grayling in the southern Athabasca Drainage. M.S. Thesis, Univ. Alberta, Edmonton. 71 pp.

Warfel, H. E., T. P. Frost and W. H. Jones. 1943. The smelt, *Osmerus mordax,* in Great Bay, New Hampshire. Trans. Amer. Fish. Soc. 72:257-262.

Warner, I. M. 1977. Herring of the Bering Sea. Alaska Seas and Coasts. 5(5):1-3.

Webster, D. A. 1962. Artificial spawning facilities for brook trout, *Salvelinus fontinalis.* Trans. Amer. Fish. Soc. 91(2): 168-174.

Weisbart, M. 1968. Osmotic and ionic regulation in embryos, alevins, and fry of five species of Pacific salmon. Canadian J. Zool. 46(3):385-397.

Weisel, G. F., D. A. Hanzel and R. L. Newell. 1973. The pygmy whitefish, *Prosopium coulteri,* in western Montana. Fish. Bull. 71(2):587-596.

Weiss, E. F., Jr. 1969. The age and growth of the marine cottid *Leptocottus armatus.* Proc. Montana Acad. Sci. 29:63-71.

Welander, A. D. 1940. Notes on the dissemination of shad, *Alosa sapidissima* (Wilson), along the Pacific coast of North America. Copeia 1940(3):221-223.

Westin, L. 1968a. The fertility of the fourhorn sculpin, *Myoxocephalus quadricornis* (L.). Rept. Inst. Freshwater Res. Drottningholm 48:67-70.

Westin, L. 1968b. Lethal limits of temperature for fourhorn sculpin *Myoxocephalus quadricornis* (L.). Rept. Inst. Freshwater Res. Drottningholm 48:71-76.

Westin, L. 1968c. Environmentally determined variation in the roe color in the fourhorn sculpin Myoxocephalus quadricornis (L.). Oikos 19:403-440.

Westin, L. 1969. The mode of fertilization, parental behavior and time of egg development in fourhorn sculpin, *Myoxocephalus quadricornis* (L.). Rept. Inst. Freshwater Res. Drottningholm 49:175-182.

Westin, L. 1970a. The food ecology and the annual food cycle in the Baltic population of fourhorn sculpin, *Myoxocephalus quadricornis* (L.) *Pisces*. Rept. Inst. Freshwater Res. Drottningholm 50:168-210.

Westin, L. 1970b. Observations on the nest digging of fourhorn sculpin *Myoxocephalus quadricornis* (L.). Rept. Inst. Freshwater Res. Drottningholm 50:211-214.

Westin, L. 1971. Locomotory activity patterns of fourhorn sculpin, *Myoxocephalus quadricornis* (L.). *(Pisces)*. Rept. Inst. Freshwater Res. Drottningholm 51:184-196.

Westrheim, S. J. 1955. Migrations of starry flounder tagged in the Columbia River. Oregon Fish Comm. Res. Briefs 6(1):33-37.

White, H. C. 1930. Some observations on the eastern brook trout *(S. fontinalis)* of Prince Edward Island. Trans. Amer. Fish. Soc. 60:101-105.

White, H. C. 1941. Migrating behavior of sea-running *Salvelinus fontinalis*. J. Fish. Res. Bd. Canada 5(3):258-264.

White, H. C. 1942. Sea life of the brook trout *(Salvelinus fontinalis)*. J. Fish. Res. Bd. Canada 5(5):471-473.

Wickett, W. P. 1959. Observations on adult pink salmon behavior. Fish. Res. Bd. Canada, Prog. Rept. Pac. Sta. 113:6-7.

Wickett, W. P. 1964. An unusually late-spawning British Columbia chum salmon. J. Fish. Res. Bd. Canada 21(3):657.

Wiebe, J. P. 1968a. The effects of temperature and daylength on the reproductive physiology of the viviparous seaperch, *Cymatogaster aggregata* Gibbons. Canad. J. Zool. 46(6): 1207-1219.

Wiebe, J. P. 1968b. The reproductive cycle of the viviparous seaperch *Cymatogaster aggregata* Gibbons. Canad. J. Zool. 46(6):1221-1234.

Wigutoff, N. B., and C. J. Carlson. 1950.A survey of the commercial fishing possibilities of Seward peninsula area, Kotzebue Sound, and certain inland rivers and lakes in Alaska. U.S. Fish Wildl. Serv. Fishery Leaflet 375. 24 pp.

Wilimovsky, N. J. 1964. Inshore fish fauna of the Aleutian Archipelago. Proc. Alaska Sci. Conf. 14:172-190.

Williams, F. T. 1968. Inventory and cataloging of sport fish and sport fish waters of the Copper River and Prince William Sound drainages, and the upper Susitna River. Alaska Dept. Fish Game. Fed. Aid Fish Restor., Ann. Rept. Progress 1967-1968, Project F-5-R-9, Job 14-A. 9:241-256.

Williams, F. T. 1969. Inventory and cataloging of the sport fish and sport fish waters of the Copper River, Prince William Sound, and the upper Susitna River drainages. Alaska Dept. Fish Game. Fed. Aid Fish Restor., Ann. Rept. Progress 1968-1969, Project F-9-1, Job 14-A. 10:275-289.

Wilson, D. C., and R. E. Millemann. 1969. Relationship of female age and size to embryo number and size in the shiner perch, *Cymatogaster aggregata*. J. Fish. Res. Bd. Canada 26(9):2339-2344.

Winslow, P. C. 1968. Notes on the biology of Wulik River char. Unpubl. Res. Rept., Alaska Dept. Fish Game, Fairbanks.

Winslow, P. C. 1969a. Comments on the proposed Wulik River commercial fishery with recommendations. Unpubl. Res. Rept., Alaska. Dept. Fish Game, Fairbanks.

Winslow, P. C. 1969b. Investigation and cataloging of sport fish and sport fish waters in interior Alaska—Char in northwestern Alaska. Alaska Dept. Fish Game. Fed. Aid Fish Restor., Ann. Rept. Progress, Project F-9-1. 10:319-332.

Winslow, P. C., and E. A. Roguski. 1970. Monitoring and evaluation of Arctic waters with emphasis on North Slope drainages. Alaska Dept. Fish Game. Fed. Aid Fish Restor., Ann. Rept. Progress 1969-1970, Project F-9-2, Job 15-C. 11:279-301.

Withler, I. L. 1965. Variability in life history characteristics of steelhead trout *(Salmo gairdneri)* along the Pacific coast of North America. J. Fish. Res. Bd. Canada 23(3):365-393.

Wojcik, F. J. 1955. Life history and management of the grayling in interior Alaska. M.S. Thesis, Univ. Alaska, College. 54 pp.

Wootton, R. J. 1973a. The effect of size of food ration on egg production in the female three-spined stickleback, *Gasterosteus aculeatus* L. J. Fish Biol. 5(1):89-96.

Wootton, R. J. 1973b. Fecundity of the three-spined stickleback, *Gasterosteus aculeatus* (L.). J. Fish Biol. 5(6):683-688.

Wootton, R. J. 1976. The biology of the sticklebacks. Academic Press, N.Y. 387 p.

Wootton, R. J., and G. W. Evans. 1976. Cost of egg production in the three-spined stickleback *(Gasterosteus aculeatus* L.). J. Fish Biol. 8(5):385-395.

Wydoski, R. S., and E. L. Cooper. 1966. Maturation and fecundity of brook trout from infertile streams. J. Fish. Res. Bd. Canada 23(5):623-649.

Wynne-Edwards, V. C. 1952. Freshwater vertebrates of the arctic and subarctic. Bull. Fish. Res. Bd. Canada 94. 26 pp.

Yancey, R. M., and F. V. Thorsteinson. 1963. The king salmon of Cook Inlet, Alaska. U.S. Fish Wildl. Serv. Spec. Sci. Rept. Fisheries. 440. 18 pp.

Yap-Chionggo, J. V. 1941. *Hypomesus pretiosus:* Its development and early life history. Ph.D. Thesis, Univ. Washington, Seattle. 123 pp.

Yoshihara, H. T. 1973. Monitoring and evaluation of Arctic waters with emphasis on the North Slope drainages. A. Some life history aspects of Arctic char. Alaska Dept. Fish Game. Fed. Aid Fish Restor., Ann. Progress Rept., Project F-9-5, Study G-III-A. 14:1-63.

GLOSSARY

Adipose fin—a small fleshy finlike structure, without supporting elements, located on the midline of the back between the dorsal fin and the tail (Figure 4A, page 3).

Adipose lid—a more or less transparent fatty tissue partly covering the eye, found especially in herrings and their relatives.

Ammocoete—the larval stage of a lamprey.

Anadromous—breeding in fresh water but spending at least part of the life cycle in the ocean.

Anal fin—an unpaired fin located on the midline of the belly behind the anus (Figure 4A, page 3).

Anterior—forward; toward the head.

Axillary process—an enlarged, more or less elongate, scale found in the angle between the body and the pelvic fin of some fishes (Figure 4A, page 3).

Basibranchials—the three median bones on the floor of the gill chamber, joined by the lower ends of the gill arches.

Benthic—occurring at the bottom of a body of water.

Branchiostegal rays (or branchiostegals)—bony or cartilaginous supports of the gill membranes below the gill covers.

Caniniform—shaped like a canine tooth.

Caudal fin—tail fin (Figure 4A, page 3).

Caudal peduncle—the wristlike region behind the anal fin and ahead of the caudal fin.

Cirrus—a slender, usually flexible, appendage.

Compressed—more or less flattened on the sides.

Crenulate—having a margin of small rounded scallops.

Ctenoid (scales)—having toothlike projections on the posterior part, as opposed to cycloid.

Cusp—an elevation that may or may not be pointed.

Cycloid (scales)—having smooth edges, as opposed to ctenoid.

Deciduous—falling off easily.

Decurved—bent downwards.

Demersal—bottom-dwelling.

Denticle—a small tooth or conical projection.

Dimorphism—the occurrence of two distinct forms, shapes or colors in animals of the same species.

Dorsal—pertaining to the back; toward the back.

Dorsal fin—an unpaired fin, sometimes in several parts, located on the midline of the back (Figure 4A, page 3).

Emarginate—having a notched margin.

Endemic—native to a particular area.

Eutrophic—rich in dissolved nutrients, but often shallow and having a seasonal shortage of oxygen. Said of lakes.

Falcate—hooked or curved; sickle-shaped.

Fin base—the part of the fin attached to the body.

Fork length—the straight-line distance from the tip of the snout or lower jaw to the tip of the middle rays of the caudal fin.

Fusiform—spindle-shaped; when referring to fish indicates a body tapered at both ends and sides flattened only slightly or not at all.

Gape—the extent of the jaws.

Gill cover—the group of bones covering the gill chamber on each side of the head of a fish.

Gill raker—bony projections on the anterior side of the gill arches. Gill raker counts are made on the first arch on the left side and are given either as the total count or as a separate count of the upper and lower parts of the arch. In such a case a raker at the angle of the arch is counted with the lower part (Figure 4C, page 3).

Gravid—pregnant; full of eggs or embryos.

Ground water—water present below the surface of the ground.

Gulf of Alaska gyre—the great counterclockwise, circular current in the Gulf of Alaska.

Gurry—fish waste (heads, fins, guts, bones) especially from canneries or fileting plants.

Heterocercal (tail or caudal fin)—having the upper lobe longer than the lower, with the end of the vertebral column prolonged and extending into the upper lobe.

Holotype—the single specimen, also called type specimen, on which the description of a new species is based.

Hypolimnion—the cold deep water of a lake.

Immaculate—unspotted.

Interorbital (or interorbital width)—the distance between the eyes, measured in a straight line across the top of the head.

Isotherm—a line connecting points of equal temperature on a chart.

Keeled—having a raised longitudinal shelf or projection resembling the keel of a boat.

Kype—the hooked jaw developed at spawning time by the males of certain salmonid fishes.

Lateral—on or referring to the side.

Lateral line—a sense organ that detects, among other things, low-frequency vibrations. The lateral line appears as a row of pores, generally along the middle of the side of the body (Figure 4A, page 3).

Laterally compressed—flattened from side to side; slab-sided.

Maxilla or maxillary—the rearmost bone of the upper jaw (Figure 4A, page 3).

Median—along the center; lying in the middle between the right and left halves.

Median dorsal line—hypothetic line along the middle of the back, from snout to tail.

Metalimnion—thermocline; the layer of water below the surface of a lake or ocean in which temperature drops rapidly. Above the metalimnion is the warm epilimnion; below is the cold hypolimnion.

Midventral—along the mid-line of the belly.

Mode—the most frequent value in a frequency distribution.

Myotome—a muscle segment.

Nuchal hump—a hump of tissue behind the head.

Opercle or operculum—the most posterior bone in the gill cover (Figure 4A, page 3).

Origin (of a fin)—the point where the forward edge of the fin meets the body.

Otolith—a calcareous mass found in the inner ear; an ear stone.

Ovarian eggs—eggs still in the ovary.

Ovipositor—a specialized organ for depositing eggs.

Paired fins—the pectoral and pelvic fins, which correspond, respectively, to the front and hind legs of land animals.

Palatines—a pair of bones in the roof of a fish's mouth. Teeth on these bones may be buried in mucus but may be felt by stroking with a needle (Figure 4B, page 3).

Papilla (plural: papillae)—a small fleshy projection.

Parr marks—dark marks on the sides of the young of certain salmonids.

Pearl organs—tubercles that appear on the scales of some fishes, notably coregonids, at spawning; breeding tubercles.

Pectoral fins—the paired "shoulder fins" located just behind the head. Correspond to the front legs of land animals (Figure 4A, page 3).

Pedicle—a narrow part by which a larger part or organ is suspended; a small, footlike organ.

Peduncle—a narrow part to which a larger part is attached. See **Caudal peduncle.**

Pelagic—of, relating to, or occurring in, open water; away from shore.

Pelvic fins—paired fins, with one on each side of the belly. The pelvic fins correspond to the hind limbs of land animals but may be located in front of the anal fin or somewhat below the pectoral fin or on the throat in front of the pectoral fin (Figure 4A, page 3).

pH—degree of acidity.

Pharyngeal teeth—bony toothlike projections from the fifth gill arch.

Pharyngobranchials—bones of gill arches immediately behind basibranchials.

Pharynx (adjective: pharyngeal)—a tube or cavity in back of the mouth that forms the first part of the digestive tract.

Phototropic—moving in a particular direction with regard to light. Positively phototropic: moving toward light.

Pored scales—scales that are in the lateral line and have small holes or pores.

Posterior—backward; toward the tail.

Postorbital distance—the distance from the posterior edge of the eye to the posterior edge of the gill cover.

Premaxilla or premaxillary—the paired bones, usually bearing teeth, in the front of the upper jaws in salmonids or, in higher spiny-rayed fishes, the paired bones that form the entire lower border of the upper jaw.

Preopercle—the "cheekbone" of fishes; part of the gill cover, lying in front of the opercle (Figure 4A, page 3).

Principal rays—the longer, obvious fin rays (at least three quarters of the height of the fin), as opposed to short, anterior rudiments that often are not visible.

Produced—extended; elongate.

Protractile—capable of being protruded or pushed out.

Pyloric caeca—small fingerlike sacs attached to the intestine just behind the stomach.

Rays—soft flexible supporting rods in the fins (Figure 4A, page 3).

Regression (of scales)—diminishing of size.

Sac fry—young fish just after hatching, with the yolk sac still present.

Salinity gradient—the change in the degree of saltiness of water, for example from the fresh water of a river through increasing saltiness down the estuary to the sea.

Scute—a bony plate or shield.

Serrate—notched or toothed on the edge.

Skein of eggs—a mass of eggs, usually in the ovary.

Slurry—a watery mixture.

Smolt—young salmon ready to go to sea. The life stage following the parr.

Smolt up—to lose the parr marks and become silvery and ready to go to sea. Said of salmonids.

Snout—the distance from the anterior tip of the upper jaw to the anterior margin of the eye (Figure 4A, page 3).

Somite—a segment of the body. All fish have somites but they usually are not visible until the fish has been skinned.

Spines—stiff sharp supporting rods, generally rather strong, which occur in some fins, especially the dorsal and anal (Figure 4A, page 3).

Standard length—the straight-line distance from the tip of the snout to the base of the caudal fin.

Striae—minute grooves, especially parallel grooves in a series.

Subcylindrical—nearly round in cross-section.

Subterminal—not quite at the end. **Mouth subterminal** means that the lower jaw is shorter than the upper, so that the mouth opening is below and behind the tip of the snout.

Superior—upward or dorsal. **Mouth superior** means that the lower jaw is somewhat longer than the upper, so that the mouth opens upward.

Swim bladder—an air bladder or gas bladder which, when present, lies along the dorsal region of the fish's body cavity.

Tactile—sensitive to touch.

Terete—more or less cylindrical but tapered at the ends.

Terminal—at the end. **Mouth terminal** means that the upper and lower jaws are of equal length, so that the mouth opens directly to the front.

Thermocline—see **Metalimnion.**

Topotype—a specimen, other than the holotype, used in describing a new species and captured at the same place as the holotype.

Total length—the straight-line distance from the tip of the snout or lower jaw to the most posterior part of the caudal fin.

Transverse—extending across; from side to side.

Truncate—cut off squarely.

Tubercle—a small knob or prominence; a bump.

UAFC and SUFC—Abbreviations for University of Alaska Fish Collection and Stanford University Fish Collection. Number is number of specimen in the collection.

Ventral—below; toward the belly.

Ventrolateral—on the side, but below the middle.

Vertical fins—the dorsal, anal and caudal fins (Figure 4A, page 3).

Vomer—a bone in the center of the roof of the mouth separating the palatines. The vomer may have teeth only on the anterior part (the head) or also on the posterior part (the shaft) or may be completely toothless (Figure 4B, page 3).

Year class—all the individuals of a population born or hatched in a given year.

Yolk-sac larvae—young fish which still have the yolk sac; sac fry.

Young-of-the year—young fish in their first year of life; 0+ age group.

INDEX